ENCYCLOPAEDIA
OF
MYSTICISM

ENCYCLOPAEDIA
OF
MYSTICISM

Dr Rana Purushottam Kumar Singh

MD PUBLICATIONS PVT LTD
NEW DELHI
www.mdppl.com

Published by :

MD Publications Pvt Ltd
'MD House', 11, Darya Ganj
New Delhi - 110 002
Phone : +91-11-41563325 (Customer Service)
+91-11-41562846 (Editorial)
E-mail (orders): contact@mdppl.com
Website: www.mdppl.com

ISBN : 978-81-7533-164-8

Published and Printed by Mrs. Rajni Gupta on behalf of **MD Publications Pvt Ltd** t Times Press, New Delhi.

CONTENTS

PREFACE

Mysticism is the pursuit of communion with, identity with, or conscious awareness of an ultimate reality, divinity, spiritual truth, or God through direct experience, intuition, or insight. Mysticisms usually center around a practice or practices intended to nurture that experience or awareness, and their teachings are often designed to create a mindset in practitioners rather than convey specific knowledge. Mysticisms may be dualistic, maintaining a distinction between the self and the divine, or they may be nondualistic. Differing religious traditions have conceived this fundamental mystical experience in different ways.

The term mysticism is used to refer to beliefs and practices which go beyond the liturgical and devotional forms of worship of mainstream faith, often by seeking out inner or esoteric meanings of conventional religious doctrine. For example, Vedanta reaches for the inner teachings of Hindu philosophy encapsulated in the Vedas, Kabbalah (based in Judaism) seeks out deeper interpretations of the Torah, Sufism (in Islam) extends and amplifies the teachings of the Quran in the spirit of universal love. Often mysticisms center on the teachings of individuals who are considered to have special insight, and in some cases entire non-mystical (doctrine-based) faiths have arisen around these leaders and their teachings, with few or no mystical practitioners remaining.

Different faiths have been differing relationships to mystical thought. Hinduism has many mystical sects, in part due to its historic reliance on gurus (individual teachers of insight) for transmission of its philosophy. Mysticism in Buddhism is largely monastic, since most buddhists consider dhyana (meditation) to be an advanced technique used only after many lifetimes. Mysticism in Abrahamic religions is largely marginalized, from the tolerance mainstream Muslims grant to Sufism to the active fears of cultism prevalent among western Christians.

I am very grateful to Mr. Pranav Gupta, Director, MD Publications Pvt Ltd for his cooperation and support for this book.

Dr Rana Purushottam Kumar Singh

1

MYSTICISM
AN INTRODUCTION

Mysticism is the pursuit of achieving communion, identity with, or conscious awareness of ultimate reality, the other, divinity, spiritual truth, or God through direct experience, intuition, or insight.

In many cases, the purpose of mysticism and mystical disciplines such as the use of entheogens or meditation, is to reach a state of return or re-integration with the Godhead. A common theme in mysticism is that the mystic and all of reality or God are a unity, termed Unio Mystica "mystical union". The purpose of mystical practices is to achieve that oneness in experience, to achieve a larger identity and re-identify with the all that is. Terms for this fundamental experience occur with various connotations in most or all religious traditions,

- Theosis (Christianity)
- Henosis (Neoplatonism)
- Irfan (Islam)
- Nirvana, Satori, Samadhi (Buddhism)
- Samadhi, Moksha (Hinduism)
- Moksha (Jainism)

Enlightenment or Illumination are generic English terms for the phenomenon, translating Latin *illuminatio* applied to Christian prayer in the 15th century *De Imitatione*, but equally to the four stages of enlightenment in Buddhism etc.

Mystic traditions often form a sub-current within larger religious traditions such as Kabbalah within Judaism, Sufism within Islam, Vedanta within Hinduism, Christian mysticism within Christianity.

TERMINOLOGY

The term "mysticism" is often used to refer to beliefs which go beyond the purely exoteric practices of mainstream religions, while still being related to or based in a mainstream religious doctrine. For example, Kabbalah is a significant mystical movement within Judaism, and Sufism is a significant mystical movement within Islam. Gnosticism refers to various mystical sects of classical/late antiquity that were influenced by Platonism, Judaism and Christianity. Some have argued that Christianity itself was a mystical sect that arose out of Judaism. Non-traditional knowledge and ritual are considered as Esotericism, for example Buddhism's Vajrayana. Vedanta, the Naths (North India), the Natha (South India), Siddhar, Nagas are considered the several mystical branches of Hinduism. Hinduism, being an ancient religion and a rather broad 'all-paths' embracing philosophy, has many mystical branches.

Mystical doctrines may reference religious texts that are non-canonical, as well as more mainstream canon (Christian example of the former, Dark Night of the Soul, and the latter Book of Revelation), and generally require a more committed intellectual, psychological and physical approach from spiritual devotees. Most mystical teachers typically have some history or connection with a mainstream religious branch—controversial or otherwise, but gather followers through reinterpreting sacred texts or developing new spiritual approaches from their own unique experience.

PRACTICE

Mystics hold that there is a deeper, more fundamental state of existence hidden beneath the appearances of day–to–day living (which may become, to the mystic, superficial or epiphenomenal). For the authentic mystic, unity is both the internal and external focus as one seeks the truth about oneself, one's relationship to others and reality (both the world at large and the unseen realm). The mystic's motivation for such an arduous endeavor appears to be unique to the individual and culture, and sometimes a new religion, order or sect may be the legacy. Generally approached through the purification processes of prayer, meditation, contemplation (communion with Reality), ingestion of entheogens (to raise consciousness and loosen the ego), and a wide variety of other means, the mystic seeks to transcend any constraint to his direct experience of the divine.

The processes/experiences undertaken to achieve unity are described variously as the path, theosis, faqr (Sufism), Makhafah/Mahabbah/Ma'rifah (fear/love/knowledge, Sufism/Egypt), fana (Sufism/Arab and Persian), enlightenment, the way, transcendence, the Fourth Way (G. I. Gurdjieff), salvation through the Christ self, satori (Zen Buddhism), dhyana or bhakti (Hinduism), wu-wei (Taoism), etc. Every culture develops traditions and myths pointing the way to the transcendent heroic Self; the process may be embodied in visual symbolism (Hindu "Shiva"/Christian "Stations of the Cross") or detailed psychologically in powerful stories such as Theseus and Odysseus, etc.

The divine realm has been expressed in any of various ways across cultures—as God/Allah/Brahma/Creator, baqa' (Sufism), the perfect goodness, ultimate reality, hal (Persian sufism), a universal presence, force (Neoplatonicism's Monad) or divine principle. The ultimate unification with the divine may be experienced by the mystic as psychological emancipation, samadhi, being born again, wahdat al-wujud(Sufism) or unity consciousness, but in practical terms it can be described as a surrendered egoless state in which the external world synchronizes with the mystic's true nature and purpose. The term, heaven/nirvana, while generally considered an after-death experience in Islam, Judaism, Christianity, Hinduism and Buddhism is seen by the mystic as a non-physical realm or "field" with physical effects in the eternal "now." Severe cultural alienation often accompanies this effort as the mystic turns away from the world (fasting/emptying) seeking reunion with the Creator or Godhead within.

Mysticism is usually understood in a religious context, but as William James and Ken Wilber point out, transcendent experiences may happen to anyone, regardless of religious training or inclinations. Such experiences can occur unbidden and without preparation at any time, and might not be understood as religious experiences at all. A momentary unity may be experienced by the artist or athlete as a perceived interconnection with existence or a loss of self accompanied by feelings of euphoria, by the scientist as a spontaneous ecstatic inspiration, by an ordinary individual as a shift in physical reality after experiencing a temporary unconflicted state of mind, by a prophet as an open channel of knowledge or even dismissed as psychological disturbances in modern times. But, the authentic mystic's ultimate goal is a sustained stable state of full consciousness, wholeness/holiness through self-knowledge. First, the observer role (Seer, Watcher) must be stabilized before he/she can return to being, merge with the preexistent field—the Divine, allowing him to fulfill his purpose or realize his passion. With that in mind, the word *mysticism*, is best used to point to conscious and systematic attempts to gain transcendent insights/experiences through studies and practice. Possible techniques include meditation, contemplation (of causality), prayer, asceticism (fasting from the world), devotions, Dhikr, Sama, the chanting of mantras or holy names, communion with entheogens, and intellectual investigation. Mystics typically go beyond specific religious perspectives or dogmas in their teachings, espousing an inclusive and universal perspective that rises above traditional sectarian differences because they comprehend the shared basis of other religious traditions beneath the superficial.

James points out that a mystical experience displays the world through a different lens than ordinary experience. The experience, in his words, is "ineffable" and "noetic"; placed beyond the descriptive abilities of language. While there is debate over what this implies, and whether the experience actually transcends the phenomenal or material world of ordinary perception, or rather transcends the capacities of ordinary perception to bring the phenomenal and material world into full view, it should be remembered that a complete absence of terminology—related to modern psychology, biology and physics—existed during the evolution of mankind's sacred texts and earliest attempts to communicate the unity experience. Ancient religious and mystical language may become more accessible with modern terminology and understanding in future translations and interpretations. However, mystics generally focus on the experience itself, and rarely concern themselves with ontological discussions assuming that the initiate understands, or will grasp the semantics as they progress. One example of the opposite can be found in Meister Eckhart, the 14th century Christian mystic, who was brought before the Inquisition for heresy because his interpretation of Christ's teachings as psychological metaphors linking mind with the Real were considered dangerous to laymen.

THE MYSTICAL PERSPECTIVE

Process

Author and mystic, Evelyn Underhill outlines the *universal mystic way*, the actual process by which the mystic arrives at union with the absolute. She identifies *five stages of this process*. First is the awakening, the stage in which one begins to have some *consciousness of absolute or divine reality*. The second stage is one of purgation which is characterized by an *awareness of one's own imperfections and finiteness*. The response in this stage is one of self-discipline and mortification. The third stage, illumination, is one reached by artists and visionaries as well as being the final stage of some mystics. It is marked by a consciousness of a transcendent order and a *vision of a new heaven* and a *new earth*. The great mystics go beyond the stage of illumination to a fourth stage which Underhill, borrowing the language of St. John of the Cross, calls the dark night of the soul.

This stage, experienced by the few, is one of final and complete purification and is marked by confusion, helplessness, stagnation of the will, and a sense of the withdrawal of God's presence. It is the period of final "unselfing" and the surrender to the hidden purposes of the divine will. The final and last stage is one of union with the object of love, the one Reality, God. Here the self has been permanently established on a transcendental level and liberated for a new purpose. Filled up with the Divine Will, it immerses itself in the temporal order, the world of appearances in order to incarnate the eternal in time, to become the mediator between humanity and eternity.

Ambiguities of Meaning

The mystic interprets the world through a different lens than is present in ordinary experience, which can prove to be a significant obstacle to those who research mystical teachings and paths. Much like poetry, the words of mystics are often idiosyncratic and esoteric, can seem confusing and opaque, simultaneously over-simplified and full of subtle meanings hidden from the unenlightened. To the mystic, however, they are pragmatic statements, without subtext or weight; simple obvious truths of experience. One of the more famous lines from the Tao Te Ching, for instance, reads:

> My words are very easy to know, and very easy to practice;
> but there is no one in the world who is able to know and able to practice them.

References to "the world" are common in mystical and religious traditions including admonitions to be separate and the call to detachment which is analogous to emptiness. One key to enigmatic expressions lies in the perspective that "the world" of appearances reflects only learned beliefs-based on the limitations of time, culture and relationships—and that unquestioned faith in those misperceptions limits one's return to the divine state. The cloaking of such insights to the uninitiated is an age-old tradition; the malleableness of reality was thought to pose a significant danger to those harboring impurities.

Readers frequently encounter seemingly open-ended statements among studies of mysticism throughout its history. In his work, *Kabbalah*, Gershom Scholem, a prominent 20th century scholar of that field, stated: *The Kabbalah is not a single system with basic principles which can be explained in a simple and straightforward fashion, but consists rather of a multiplicity of different approaches, widely separated from one another and sometimes completely contradictory*

Strategies

Aphorisms, Poetry, and etc.

Semi-artistic efforts to crystalize some particular description or aspect of the mystical experience in words

- *God is Love* (Christian and Sufi in particular), *Atman is Brahman* (Advaitan), Zen haiku, Rumi's love poems (Sufism). Over time many of these have become trite slogans, losing their core meaning as depictions of practical experience, i.e. "God is Love"—describing the power of creation inherent in pure desire/unconflicted singlemindedness of will.

Koans, Riddles, and Metaphysical Contradictions

Irresolvable tasks or lines of thought designed to direct one away from intellectualism and effort towards direct experience.

- The classic "What is the sound of one hand clapping?" (Zen) or "How many angels can stand on the head of a pin?" (Christian). Sometimes these are dismissed as mere incomprehensible silliness; sometimes they are taken (erroneously) as serious questions whose answers would have mystical significance. In either case, the intention is lost; the point being that excessive effort in contemplating the impossible leads the initiate to give up the ego pursuit of doing/getting as opposed to the unity experience of being/having.
- The evocative Taoist phrase—To yield is to be preserved whole, to be bent is to become straight, to be empty is to be full, to have little is to possess—is another example of a metaphysical contradiction describing the path of emptying of the learned self.

Humor and Humorous Stories

Teachings which simultaneously draw one away from serious discussion and highlight metaphysical points

- Primary examples are the Nasrudin tales, many of which focus on the unreliability of perception, e.g. someone shouts at Nasrudin sitting on a river bank, "How do I get across?" "You are across." he replies; Bektashi jokes (Islam) which serve as a means of opposing the pressures put on society by Orthodox Islam, and the Trickster or Animal Spirit stories passed down in Native American, Australian Aboriginal, and African Tribal folklore. Even the familiar "Br'er Rabbit and the Tar Baby", for example, is fairly acute psychology wrapped in a children's tale. Humor of this sort is often corrupted into mere jokes: some Nasrudin tales have a clear metaphysics built in, while others have devolved into little more than depictions of a crazy, dimwitted old man.

Parables and Metaphor

Stories designed to teach a particular but unconventional metaphysical view of reality indirectly, by using analogy

- One familiar example—the Garden of Eden story of Adam and Eve being cast out in shame—has lost its metaphorical meaning over time; the psychological/metaphysical consequences of shame when the innocent creative ego (feminine aspect) is tempted to reach for power and subsequently enters the belief in duality (eating of the tree of good and evil) because reason (masculine aspect of mind) has yet to waken. In the story, return to the Garden and Tree of Eternal

Aliveness (divine reality) is only possible through purification of mind (the gate is protected by the lone innocent cherubim/Self wielding a flaming sword.) Compare this to the symbols of fire, masculine/feminine unity, time, fearlessness, and ego transcendence found in images of "Shiva the Destroyer" (Hindu) where the transformational process is described by visual metaphors. Christ is well-known for his use of parables, consistently using them to teach compassion and inclusion, while many contain hidden metaphorical content for "those who have ears to hear." In one of the most enigmatic stories from the Gospel of Thomas, he describes the Kingdom of Heaven as like an old woman returning home after a long journey, carrying all she values—a bag full of grain—on her back. A tear allows the grain to escape during the journey and she arrives home to discover it empty. Very Buddhist in tone, each word of the story has significance in describing the return path to the divine through a gradual emptying of earthbound value concepts and subtle internal conflicts. The old woman is a common metaphor related to the mind's creative incapacity when controlled by ego values.

These categories are, of course, intended only as guidelines; many mystical teachings cover the gamut. For instance, Yunus Emre's famous passage:

I climbed into the plum tree
and ate the grapes I found there.
The owner of the garden called to me,
"Why are you eating my walnuts?"

is humor, parable, poem, and koan all at once as it describes the human potential for timelessness and moving beyond the vagaries of perception and levels.

Relation to Philosophy and Sciences

To an extent, mysticism and the modern sciences appear antithetical. Mysticism is generally considered experiential and holistic, and mystical experiences held to be beyond expression; modern philosophy, psychology, biology and physics being overtly analytical, verbal, and reductionist. However, through much of history mystical and philosophical thought were closely entwined. Plato and Pythagoras, and to a lesser extent Socrates, had clear mystical elements in their teachings; many of the great Christian mystics were also prominent philosophers, and certainly Buddha's Sutras and Shankara's 'Crest Jewel of Discrimination' (fundamental texts in Buddhism and Advaitan Hinduism, respectively) display highly analytical treatments of mystical ideas. Baruch de Spinoza, the 17th c. philosopher, while supporting the new discoveries of science and eschewing traditional Jewish concepts of God and miracles, espoused that Nature/Universe was one holistic reality with the highest virtue—the power inherent in preserving essence (being) or "conatus," and the highest form of knowledge—the intuitive knowing of the Real. These shared understandings occur again and again in the field of philosophy and yet some persist in disparaging the one over the other.

The pursuit of knowledge in the realm of physics has been accepted for much of history as inseparable from understanding the mind of God—including the 20th c. comment by Albert Einstein that "God does not play dice," referring to the unfathomable discoveries of quantum physics. The rift between mysticism and the modern sciences derives mainly from elements of scientism in the latter: certain branches of the natural sciences, broadly disavow subjective experience as meaningless, misunderstanding the limitations of the ancient languages. That said, several areas of study in biology (work of Mae Wan Ho and Lynn Margulis are two examples) and philosophy address the same issues that concern the mystic, and modern physicists now struggle to understand a multiple dimensional reality that mystics' have attempted to describe for millennia. Physicist David Bohm speaking of consciousness expressing itself as matter and/or energy would be completely understood by the mystic, whatever his cultural/religious heritage.

Furthermore, Continental philosophy tends to be concerned with issues closely related to mysticism, such as the subjective experience of existence in Existentialism. It should be noted that while existentialism suggests a nothingness rather than a oneness, the mystic's pursuit of emptiness—despite its fear producing angst—for the sake of union with the Divine, points directly toward a potential unity between physics and psychology that does not at present exist. The mystic's attempt to describe cause and effect between one's internal state and the miraculous, hints at a close connection between psychological stability (ego transcendence) and the mysterious realm of causality quantum physicists are now deciphering—dimensional reality shifts that synchronize with states of consciousness and unconflicted choices.

Ontology, Epistemology and Phenomenology

While the three philosophical fields—the nature of reality, knowledge and phenomenon—would appear to all relate to aspects of mystical experience, they have not as yet been correlated in a systematic way. Traditional use of the term ontology makes it a synonym of metaphysics. Prior to Immanuel Kant's theoretical separation of "reality" from the "appearance of reality," with human knowledge limited to the latter, the field of ontology/metaphysics concerned itself with the overall structure or nature of reality. Afterword, philosophical and mystical approaches were seemingly separated in a permanent way. 'The general focus on experience in mysticism tends to belie ontological questions; mystical ontology is rarely stated in clear affirmative particulars. Often, it consists of generalized, transcendent identity statements—*"Atman is Brahman"*, *"God is Love"*, *"There is only One without a Second"*—or other phrases suggestive of immanence. Sometimes it is stated in negative terms, from the Hindu tradition for instance, the word

Brahman is usually defined as *God 'without' characteristics or attributes*. Buddhist teachings explicitly discourage ontological beliefs, Taoist philosophy consistently reminds that ontos is knowable but inexpressible, and certain 'psychological' schools—spiritual schools following after Carl Jung, and philosophical schools derived from Husserl—concern themselves more with the transformation of perceptions within consciousness than the connection between transformed consciousness and the external Real.

Mysticism is related to epistemology to the extent that both are concerned with the nature, acquisition and limitations of knowledge. However, where epistemology struggles with foundational issues—*how* do we know that our knowledge is true or our beliefs justified—mystics often appear more concerned with process as the means to true knowing. However, every mystical path has necessarily as its ontological purpose, the discernment between truth and illusion, and many approaches emphasize the total discarding of beliefs as the prerequisite to knowledge in the phenomenological sense. Foundational questions are generally answered, in mystical thought, by mystical experiences. Their focus, less on finding procedures of reason that will establish clear relations between ontos and episteme, but rather on finding practices that will yield clear perception. The goals therefore are the same, but the mystic's awareness of evolving levels of consciousness encompass another realm altogether. At least one branch of epistemology claims that non-rational procedures (e.g. statements of desire, random selection, or intuitive processes) are in some cases acceptable means of arriving at beliefs, while the mystic's goal is discarding said beliefs as a limit to knowledge. The term "mysticism" is also used in a pejorative sense in epistemology to refer to beliefs that cannot be justified empirically, and thus considered irrational. According to Schopenhauer, mystics arrive at a condition in which there is no knowing subject and known object:

> ... we see all religions at their highest point end in mysticism and mysteries, that is to say, in darkness and veiled obscurity. These really indicate merely a blank spot for knowledge, the point where all knowledge necessarily ceases. Hence for thought this can be expressed only by negations, but for sense-perception it is indicated by symbolical signs, in temples by dim light and silence, in Brahmanism even by the required suspension of all thought and perception for the purpose of entering into the deepest communion with one's own self, by mentally uttering the mysterious *Om*. In the widest sense, mysticism is every guidance to the immediate awareness of that which is not reached by either perception or conception, or generally by any knowledge. The mystic is opposed to the philosopher by the fact that he begins from within, whereas the philosopher begins from without. The mystic starts from his inner, positive, individual experience, in which he finds himself as the eternal and only being, and so on. But nothing of this is communicable except the assertions that we have to accept on his word; consequently he is unable to convince.
>
> – *Schopenhauer, The World as Will and Representation, Vol. II, Ch. XLVIII*

The emphasis most accolytes place on the "mysteriousness" of the encounter with the divine and otherworldly transcendent goal of unity, leave most scientists and laymen behind for lack of interest in "mumbo-jumbo"—despite the seemingly causal relationship between self knowledge/accurate perception and the subsequent Real effects as described by not only the mystic, but the pychologist and philosopher as well.

Phenomenology is perhaps the closest philosophical perspective to mystical thinking, and shares many of the difficulties in comprehension that plague mysticism itself. Husserl's phenomenology, for instance, insists on the same first-person, experiential stance that mystics try to achieve: his notion of phenomenological *epoché*, or bracketing, precludes assumptions or questions about the extra-mental existence of perceived phenomena. Heidegger goes a step beyond: rather than merely bracketing phenomena to exclude ontological questions, he asserts that only 'beingness' has ontological reality (similar to Baruch de Spinoza's suppositions) and thus only investigation and experiencing of the self can lead to authentic existence. Christian mystics would assert that "the Kingdom of Heaven is within" references the same approach. Phenomenology and most forms of mysticism part ways, however, in their understanding of the experience. Phenomenology (and in particular existentialist phenomenology) is pre-conditioned by angst (existential dread) which arises from the discovery of the essential emptiness of 'the real' and can go no further; mystics, by contrast take the step beyond to "being" and describe the peace or bliss that derives from their final active connection to 'the Real'. Those who adopt a phenomenological approach to mysticism believe that an argument can be made for concurrent lines of thought throughout mysticism, regardless of interaction.

Other Perspectives

The philosopher Ken Wilber who has also studied mysticism and mystical philosophies in some depth comments that:

> "There is nothing spooky or occult about this. We have already seen identity shift from matter to body to mind, each of which involved a decentering or dis-identifying with the lesser dimension... consciousness is simply continuing this process and dis-identifying with the mind itself, which is precisely why it can witness the mind, see the mind, experience the mind. The mind is no longer a subject, it is starting to become an object [in the perception of] the observing self. And so the mystical, contemplative and yogic traditions pick up where the mind leaves off... with the observing self as it begins to transcend the mind."

> "The contemplative traditions are based upon a series of experiments in awareness: what if you pursue this Witness to its source? What if you inquire within, pushing deeper and deeper into the source of awareness itself? What do you find? As a repeatable, reproducible experiment in awareness? One of the most famous answers to that question. begins, *There is a subtle essence*

that pervades all reality. It is the reality of all that is, and the foundation of all that is. That essence is all. That essence is the real. And thou, thou art that. In other words, the observing self eventually discloses its own source, which is Spirit itself, Emptiness itself... and the stages of transpersonal growth and development are basically the stages of following this observing self to its ultimate abode."

Q. "How do you know these phenomena actually exist?

A. "As the observing self begins to transcend... deeper or higher dimensions of consciousness come into focus. All of the items on that list are objects that can be directly perceived in that worldspace. Those items are as real in [that] worldspace as rocks are in the sensorimotor worldspace and concepts are in the mental worldspace. If cognition awakens or develops to this level, you simply perceive these new objects as simply as you would perceive rocks in the sensory world or images in the mental world. They are simply given to awareness, they simply present themselves, and you don't have to spend a lot of time trying to figure out if they're real or not."

"Of course, if you haven't awakened to [this] cognition, then you will see none of this, just as a rock cannot see mental images. And you will probably have unpleasant things to say about people who do see them".

According to author Joseph Chilton Pearce, author of "The Crack in the Cosmic Egg" and "Evolution's End," we have transcendence itself as our biological imperative:

"...Spiritual transcendence and religion have little in common. In fact, if we look closely, we can see that these two have been the fundamental antagonists in our history, splitting our mind into warring camps. Neither our violence nor our transcendence is a moral or ethical matter of religion, but rather an issue of biology. We actually contain a built-in ability to rise above restriction, incapacity, or limitation and, as a result of this ability, possess a vital adaptive spirit that we have not yet fully accessed."

"Historically our transcendence has been sidetracked... by our projection of these transcendent potentials rather than our development of them. We project when we intuitively recognize a possibility or tendency within ourselves but perceive this as a manifestation or capacity of some person, force, or being outside of ourselves. We seem invariably to project onto each other our negative tendencies..., while we project our transcendent potentials onto principalities and powers "out there" on cloud nine or onto equally nebulous scientific laws...we wander in a self-made hall of mirrors, overwhelmed by inaccessible reflections of our own mind."

"Culture has been defined by anthropologists as a collection of learned survival strategies passed on to our young through teaching and modeling...as the collected embodiment of our survival ideation, is the mental environment to which we must adapt, the state of mind with which we identify. The nature or character of a culture is colored by the myths and religions that arise within it, and abandoning one myth or religion to embrace another has no effect on culture because it both produces and is produced by these elements...That we are shaped by the culture we create makes it difficult to see that our culture is what must be transcended, which means we must rise above our notions and techniques of survival itself, if we are to survive. Thus the paradox that only as we lose our life do we find it."

"A new breed of biologists and neuroscientists have revealed why we behave in so paradoxical a manner that we continually say one thing, feel something else, and act from an impulse different from either of these...A major clue to our conflict is the discovery...that we have five different neural structures, or brains, within us. These five...represent the whole evolution of life preceding us; reptilian, old mammalian, and human. Nature never abandons a good idea but instead builds new structures upon it...Thus, while we refer to transcendence in rather mystical, ethereal terms, to the intelligence of life, transcendence may be simply the next intelligent move to make."

"...Neurocardiology, a new field of medical research, has discovered in our heart a major brain center that functions in dynamic with the fourfold brain in our head. Outside our conscious awareness, this heart-head dynamic reflects, determines, and affects the very nature of our resulting awareness even as it is, in turn, profoundly affected."

Goals Sought and Reasons for Seeking

Theistic, pantheistic, and panentheistic metaphysical systems most often understand mystical experience as individual communion with a God. One can receive these very subjective experiences as visions, miracles, dreams, revelations, or prophecies, for example.

Going beyond "natural theology" (*theologia naturalis*) to direct experience of God is "mystical theology" (*theologia mystica*) or, as Thomas Aquinas defined it, "experiential knowledge of God" (*cognitio dei experimentalis*). In Catholicism the mystical experience is not sought for its own sake, and is always informed by revelation (not of necessity visions or supernatural occurrences) and ascetical theology. The effort being analogous to reentering a divine "field" which we misperceive we have been excluded—by sin/shame/remorse. Repentance (awareness of lower-self attachments) and ascetics (giving up the thoughts/behaviors) is the requirement for reestablishing divine communion/unity/grace.

Enlightenment is becoming aware of the nature of the self through observation. By examination of the interior thought system and emotions with detachment, one becomes aware of its processes without being controlled by them, allowing one greater creative capacity and ease of interaction with others and the environment.

Hence the saying: If you know the enemy and know yourself, you need not fear the result of a hundred battles. If you know yourself but not the enemy, for every victory gained you will also suffer a defeat. If you know neither the enemy nor yourself, you will succumb in every battle.

Sun Tzu, the Art of War

Terms descriptive of a desired "afterlife" include Moksha (*liberation* or *release*), Heaven (traditionally understood as a gathering place for goodly spirits, near to God and other holy beings), and Nirvana (literally *extinguishing* of the mental fetters or *unbinding* of the mind), but in mystical parlance these reference an experience of reality "different from the present here and now." "Afterlife" is not related to an extension of life after physical death, but sought as a direct experience of the perfect, the divine reality in the present life. The goal is generally established through an "accidental" revelatory or miraculous experience such as a dimensional shift between one structure of reality to another. Once this "potentiality" has been experienced/received/observed, understanding how and why it has occurred becomes the goal of the individual and permanently stabilizing this "direct experience of God" is obsessively pursued. Because terms descriptive of the divine "goal" are defined differently—even by individuals within a given religion—and their usage within mysticism is often no less imprecise, it is extremely difficult for anyone, who has not experienced the simultaneity of the "shift in awareness/ reality" to translate mystical language in a useful way.

Types of Experience

The Stanford Encyclopedia of Philosophy describes three common classifications of Religious experience:

- **Extrovertive** – mystical consciousness of the unity of nature overlaid onto one's sense perception of the world.
- **Introvertive** – any experience that includes sense-perceptual, somatosensory, or introspective content. An experience of "nothingness" or "emptiness", in some mystical traditions, are examples of introvertive experiences.
- **Theistic** – experiences of God.

External or Internal Divinity

From the inner light of the Quakers to the Atman of the Hindu, many have found a soul or other essential essence within themselves to be a center of focus. Even the buddhist who seeks Buddhahood through anatta places a great deal of emphasis on their inner world.

In contrast some (particularly some gnostics and dualists) see the learned self (as opposed to essence) as wicked and deserving of punishment or extreme neglect through asceticism, with positive values placed only upon the transcendent true self.

Mysticism and the Soul

Abrahamic religions conceive of a soul that lies within each individual, which is of great spiritual significance. However, Judaism, placing more focus on this world than others, has resulted in multiple views... that man is a partner in God, all the way to the mystical esoteric knowledge of numerology and the Kabbalah.

Christian mysticism has diverse takes on the relationship between God and the soul with purification and reunion the goal and the soul synonymous with the Christ Self or one's true God-given nature. In Catholicism, saints and other beatific individuals are sometimes said to have received the Holy Spirit—Who grants them miraculous, prophetic, or other transcendent abilities—and this belief is taken up in certain charismatic and evangelical faiths that seek out testaments to divine revelation through spontaneous speaking in tongues, faith healing, the casting out of demons, etc. However, the practice is generally unrelated to a disciplined mystical approach.

In the Quaker view, the soul is inner light, an inherent presence of God within the individual. Other Christian traditions, such as Catholicism, hold a more distinct division between the individual soul and God, given the traditional belief that the salvation of the soul and union with God will occur only at the resurrection after physical death, but these faiths generally hold that righteousness is possible and necessary during life. Eastern Orthodoxy holds that union with God happens in this life during baptism and continues via the process of theosis. Christian mystics seek this unity state of the soul while in the body, variously, through intense prayer, ascetism (purification), contemplation and meditation, to achieve resurrection of the Christ Self/nature in this life.

The Jainist view of soul is perceivable non-matter which has the ability to connect to infinite knowledge but cannot receive that knowledge without removal of the blanket of karma, but as self knowledge is gained, the hold of karma is loosened, everything can be seen clearly and nirvana(salvation) is achieved. The pure soul—divine unity—is accomplished when all the power of karma is destroyed.

Islam shares this conception of a distinct soul, but with less focus on miraculous powers; the Muslim world emphasizes remembrance (dhikr, zikr): the recalling of one's original and innate connection to Allah's grace. In traditional Islam this connection is maintained by angels, who carry out God's will—returning the soul to one's authentic origin—though only prophets have the ability to see and hear them directly. In Islam the mystical path is incorporated within Sufi and the Self/Soul is embattled (jihad) with the infidel/ego. Sufism holds that God can be experienced directly as a universal love that pervades the universe. Remembrance, for Sufis, explicitly means remembrance of the soul's love/purpose or returning to one's original divine state, and Sufis are particularly noted for the artistic turn their forms of worship often take.

Eastern philosophies, such as Hinduism, Buddhism, and Taoism are concerned with the individual soul's dissolution of ego (moksha) into transcendent reality (generally Brahmanor Ishvara). In the mystical aspects of the Vedic tradition Atman (something not entirely different from the western conception of the soul) is believed to be identical with Brahman. Hindu mystical practices aim for *God-consciousness* and loss of lower self.

Buddhist teaching holds that all suffering (dukkha) in the world comes from craving, aversion and ignorance ('raga', 'dosa', 'moha'), and that freedom from suffering comes from the extinction ('nirodha') of these poisons which are the source of mental defilements ('klesha'), through the development of insight and equanimity. The doctrine of 'anatta' suggests that the perception of an unchanging and cohesive self (the 'me'), is itself a mere mental construct ('vijnana') to which one may be attached, and is thus also a major source of suffering. While Mahayana and Vajrayana Buddhist schools invoke various deities and venerated beings, the mystical sects of Buddhism are generally not concerned with, and even overtly deny, the existence of a permanent or unchanging self, or of a permanent or unchanging deity. There is no term equivalent to the Christian idea of 'soul' in the Buddhist lexicon however belief in rebirth is assumed throughout the Buddhist world.

Taoism is largely unconcerned with the soul. Instead, Taoism centers around the tao ('the way' or 'the path'). The human tendency, according to Taoism, is to conceive of dualisms; the Taoist mystical practice is to recapture and conform with that original unity (called te, de, which is translated as virtue).

Regardless of particular conceptions of the soul, a common thread of mysticism is the experience of a collective peace, joy, compassion or love.

Differences of Terms and Interpretation

Pantheism, Acosmism, Dualism, Non-dualism, Syncretism

Pantheism means "God is The All" and "All is God". It is the idea that natural law, existence, and/or the universe (the sum total of all that is, was, and shall be) is represented or personified in the theological principle of 'God'.

In contrast Acosmism denies the reality of the universe, seeing it as ultimately illusory (maya), with only the infinite unmanifest Absolute as real.

There are also dualist conceptions, often with an evil (though existent) material world of the ego competing with a transcendent and perfect spiritual plane aligned with the true self/essence. Gnosticism is a term for various mystical initiatory religions, sects and knowledge schools which were most active in the first few centuries of the Christian/Common Era around the Mediterranean and extending into central Asia. These systems typically recommend the pursuit of special knowledge (*gnosis*) as the central goal of life. They also commonly depict creation as a dualistic struggle between competing forces of light and dark, and posit a marked division between the material realm, which is typically depicted as under the governance of malign forces, and the higher spiritual realm from which it is divided. As a result of these traits, dualism, anticosmism and body-hatred are sometimes present within Gnosticism. There is, however, variety, subtlety, and complexity in the traditions involved.

Mysticism is often found in common with nondual worldviews and many mystics, from whichever religion or tradition they originally came, also describe in many ways a non-dual view of existence. Ramesh Balsekar comments on nonduality and mysticism, that it is in order for phenomenae to occur, that the illusion of personal existence and doer-ship (ego) is present, and explains mysticism and nonduality in fairly accessible (conventional) terms:

> "Consciousness-at-rest is not aware of Itself only the force around it. It becomes aware of Itself only when this sudden feeling, I-am, arises, the impersonal sense of being aware. And that is when Consciousness-at-rest becomes Consciousness-in-movement, Potential energy becomes actual energy. They are not two. Nothing separate comes out of Potential energy becoming the one true being... That moment that science calls the Big Bang, the mystic calls the sudden arising of awareness..."

Related to syncretism, mystics of different traditions report similar experiences of a world/reality outside conventional perception, although this does not infer an abandonment of knowledge understood through normal means. Mystics describe the same unity experience across history, culture and religion—despite the extreme individuality of the experience. If the attempt of religion, philosophy and science to describe reality is comparative to the fable of five blind men attempting to define an elephant by describing its parts, the mystic of every religion and culture sees the elephant despite the individuality of approach and differences in culture and language. Elements of mysticism exist at the core of all religions and in many philosophies, including those where the majority of the followers have no awareness of this. Some mystics perceive a common thread of divine influence in all religions and philosophies. The Vedic tradition is inherently mystic; the Christian apocalyptic Book of Revelation is clearly mystical, as with Ezekiel's or Daniel's visions of Judaism, and Muslims believe that the angel Gabriel revealed the Qur'an in a miraculous manner. Indigenous cultures also have cryptic revelations pointing toward a universal flow of love or unity, usually following a vision quest or similar ritual. Mystical philosophies thus can exhibit a strong tendency towards syncretism.

Mysticism and Traditional Religions

Conventional religions by definition, are marked by strong institutional structures. A religion will generally include most or all of the following:

- an established hierarchy
- a definitive creed
- a set of approved central texts

- regular public services
- an accumulation of rites, rituals, and holy days
- a clearly stated ethical code or set of moral laws

Adherents of the faith are expected to respect or follow each of these closely. Most mystical paths arise in the context of some particular religion but tend to set aside or move beyond these institutional structures, often believing themselves to be following the 'purest' or 'deepest' representations of that faith. Thus, to the extent that a mystical path has a hierarchy, it is generally limited to teacher/student relationships; to the extent that they use a central text or ethical code, they view them as interpretable guidelines rather than established law. Conventional religious perspectives towards mystics varies between and within faiths. Sometimes (as with the Catholic church and Vedantic Hinduism) mystics are incorporated into the church hierarchy, with criteria set up for validation of mystical experiences and veneration of those who achieve that status. In other cases, mystical paths follow a separate but parallel course. Traditionally, Buddhist monks were closely interwoven into the fabric of village life through most of Asia, but had no authoritative position in the community; almost all the traditional Islamic 'orthodox' scholars, however, were Sufis, including Al-Shafi'i, Imam Nawawi, and Al-Ghazali.

Some systems of mysticism are found within specific religious traditions and do not relinquish doctrinal principles as a part of mystical experience. In some definite cases, theology remains a distinct source of insight that guides and informs the mystical experience. Christian Science, based on the mystical experience and writings of founder Mary Baker Eddy is one such example. Some faiths—including most Protestant Christian sects—find mystical practices disreputable; so called mystic "practices" and beliefs generally restricted to specific sects, such as the Society of Friends or certain Charismatic groups, which have implicitly incorporated them.

The mystic's disregard of religious institutional structures often lends a quasi-revolutionary aspect to mystical teaching, and this occasionally leads to conflict with established religious and political structures, or the creation of splinter groups or new faiths. The relation of mysticism to ethics and morality is more complex than is usually assumed. Mystical experiences do not guarantee that mystics will be compassionate or moral, nor on the other hand is a mystical state incompatible with being morally concerned with others. Rather, a given mystic's ethics will depend on the factual beliefs and values espoused in that mystic's religious tradition..

New Religious Movements, Perennial Philosophy and Entheogens

The late 19th century saw a significant increase of interest in mysticism in the West that combined with increased interest in Occultism and Eastern Philosophy. Theosophy became a major movement in the popularization of these interests. Madame Blavatsky functioned as a central figure of the theosophy movement. This trend later became absorbed in the rise of the New Age movement which included a major surge in the popularity of psychological self-awareness groups such as EST and many others. At the end of the twentieth century books like A Course in Miracles (purported to be a channeled course of study dictated by Jesus) and Conversations with God (in which the author describes his direct communication with God) became popularized.

The term perennial philosophy, coined by Leibniz and popularized by Aldous Huxley, relates to what some take to be the mystic's primary concern:

> With the one, divine reality substantial to the manifold world of things and lives and minds. But the nature of this one reality is such that it cannot be directly or immediately apprehended except by those who have chosen to fulfill certain conditions, making themselves loving, pure in heart, and poor in spirit.

Some mystics use the term to refer to a manner wherein the mystic strives to plumb the depths of the self and reality in a radical process of meditative self-exploration, with the aim of experiencing the true nature of reality.

In some cultures and traditions, mind-altering substances—often referred to as entheogens—have been used as a guide; the Uniao do Vegetal being a notable modern example.

It is important to note that many of the self-styled mystical belief systems arising in recent decades essentially differ from mysticism proper in that they rely on the individual seeker's power and will, whereas in the mystic traditions, the states cannot be initiated by the seeker himself, but only by the Ultimate Being.

In Rosicrucianism, Masonry and Golden Dawn

The Rosicrucian Order is a legendary and secretive Order publicly documented in the early 17th century. It is associated with the symbol of the Rose Cross, which is also found in certain rituals beyond "Craft" or "Blue Lodge" Freemasonry. The Rosicrucian Order is viewed among earlier and many modern Rosicrucianists as an inner worlds Order, composed of great "Adepts." When compared to human beings, the consciousness of these Adepts is said to be like that of *demi-gods.* This "College of Invisibles" is regarded as the source permanently behind the development of the Rosicrucian movement.

Freemasonry is a worldwide fraternal organization. Members are joined together by shared ideals of both a moral and metaphysical nature and, in most of its branches, by a constitutional declaration of belief in a Supreme Being. Freemasonry is an esoteric society, in that certain aspects of its internal work are not generally disclosed to the public, but it is not an occult system. The private aspects of modern Freemasonry deal with elements of ritual and the modes of recognition amongst members within the ritual.

The Hermetic Order of the Golden Dawn (or Golden Dawn, as it is commonly referred to) is a tradition of magical theurgy and spiritual development, probably the single greatest influence on twentieth century western occultism and many other traditions, including Wicca, Thelema and other forms of magical spirituality popular today. By the mid 1890s, the Golden Dawn was well established in Great Britain, with membership rising to over a hundred from every class of Victorian society. In its heyday, many cultural celebrities belonged to the Golden Dawn, such as actress Florence Farr, Arthur Machen, William Butler Yeats, Evelyn Underhill, and Aleister Crowley. Many men and women of the 19th century Fin de siècle social culture were members of the Golden Dawn.

Mystical Traditions

Examples of major traditions and philosophies with strong elements of mysticism are:

- Ego death
- Divine Science
- Faith healing
- The Fourth Way
- Ghost Dance (Nineteenth century Native American)
- Mystery religions
- National mysticism
- Nazi mysticism
- Near-death experience
- New Thought
- Occult
- Psychedelic experience
- Religious Science
- Religious Society of Friends
- The Rosicrucian Cosmo-Conception (Rosicrucian)
- Theistic Satanism
- Thelemic mysticism (Thelema)
- Transcendentalism (Unitarianism)
- Unity

- Wicca
- Ascetism
- Christian mysticism
- Yoga (Hinduism)
- Vedanta (Hinduism)
- Tibetan Buddhism
- Zen (Buddhism)
- Gnosticism (Christian)
- Hesychasm (Eastern Orthodox)
- Kabbalah (Judaism)
- Christian Kabbalah (Christian)
- Sufism (Islam)
- Taoism
- Bahá'í Faith

2

THE CHARACTERISTICS OF MYSTICISM

The spiritual history of man reveals two distinct and fundamental attitudes towards the unseen; and two methods whereby he has sought to get in touch with it. For our present purpose I will call these methods the "way of magic" and the "way of mysticism." Having said this, we must at once add that although in their extreme forms these methods are sharply contrasted, their frontiers are far from being clearly defined: that, starting from the same point, they often confuse the inquirer by using the same language, instruments, and methods. Hence, much which is really magic is loosely and popularly described as mysticism. They represent as a matter of fact the opposite poles of the same thing: the transcendental consciousness of humanity. Between them lie the great religions, which might be described under this metaphor as representing the ordinarily habitable regions of that consciousness. Thus, at one end of the scale, pure mysticism "shades off" into religion—from some points of view seems to grow out of it. No deeply religious man is without a touch of mysticism; and no mystic can be other than religious, in the psychological if not in the theological sense of the word. At the other end of the scale, religion, no less surely, shades off into magic.

The fundamental difference between the two is this: magic wants to get, mysticism wants to give—immortal and antagonistic attitudes, which turn up under one disguise or another in every age of thought. Both magic and mysticism in their full development bring the whole mental machinery, conscious and unconscious, to bear on their undertaking: both claim that they give their initiates powers unknown to ordinary men. But the centre round which that machinery is grouped, the reasons of that undertaking, and the ends to which those powers are applied differ enormously. In mysticism the will is united with the emotions in an impassioned desire to transcend the sense-world, in order that the self may be joined by love to the one eternal and ultimate Object of love; whose existence is intuitively perceived by that which we used to call the soul, but now find it easier to refer to as the "cosmic" or "transcendental" sense. This is the poetic and religious temperament acting upon the plane of reality. In magic, the will unites with the intellect in an impassioned desire for supersensible knowledge. This is the intellectual, aggressive, and scientific temperament trying to extend its field of consciousness, until it includes the supersensual world: obviously the antithesis of mysticism, though often adopting its title and style.

It will be our business later to consider in more detail the characteristics and significance of magic. Now it is enough to say that we may class broadly as magical all forms of self-seeking transcendentalism. It matters little whether the apparatus which they use be the incantations of the old magicians, the congregational prayer for rain of orthodox Churchmen, or the consciously self-hypnotizing devices of "New Thought": whether the end proposed be the evocation of an angel, the power of transcending circumstance, or the healing of disease. The object is always the same: the deliberate exaltation of the will, till it transcends its usual limitations and obtains for the self or group of selves something which it or they did not previously possess. It is an individualistic and acquisitive science: in all its forms an activity of the intellect, seeking Reality for its own purposes, or for those of humanity at large.

Mysticism, whose great name is too often given to these supersensual activities, has nothing in common with this. It is non-individualistic. It implies, indeed, the abolition of individuality; of that hard separateness, that "I, Me, Mine" which makes of man a finite isolated thing. It is essentially a movement of the heart, seeking to transcend the limitations of the individual standpoint and to surrender itself to ultimate Reality; for no personal gain, to satisfy no transcendental curiosity, to obtain no other-worldly joys, but purely from an instinct of love. By the word *heart,* of course we here mean not merely "the seat of the affections," "the organ of tender emotion," and the like: but rather the inmost sanctuary of personal being, the deep root of its love and will, the very source of its energy and life. The mystic is "in love with the Absolute" not in any idle or sentimental manner, but in that vital sense which presses at all costs and through all dangers towards union with the object beloved. Hence, whilst the practice of magic—like the practice of science—does not necessarily entail passionate emotion, though of course it does and must entail interest of some kind, mysticism, like art, cannot exist without it. We must feel, and feel acutely, before we want to act on this hard and heroic scale.

We see, then, that these two activities correspond to the two eternal passions of the self, the desire of love and the desire of knowledge: severally representing the hunger of heart and intellect for ultimate truth. The third attitude towards the supersensual world, that of transcendental philosophy, hardly comes within the scope of the present inquiry;

since it is purely academic, whilst both magic and mysticism are practical and empirical. Such philosophy is often wrongly called mysticism, because it tries to make maps of the countries which the mystic explores. Its performances are useful, as diagrams are useful, so long as they do not ape finality; remembering that the only final thing is personal experience—the personal and costly exploration of the exalted and truth-loving soul.

What then do we really mean by mysticism? A word which is impartially applied to the performances of mediums and the ecstasies of the saints, to "menticulture" and sorcery, dreamy poetry and mediaeval art, to prayer and palmistry, the doctrinal excesses of Gnosticism, and the tepid speculations of the Cambridge Platonists—even, according to William James, to the higher branches of intoxication—soon ceases to have any useful meaning. Its employment merely confuses the inexperienced student, who ends with a vague idea that every kind of supersensual theory and practice is somehow "mystical." Hence the need of fixing, if possible, its true characteristics and restating the fact that Mysticism, in its pure form, is the science of ultimates, the science of union with the Absolute, and nothing else, and that the mystic is the person who attains to this union, not the person who talks about it. Not to *know about* but to *Be,* is the mark of the real initiate.

The difficulty lies in determining the point at which supersensual experience ceases to be merely a practical and interesting extension of sensual experience—an enlarging, so to speak, of the boundaries of existence—and passes over into that boundless life where Subject and Object, desirous and desired, are *one.* No sharp line, but rather an infinite series of gradations separate the two states. Hence we must look carefully at all the pilgrims on the road; discover, if we can, the motive of their travels, the maps which they use, the luggage which they take, the end which they attain.

Now we have said that the end which the mystic sets before him is conscious union with a living Absolute. That Divine Dark, that Abyss of the Godhead, of which he sometimes speaks as the goal of his quest, is just this Absolute, the Uncreated Light in which the Universe is bathed, and which—transcending, as it does, all human powers of expression—he can only describe to us as *dark.* But there is—must be—contact "in an intelligible where" between every individual self and this Supreme Self, this Ultimate. In the mystic this union is conscious, personal, and complete. "He enjoys," says St. John of the Cross, "a certain contact of the soul with the Divinity; and it is God Himself who is then felt and tasted." More or less according to his measure, he has touched—or better, been touched by—the substantial Being of Deity, not merely its manifestation in life. This it is which distinguishes him from the best and most brilliant of other men, and makes his science, in Patmore's words, "the science of self-evident Reality." Gazing with him into that unsearchable ground whence the World of Becoming comes forth "eternally generated in an eternal Now," we may see only the icy darkness of perpetual negations: but he, beyond the coincidence of opposites, looks upon the face of Perfect Love.

As genius in any of the arts is—humanly speaking—the final term of a power of which each individual possesses the rudiments, so mysticism may be looked upon as the final term, the active expression, of a power latent in the whole race: the power, that is to say, of so perceiving transcendent reality. Few people pass through life without knowing what it is to be at least touched by this mystical feeling. He who falls in love with a woman and perceives—as the lover really does perceive—that the categorical term "girl" veils a wondrous and unspeakable reality: he who, falling in love with nature, sees the landscape "touched with light divine,"—a charming phrase to those who have not seen it, but a scientific statement to the rest—he who falls in love with the Holy, or as we say "undergoes conversion": all these have truly known for an instant something of the secret of the world.

"... Ever and anon a trumpet sounds
From the hid battlement of Eternity,
Those shaken mists a space unsettle, then
Round the half-glimpsèd turrets slowly wash again."

At such moments "Transcendental Feeling, welling up from another 'Part of the Soul' whispers to Understanding and Sense that they are leaving out something. What? Nothing less than the secret plan of the Universe. And what is that secret plan? The other 'Part of the Soul' indeed comprehends it in silence as it is, but can explain it to the Understanding only in the symbolical language of the interpreter, Imagination—in Vision."

Here, in this spark or "part of the soul" where the spirit, as religion says, "rests in God who made it," is the fountain alike of the creative imagination and the mystic life. Now and again something stings it into consciousness, and man is caught up to the spiritual level, catches a glimpse of the "secret plan." Then hints of a marvellous truth, a unity whose note is ineffable peace, shine in created things; awakening in the self a sentiment of love, adoration, and awe. Its life is enhanced, the barrier of personality is broken, man escapes the sense-world, ascends to the apex of his spirit, and enters for a brief period into the more extended life of the All.

This intuition of the Real lying at the root of the visible world and sustaining its life, is present in a modified form in the arts perhaps it were better to say, *must* be present if these arts are so justify themselves as heightened forms of experience. It is this which gives to them that peculiar vitality, that strange power of communicating a poignant emotion, half torment and half joy, which baffle their more rational interpreters. We know that the picture which is "like a photograph," the building which is at once handsome and commodious, the novel which is a perfect transcript of life, fail to satisfy us. It is difficult to say why this should be so, unless it were because these things have neglected their true business; which was not to reproduce the illusions of ordinary men but to catch and translate for us something of that "secret plan," that reality which the artistic consciousness is able, in a measure, to perceive. "Painting as well as music and poetry exists and exults in immortal thoughts," says Blake. That "life-enhancing power" which has been recognized as the supreme quality of good painting, has its origin in this contact of the artistic mind with the archetypal—or, if you like, the transcendental—world, the underlying verity of things.

A critic, in whom poetic genius has brought about the unusual alliance of intuition with scholarship, testifies to this same truth when he says of the ideals which governed early Chinese painting, "In this theory every work of art is thought of as an incarnation of the genius of rhythm, manifesting the living spirit of things with a clearer beauty and intenser power than the gross impediments of complex matter allow to be transmitted to, our senses in the visible world around us. A picture is conceived as a *sort of apparition from a more real world of essential life."*

That "more real world of essential life" is the world in which the "free soul" of the great mystic dwells; hovering like the six-winged seraph before the face of the Absolute. The artist too may cross its boundaries in his brief moments of creation: but he cannot stay. He comes back to us, bearing its tidings, with Dante's cry upon his lips—

"... Non eran da ciò le proprie penne
se non che la mia mente fu percossa
da un fulgore, in che sua voglia venne."

The mystic may say—is indeed bound to say—with St. Bernard, "My secret to myself." Try how he will, his stammering and awestruck reports can hardly be understood but by those who are already in the way. But the artist cannot act thus. On him has been laid the duty of expressing something of that which he perceives. He is bound to tell his love. In his worship of Perfect Beauty faith must be balanced by works. By means of veils and symbols he must interpret his free vision, his glimpse of the burning bush, to other men. He is the mediator between his brethren and the divine, for art is the link between appearance and reality.

But we do not call every one who has these partial and artistic intuitions of reality a mystic, any more than we call every one a musician who has learnt to play the piano. The true mystic is the person in whom such powers transcend the merely artistic and visionary stage, and are exalted to the point of genius, in whom the transcendental consciousness can dominate the normal consciousness, and who has definitely surrendered himself to the embrace of Reality. As artists stand in a peculiar relation to the phenomenal world, receiving rhythms and discovering truths and beauties which are hidden from other men, so this true mystic stands in a peculiar relation to the transcendental world, there experiencing actual, but to us unimaginable tension and delight. His consciousness is transfigured in a particular way, he lives at different levels of experience from other people: and this of course means that he sees a different world, since the world as we know it is the product of certain scraps or aspects of reality acting upon a normal and untransfigured consciousness. Hence his mysticism is no isolated vision, no fugitive glimpse of reality, but a complete system of life carrying its own guarantees and obligations. As other men are immersed in and react to natural or intellectual life, so the mystic is immersed in and reacts to spiritual life. He moves towards that utter identification with its interests which he calls "Union with God." He has been called a lonely soul. He might more properly be described as a lonely body, for his soul, peculiarly responsive, sends out and receives communications upon every side.

The earthly artist, because perception brings with it the imperative longing for expression, tries to give us in colour, sound or words a hint of his ecstasy, his glimpse of truth. Only those who have tried, know how small a fraction of his vision he can, under the most favourable circumstance, contrive to represent. The mystic, too, tries very hard to tell an unwilling world his secret. But in his case, the difficulties are enormously increased. First, there is the huge disparity between his unspeakable experience and the language which will most nearly suggest it. Next, there is the great gulf fixed between his mind and the mind of the world. His audience must be bewitched as well as addressed, caught up to something of his state, before they can be made to understand.

Were he a musician, it is probable that the mystic could give his message to other musicians in the terms of that art, far more accurately than language will allow him to do, for we must remember that there is no excuse but that of convenience for the pre-eminence amongst modes of expression which we accord to words. These correspond so well to the physical plane and its adventures, that we forget that they have but the faintest of relations with transcendental things. Even the artist, before he can make use of them, is bound to re-arrange them in accordance with the laws of rhythm, obeying unconsciously the rule by which all arts "tend to approach the condition of music."

So too the mystic. Mysticism, the most romantic of adventures, from one point of view the art of arts, their source and also their end, finds naturally enough its closest correspondences in the most purely artistic and most deeply significant of all forms of expression. The mystery of music is seldom realized by those who so easily accept its gifts. Yet of all the arts music alone shares with great mystical literature the power of waking in us a response to the life-movement of the universe brings us—we know not how—news of its exultant passions and its incomparable peace. Beethoven heard the very voice of Reality, and little of it escaped when he translated it for our ears.

The mediaeval mind, more naturally mystical than ours, and therefore more sharply aware of the part which rhythmic harmony plays in the worlds of nature and of grace, gave to music a cosmic importance, discerning its operation in many phenomena which we now attribute to that dismal figment, Law. "There are three kinds of music," says Hugh of St. Victor, "the music of the worlds, the music of humanity, the music of instruments. Of the music of the worlds, one is of the elements, another of the planets, another of Time. Of that which is of the elements, one is of number, another of weights, another of measure. Of that which is of the planets, one is of place, another of motion, another of nature. Of that which is of Time, one is of the days and the vicissitudes of light and darkness; another of the months and the waxing and waning of the moon; another of the years and the changes of spring, summer, autumn and winter. Of the music of humanity, one is of the body, another of the soul, another in the connexion that is between them." Thus the life of the visible and invisible universe consists in a supernal fugue.

One contemplative at least, Richard Rolle of Hampole, "the father of English mysticism," was acutely aware of this music of the soul, discerning in it a correspondence with the measured harmonies of the spiritual universe. In those enraptured descriptions of his inward experience which are among the jewels of mystical literature, nothing is more remarkable than his constant and deliberate employment of musical imagery. This alone, it seems, could catch and translate for him the character of his experience of Reality. The condition of joyous and awakened love to which the mystic passes when his purification is at an end is to him, above all else, the state of Song. He does not "see" the spiritual world: he "hears" it. For him, as for St. Francis of Assisi, it is a "heavenly melody, intolerably sweet."

"Song I call," he says, "when in a plenteous soul the sweetness of eternal love with burning is taken, and thought into song is turned, and the mind into full sweet sound is changed." Richard Rolle, In this and subsequent quotations from Rolle's *Incendium Amoris* I have usually adopted Misyn's fifteenth-century translation; slightly modernizing the spelling, and, where necessary, correcting from the Latin his errors and obscurities. He who experiences this joyous exaltation "says not his prayers like other righteous men" but "is taken into marvellous mirth: and, goodly sound being descended into him, as it were with notes his prayers he sings." o Gertrude More—"O lett me sitt alone, silent to all the world and it to me, that I may learn the song of Love."

Rolle's own experience of mystic joy seems actually to have come to him in this form: the perceptions of his exalted consciousness presenting themselves to his understanding under musical conditions, as other mystics have received them in the form of pictures or words. I give in his own words the classic description of his passage from the first state of "burning love" to the second state of "songful love"—from *Calor* to *Canor*— when "into song of joy meditation is turned." "In the night, before supper, as I my psalms sung, as it were the sound of readers or rather singers about me I beheld. Whilst, also praying, to heaven with all desire I took heed, suddenly, in what manner I wot not, in me the sound of song I felt; and likeliest heavenly melody I took, with me dwelling in mind. Forsooth my thought continually to mirth of song was changed, and my meditation to praise turned; and my prayers and psalm-saying, in *sound* I showed."

The song, however, is a mystic melody having little in common with its clumsy image, earthly music. Bodily song "lets it"; and "noise of janglers makes it turn again to thought," "for sweet ghostly song accords not with outward song, which in churches and elsewhere is used. It discords much: for all that is man's voice is formed with bodily ears to be heard; but among angels' tunes it has an acceptable melody, and with marvel it is commended of them that have known it." To others it is incommunicable. "Worldly lovers soothly words or ditties of our song may know, for the words they read: but the tone and sweetness of that song they may not learn."

Such symbolism as this—a living symbolism of experience and action, as well as of statement—seems almost essential to mystical expression. The mind must employ some device of the kind if its transcendental perceptions—wholly unrelated as they are to the phenomena with which intellect is able to deal—are ever to be grasped by the surface consciousness. Sometimes the symbol and the perception which it represents become fused in that consciousness; and the mystic's experience then presents itself to him as "visions" or "voices" which we must look upon as the garment he has himself provided to veil that Reality upon which no man may look and live. The nature of this garment will be largely conditioned by his temperament—as in Rolle's evident bias towards music, St. Catherine of Genoa's leaning towards the abstract conceptions of fire and light—and also by his theological education and environment. Cases in point are the highly dogmatic visions and auditions of St. Gertrude, Suso, St. Catherine of Siena, the Blessed Angela of Foligno; above all of St. Teresa, whose marvellous self-analyses provide the classic account of these attempts of the mind to translate transcendental intuitions into concepts with which it can deal.

The greatest mystics, however—Ruysbroeck, St. John of the Cross, and St. Teresa herself in her later stages—distinguish clearly between the ineffable Reality which they perceive and the image under which they describe it. Again and again they tell us with Dionysius and Eckhart, that the Object of their contemplation "hath no image": or with St. John of the Cross that "the soul can never attain to the height of the divine union, so far as it is possible in this life, through the medium of any forms or figures." Therefore the attempt which has sometimes been made to identify mysticism with such forms and figures—with visions, voices, "supernatural favours" and other abnormal phenomena—is clearly wrong.

"The highest and most divine things which it is given us to see and to know," says Dionysius the Areopagite plainly, "are but the symbolic language of things subordinate to Him who Himself transcendeth them all, through which things His incomprehensible Presence is shown, walking on those heights of His Holy Places which are perceived by the mind.

The mystic, as a rule, cannot wholly do without symbol and image, inadequate to his vision though they must always be: for his experience must be expressed if it is to be communicated, and its actuality is inexpressible except in some side-long way, some hint or parallel which will stimulate the dormant intuition of the reader, and convey, as all poetic language does, something beyond its surface sense. Hence the large part which is played in all mystical writings by symbolism and imagery, and also by that rhythmic and exalted language which induces in sensitive persons something of the languid ecstasy of dream. The close connection between rhythm and heightened states of consciousness is as yet little understood. Its further investigation will probably throw much light on ontological as well as psychological problems. Mystical, no less than musical and poetic perception, tends naturally—we know not why—to present itself in rhythmical periods, a feature which is also strongly marked in writings obtained in the automatic state. So constant is this law in some subjects that Baron von Hügel adopted the presence or absence of rhythm as a test whereby to distinguish the genuine utterances of St. Catherine of Genoa from those wrongly attributed to her by successive editors of her legend.

All kinds of symbolic language come naturally to the articulate mystic, who is often a literary artist as well so naturally, that he sometimes forgets to explain that his utterance is but symbolic—a desperate attempt to translate the truth of that world into the beauty of this. It is here that mysticism joins hands with music and poetry, had this fact always been recognized by its critics, they would have been saved from many regrettable and some ludicrous misconceptions. Symbol—the clothing which the spiritual borrows from the material plane—is a form of artistic expression. That is to say, it is not literal but suggestive: though the artist who uses it may sometimes lose sight of this distinction. Hence the persons who imagine that the "Spiritual Marriage" of St. Catherine or St. Teresa veils a perverted sexuality, that the vision of the Sacred Heart involved an incredible anatomical experience, or that the divine inebriation of the Sufis is the apotheosis of drunkenness, do but advertise their ignorance of the mechanism of the arts: like the lady who thought that Blake *must* be mad because he said that he had touched the sky with his finger.

Further, the study of the mystics, the keeping company however humbly with their minds, brings with it as music or poetry does—but in a far greater degree—a strange exhilaration, as if we were brought near to some mighty source of Being, were at last on the verge of the secret which all seek. The symbols displayed, the actual words employed, when we analyse them, are not enough to account for such effect. It is rather that these messages from the waking transcendental self of another, stir our own deeper selves in their sleep. It were hardly an extravagance to say, that those writings which are the outcome of true and first-hand mystical experience may be known by this power of imparting to the reader the sense of exalted and extended life. "All mystics," says Saint-Martin, "speak the same language, for they come from the same country." The deep undying life within us came from that country too: and it recognizes the accents of home, though it cannot always understand what they would say.

Now, returning to our original undertaking, that of defining if we can the characteristics of true mysticism, I think that we have already reached a point at which William James's celebrated "four marks" of the mystic state, Ineffability, Noetic Quality, Transiency, and Passivity, will fail to satisfy us. In their place I propose to set out, illustrate and, I hope, justify four other rules or notes which may be applied as tests to any given case which claims to take rank amongst the mystics.

1. True mysticism is active and practical, not passive and theoretical. It is an organic life-process, a something which the whole self does; not something as to which its intellect holds an opinion.
2. Its aims are wholly transcendental and spiritual. It is in no way concerned with adding to, exploring, re-arranging, or improving anything in the visible universe. The mystic brushes aside that universe, even in its supernormal manifestations. Though he does not, as his enemies declare, neglect his duty to the many, his heart is always set upon the changeless One.
3. This One is for the mystic, not merely the Reality of all that is, but also a living and personal Object of Love; never an object of exploration. It draws his whole being homeward, but always under the guidance of the heart.
4. Living union with this One—which is the term of his adventure—is a definite state or form of enhanced life. It is obtained neither from an intellectual realization of its delights, nor from the most acute emotional longings. Though these must be present they are not enough. It is arrived at by an arduous psychological and spiritual process—the so-called Mystic Way—entailing the complete remaking of character and the liberation of a new, or rather latent, form of consciousness; which imposes on the self the condition which is sometimes inaccurately called "ecstasy," but is better named the Unitive State.

Mysticism, then, is not an opinion: it is not a philosophy. It has nothing in common with the pursuit of occult knowledge. On the one hand it is not merely the power of contemplating Eternity: on the other, it is not to be identified with any kind of religious queerness. It is the name of that organic process which involves the perfect consummation of the Love of God: the achievement here and now of the immortal heritage of man. Or, if you like it better—for this means exactly the same thing—it is the art of establishing his conscious relation with the Absolute.

The movement of the mystic consciousness towards this consummation, is not merely the sudden admission to an overwhelming vision of Truth: though such dazzling glimpses may from time to time be vouchsafed to the soul. It is rather an ordered movement towards ever higher levels of reality, ever closer identification with the Infinite. "The mystic experience," says Récéjac, "ends with the words, 'I live, yet not I, but God in me.' This feeling of identification, which is the term of mystical activity, has a very important significance. In its early stages the mystic consciousness feels the Absolute in opposition to the Self... as mystic activity goes on, it tends to abolish this opposition.... When it has reached its term the consciousness finds itself possessed by the sense of a Being at one and the same time greater than the Self and identical with it: great enough to be God, intimate enough to be me."

This is that mystic union which is the only possible fulfilment of mystic love: since

"All that is not One must ever
Suffer with the wound of Absence
And whoever in Love's city
Enters, finds but room for One
And but in One-ness, Union."

The history of mysticism is the history of the demonstration of this law upon the plane of reality. Now, how do these statements square with the practice of the great mystics; and with the various forms of activity which have been classified at one time or another as mystical?

MYSTICISM IS PRACTICAL, NOT THEORETICAL

This statement, taken alone, is not, of course, enough to identify mysticism; since it is equally true of magic, which also proposes to itself something to be done rather than something to be believed. It at once comes into collision, however, with the opinions of those who believe mysticism to be "the reaction of the born Platonist upon religion."

The difference between such devout philosophers and the true mystic, is the difference which George Tyrrell held to distinguish revelation from theology. Mysticism, like revelation, is final and personal. It is not merely a beautiful and suggestive diagram but experience in its most intense form. That experience, in the words of Plotinus, is the soul's solitary adventure "the flight of the Alone to the Alone." It provides the material, the substance, upon which mystical philosophy cogitates; as theologians cogitate upon the revelation which forms the basis of faith. Hence those whom we are to accept as mystics must have received, and acted upon, intuitions of a Truth which is for them absolute. If we are to acknowledge that they "knew the doctrine" they must have "lived the life"; submitted to the interior travail of the Mystic Way, not merely have reasoned about the mystical experiences of others. We could not well dispense with our Christian Platonists and mystical philosophers. They are our stepping-stones to higher things; interpret to our dull minds, entangled in the sense-world, the ardent vision of those who speak to us from the dimension of Reality. But they are no more mystics than the milestones on the Dover Road are travellers to Calais. Sometimes their words—the wistful words of those who know but cannot be—produce mystics; as the sudden sight of a signpost pointing to the sea will rouse the spirit of adventure in a boy. Also there are many instances of true mystics, such as Eckhart, who have philosophized upon their own experiences, greatly to the advantage of the world; and others—Plotinus is the most characteristic example—of Platonic philosophers who have passed far beyond the limits of their own philosophy, and abandoned the making of diagrams for an experience, however imperfect, of the reality at which these diagrams hint. It were more accurate to reverse the epigram above stated, and say, that Platonism is the reaction of the intellectualist upon mystical truth.

Over and over again the great mystics tell us, not how they speculated, but how they acted. To them, the transition from the life of sense to the life of spirit is a formidable undertaking, which demands effort and constancy. The paradoxical "quiet" of the contemplative is but the outward stillness essential to inward work. Their favourite symbols are those of action: battle, search, and pilgrimage.

"In an obscure night
Fevered with love's anxiety
(O hapless, happy plight!)
I *went*, none seeing me
Forth from my house, where all things quiet be,"

said St. John of the Cross, in his poem of the mystic quest.

Those who suppose mystical experience to be merely a pleasing consciousness of the Divine in the world, a sense of the "otherness" of things, a basking in the beams of the Uncreated Light, are only playing with Reality. True mystical achievement is the most complete and most difficult expression of life which is as yet possible to man. It is at once an act of love, an act of surrender, and an act of supreme perception; a trinity of experiences which meets and satisfies the three activities of the self. Religion might give us the first and metaphysics the third of these processes. Only Mysticism can offer the middle term of the series; the essential link which binds the three in one. "Secrets," says St. Catherine of Siena, "are revealed to a friend who has become one thing with his friend and not to a servant."

MYSTICISM IS AN ENTIRELY SPIRITUAL ACTIVITY

This rule provides us with a further limitation, which of course excludes all the practisers of magic and of magical religion: even in their most exalted and least materialistic forms. When we come to consider these persons, their object—not necessarily an illegitimate one—is to improve and elucidate the visible by help of the invisible: to use the supernormal powers of the self for the increase of power, virtue, happiness or knowledge. The mystic never turns back on himself in this way, or tries to combine the advantages of two worlds. At the term of his development he knows God by communion, and this direct intuition of the Absolute kills all lesser cravings. He possesses God, and needs nothing more. Though he will spend himself unceasingly for other men, become "an agent of the Eternal Goodness," he is destitute of supersensual ambitions and craves no occult knowledge or power. Having his eyes set on eternity, his consciousness steeped in it, he can well afford to tolerate the entanglements of time. "His spirit," says Tauler, "is as it were sunk and lost in the Abyss of the Deity, and loses the consciousness of all creature-distinctions. All things are gathered together in one with the divine sweetness, and the man's being is so penetrated with the divine substance that he loses himself therein, as a drop of water is lost in a cask of strong wine. And thus the man's spirit is so sunk in God in divine union, that he loses all sense of distinction... and there remains a secret, still union, without cloud or colour." "I wish not," said St. Catherine of Genoa, "for anything that comes forth from Thee, but only for Thee, oh sweetest Love!" "Whatever share of this world," says Rabi'a, "Thou dost bestow on me, bestow it on Thine enemies, and whatever share of the next world thou dost give me, give it to Thy friends. Thou art enough for me!" "The Soul," says Plotinus in one of his most profound passages, "having now arrived at the desired end, and participating of Deity, will know that the Supplier of true life is then present. She will likewise then require nothing farther; for, on the contrary it will be requisite to lay aside other things, to stop in this alone, amputating everything else with which she is surrounded."

THE BUSINESS AND METHOD OF MYSTICISM IS LOVE

Here is one of the distinctive notes of true mysticism; marking it off from every other kind of transcendental theory and practice and providing the answer to some of the question. It is the eager, outgoing activity whose driving power is generous love, not the absorbent, indrawing activity which strives only for new knowledge, that is fruitful in the spiritual as well as in the physical world.

Having said this, however, we must add—as we did when speaking of the "heart"—that the word Love as applied to the mystics is to be understood in its deepest, fullest sense; as the ultimate expression of the self's most vital tendencies, not as the superficial affection or emotion often dignified by this name. Mystic Love is a total dedication of the will; the deep-seated desire and tendency of the soul towards its Source. It is a condition of humble access, a life-movement of the self: more direct in its methods, more valid in its results—even in the hands of the least lettered of its adepts—than the most piercing intellectual vision of the greatest philosophic mind. Again and again the mystics insist upon this. "For silence is not God, nor speaking is not God; fasting is not God nor eating is not God; onliness is not God nor company is not God; nor yet any of all the other two such quantities, He is hid between them, and may not be found by any work of thy soul, but all only by love of thine heart. He may not be known by reason, He may not be gotten by thought, nor concluded by understanding; but he may be loved and chosen with the true lovely will of thine heart.... Such a blind shot with the sharp dart of longing love may never fail of the prick, the which is God."

"'Come down quickly,'" says the Incomprehensible Godhead to the soul that has struggled like Zaccheus to the topmost branches of the theological tree, "'for I would dwell with you to-day.' And this hasty descent to which he is summoned by God is simply a descent by love and desire in to that abyss of the Godhead which the intellect cannot understand. But where intelligence must rest without, love and desire can enter in."

Volumes of extracts might be compiled from the works of the mystics illustrative of this rule, which is indeed their central principle. "Some there are," says Plotinus, "that for all their effort have not attained the Vision; the soul in them has come to no sense of the splendour there. It has not taken warmth; it has not felt burning within itself the flame of love for what is there to know." "Love," says Rolle, "truly suffers not a loving soul to bide in itself, but ravishes it out to the Lover, that the soul is more there where it loves, than where the body is that lives and feels it." "Oh singular joy of love everlasting," he says again, "that ravishes all his to heavens above all worlds, them binding with bands of virtue! Oh dear charity, in earth that has thee not is nought wrought, whatever it hath! He truly in thee that is busy, to joy above earthly is soon lifted! Thou makest men contemplative, heaven-gate thou openest, mouths of accusers thou dost shut, God thou makest to be seen and multitude of sins thou hidest. We praise thee, we preach thee, by thee the world we quickly overcome, by whom we joy and the heavenly ladder we ascend."

Love to the mystic, then, is (a) the active, conative, expression of his will and desire for the Absolute; (b) his innate tendency to that Absolute, his spiritual weight. He is only thoroughly natural, thoroughly alive, when he is obeying its voice. For him it is the source of joy, the secret of the universe, the vivifying principle of things. In the words of Récéjac, "Mysticism claims to be able to know the Unknowable without any help from dialectics; and believes that, by the way of love and will it reaches a point to which thought alone is unable to attain." Again, "It is the heart and never the reason which leads us to the Absolute." Hence in St. Catherine of Siena's exquisite allegory it is the feet of the soul's affection which brings it first to the Bridge, "for the feet carry the body as affection carries the soul."

The jewels of mystical literature glow with this intimate and impassioned love of the Absolute; which transcends the dogmatic language in which it is clothed and becomes applicable to mystics of every race and creed. There is little difference in this between the extremes of Eastern and Western thought: between A Kempis the Christian and Jalalu 'd Din the Moslem saint.

"How great a thing is Love, great above all other goods: for alone it makes all that is heavy light, and bears evenly all that is uneven....

"Love would be aloft, nor will it be kept back by any lower thing. Love would be free, and estranged from all worldly affection, that its inward sight be not hindered: that it may not be entangled by any temporal comfort, nor succumb to any tribulation.

"Nought is sweeter than love, nought stronger, nought higher, nought wider: there is no more joyous, fuller, better thing in heaven or earth. For love is born of God, and cannot rest save in God, above all created things.

"The lover flies, runs, and, rejoices: he is free, and cannot be restrained. He gives all for all, and has all in all; for he rests in One Supreme above all, from whom all good flows and proceeds.

"He looks not at the gift, but above all goods turns himself to the giver.

"... He who loves knows the cry of this voice. For this burning affection of the soul is a loud cry in the ears of God when it saith 'My God, My Love, Thou art all mine, and I am all Thine.'"

So much for the Christian. Now for the Persian mystic.

"While the thought of the Beloved fills our hearts
All our work is to do Him service and spend life for Him.
Wherever He kindles His destructive torch
Myriads of lovers' souls are burnt therewith.

The lovers who dwell within the sanctuary
Are moths burnt with the torch of the Beloved's face.
O heart, hasten thither! for God will shine upon you,
And seem to you a sweet garden instead of a terror.
He will infuse into your soul a new soul,
So as to fill you, like a goblet, with wine.
Take up your abode in His Soul!
Take up your abode in heaven, oh bright full moon!
Like the heavenly Scribe, He will open your heart's book
That he may reveal mysteries unto you."

Well might Hilton say that "Perfect love maketh God and the soul to be as if they both together were but one thing," and Tauler that "the well of life is love, and he who dwelleth not in love is dead."

These, nevertheless, are objective and didactic utterances; though their substance may be—probably is—personal, their form is not. But if we want to see what it really means to be "in love with the Absolute,"—how intensely actual to the mystic is the Object of his passion, how far removed from the spheres of pious duty or philosophic speculation, how concrete, positive and dominant such a passion may be—we must study the literature of autobiography, not that of poetry or exhortation. I choose for this purpose, rather than the well-known self-analyses of St. Augustine, St. Teresa or Suso, which are accessible to every one, the more private confessions of that remarkable mystic Dame Gertrude More, contained in her "Spiritual Exercises."

This nun, great-great-granddaughter of Sir Thomas More, and favourite pupil of the celebrated Benedictine contemplative, the Ven. Augustine Baker, exhibits the romantic and personal side of mysticism more perfectly than even St. Teresa, whose works were composed for her daughters' edification. She was an eager student of St. Augustine, "my deere deere Saint," as she calls him more than once. He had evidently influenced her language; but her passion is her own.

Remember that Gertrude More's confessions represent the most secret conversations of her soul with God. They were not meant for publication; but, written for the most part on blank leaves in her breviary, were discovered and published after her death. "She called them," says the title-page with touching simplicity, " *Amor ordinem nescit:* an Ideot's Devotions. Her only spiritual father and directour, Father Baker, styled them *Confessiones Amantis,* A Lover's Confessions. *Amans Deum anima sub Deo despicit universa.* A soul that loveth God despiseth all things that be inferiour unto God."

The spirit of her little book is summed up in two epigrams, epigrams of which her contemporary, Crashaw, might have been proud. "To give all for love is a most sweet bargain." "O let me love, or not live!" Love indeed was her life: and she writes of it with a rapture which recalls at one moment the exuberant poetry of Jacopene da Todi, at another the love songs of the Elizabethan poets.

"Never was there or can there be imagined such a Love, as is between an humble soul and thee. Who can express what passeth between such a soul and thee? Verily neither man nor Angell is able to do it sufficiently.... In thy prayse I am only happy, in which, my Joy, I will exult with all that love thee. For what can be a comfort while I live separated from thee, but only to remember that my God, who is more myne than I am my owne, is absolutely and infinitely happy?... Out of this true love between a soul and thee, there ariseth such a knowledge in the soul that it loatheth all that is an impediment to her further proceeding in the Love of thee. O Love, Love, even by naming thee, my soul loseth itself in thee.... Nothing can Satiate a reasonable soul but only thou: and having of thee, who art indeed all, nothing could be said to be wanting to her.... *Blessed are the cleans of hart for they shall see God.* O sight to be wished, desired, and longed for; because once to have seen thee is to have learnt all things. Nothing can bring us to this sight but love. But what love must it be? not a sensible love only, a childish love, a love which seeketh itself more than the beloved. No, no, but it must be an ardent love, a pure love, a courageous love, a love of charity, an humble love, and a constant love, not worn out with labours, not daunted with any difficulties.... For that soul that hath set her whole love and desire on thee, can never find any true satisfaction, but only in thee."

Who will not see that we have here no literary exercise, but the fruits of an experience of peculiar intensity? It answers exactly to one of the best modern definitions of mysticism as "in essence, the concentration of all the forces of the soul upon a supernatural Object, conceived and loved as a living Person." "Love and desire," says the same critic, "are the fundamental necessities; and where they are absent man, even though he be a visionary, cannot be called a mystic." Such a definition, of course, is not complete. It is valuable however, because it emphasizes the fact that all true mysticism is rooted in personality, and is therefore fundamentally a science of the heart.

Attraction, desire, and union as the fulfilment of desire, this is the way Life works, in the highest as in the lowest things. The mystic's outlook, indeed, is the lover's outlook. It has the same element of wildness, the same quality of selfless and quixotic devotion, the same combination of rapture and humility. This parallel is more than a pretty fancy, for mystic and lover, upon different planes, are alike responding to the call of the Spirit of Life. The language of human passion is tepid and insignificant beside the language in which the mystics try to tell the splendours of their love. They force upon the unprejudiced reader the conviction that they are dealing with an ardour far more burning for an Object far more real.

"This monk can give lessons to lovers!" exclaimed Arthur Symons in astonishment of St. John of the Cross. It would be strange if he could not; since their finite passions are but the feeble images of his infinite one, their beloved the imperfect symbol of his First and only Fair. "I saw Him and sought Him: I had Him and I wanted Him," says Julian of Norwich, in a phrase which seems to sum up all the ecstasy and longing of man's soul. Only this mystic passion can lead us from our prison. Its brother, the desire of knowledge, may enlarge and improve the premises to an extent as yet undreamed of but it can never unlock the doors.

MYSTICISM ENTAILS A DEFINITE PSYCHOLOGICAL EXPERIENCE

That is to say, it shows itself not merely as an attitude of mind and heart, but as a form of organic life. It is not only a theory of the intellect or a hunger, however passionate, of the heart. It involves the organizing of the whole self, conscious and unconscious, under the spur of such a hunger: a remaking of the whole character on high levels in the interests of the transcendental life. The mystics are emphatic in their statement that spiritual desires are useless unless they initiate this costly movement of the whole self towards the Real.

Thus in the visions of Mechthild of Magdeburg, "The soul spoke thus to her Desire, 'Fare forth and see where my Love is. Say to him that I desire to love.' So Desire sped forth, for she is quick of her nature, and came to the Empyrean and cried, 'Great Lord, open and let me in!' Then said the Householder of that place, 'What means this fiery eagerness?' Desire replied, 'Lord I would have thee know that my lady can no longer bear to live. If Thou wouldst flow forth to her, then might she swim: but the fish cannot long exist that is left stranded on the shore.' 'Go back,' said the Lord, 'I will not let thee in unless thou bring to me that hungry soul, for it is in this alone that I take delight.'"

We have said that the full mystic consciousness is extended in two distinct directions. So too there are two distinct sides to the full mystical experience. (A) The vision or consciousness of Absolute Perfection. (B) The inward transmutation to which that Vision compels the mystic, in order that he may be to some extent worthy of that which he has beheld: may take his place within the order of Reality. He has seen the Perfect; he wants to be perfect too. The "third term," the necessary bridge between the Absolute and the Self, can only, he feels, be moral and spiritual transcendence—in a word, *Sanctity*— for "the only means of attaining the Absolute lies in adapting ourselves to It." The moral virtues are for him, then, the obligatory "ornaments of the Spiritual Marriage" as Ruysbroeck called them: though far more than their presence is needed to bring that marriage about. Unless this impulse for moral perfection be born in him, this travail of the inner life begun, he is no mystic: though he may well be a visionary, a prophet, a "mystical" poet.

Moreover, this process of transmutation, this rebuilding of the self on higher levels, will involve the establishment within the field of consciousness, the making "central for life," of those subconscious spiritual perceptions which are the primary material of mystical experience. The end object of this "inward alchemy" will be the raising of the whole self to the condition in which conscious and permanent union with the Absolute takes place and man, ascending to the summit of his manhood, enters into that greater life for which he was made. In its journey towards this union, the subject commonly passes through certain well-marked phases, which constitute what is known as the "Mystic Way." This statement rules out from the true mystic kingdom all merely sentimental and affective piety and visionary poetry, no less than mystical philosophy. It brings us back to our first proposition—the concrete and practical nature of the mystical act.

More than the apprehension of God, then, more than the passion for the Absolute, is needed to make a mystic. These must be combined with an appropriate psychological make-up, with a nature capable of extraordinary concentration, an exalted moral emotion, a nervous organization of the artistic type. All these are necessary to the successful development of the mystic life process. In the experience of those mystics who have left us the records of their own lives, the successive stages of this life process are always traceable. In the second part of this book, they will be found worked out at some length. Rolle, Suso, St. Teresa, and many others have left us valuable self-analyses for comparison and from them we see how arduous, how definite, and how far removed from mere emotional or intellectual activity, is that educational discipline by which "the eye which looks upon Eternity" is able to come to its own. "One of the marks of the true mystic," says Leuba—by no means a favourable witness—"is the tenacious and heroic energy with which he pursues a definite moral ideal "He is," says Pacheu, "the pilgrim of an inward Odyssey." Though we may be amazed and delighted by his adventures and discoveries on the way, to him the voyage and the end are all. "The road on which we enter is a royal road which leads to heaven," says St. Teresa. "Is it strange that the conquest of such a treasure should cost us rather dear?"

It is one of the many indirect testimonies to the objective reality of mysticism that the stages of this road, the psychology of the spiritual ascent, as described to us by different schools of contemplatives, always present practically the same sequence of states. The "school for saints" has never found it necessary to bring its curriculum up to date. The psychologist finds little difficulty, for instance, in reconciling the "Degrees of Orison" described by St. Teresa—Recollection, Quiet, Union, Ecstasy, Rapt, the "Pain of God," and the Spiritual Marriage of the soul—with the four forms of contemplation enumerated by Hugh of St. Victor, or the Sufi's "Seven Stages" of the soul's ascent to God, which begin in adoration and end in spiritual marriage. Though each wayfarer may choose different landmarks, it is clear from their comparison that the road is one.

As a corollary to these four rules, it is perhaps well to reiterate the statement already made, that *True Mysticism is never self-seeking.* It is not, as many think, the pursuit of supernatural joys; the satisfaction of a high ambition. The mystic does not enter on his quest because he desires the happiness of the Beatific Vision, the ecstasy of union with the Absolute, or any other personal reward. That noblest of all passions, the passion for perfection for Love's sake, far outweighs the desire for transcendental satisfaction. "O Love," said St. Catherine of Genoa, "I do not wish to follow thee for sake of these delights, but solely from the motive of true love." Those who do otherwise are only, in the plain words of St. John of the Cross, "spiritual gluttons": or, in the milder metaphor here adopted, magicians of the more high-minded sort. The true mystic claims no promises and makes no demands. He goes because he must, as Galahad went towards the Grail knowing that for those who can live it, this alone is life. He never rests in that search for God which he holds to be the fulfilment of his highest duty, yet he seeks without any certainty of success. He holds with St. Bernard that "He alone is God who can never be sought in vain, not even when He cannot be found." With Mechthild of Magdeburg, he hears the Absolute saying in his soul, "O soul, before the world was I longed for thee: and I still long for thee, and thou for Me. Therefore, when our two desires unite, Love shall be fulfilled."

Like his type, the "devout lover" of romance, then, the mystic serves without hope of reward. By one of the many paradoxes of the spiritual life, he obtains satisfaction because he does not seek it; completes his personality because he gives it up. "Attainment," says Dionysius the Areopagite in words which are writ large on the annals of Christian ecstasy, "comes only by means of this sincere, spontaneous, and entire surrender of yourself and all things." Only with the annihilation of selfhood comes the fulfilment of love. Were the mystic asked the cause of his often extraordinary behaviour, his austere and steadfast quest, it is unlikely that his reply would contain any reference to sublime illumination or unspeakable delights. It is more probable that he would answer in some such words as those of Jacob Boehme, "I am not come to this meaning, or to this work and knowledge through my own reason or through my own will and purpose; neither have I sought this knowledge, nor so much as to know anything concerning it. I sought only for the heart of God, therein to hide myself."

"Whether we live or whether we die," said St. Paul, "we are the Lord's." The mystic is a realist, to whom these words convey not a dogma but an invitation, an invitation to the soul to attain that fullness of life for which she was made, to "lose herself in That which can be neither seen nor touched; giving herself entirely to this sovereign Object without belonging either to herself or to others; united to the Unknown by the most noble part of herself and because of her renouncement of knowledge; finally drawing from this absolute ignorance a knowledge which the understanding knows not how to attain. Mysticism, then, is seen as the "one way out" for the awakened spirit of man; healing that human incompleteness which is the origin of our divine unrest. "I am sure," says Eckhart, "that if a soul knew the very least of all that Being means, it would never turn away from it." The mystics have never turned away: to do so would have seemed to them a self-destructive act. Here, in this world of illusion, they say, we have no continuing city. This statement, to you a proposition, is to us the central fact of life. "Therefore, it is necessary to hasten our departure from hence, and detach ourselves in so far as we may from the body to which we are fettered, in order that with the whole of our selves, we may fold ourselves about Divinity, and have no part void of contact with Him."

Mysticism is seen to be a highly specialized form of that search for reality, for heightened and completed life, which we have found to be a constant characteristic of human consciousness. It is largely prosecuted by that "spiritual spark," that transcendental faculty which, though the life of our life, remains below the threshold in ordinary men. Emerging from its hiddenness in the mystic, it gradually becomes the dominant factor in his life; subduing to its service, and enhancing by its saving contact with reality, those vital powers of love and will, which we attribute to the heart, rather than those of mere reason and perception, which we attribute to the head. Under the spur of this love and will, the whole personality rises in the acts of contemplation and ecstasy to a level of consciousness at which it becomes aware of a new field of perception. By this awareness, by this "loving sight," it is stimulated to a new life in accordance with the Reality which it has beheld. So strange and exalted is this life, that it never fails to provoke either the anger or the admiration of other men. "If the great Christian mystics," says Leuba, "could by some miracle be all brought together in the same place, each in his habitual environment, there to live according to his manner, the world would soon perceive that they constitute one of the most amazing and profound variations of which the human race has yet been witness."

A discussion of mysticism, regarded as a form of human life, will therefore include two branches. First the life process of the mystic, the remaking of his personality, the method by which his peculiar consciousness of the Absolute is attained, and faculties which have been evolved to meet the requirements of the phenomenal, are enabled to do work on the transcendental, plane. This is the "Mystic Way" in which the self passes through the states or stages of development which were codified by the Neoplatonists, and after them by the mediaeval mystics, as Purgation, Illumination, and Ecstasy. Secondly, the content of the mystical field of perception; the revelation under which the contemplative becomes aware of the Absolute. This will include a consideration of the so called doctrines of mysticism: the attempts of the articulate mystic to sketch for us the world into which he has looked, in language which is only adequate to the world in which the rest of us dwell. Here the difficult question of symbolism, and of symbolic theology, comes in a point upon which many promising expositions of the mystics have been wrecked. It will be our business to strip off as far as may be the symbolic wrapping, and attempt a synthesis of these doctrines; to resolve the apparent contradictions of objective and subjective revelations, of the ways of negation and affirmation, emanation and immanence, surrender and deification, the Divine Dark and the Inward Light; and finally to exhibits if we can, the essential unity of that experience in which the human soul enters consciously into the Presence of God.

3

MYSTICISM AND THEOLOGY

To understand this we will have to take account of the fact that often the true mystic is also a mystical philosopher; though there are plenty of mystical philosophers who are not and could never be mystics. Because it is characteristic of the human self to reflect upon its experience, to use its percepts as material for the construction of a concept, most mystics have made or accepted a theory of their own adventures. Thus we have a mystical philosophy or theology—the comment of the intellect on the proceedings of spiritual intuition—running side by side with true or empirical mysticism: classifying its data, criticizing it, explaining it, and translating its vision of the supersensible into symbols which are amenable to dialectic.

Such a philosophy is most usually founded upon the formal creed which the individual mystic accepts. It is characteristic of him that in so far as his transcendental activities are healthy he is generally an acceptor and not a rejector of such creeds. The view which regards the mystic as a spiritual anarchist receives little support from history; which shows us, again and again, the great mystics as faithful sons of the great religions. Almost any religious system which fosters unearthly love is potentially a nursery for mystics and Christianity, Islam, Brahmanism, and Buddhism each receives its most sublime interpretation at their hands. Thus St. Teresa interprets her ecstatic apprehension of the Godhead in strictly Catholic terms, and St. John of the Cross contrives to harmonize his intense transcendentalism with incarnational and sacramental Christianity. Thus Boehme believed to the last that his explorations of eternity were consistent with the teaching of the Lutheran Church. The Sufis were good Mohammedans, Philo and the Kabalists were orthodox Jews. Plotinus even adapted—though with what difficulty—the relics of paganism to his doctrine of the Real.

Attempts, however, to limit mystical truth—the direct apprehension of the Divine Substance—by the formula of any one religion, are as futile as the attempt to identify a precious metal with the die which converts it into current coin. The dies which the mystics have used are many. Their peculiarities and excrescences are always interesting and sometimes highly significant. Some give a far sharper, more coherent, impression than others. But the gold from which this diverse coinage is struck is always the same precious metal: always the same Beatific Vision of a Goodness, Truth, and Beauty which is *one.* Hence its substance must always be distinguished from the accidents under which we perceive it, for this substance has an absolute, and not a denominational, importance.

Nevertheless, if we are to understand the language of the mystics, it is evident that we must know a little of accident as well as of substance that is to say, of the principal philosophies or religions which they have used in describing their adventures to the world. This being so, before we venture to apply ourselves to the exploration of theology proper, it will be well to consider the two extreme forms under which both mystics and theologians have been accustomed to conceive Divine Reality, that is to say, the so-called "emanation-theory" and "immanence-theory" of the transcendental world.

Emanation and Immanence are formidable words; which though perpetually tossed to and fro by amateurs of religious philosophy, have probably, as they stand, little actuality for practical modern men. They are, however, root-ideas for the maker of mystical diagrams and his best systems are but attempts towards their reconciliation. Since the aim of every mystic is union with God, it is obvious that the vital question in his philosophy must be the place which this God, the Absolute of his quest, occupies in the scheme. Briefly, He has been conceived—or, it were better to say, presented—by the great mystics under two apparently contradictory modes.

(1) The opinion which is represented in its most extreme form by the theory of *Emanations,* declares His utter transcendence. This view appears early in the history of Greek philosophy. It is developed by Dionysius, by the Kabalists, by Dante: and is implied in the language of Rulman Merswin, St. John of the Cross and many other Christian ecstatics.

The solar system is an almost perfect symbol of this concept of Reality; which finds at once its most rigid and most beautiful expression in Dante's "Paradiso." The Absolute Godhead is conceived as removed by a vast distance from the material world of sense; the last or lowest of that system of dependent worlds or states which, generated by or emanating from the Unity or Central Sun, become less in spirituality and splendour, greater in multiplicity, the further they recede from their source. That Source—the Great Countenance of the Godhead—can never, say the Kabalists, be discerned by man. It is the Absolute of the Neoplatonists, the Unplumbed Abyss of later mysticism, the Cloud of Unknowing wraps it from our sight. Only by its "emanations" or manifested attributes can we attain knowledge of it. By the outflow of these same manifested attributes and powers the created universe exists, depending in the last resort on the *latens Deitas:* Who is therefore conceived as external to the world which He illuminates and vivifies.

St. Thomas Aquinas virtually accepts the doctrine of Emanations when he writes: "As all the perfections of Creatures descend in order from God, who is the height of perfection, man should begin from the lower creatures and ascend by degrees, and so advance to the knowledge of God.... And because in that roof and crown of all things, God, we find the most perfect unity, and everything is stronger and more excellent the more thoroughly it is one; it follows that diversity and variety increase in things, the further they are removed from Him who is the first principle of all." Suso, whose mystical system, like that of most Dominicans, is entirely consistent with Thomist philosophy, is really glossing Aquinas when he writes: "The supreme and superessential Spirit has ennobled man by illuminating him with a ray from the Eternal Godhead.... Hence from out the great ring which represents the Eternal Godhead there flow forth... little rings, which may be taken to signify the high nobility of natural creatures."

Obviously, if this theory of the Absolute be accepted the path of the soul's ascent to union with the divine must be literally a transcendence: a journey "upward and outward," through a long series of intermediate states or worlds till, having traversed the "Thirty-two paths of the Tree of Life," she at last arrives, in Kabalistic language, at the Crown: fruitive knowledge of God, the Abyss or Divine Dark of the Dionysian school, the Neoplatonic One. Such a series of worlds is symbolized by the Ten Heavens of Dante, the hierarchies of Dionysius, the Tree of Life or Sephiroth of the Kabalah and receives its countersign in the inward experience, in the long journey of the self through Purgation and Illumination to Union. "We ascend," says St. Augustine, "thy ways that be in our heart, and sing a song of degrees; we glow inwardly with thy fire, with thy good fire, and we go, because we go upwards to the peace of Jerusalem."

This theory postulates, under normal and non-mystical conditions, the complete separation of the human and the divine, the temporal and the eternal worlds. "Never forget," says St. John of the Cross, "that God is inaccessible. Ask not therefore how far your powers may comprehend Him, your feeling penetrate Him. Fear thus to content yourself with too little, and deprive your soul of the agility which it needs in order to mount up to Him." The language of pilgrimage, of exile, comes naturally to the mystic who apprehends reality under these terms. To him the mystical adventure is essentially a "going forth" from his normal self and from his normal universe. Like the Psalmist "in his heart he hath disposed to ascend by steps in this vale of tears" from the less to the more divine. He, and with him the Cosmos—for to mystical philosophy the soul of the individual subject is the microcosm of the soul of the world—has got to retrace the long road to the Perfection from which it originally came forth; as the fish in Rulman Merswin's Vision of Nine Rocks must struggle upwards from pool to pool until they reach their Origin.

Such a way of conceiving Reality accords with the type of mind which William James called the "sick soul." It is the mood of the penitent, of the utter humility which, appalled by the sharp contrast between itself and the Perfect which it contemplates, can only cry "out of the depths." It comes naturally to the temperament which leans to pessimism, which sees a "great gulf fixed" between itself and its desire, and is above all things sensitive to the elements of evil and imperfection in its own character and in the normal experience of man. Permitting these elements to dominate its field of consciousness, wholly ignoring the divine aspect of the World of Becoming, such a temperament constructs from its perceptions and prejudices the concept of a material world and a normal self which are very far from God.

(2) *Immanence.* At the opposite pole from this way of sketching Reality is the extreme theory of Immanence, which plays so large a part in modern theology. To the holders of this theory, who commonly belong to James's "healthy minded" or optimistic class, the quest of the Absolute is no long journey, but a realization of something which is implicit in the self and in the universe: an opening of the eyes of the soul upon the Reality in which it is bathed. For them earth is literally "crammed with heaven." "Thou wert I, but dark was my heart, I knew not the secret transcendent," says Téwekkul Bég, a Moslem mystic of the seventeenth century. This is always the cry of the temperament which leans to a theology of immanence, once its eyes are opened on the light. "God," says Plotinus, "is not external to anyone, but is present with all things, though they are ignorant that He is so." In other and older words, "The Spirit of God is within you." The Absolute Whom all seek does not hold Himself aloof from an imperfect material universe, but dwells within the flux of things: stands as it were at the very threshold of consciousness and knocks awaiting the self's slow discovery of her treasures. "He is not far from any one of us, for in Him we live and move and have our being," is the pure doctrine of Immanence, a doctrine whose teachers are drawn from amongst the souls which react more easily to the touch of the Divine than to the sense of alienation and of sin, and are naturally inclined to love rather than to awe.

Unless safeguarded by limiting dogmas, the theory of Immanence, taken alone, is notoriously apt to degenerate into pantheism; and into those extravagant perversions of the doctrine of "deification" in which the mystic holds his transfigured self to be identical with the Indwelling God. It is the philosophical basis of that practice of introversion, the turning inward of the soul's faculties in contemplation, which has been the "method" of the great practical mystics of all creeds. That God, since He is in all—in a sense, *is* all—may most easily be found within ourselves, is the doctrine of these adventurers; who, denying or ignoring the existence of those intervening "worlds" or "planes" between the material world and the Absolute, which are postulated by the theory of Emanations, claim with Ruysbroeck that "by a simple introspection in fruitive love" they "meet God without intermediary." They hear the Father of Lights "saying eternally, without intermediary or interruption, in the most secret part of the spirit, the one, unique, and abysmal Word."

This discovery of a "divine" essence or substance, dwelling, as Ruysbroeck says, at the apex of man's soul is that fundamental experience—found in some form or degree in all genuine mystical religion—which provides the basis of the New Testament doctrine of the indwelling spirit. It is, variously interpreted, the "spark of the soul" of Eckhart, the "ground" of Tauler, the Inward Light of the Quakers, the "Divine Principle" of some modern transcendentalists; the fount and source of all true life. At this point logical exposition fails mystic and theologian alike. A tangle of metaphors takes its place. We are face to face with the "wonder of wonders"—that most real, yet most mysterious, of all the experiences of religion, the union of human and divine, in a nameless *something* which is "great enough to be God, small enough to be me." In the struggle to describe this experience, the "spark of the soul," the point of juncture, is at one moment presented to us as the divine to which the self attains: at another, as that transcendental aspect of the self which is in contact with God. On either hypothesis, it is here that the mystic encounters Absolute Being. Here is his guarantee of God's immediate presence in the human heart; and, if in the human heart, then in that universe of which man's soul resumes in miniature the essential characteristics.

According to the doctrine of Immanence, creation, the universe, could we see it as it is, would be perceived as the self-development, the self-revelation of this indwelling Deity. The world is not projected from the Absolute, but immersed in God. "I understood," says St. Teresa, "how our Lord was in all things, and how He was in the soul and the illustration of a sponge filled with water was suggested to me."

The world-process, then, is the slow coming to fruition of that Divine Spark which is latent alike in the Cosmos and in man. "If," says Boehme, "thou conceivest a small minute circle, as small as a grain of mustard seed, yet the Heart of God is wholly and perfectly therein and if thou art born in God, then there is in thyself (in the circle of thy life) the whole Heart of God undivided." The idea of Immanence has seldom been more beautifully expressed. It is worth noticing that both the theological doctrines of reality which have been acceptable to the mystics implicitly declare, as science does, that the universe is not static but dynamic; a World of Becoming. According to the doctrine of

Immanence this universe is free, self-creative. The divine action floods it, no part is more removed from the Godhead than any other part. "God," says Eckhart, "is nearer to me than I am to myself. He is just as near to wood and stone, but they do not know it."

These two apparently contradictory explanations of the Invisible have both been held, and that in their extreme form, by the mystics who have found in both adequate, and indeed necessary, diagrams by which to suggest something of their rich experience of Reality. Some of the least lettered and most inspired amongst them—for instance, St. Catherine of Siena, Julian of Norwich—and some of the most learned, as Dionysius the Areopagite and Meister Eckhart, have actually used in their rhapsodies language appropriate to both the theories of Emanation and of Immanence. It would seem, then, that both these theories convey a certain truth; and that it is the business of a sound mystical philosophy to reconcile them. It is too often forgotten by quarrelsome partisans of a concrete turn of mind that at best all these transcendental theories are only symbols, methods, diagrams, feebly attempting the representation of an experience which in its fullness is always the same, and of which the dominant characteristic is ineffability. Hence they insist with tiresome monotony that Dionysius must be wrong if Tauler be right: that it is absurd to call yourself the Friend of God if unknowableness be that God's first attribute: that Plato's Perfect Beauty and St. Catherine of Siena's Accepter of Sacrifices cannot be the same: that the "courteous and dear-worthy Lord" who said to Lady Julian, "My darling, I am glad that thou art come to Me, in all thy woe I have ever been with thee," ules out the formless and impersonal One of Plotinus, the "triple circle" of Suso and Dante. Finally, that if God be truly immanent in the material world it is either sin or folly to refuse that world in order that we may find Him; and if introversion be right, a plan of the universe which postulates intervening planes between Absolute Being and the phenomenal world must be wrong.

Now as regards the mystics, of whom we hold both these doctrines, these ways of seeing truth—for what else is a doctrine but that?—it is well to remind ourselves that their teaching about the relation of the Absolute to the finite, of God to the phenomenal world, must be founded in the first instance on what they know by experience of the relation between that Absolute and the individual self. This experience is the valid part of mysticism, the thing which gives to it its unique importance amongst systems of thought, the only source of its knowledge. Everything else is really guessing aided by analogy. When therefore the mystic, applying to the universe what he knows to be true in respect of his own soul, describes Divine Perfection as very far removed from the material world, yet linked with it by a graduated series of "emanations"—states or qualities which have each of them something of the godlike, though they be not God—he is trying to describe the necessary life-process which he has himself passed through in the course of his purgation and spiritual ascent from the state of the "natural man" to that other state of harmony with the spiritual universe, sometimes called "deification," in which he is able to contemplate, and unite with, the divine. We have in the "Divina Commedia" a classic example of such a twofold vision of the inner and the outer worlds, for Dante's journey up and out to the Empyrean Heaven is really an inward alchemy, an ordering and transmuting of his nature, a purging of his spiritual sight till—transcending all derived beatitude—it can look for an instant on the Being of God.

The mystic assumes—because he tends to assume an orderly basis for things—that there is a relation, an analogy, between this microcosm of man's self and the macrocosm of the world-self. Hence his experience, the geography of the individual quest, appears to him good evidence of the geography of the Invisible. Since he must transcend his natural life in order to attain consciousness of God, he conceives of God as essentially transcendent to the natural world. His description of that geography, however—of his path in a land where there is no time and space, no inner and no outer, up or down—will be conditioned by his temperament, by his powers of observation, by the metaphor which comes most readily to his hand, above all by his theological education. The so-called journey itself is a psychological and spiritual experience, the purging and preparation of the self, its movement to higher levels of consciousness, its unification with that more spiritual but normally unconscious self which is in touch with the transcendental order, and its gradual or abrupt entrance into union with the Real. Sometimes it seems to the self that this performance is a retreat inwards to that "ground of the soul" where, as St. Teresa says, "His Majesty awaits us": sometimes a going forth from the Conditioned to the Unconditioned, the "supernatural flight" of Plotinus and Dionysius the Areopagite. Both are but images under which the self conceives the process of attaining conscious union with that God who is "at once immanent and transcendent in relation to the Soul which shares His life."

He has got to find God. Sometimes his temperament causes him to lay most stress on the length of the search; sometimes the abrupt rapture which brings it to a close makes him forget that preliminary pilgrimage in which the soul is "not outward bound but rather on a journey to its centre." The habitations of the Interior Castle through which St. Teresa leads us to that hidden chamber which is the sanctuary of the indwelling God, the hierarchies of Dionysius, ascending from the selfless service of the angels, past the seraphs' burning love, to the God enthroned above time and space, the mystical paths of the Kabalistic Tree of Life which lead from the material world of Malkuth through the universes of action and thought, by Mercy, Justice and Beauty, to the Supernal Crown; all these are different ways of describing this same pilgrimage.

As every one is born a disciple of either Plato or Aristotle, so every human soul leans to one of these two ways of apprehending reality. The artist, the poet, every one who looks with awe and rapture on created things, acknowledges in this act the

Immanent God. The ascetic, and that intellectual ascetic the metaphysician, turning from the created, denying the senses in order to find afar off the uncreated, unconditioned Source, is really—though often he knows it not—obeying that psychological law which produced the doctrine of Emanations.

A good map then, a good mystical philosophy, will leave room for both these ways of interpreting our experience. It will mark the routes by which many different temperaments claim to have found their way to the same end. It will acknowledge both the aspects under which the *patria splendida* Truth has appeared to its lovers: the aspects which have called forth the theories of emanation and immanence and are enshrined in the Greek and Latin names of God. *Deus,* whose root means day, shining, the Transcendent Light; and *Theos,* whose true meaning is supreme desire or prayer—the Inward Love—do not contradict, but complete each other. They form, when taken together, an almost perfect definition of that Godhead which is the object of the mystic's desire, the Divine Love which, immanent in the soul spurs on that soul to union with the transcendent and Absolute Light—at once the source, the goal, the life of created things.

The true mystic—the person with a genius for God—hardly needs a map himself. He steers a compass course across the "vast and stormy sea of the divine." It is characteristic of his intellectual humility, however, that he is commonly willing to use the map of the community in which he finds himself, when it comes to showing other people the route which he has pursued. Sometimes these maps have been adequate. More, they have elucidated the obscure wanderings of the explorer; helped him; given him landmarks; worked out right. Time after time he puts his finger on some spot—some great hill of vision, some city of the soul—and says with conviction, "*Here* have I been." At other times the maps have embarrassed him, have refused to fit in with his description. Then he has tried, as Boehme did and after him Blake, to make new ones. Such maps are often wild in drawing, because good draughtsmanship does not necessarily go with a talent for exploration. Departing from the usual convention, they are hard—sometimes impossible—to understand. As a result, the orthodox have been forced to regard their makers as madmen or heretics when they were really only practical men struggling to disclose great matters by imperfect means.

Without prejudice to individual beliefs, and without offering an opinion as to the exclusive truth of any one religious system or revelation—for here we are concerned neither with controversy nor with apologetics—we are bound to allow as a historical fact that mysticism, so far, has found its best map in Christianity. Christian philosophy, especially that Neoplatonic theology which, taking up and harmonizing all that was best in the spiritual intuitions of Greece, India, and Egypt, was developed by the great doctors of the early and mediaeval Church, supports and elucidates the revelations of the individual mystic as no other system of thought has been able to do.

We owe to the great fathers of the first five centuries—to Clement of Alexandria and Irenaeus, Gregory of Nyssa and Augustine; above all to Dionysius the Areopagite, the great Christian contemporary of Proclus—the preservation of that mighty system of scaffolding which enabled the Catholic mystics to build up the towers and bulwarks of the City of God. The peculiar virtue of this Christian philosophy, that which marks its superiority to the more coldly self-consistent systems of Greece, is the fact that it re-states the truths of metaphysics in terms of personality thus offering a third term, a "living mediator" between the Unknowable God, the unconditioned Absolute, and the conditioned self. This was the priceless gift which the Wise Men received in return for their gold, frankincense, and myrrh. This solves the puzzle which all explorers of the supersensible have sooner or later to face: *come si convenne l'imago al cerchio,* the reconciliation of Infinite and intimate, both known and felt, but neither understood. Such a third term, such a stepping-stone, was essential if mysticism were ever to attain that active union that fullness of life which is its object, and develop from a blind and egoistic rapture into fruitful and self-forgetting love.

Where non-Christian mystics, as a rule, have made a forced choice between the two great dogmatic expressions of their experience, (*a*) the long pilgrimage towards a transcendent and unconditioned Absolute, (*b*) the discovery of that Absolute in the "ground" or spiritual principle of the self; it has been possible to Christianity, by means of her central doctrine of the Trinity, to find room for both of them and to exhibit them as that which they are in fact—the complementary parts of a whole. Even Dionysius, the godfather of the emanation doctrine, combines with his scheme of descending hierarchies the dogma of an indwelling God and no writer is more constantly quoted by Meister Eckhart, who is generally considered to have preached immanence in its most extreme and pantheistic form.

Further, the Christian atmosphere is the one in which the individual mystic has most often been able to develop his genius in a sane and fruitful way; and an overwhelming majority of the great European contemplatives have been Christians of a strong impassioned and personal type. This alone would justify us in regarding it as embodying, at any rate in the West, the substance of the true tradition providing the "path of least resistance" through which that tradition flows. The very heretics of Christianity have often owed their attraction almost wholly to the mystical element in their teachings. The Gnostics, the Fraticelli, the Brethren of the Free Spirit, the Quietists, the Quakers, are instances of this. In others, it was to an excessive reliance on reason when dealing with the suprarational, and a corresponding absence of trust in mystical intuition that heresy was due. Arius and Pelagius are heretics of this type.

The greatest mystics, however, have not been heretics but Catholic saints. In Christianity the "natural mysticism" which like "natural religion," is latent in humanity, and at a certain point of development breaks out in every race, came to itself; and attributing for the first time true and distinct personality to its Object, brought into focus the confused and unconditioned God which Neoplatonism had constructed from the abstract concepts of philosophy blended with the intuitions of Indian ecstatics, and made the basis of its meditations on the Real. It is a truism that the chief claim of Christian philosophy on our respect does not lie in its exclusiveness but in its Catholicity: in the fact that it finds truth in a hundred different systems, accepts and elucidates Greek, Jewish, and Indian thought, fuses them in a coherent theology, and says to speculative thinkers of every time and place, "Whom therefore ye ignorantly worship, Him declare I unto you."

The voice of that Truth which spoke once for all on Calvary, and there declared the ground plan of the universe, was heard more or less perfectly by all the great seers, the intuitive leaders of men, the possessors of genius for the Real. There are few of the Christian names of God which were not known to the teachers of antiquity. To the Egyptians He was the Saviour, to the Platonists the Good, Beautiful and True, to the Stoics the Father and Companion. The very words of the Fourth Gospel are anticipated by Cleanthes. Heracleitus knew the Energizing Fire of which St. Bonaventura and Mechthild of Magdeburg speak. Countless mystics, from St. Augustine to St. John of the Cross, echo again and again the language of Plotinus. It is true that the differentia which mark off Christianity from all other religions are strange and poignant but these very differentia make of it the most perfect of settings for the mystic life. Its note of close intimacy, of direct and personal contact with a spiritual reality given here and now—its astonishing combination of splendour and simplicity, of the sacramental and transcendent—all these things minister to the needs of the mystical type.

Hence the Christian system, or some colourable imitation of it, has been found essential by almost all the great mystics of the West. They adopt its nomenclature, explain their adventures by the help of its creed, identify their Absolute with the Christian God. Amongst European mystics the most usually quoted exception to this rule is Blake; yet it is curious to notice that the more inspired his utterance, the more passionately and dogmatically Christian even this hater of the Churches becomes:

"We behold
Where Death eternal is put off eternally. O Lamb
Assume the dark satanic body in the Virgin's womb!
O Lamb divine ! it cannot thee annoy! O pitying One
Thy pity is from the foundation of the world, and thy Redemption
Begins already in Eternity."

This is the doctrine of the Incarnation in a nutshell, here St. Thomas himself would find little to correct. Of the two following extracts from "Jerusalem," the first is but a poet's gloss on the Catholic's cry, *"O felix culpa!"* the second is an almost perfect epitome of Christian theology and ethics:

"If I were pure, never could I taste the sweets
Of the forgiveness of sins. If I were holy I never could behold the tears
Of Love... O Mercy! O divine Humanity!
O Forgiveness, O Pity and Compassion! If I were pure I should never
Have known Thee."

"Wouldst thou love one who never died
For thee, or ever die for one who had not died for thee?
And if God dieth not for man, and giveth not Himself
Eternally for Man, Man could not exist, for Man is Love
As God is Love. Every kindness to another is a little death
In the Divine Image, nor can Man exist but by brotherhood."

Whether the dogmas of Christianity be or be not accepted on the scientific and historical plane, then, those dogmas are necessary to an adequate description of mystical experience—at least, of the fully developed dynamic mysticism of the West. We must therefore be prepared in reading the works of the contemplatives for much strictly denominational language; and shall be wise if we preface the encounter by some consideration of this language, and of its real meaning for those who use and believe it.

No one needs, I suppose, to be told that the two chief features of Christian schematic theology are the dogmas of the Trinity and the Incarnation. They correlate and explain each other: forming together, for the Christian, the "final key" to the riddle of the world. The history of practical and institutional Christianity is the history of the attempt to exhibit their meaning in space and time. The history of mystical philosophy is the history—still incomplete—of the demonstration of their meaning in eternity.

Some form of Trinitarian dogma is found to be essential, as a method of describing observed facts, the moment that mysticism begins either (*a*) to analyse its own psychological conditions, or (*b*) to philosophize upon its intuitive experience of God. It must, that is to say, divide the aspects under which it knows the Godhead, if it is to deal with them in a fruitful or comprehensible way. The Unconditioned One, which is, for Neoplatonic and Catholic mystic alike, the final object of their quest, cannot of itself satisfy the deepest instincts of humanity: for man is aware that diversity in unity is a necessary condition if perfection of character is to be expressed. Though the idea of unity alone may serve to define the End—and though the mystics return to it again and again as a relief from that "heresy of multiplicity" by which they are oppressed—it cannot by itself be adequate to the description of the All.

The first question, then, must be—How many of such aspects are necessary to a satisfactory presentment of the mystic's position? How many faces of Reality does he see? We observe that his experience involves at least a twofold apprehension. (*a*) That Holy Spirit within, that Divine Life by which his own life is transfused and upheld, and of which he becomes increasingly conscious as his education proceeds. (*b*) That Transcendent Spirit without, the "Absolute," towards union with which the indwelling and increasingly dominant spirit of love presses the developing soul. In his ecstasy, it seems to the mystic that these two experiences of God become one. But in the attempt to philosophize on his experiences he is bound to separate them. Over and over again the mystics and their critics acknowledge, explicitly or implicitly, the necessity of this discrimination for human thought.

Thus even the rigid monotheism of Israel and Islam cannot, in the hands of the Kabalists and the Sufis, get away from an essential dualism in the mystical experience. According to the Zohar "God is considered as immanent in all that has been created or emanated, and yet is transcendent to all." So too the Sufis. God, they say, is to be contemplated *(a)* outwardly in the imperfect beauties of the earth; (*b*) inwardly, by meditation. Further, since He is One, and in all things, "to conceive one's self as separate from God is an error: yet *only when one sees oneself as separate from God, can one reach out to God."*

Thus Delacroix, speaking purely as a psychologist, and denying to the mystical revelation—which he attributes exclusively to the normal content of the subliminal mind—any transcendental value, writes with entire approval of St. Teresa, that she "set up externally to herself the definite God of the Bible, at the same time as she set up within her soul the confused God of the Pseudo-Areopagite, the One of Neoplatonism. The first is her guarantee of the orthodoxy of the second, and prevents her from losing herself in an indistinction which is non-Christian. The confused God within is highly dangerous.... St. Teresa knew how to avoid this peril, and, served by her rich subconscious life, by the exaltation of her mental images, by her faculty of self-division on the one hand, on the other by her *rare powers of unification,* she realized simultaneously a double state in which the two Gods [*i.e.,* the two ways of apprehending God, transcendence and immanence] were guarantees of each other, mutually consolidating and enriching one another, such is the intellectual vision of the Trinity in the Seventh Habitation."

It is probable that St. Teresa, confronted by this astonishing analysis, would have objected that her Trinity, unlike that of her eulogist, consisted of three and not two Persons. His language concerning confused interior and orthodox exterior Gods would certainly have appeared to her delicate and honest mind both clumsy and untrue: nor could she have allowed that the Unconditioned One of the Neoplatonists was an adequate description of the strictly personal Divine Majesty, Whom she found enthroned in the inmost sanctuary of the Castle of the Soul. What St. Teresa really did was to actualize in her own experience, apprehend in the "ground of her soul" by means of her extraordinarily developed transcendental perceptions, the three distinct and personal Aspects of the Godhead which are acknowledged by the Christian religion.

First, the Father, pure transcendent Being, creative Source and Origin of all that Is: the Unconditioned and Unknowable One of the Neoplatonists: Who is "neither This nor That" and must be conceived, *pace* M. Delacroix, as utterly transcendent to the subject rather than "set up within the soul."

Secondly, in the Person of Christ, St. Teresa isolated and distinguished the Logos or Creative Word; the expression, or outbirth, of the Father's thought. Here is the point at which the Divine Substance first becomes apprehensible by the spirit of man, that mediating principle "raised up between heaven and earth" which is at once the Mirror of Pure Being and the Light of a finite world. The Second Person of the Christian Trinity is for the believer not only the brightness or express image of Deity, but also the personal, inexhaustible, and responsive Fount of all life and Object of all love: Who, because of His taking up (in the Incarnation) of humanity into the Godhead, has become the Bridge between finite and infinite, between the individual and the Absolute Life, and hence in mystic language the "true Bridegroom" of every human soul.

Thirdly, she recognized within herself the germ of that Absolute Life, the indwelling Spirit which is the source of man's transcendental consciousness and his link with the Being of God. That is to say, the Holy Spirit of Divine Love, the Real Desirous seeking for the Real Desired, without Whose presence any knowledge of or communion with God on man's part would be inconceivable.

In the supreme Vision of the Trinity which was vouchsafed to St. Teresa in the Seventh Habitation of the soul, these three aspects became fused in One. In the deepest recesses of her spirit, in that abyss where selfhood ceases to have meaning, and the individual soul touches the life of the All, distinction vanished and she "saw God in a point." Such an experience, such an intuition of simple and undifferentiated Godhead—the Unity—beyond those three centres of Divine Consciousness which we call the Trinity of Persons, is highly characteristic of mysticism. The German mystics—temperamentally miles asunder from St. Teresa—described it as the attainment of the "still wilderness" or "lonely desert of Deity" the limitless Divine Abyss, impersonal, indescribable, for ever hid in the Cloud of Unknowing, and yet the true Country of the Soul.

These statements, which appear when thus laid down to be hopelessly academic, violently divorced from life, were not for St. Teresa or any other Christian mystic abstract propositions but attempts towards the description of first-hand experience.

"By some mysterious manifestation of the truth," she says, "the three Persons of the most Blessed Trinity reveal themselves, preceded by an illumination which shines on the spirit like a most dazzling cloud of light. The three Persons are distinct from one another; a sublime knowledge is infused into the soul, imbuing it with a certainty of the truth that the Three are of one substance, power, and knowledge, and are one God. Thus that which we hold as a doctrine of faith, the soul now, so to speak, understands by sight, though it beholds the Blessed Trinity neither by the eyes of the body nor of the soul, this being no imaginary vision. All the Three Persons here communicate Themselves to the soul, speak to it, and make it understand the words of our Lord in the Gospel, that He and the Father and the Holy Ghost will come and make their abode with the soul which loves Him and keeps His commandments.

O my God, how different from merely hearing and believing these words is it to realize their truth in this way! Day by day a growing astonishment takes possession of this soul, for the three Persons of the Blessed Trinity seem never to depart; that They dwell far within its own centre and depths; though for want of learning it cannot describe how, it is conscious of the indwelling of these divine Companions."

Mystical writers constantly remind us that life as perceived by the human minds shows an inveterate tendency to arrange itself in triads: that if they proclaim the number Three in the heavens, they can also point to it as dominating everywhere upon the earth. Here Christianity did but give form to a deep instinct of the human mind, an instinct which made Pythagoras call Three the number of God, because beginning, middle, and end were contained therein. Thus to Hindu thought the Absolute Godhead was unknowable, but He disclosed three faces to man—Brahma the Creator, Shiva the Destroyer, Krishna the Repairer—and these three were One. So too the Neoplatonists distinguished three worlds; the Sensible or Phenomenal, the Rational or Intellectual, the Intelligible or Spiritual; and three aspects of God—the Unconditioned Absolute, the Logos or Artificer, and the divine Essence or Soul of the World which is both absolute and created. Perhaps we have in such triads a first sketch of the Christian Trinity; though falling far short of the requirements of man's spiritual experience. The dry bones await the breath of more abundant life. Corresponding with this diagram of God's nature the Platonists see also three grades of beauty; the Corporeal, the Spiritual, and the Divine.

Man, that "thing of threes," of body, soul and spirit, of understanding, memory and will, follows in his path towards unity the Threefold Way: for "our soul," says Lady Julian, "is made-trinity like to the unmade blissful Trinity, known and loved from without beginning, and in the making oned to the Maker." We still tend to analyse our psychic life into emotional, volitional, and intellectual elements. Even the Subject and Object implied in every experience required a third term, the relation between them, without which no thought can be complete. Thus the very principle of analogy imposes upon man a Trinitarian definition of Reality as the one with which his mind is best able to cope. It is easy for the hurried rationalist to demonstrate the absurdity of this fact but he will find it a very different matter when it comes to disproving it.

"I could wish," says St. Augustine, "that men would consider these three things that are in themselves... To Be, to Know, and to Will. For I am, and I know, and I will, I am knowing and willing, and I know myself to be and to will; and I will to be and to know. In these three therefore let him who can, see how inseparable a life there is—even one life, one mind, one essence, finally how inseparable is the distinction, and yet a distinction. Surely a man hath it before him, let him look into himself and see and tell me. But when he discovers and can see anything of these, let him not think that he has discovered that which is above these Unchangeable: which Is unchangeably and Knows unchangeably and Wills unchangeably."

In a well-known passage, Julian of Norwich tells us how she saw the Trinity of the Divine Nature shining in the phenomenal as well as in the spiritual world. "He showed me," she says, "a little thing, the quantity of an hazel nut, in the palm of my hand and it was as round as a ball. I looked thereupon with the eye of my understanding, and thought, *What may this be?* And it was answered generally thus: *It is all that is made....* In this Little Thing I saw three properties. The first is that God made it, the second is that God loveth it, the third is that God keepeth it. But what is to me verily the Maker, the Keeper, and the Lover, I cannot tell."

Julian, a simple and deeply human Englishwoman of middle age dwelling alone in her churchyard cell, might well be called the poet of the Trinity. She treats this austere and subtle dogma—of which the mediaeval mystics write with a passion little understood by those who look upon it as "orthodoxy reduced to mathematics"—with an intimacy and vigour which carry with them a conviction of her own direct and personal apprehension of the theological truth she struggles to describe. "I beheld," she says of a vision which is close to that of St. Teresa in the "Seventh Habitation of the Soul," and more lucidly if less splendidly expressed, "the working of all the blessed Trinity: in which beholding, I saw and understood these three properties: the property of the Fatherhood, the property of the Motherhood, and the property of the Lordhood, in one God. In our Father Almighty we have our keeping and our bliss as anent our natural Substance, which is to us by our making, without beginning. And in the Second Person in wit and wisdom we have our keeping as anent our Sense-soul: our restoring and our saving; for He is our Mother, Brother, and Saviour. And in our good Lord, the Holy Ghost, we have our rewarding and our meed-giving for our living and our travail, and endless overpassing of all that we desire, in His marvellous courtesy of His high plenteous grace. For all our life is in *three:* in the first we have our Being, in the second we have our Increasing, and in the third we have our Fulfilling; the first is Nature, the second is Mercy, and the third is Grace. The high Might of the Trinity is our Father, and the deep Wisdom of the Trinity is our Mother, and the great Love of the Trinity is our Lord: and all this we have in Nature and in our Substantial Making." Again, in a passage of exquisite tenderness, "As verily as God is our Father, so verily God is our Mother; and that shewed He in all [her revelations] and especially in these sweet words where He saith: *I it am.* That is to say, *I it am, the Might and the Goodness of the Fatherhood; I it am, the Wisdom of the Motherhood, I it am the Light and the Grace that is all blessed Love. I it am, the Trinity, I it am, the Unity: I am the sovereign Goodness of all manner of things. I am that maketh thee to love. I am that maketh thee to long: I it am, the endless fulfilling of all true desires.*"

So Christopher Hervey—

"The whole world round is not enough to fill
The heart's three corners, but it craveth still.
Only the Trinity that made it can
Suffice the vast triangled heart of Man."

Any attempt towards a definition of God which does not account for and acknowledge these three aspects is found in experience to be incomplete. They provide objectives for the heart, the intellect, and the will, for they offer to the Self material for its highest love, its deepest thought, its act of supreme volition. Under the familiar Platonic terms of Goodness, Truth, and Beauty, they represent the divine source and end of Ethics, Science, and Art, the three supreme activities of man. Thus the ideals of artist, student, and philanthropist, who all seek under different modes the same reality, are gathered up in the mystic's One; as the pilgrimage of the three kings ended in the finding of one Star

"What is God?" says St. Bernard. "Length, breadth, height, and depth. 'What,' you say, 'you do after all profess to believe in the fourfold Godhead which was an abomination to you?' Not in the least.... God is designated One to suit our comprehension, not to describe his character. *His character is capable of division, He Himself is not.* The words are different, the paths are many, but one thing is signified; the paths lead to one Person."

All possible ways of conceiving this One Person in His living richness are found in the end to range themselves under three heads. He is "above all and through all and in you all," said St. Paul, anticipating the Councils in a flash of mystic intuition and giving to the infant Church the shortest and most perfect definition of its Triune God. Being, which is above all, manifests itself as Becoming; as the dynamic omnipresent Word of Life. The Divine Love immanent in the heart and in the world comes forth from, and returns to, the Absolute One. "Thou, my God, who art Love," says Nicolas of Cusa, "art Love that loveth, and Love that is loveable, and Love that is the bond between these twain." Thus is completed "the Eternal Circle from Goodness, through Goodness, to Goodness."

It is true that to these fundamental respects of the perceived Godhead—that Being, Becoming, and Desire whereto the worlds keep time—the mystics have given many and various names; for they have something of the freedom of true intimates in treating of the Reality which they love. In particular, those symbols of the Absolute which are drawn from the great and formless forces of the universe, rather than from the orthodox but necessarily anthropomorphic imagery of human relationship, have always appealed to them. Their intense apprehension of Spirit seems to find freer and more adequate expression in such terms, than in those in which the notion of space is involved, or which suggest a concrete picture to the mind. Though they know as well as the philosophers that "there must always be something symbolic in our way of expressing the spiritual life," since "that unfathomable infinite whose spiritual character is first recognized in our human experience, can never reveal itself fully and freely under the limitations of our earthly existence" yet they ever seek, like the artists they are, some new and vital image which is not yet part of the debased currency of formal religion, and conserves its original power of stinging the imagination to more vivid life.

Thus "the Kingdom of Heaven," says Law, "stands in this threefold life, where three are one, because it is a manifestation of the Deity, which is Three and One; the Father has His distinct manifestation in the Fire, which is always generating the Light; the Son has His distinct manifestation in the Light, which is always generated from the Fire; the Holy Ghost has His manifestation in the Spirit, that always proceeds from both, and is always united with them. It is this eternal unbeginning Trinity in Unity of Fire, Light, and Spirit, that constitutes Eternal Nature, the Kingdom of Heaven, the heavenly Jerusalem, the Divine Life, the Beatific Visibility, the majestic Glory and Presence of God. Through this Kingdom of Heaven, or Eternal Nature, is the invisible God, the incomprehensible Trinity, eternally breaking forth and manifesting itself in a boundless height and depth of blissful wonders, opening and displaying itself to all its creatures as in an infinite variation and endless multiplicity of its powers, beauties, joys, and glories."

Perhaps an easier, better, more beautiful example of these abstract symbols of the Trinity than Law's Fire, Light, and Spirit is that of Light, Life, and Love: a threefold picture of the Real which is constantly dwelt upon and elaborated by the Christian mystics. Transcendent Light, intangible but unescapable, ever emanating Its splendour through the Universe: indwelling, unresting, and energizing Life: desirous and directive Love—these are cardinal aspects of Reality to which they return again and again in their efforts to find words which will express something of the inexpressible truth.

(*a*) LIGHT, ineffable and uncreated, the perfect symbol of pure undifferentiated Being: above the intellect, as St. Augustine reminds us, but known to him who loves. This Uncreated Light is the "deep yet dazzling darkness" of the Dionysian school, "dark from its surpassing brightness... as the shining of the sun on his course is as darkness to weak eyes." It is St. Hildegarde's *lux vivens,* Dante's *somma luce,* wherein he saw multiplicity in unity, the ingathered leaves of all the universe: the Eternal Father, or Fount of Things. "For well we know," says Ruysbroeck "that the bosom of the Father is our ground and origin, wherein our life and being is begun."

(*b*) LIFE, the Son, hidden Steersman of the Universe, the Logos, Fire, or cosmic Soul of Things. This out-birth or Concept of the Father's Mind, which He possesses within Himself, as Battista Vernazza was told in her ecstasy, "The Mystical Element of Religion," is that Word of Creation which since It is alive and infinite, no formula can contain the Word eternally "spoken" or generated by the Transcendent Light. "This is why," says Ruysbroeck again, "all that lives in the Father unmanifested in the Unity, is also in the Son actively poured forth in manifestation." This life, then, is the flawless expression or character of the Father, *Sapientia Patris.* It is at once the personal and adorable comrade of the mystic's adventure and the inmost principle, the sustaining power, of a dynamic universe; for that which intellect defines as the Logos or Creative Spirit, contemplative love *knows* as Wonderful, Counsellor, and Prince of Peace.

Since Christ, for the Christian philosopher, is Divine Life Itself—the drama of Christianity expressing this fact and its implications "in a point"—it follows that His active spirit is to be discerned, not symbolically, but in the most veritable sense, in the ecstatic and abounding life of the world. In the rapturous vitality of the birds, in their splendid glancing flight: in the swelling of buds and the sacrificial beauty of the flowers: in the great and solemn rhythms of the sea—there is somewhat of Bethlehem in all these things, somewhat too of Calvary in their self-giving pains. It was this re-discovery of Nature's Christliness which Blake desired so passionately when he sang—

"I will not cease from mental fight,
Nor shall my sword sleep in my hand
Till we have built Jerusalem
In England's green and pleasant land."

Here then it is, on this pinnacle of faith, at the utmost boundaries of human speech, that mystical theology suddenly shows herself—not as the puzzle-headed constructor of impossible creeds, but as accepting and transmuting to a more radiant life those two profound but apparently contradictory metaphysical definitions of Reality which we have already discussed. Eternal Becoming, God immanent and dynamic, striving with and in His world: the unresting "flux of things" of Heracleitus, the crying aloud of that Word "which is through all things everlastingly"—the evolutionary world-process beloved of modern philosophers—is here placed once for all in true relation with pure transcendent and unmoved Being; the Absolute One of Xenophanes and the

Platonists. This Absolute is discerned by mystic intuition as the "End of Unity" in whom all diversities must cease; the Ocean to which that ceaseless and painful Becoming, that unresting river of life, in which we are immersed, tends to return: the Son going to the Father.

(*c*) LOVE, the principle of attraction, which seems to partake at once of the transcendental and the created worlds. If we consider the Father as Supreme Subject—"origin," as Aquinas says, "of the entire procession of Deity"—and the Son or generated Logos as the Object of His thought, in whom, says Ruysbroeck, "He contemplates Himself and all things in an eternal Now"; then this personal Spirit of Love, *il desiro e il velle,* represents the relation between the two, and constitutes the very character of God. "The heavenly Father," says Ruysbroeck, "as a living Ground, with all that lives in Him, is actively turned towards His Son as to His own Eternal Wisdom. And that same Wisdom, with all that lives in it, is actively turned back towards the Father, that is towards that very ground from which it comes forth. And of this meeting is born the third Person, between the Father and the Son, that is the Holy Spirit, their mutual Love." Proceeding, according to Christian doctrine, from Light and Life, the Father and Son—implicit, that is, in both the Absolute Source and dynamic flux of things—this divine spirit of desire is found enshrined in our very selfhood; and is the agent by which that selfhood is merged in the Absolute Self. "My love is my weight," said St. Augustine. It is the spiritual equivalent of that gravitation which draws all things to their place. Thus Bernard Holland says in his Introduction to Boehme's "Dialogues," "In a deep sense, the desire of the Spark of Life in the Soul to return to its Original Source is part of the longing desire of the universal Life for its own heart or centre. Of this longing, the universal attraction striving against resistance, towards a universal centre, proved to govern the phenomenal or physical world, is but the outer sheath and visible working." Again, "Desire is everything in Nature; does everything. Heaven is Nature filled with divine Life attracted by Desire."

"The best masters say," says Eckhart, "that the love wherewith we love is the Holy Spirit. Some deny it. But this is always true: all those motives by which we are moved to love, in these is nothing else than the Holy Spirit." "God wills," says Ruysbroeck, gathering these scattered symbols to unity again, "that we should come forth from ourselves in this Eternal Light; that we should reunite ourselves in a supernatural manner with that image which is our true Life, and that we should possess it with Him actively and fruitively in eternal blessedness... this going forth of the contemplative is also in Love: for by fruitive love he overpasses his created being and finds and tastes the riches and delights which are God Himself, and which He causes to pour forth without ceasing in the most secret chamber of the soul, at that place where it is most like unto the nobility of God."

Here only, in the innermost sanctuary of being, the soul's "last habitation," as St. Teresa said, is the truth which these symbols express truly known for "as to how the Trinity is one and the Trinity in the Unity of the nature is one, whilst nevertheless the Trinity comes forth from the Unity, this cannot be expressed in words," says Suso, "owing to the simplicity of that deep abyss. Hither it is, into this intelligible *where* that the spirit, spiritualizing itself, soars up; now flying in the measureless heights, now swimming in the soundless deeps, of the sublime marvels of the Godhead!"

Mystical philosophy, then, has availed itself gladly of the doctrine of the Trinity in expressing its vision of the nature of that Absolute which is found, by those who attain the deep Abyss of the Godhead, to be essentially One. But it is by the complementary Christian dogma of the Incarnation that it has best been able to describe and explain the nature of the inward and personal mystic experience. The Incarnation, which is for traditional Christianity synonymous with the historical birth and earthly life of Christ, is for mystics of a certain type, not only this but also a perpetual Cosmic and personal process. It is an everlasting bringing forth, in the universe and also in the individual ascending soul, of the divine and perfect Life, the pure character of God, of which the one historical life dramatized the essential constituents. Hence the soul, like the physical embryo, resumes in its upward progress the spiritual life-history of the race. "The one secret, the greatest of all," says Patmore, is "the doctrine of the Incarnation, regarded not as an historical event which occurred two thousand years ago, but as an event which is renewed in the body of every one who is in the way to the fulfilment of his original destiny."

We have seen that for mystical theology the Second Person of the Trinity is the Wisdom of the Father, the Word of Life. The fullness of this Word could therefore only be communicated to the human consciousness by a Life. In the Incarnation this Logos, this divine character of Reality, penetrated the illusions of the sensual world—in other words, the illusions of all the selves whose ideas compose that world—and "saved" it by this infusion of truth. A divine, suffering, self-sacrificing Personality was then shown as the sacred heart of a living, striving universe and for once the Absolute was exhibited in the terms of finite human existence. Some such event as this breaking through of the divine and archetypal life into the temporal world is perceived by the mystical philosopher to be a necessity, if man was ever to see in terms of life that greatness of life to which he belongs: learn to transcend the world of sense, and rebuild his life upon the levels of reality. "For Thou art," says Nicolas of Cusa, "the Word of God humanified, and Thou art man deified." Thus it is that the Catholic priest in the Christmas Mass gives thanks, not for the setting in hand of any commercial process of redemption, but for a revelation of reality, "Quia per incarnati Verbi mysterium nova mentis nostrae oculis lux tuae claritatis infulsit: ut dum visibiliter Deum cognoscimus, per hunc in invisibilium amorem rapiamur." The essence of mystical Christianity seems to be summed up in these lovely words.

"The Son of God, the Eternal Word in the Father, who is the glance, or brightness, and the power of the light eternity" says Boehme, "must become man and be born in you, if you will know God: otherwise you are in the dark stable and go about groping." "The Word," says Ruysbroeck finely, "is no other than See. And this is the coming forth and the birth of the Son of the Eternal Light, in Whom all blessedness is seen and known." Once at any rate, they say in effect, the measure of that which it was possible for the Spirit of Life to do and for living creatures to be, was filled to the brim. By this event, all were assured that the ladder of Creation was made whole; in this hypostatic union, the breach between appearance and reality, between God and man, was healed. The Bridge so made—to use St. Catherine of Siena's allegory again—is eternal, since it was "laid before the foundation of the world" in the "Eternal Now." Thus the voice of the Father says to her in that vision, "I also wish thee to look at the Bridge of My only-begotten Son, and see the greatness thereof, for it reaches from Heaven to earth; that is, that the earth of your humanity is joined to the greatness of the Deity thereby. I say, then, that this Bridge reaches from Heaven to earth, and constitutes the union which I have made with man.... So the height of the Divinity, humbled to the earth, and joined with your humanity made the Bridge and reformed the road. Why was this done? In order that man might come to his true happiness with the angels. And observe that it is not enough, in order that you should have life, that My son should have made you this Bridge, unless you walk thereon." "Our high Father God Almighty, which is Being," says Lady Julian, "He knew and loved us from afore any time. Of which knowing, in His marvellous deep charity, and the foreseeing counsel of all the blessed Trinity, He willed that the Second Person should become our Mother."

It is of course this assertion of the quickening communication of grace to nature, of God to man—an influx of ultimate reality, possible of assimilation by all—which constitutes the strength of the Christian religion. Instead of the stony diet of the philosophers, it offers to the self hungry for the Absolute that *Panis Angelorum,* the vivifying principle of the world. That is to say, it gives concrete and experimental knowledge of a supreme Personality—absorption into His mystical body—instead of the artificial conviction produced by concentration on an idea. It knits up the universe; shows the phenomenal pierced in all directions by the real, the natural as the vehicle of the supernatural. It provides a solid basis for mysticism, a basis which is at once metaphysical and psychological: and shows that state towards which the world's deepest minds have always instinctively aspired, as a part of the cosmic return through Christ to God.

"Quivi è la sapienza e la possanza
ch' aprì le strade intra il cielo e la terra
onde fu già sì lunga disianza."

This is what the Christian mystics mean to express when they declare over and over again that the return to the Divine Substance, the Absolute, which is the end of the soul's ascent, can only be made through the humanity of Christ. The Son, the Word, is the character of the Father: that in which the Ineffable Godhead knows Himself, as we only know ourselves in our own characters. He is thus a double link: the means of God's self-consciousness, the means of man's consciousness of God. How then, asks mystic theology, could such a link complete its attachments without some such process as that which the Incarnation dramatized in time and space? The Principle of Life is also the Principle of Restitution; by which the imperfect and broken life of sense is mended and transformed into the perfect life of spirit. Hence the title of Repairer applied by Boehme to the Second Person of the Trinity.

In the last resort, the doctrine of the Incarnation is the only safeguard of the mystics against the pantheism to which they always tend. The Unconditioned Absolute, so soon as it alone becomes the object of their contemplation, is apt to be conceived merely as Divine Essence; the idea of Personality evaporates. The union of the soul with God is then thought of in terms of absorption. The distinction between Creator and creature is obliterated and loving communion is at an end. This is probably the reason why many of the greatest contemplatives—Suso and St. Teresa are cases in point—have found that deliberate meditation upon the humanity of Christ, difficult and uncongenial as this concrete devotion sometimes is to the mystical temperament, was a necessity if they were to retain a healthy and well-balanced inner life.

Further, these mystics see in the historic life of Christ an epitome—or if you will, an exhibition—of the essentials of all spiritual life. There they see dramatized not only the cosmic process of the Divine Wisdom, but also the inward experience of every soul on her way to union with that Absolute "to which the whole Creation moves." This is why the expressions which they use to describe the evolution of the mystical consciousness from the birth of the divine in the spark of the soul to its final unification with the Absolute Life are so constantly chosen from the Drama of Faith. In this drama they see described under veils the necessary adventures of the spirit. Its obscure and humble birth, its education in poverty, its temptation, mortification and solitude, its "illuminated life" of service and contemplation, the desolation of that "dark night of the soul" in which it seems abandoned by the Divine: the painful death of the self, its resurrection to the glorified existence of the Unitive Way, its final reabsorption in its Source—all these, they say, were lived once in a supreme degree in the flesh. Moreover, the degree of closeness with which the individual experience adheres to this Pattern is always taken by them as a standard of the healthiness, ardour, and success of its transcendental activities.

"Apparve in questa forma
Per dare a noi la norma."

sang Jacopone da Todi. "And he who vainly thinketh otherwise," says the "Theologia Germanica" with uncompromising vigour, "is deceived. And he who saith otherwise, lieth."

Those to whom such a parallel seems artificial should remember that according to the doctrine of mysticism that drama of the self-limitation and self-sacrifice of the Absolute Life, which was once played out in the phenomenal world—forced, as it were, upon the consciousness of dim-eyed men—is eternally going forward upon the plane of reality. To them the Cross of Calvary is implicit in the Rose of the World. The law of this Infinite Life which was in the Incarnation expressing Its own nature in human terms, must then also be the law of the finite life; in so far as that life aspires to transcend individual limitations, rise to freedom, and attain union with Infinity. It is this governing idea which justifies the apparently fanciful allegorizations of Christian history which swarm in the works of the mystics.

To exhibit these allegorizations in detail would be tedious. All that is necessary is that the principle underlying them should be understood. I give, then, but one example that which is referred by mystical writers to the Nativity, and concerns the eternal Birth or Generation of the Son or Divine Word.

This Birth is in its first, or cosmic sense, the welling forth of the Spirit of Life from the Divine Abyss of the unconditioned Godhead. "From our proper Ground, that is to say from the Father and all that which lives in Him, there shines," says Ruysbroeck, "an eternal Ray, the which is the Birth of the Son." It is of this perpetual generation of the Word that Meister Eckhart speaks, when he says in his Christmas sermon, "We are celebrating the feast of the Eternal Birth which God the Father has borne and *never ceases to bear* in all Eternity: whilst this birth also comes to pass in Time and in human nature. Saint Augustine says this Birth is ever taking place." At this point, with that strong practical instinct which is characteristic of the mystics, Eckhart turns abruptly from speculation to immediate experience, and continues "But if it takes not place in me, what avails it? Everything lies in this, that it should take place in me." Here in a few words the two-fold character of this Mystic Birth is exhibited. The interest is suddenly deflected from its cosmic to its personal aspect; and the individual is reminded that in him, no less than in the Archetypal Universe, real life must be born if real life is to be lived. "When the soul brings forth the Son," says Eckhart in another place, "it is happier than Mary."

Since the soul, according to mystic principles, can only perceive Reality in proportion as she is real, know God by becoming Godlike, it is clear that this birth is the initial necessity. The true and definitely directed mystical life does and must open with that most actual, though indescribable phenomenon, the coming forth into consciousness of man's deeper, spiritual self, which ascetical and mystical writers of all ages have agreed to call Regeneration or Re-birth. Nothing that is within him is able of its own power to achieve this. It must be evoked by an energy, a quickening Spirit, which comes from beyond the soul, and "secretly initiates what He openly crowns."

We have already considered the New Birth in its purely psychological aspect, as the emergence of the transcendental sense. Here its more profound and mystical side is exhibited. By a process which may indifferently be described as the birth of something new or the coming forth of something which has slept—since both these phrases are but metaphors for another and more secret operation—the eye is opened on Eternity, the self, abruptly made aware of Reality, comes forth from the cave of illusion like a child from the womb and begins to live upon the supersensual plane. Then she feels in her inmost part a new presence, a new consciousness—it were hardly an exaggeration to say a new Person—weak, demanding nurture, clearly destined to pass through many phases of development before its maturity is reached; yet of so strange a nature, that in comparison with its environment she may well regard it as Divine.

"This change, this upsetting, is called re-birth. *To be born* simply means to enter into a world in which the senses dominate, in which wisdom and love languish in the bonds of individuality. To be *re-born* means to return to a world where the spirit of wisdom and love governs and animal-man obeys." So Eckartshausen. It means, says Jane Lead, "the bringing forth of a new-created Godlike similitude in the soul." He is brought forth, says Eckartshausen again, in the stable previously inhabited by the ox of passion and the ass of prejudice. His mother, says Boehme, is the Virgin Sophia, the Divine Wisdom, or Mirror of the Being of God. With the emergence of this new factor into the conscious field—this spiritual birth—the mystic life begins: as the Christian epoch began with the emergence of Divine Spirit in the flesh. Paradise, says Boehme, is still in the world, but man is not in Paradise unless he be born again. In that case, he stands therein in the New Birth, and tastes here and now that Eternal Life for which he has been made.

Here then are some characteristics of the map which the Christian mystics are most inclined to use. There are, of course, other great landmarks upon it and these we shall meet as we follow in detail the voyages of the questing soul. One warning, however, must be given to amateur geographers before we go on. Like all other maps, this one at its best can but represent by harsh outline and conventional colour the living earth which those travellers trod and the mysterious seas on which they sailed. It is a deliberately schematic representation of Reality, a flat and sometimes arid symbol of great landscapes, rushing rivers, awful peaks: dangerous unless these its limitations be always kept in mind. The boy who defined Canada as "very pink" was not much further off the track than those who would limit the Adorable Trinity to the definitions of the "Athanasian" Creed; however useful that chart may be, and is, within the boundaries imposed by its form.

Further, all such maps, and we who treat of them, can but set down in cold blood and with a dreadful pretence of precision, matters which the true explorers of Eternity were only able to apprehend in the ardours of such a passion, in the transports of such a union as we, poor finite slaves of our frittered emotions, could hardly look upon and live. "If you would truly know how these things come to pass," says St. Bonaventura, in a passage which all students of theology should ever keep in mind, "ask it of grace, not of doctrine; of desire, not of intellect; of the ardours of prayer, not of the teachings of the schools; of the Bridegroom, not of the Master; of God, not of man; of the darkness, not of the day; not of illumination, but of that Fire which enflames all and wraps us in God with great sweetness and most ardent love. Thus the Fire most truly is God, and the hearth thereof is in Jerusalem."

4

MYSTICISM AND PSYCHOLOGY

We come now to consider the mental apparatus which is at the disposal of the self, to ask what it can tell us of the method by which she may escape from the prison of the sense-world, transcend its rhythm, and attain knowledge of—or conscious contact with—a supra-sensible Reality. We have seen the normal self shut within that prison, and making, by the help of science and of philosophy, a survey of the premises and furniture, testing the thickness of the walls and speculating on the possibility of trustworthy news from without penetrating to her cell. Shut with her in that cell, two forces, the desire to know more and the desire to love more, are ceaselessly at work. Where the first of these cravings predominates, we call the result a philosophical or a scientific temperament; where it is overpowered by the ardour of unsatisfied love, the self's reaction upon things becomes poetic, artistic, and characteristically—though not always explicitly—religious.

We have seen further that a certain number of persons declare that they have escaped from the prison. Have they done so, it can only be in order to satisfy these two hungry desires, for these, and these only, make that a prison which might otherwise be a comfortable hotel; and since, in varying degrees, these desires are in all of us, active or latent, it is clearly worth while to discover, if we can, the weak point in the walls, and method of achieving this one possible way of escape.

Before we try to define in psychological language the way in which the mystic slips the fetters of sense, sets out upon his journey towards home, it seems well to examine the machinery which is at the disposal of the normal, conscious self: the creature, or part of a creature, which we recognize as "ourselves." The older psychologists were accustomed to say that the messages from the outer world awaken in that self three main forms of activity. (1) They arouse movements of attraction or repulsion, of desire or distaste; which vary in intensity from the semi-conscious cravings of the hungry infant to the passions of the lover, artist, or fanatic. (2) They stimulate a sort of digestive process, in which she combines and cogitates upon the material presented to her; finally absorbing a certain number of the resulting concepts and making them part of herself or of her world, (3) The movements of desire, or the action of reason, or both in varying combinations, awaken in her a determination by which percept and concept issue in action; bodily, mental, or spiritual. Hence, the main aspects of the self were classified as Emotion, Intellect, and Will and the individual temperament was regarded as emotional, intellectual, or volitional, according to whether feeling, thought, or will assumed the reins.

Modern psychologists have moved away from this diagramnıatic conception, and incline more and more to dwell upon the unity of the psyche—that hypothetical self which none have ever seen—and on some aspect of its energetic desire, its *libido,* or "hormic drive" as the ruling factor of its life. These conceptions are useful to the student of mysticism, though they cannot be accepted uncritically or regarded as complete.

Now the unsatisfied psyche in her emotional aspect wants, as we have said, to love more; her curious intellect wants to know more. The awakened human creature suspects that both appetites are being kept on a low diet; that there really is more to love, and more to know, somewhere in the mysterious world without, and further that its powers of affection and understanding are worthy of some greater and more durable objective than that provided by the illusions of sense. Urged therefore by the cravings of feeling or of thought, consciousness is always trying to run out to the encounter of the Absolute, and always being forced to return. The neat philosophical system, the diagrams of science, the "sunset-touch," are tried in turn. Art and life, the accidents of our humanity, may foster an emotional outlook; till the moment in which the neglected intellect arises and pronounces such an outlook to have no validity. Metaphysics and science seem to offer to the intellect an open window towards truth; till the heart looks out and declares this landscape to be a chill desert in which she can find no nourishment. These diverse aspects of things must be either fused or transcended if the whole self is to be satisfied; for the reality which she seeks has got to meet both claims and pay in full.

When Dionysius the Areopagite divided those angels who stand nearest God into the Seraphs who are aflame with perfect love, and the Cherubs who are filled with perfect knowledge, he only gave expression to the two most intense aspirations of the human soul, and described under an image the two-fold condition of that Beatific Vision which is her goal. There is a sense in which it may be said, that the desire of knowledge is a part of the desire of perfect love: since one aspect of that all inclusive passion is clearly a longing to know, in the deepest, fullest, closest sense, the thing adored. Love's characteristic activity—for Love, all wings, is inherently active, and "cannot be lazy," as the mystics say—is a quest, an outgoing towards an object desired, which only when possessed will be fully known, and only when fully known can be perfectly adored. Intimate communion, no less than worship, is of its essence. Joyous fruition is its proper end. This is true of all Love's quests, whether the Beloved be human or divine—the bride, the Grail, the Mystic Rose, the Plenitude of God. But there is no sense in which it can be said that the desire of love is merely a part of the desire of perfect knowledge: for that strictly intellectual ambition includes no adoration, no self-spending, no reciprocity of feeling between Knower and Known. Mere knowledge, taken alone, is a matter of receiving, not of acting: of eyes, not wings: a dead alive business at the best. There is thus a sharp distinction to be drawn between these two great expressions of life: the energetic love, the passive knowledge. One is related to the eager, outgoing activity, the dynamic impulse to *do* somewhat, physical, mental, or spiritual, which is inherent in all living things and which psychologists call *conation:* the other to the indwelling consciousness, the passive knowing somewhat, which they call *cognition.*

Now "conation" is almost wholly the business of will, but of will stimulated by emotion: for wilful action of every kind, however intellectual it may seem, is always the result of interest, and interest involves feeling. We act because we feel we want to feel we must. Whether the inspiring force be a mere preference or an overwhelming urge, our impulse to "do" is a synthesis of determination and desire. All man's achievements are the result of conation, never of mere thought. "The intellect by itself moves nothing," said Aristotle, and modern psychology has but affirmed this law. Hence his quest of Reality is never caused, though it may be greatly assisted, by the intellectual aspect of his consciousness; for the reasoning powers as such have little initiative. Their province is analytic, not exploratory. They stay at home, dissecting and arranging matter that comes to hand; and do not adventure beyond their own region in search of food. Thought does not penetrate far into an object in which the self feels no interest— *i.e.,* towards which she does not experience a "conative" movement of attraction, of desire—for interest is the only method known to us of arousing the will, and securing the fixity of attention necessary to any intellectual process. None think for long about anything for which they do not care; that is to say, which does not touch some aspect of their emotional life. They may hate it, love it, fear it, want it; but they must have some feeling about it. Feeling is the tentacle we stretch out to the world of things.

Here the lesson of psychology is the same as that which Dante brought back from his pilgrimage; the supreme importance and harmonious movement of *il desiro* and *il velle. Si come rota ch'egualmente è mossa,* these move together to fulfil the Cosmic Plan. In all human life, in so far as it is not merely a condition of passive "awareness," the law which he found implicit in the universe is the law of the individual mind.

Not logic, not "common sense,"but *l'amor che move il sole e le altre stelle* the motive force of the spirit of man: in the inventors, the philosophers, and the artists, no less than in the heroes and in the saints.

The vindication of the importance of feeling in our life, and in particular its primacy over reason in all that has to do with man's contact with the transcendental world, has been one of the great achievements of modern psychology. In the sphere of religion it is now acknowledged that "God known of the heart" gives a better account of the character of our spiritual experience than "God guessed at by the brain"; that the loving intuition is more fruitful and more trustworthy than the dialectic proof. One by one the commonplaces of mysticism are thus rediscovered by official science, and given their proper place in the psychology of the spiritual life. Thus Leuba, hardly a friendly witness, is found to agree with the Fourth Evangelist that "Life, more life, a larger, richer, more satisfying life, is in the last analysis the end of religion," and we have seen that life, as we know it, has the character of a purposive striving, more directly dependent on will and feeling then on thought. Of this drive, this urge, thought indeed is but the servant; a skilled and often arrogant servant, with a constant tendency to usurpation. Some form of feeling—interest, desire, fear, appetite—must supply the motive power. Without this, the will would be dormant, and the intellect lapse into a calculating machine.

Further, "the heart has its reasons which the mind knows not of." It is a matter of experience that in our moments of deep emotion, transitory though they be, we plunge deeper into the reality of things than we can hope to do in hours of the most brilliant argument. At the touch of passion doors fly open which logic has battered on in vain: for passion rouses to activity not merely the mind, but the whole vitality of man. It is the lover, the poet, the mourner, the convert, who shares for a moment the mystic's privilege of lifting that Veil of Isis which science handles so helplessly, leaving only her dirty fingermarks behind. The heart, eager and restless, goes out into the unknown, and brings home, literally and actually, "fresh food for thought." Hence those who "feel to think" are likely to possess a richer, more real, if less orderly, experience than those who "think to feel."

This psychological law, easily proved in regard to earthly matters, holds good also upon the supersensual plane. It was expressed once for all by the author of "The Cloud of Unknowing" when he said of God, "By love He may be gotten and holden, but by thought of understanding, never." That exalted feeling, that "secret blind love pressing," not the neat deductions of logic, the apologist's "proofs" of the existence of the Absolute, unseals the eyes to things unseen before. "Therefore," says the same mystic "what time that thou purposest thee to this work, and feelest by grace that thou art called of God, lift then up thine heart unto God with a meek stirring of love; and mean God that made thee and bought thee, and that graciously hath called thee to thy degree and receive none other thought of God. And yet not all these but if thou list; for it sufficeth thee enough, a naked intent direct unto God without any other cause than Himself." Here we see emotion at its proper work; the movement of desire passing over at once into the act of concentration, the gathering up of all the powers of the self into a state of determined attention, which is the business of the Will. "This driving and drawing," says Ruysbroeck, "we feel in the heart and in the unity of all our bodily powers, and especially in the desirous powers." This act of perfect concentration, the passionate focussing of the self upon one point, when it is applied "with a naked intent" to real and transcendental things, constitutes in the technical language of mysticism the state of recollection, a condition which is peculiarly characteristic of the mystical consciousness, and is the necessary prelude of pure contemplation, that state in which the mystic enters into communion with Reality.

We have then arrived so far in our description of the mechanism of the mystic. Possessed like other men of powers of feeling, thought, and will, it is essential that his love and his determination, even more than his thought, should be set upon Transcendent Reality. He must feel a strong emotional attraction toward the supersensual Object of his quest: that love which scholastic philosophy defined as the force or power which causes every creature to follow out the trend of its own nature. Of this must be born the will to attain communion with that Absolute Object. This will, this burning and active desire, must crystallize into and express itself by that definite and conscious concentration of the whole self upon the Object, which precedes the contemplative state. We see already how far astray are those who look upon the mystical temperament as passive in type.

Our next concern, then, would seem to be with this condition of contemplation: what it does and whither it leads. What is (*a*) its psychological explanation and (*b*) its empirical value? Now, in dealing with this, and other rare mental conditions, we are of course trying to describe from without that which can only adequately be described from within; which is as much as to say that only mystics can really write about mysticism. Fortunately, many mystics have so written; and we, from their experiences and from the explorations of psychology upon another plane, are able to make certain elementary deductions. It appears generally from these that the act of contemplation is for the mystic a psychic gateway; a method of going from one level of consciousness to another. In technical language it is the condition under which he shifts his "field of perception" and obtains his characteristic outlook on the universe. That there is such a characteristic outlook, peculiar to no creed or race, is proved by the history of mysticism; which demonstrates plainly enough that in some men another sort of consciousness, another "sense," may be liberated beyond the normal powers we have discussed. This "sense" has attachments at each point to emotion, to intellect, and to will.

It can express itself under each of the aspects which these terms connote. Yet it differs from and transcends the emotional, intellectual, and volitional life of ordinary men. It was recognized by Plato as that consciousness which could apprehend the real world of the Ideas. Its development is the final object of that education which his "Republic" describes. It is called by Plotinus "Another intellect, different from that which reasons and is denominated rational." Its business, he says, is the perception of the supersensual—or, in Neoplatonic language, the *intelligible* world. It is the sense which, in the words of the "Theologia Germanica," has "the power of seeing into eternity," the "mysterious eye of the soul" by which St. Augustine saw "the light that never changes." It is, says Al Ghazzali, a Persian mystic of the eleventh century, "like an immediate perception, as if one touched its object with one's hand." In the words of his great Christian successor, St. Bernard, "it may be defined as the soul's true unerring intuition, the unhesitating apprehension of truth": which "simple vision of truth," says St. Thomas Aquinas, "ends in a movement of desire."

It is infused with burning love, for it seems to its possessors to be primarily a movement of the heart with intellectual subtlety, for its ardour is wholly spent upon the most sublime object of thought with unflinching will, for its adventures are undertaken in the teeth of the natural doubts, prejudices, languors, and self-indulgence of man. These adventures, looked upon by those who stay at home as a form of the Higher Laziness, are in reality the last and most arduous labours which the human spirit is called to perform. They are the only known methods by which we can come into conscious possession of all our powers; and, rising from the lower to the higher levels of consciousness, become aware of that larger life in which we are immersed, attain communion with the transcendent Personality in Whom that life is resumed.

Mary has chosen the better, not the idler part; for her gaze is directed towards those First Principles without which the activity of Martha would have no meaning at all. In vain does sardonic common sense, confronted with the contemplative type, reiterate the sneer of Mucius, "Encore sont-ils heureux que la pauvre Marthe leur fasse la cuisine." It remains a paradox of the mystics that the passivity at which they appear to aim is really a state of the most intense activity: more, that where it is wholly absent no great creative action can take place. In it, the superficial self compels itself to be still, in order that it may liberate another more deep-seated power which is, in the ecstasy of the contemplative genius, raised to the highest pitch of efficiency.

"This restful travail," said Walter Hilton, "is full far from fleshly idleness and from blind security. It is full of ghostly work but it is called rest, for grace looseth the heavy yoke of fleshly love from the soul and maketh it mighty and free through the gift of the holy ghostly love for to work gladly, softly, and delectably.... Therefore is it called an holy idleness and a rest most busy; and so is it in *stillness* from the great crying and the beastly noise of fleshly desires."

If those who have cultivated this latent power be correct in their statements, the self was mistaken in supposing herself to be entirely shut off from the true external universe. She has, it seems certain tentacles which, once she learns to uncurl them, will stretch sensitive fingers far beyond that limiting envelope in which her normal consciousness is contained, and give her news of a higher reality than that which can be deduced from the reports of the senses. The fully developed and completely conscious human soul can open as an anemone does, and *know* the ocean in which she is bathed. This act, this condition of consciousness, in which barriers are obliterated, the Absolute flows in on us, and we, rushing out to its embrace, "find and feel the Infinite above all reason and above all knowledge," is the true "mystical state." The value of contemplation is that it tends to produce this state, release this transcendental sense; and so turns the "lower servitude" in which the natural man lives under the sway of his earthly environment to the "higher servitude" of fully conscious dependence on that Reality "in Whom we live and move and have our being."

What then, we ask, is the nature of this special sense—this transcendental consciousness—and how does contemplation liberate it?

Any attempt to answer this question brings upon the scene another aspect of man's psychic life: an aspect of paramount importance to the student of the mystic type. We have reviewed the chief ways in which our surface consciousness reacts upon experience: a surface consciousness which has been trained through long ages to deal with the universe of sense. We know, however, that the personality of man is a far deeper and more mysterious thing than the sum of his conscious feeling, thought and will: that this superficial self—this Ego of which each of us is aware—hardly counts in comparison with the deeps of being which it hides. "There is a root or depth in thee," says Law, "from whence all these faculties come forth as lines from a centre, or as branches from the body of a tree. This depth is called the centre, the fund, or bottom, of the soul. This depth is the unity, the Eternity, I had almost said the infinity of thy soul, for it is so infinite that nothing can satisfy it, or give it any rest, but the infinity of God."

Since normal man is utterly unable to set up relations with spiritual reality by means of his feeling, thought, and will, it is clearly in this depth of being—in these unplumbed levels of personality—that we must search, if we would find the organ, the power, by which he is to achieve the mystic quest. That alteration of consciousness which takes place in contemplation can only mean the emergence from this "fund or bottom of the soul" of some faculty which diurnal life keeps hidden "in the deeps."

Modern psychology, in its doctrine of the unconscious or subliminal personality, has acknowledged this fact of a range of psychic life lying below and beyond the conscious field. Indeed, it has so dwelt upon and defined this shadowy region—which is really less a "region" than a useful name—that it sometimes seems to know more about the unconscious than about the conscious life of man. There it finds, side by side, the sources of his most animal instincts, his least explicable powers, his most spiritual intuitions: the "ape and tiger," and the "soul." Genius and prophecy, insomnia and infatuation, clairvoyance, hypnotism, hysteria, and "Christian" science—all are explained by the "unconscious mind." In his destructive moods the psychologist has little apparent difficulty in reducing the chief phenomena of religious and mystical experience to activities of the "unconscious," seeking an oblique satisfaction of repressed desires. Where he undertakes the more dangerous duties of apologetic, he explains the same phenomena by saying that "God speaks to man in the subconsciousness," by which he can only mean that our apprehensions of the eternal have the character of intuition rather than of thought. Yet the "unconscious" after all is merely a convenient name for the aggregate of those powers, parts, or qualities of the whole self which at any given moment are not conscious, or that the Ego is not conscious of. Included in the unconscious region of an average healthy man are all those automatic activities by which the life of the body is carried on: all those "uncivilized" instincts and vices, those remains of the ancestral savage, which education has forced out of the stream of consciousness and which now only send their messages to the surface in a carefully disguised form. There too work in the hiddenness those longings for which the busy life of the world leaves no place; and there lies that deep pool, that heart of personality, from which in moments of lucidity a message may reach the conscious field. Hence in normal men the best and worst, most savage and most spiritual parts of character, are bottled up "below the threshold." Often the partisans of the "unconscious" forget to mention this.

It follows, then, that whilst we may find it convenient and indeed necessary to avail ourselves of the symbols and diagrams of psychology in tracking out the mystic way, we must not forget the large and vague significance which attaches to these symbols, and the hypothetical character of many of the entities they represent. Nor must we allow ourselves to use the "unconscious" as the equivalent of man's transcendental sense. Here the mystics have surely displayed a more scientific spirit, a more delicate power of analysis, than the psychologists. They, too, were aware that in normal men the spiritual sense lies below the threshold of consciousness. Though they had not at their command the spatial metaphors of the modern school, and could not describe man's ascent toward God in those picturesque terms of levels and uprushes, margins and fields, projection, repression, and sublimation, which now come so naturally to investigators of the spiritual life, they leave us in no doubt as to their view of the facts.

Further, man's spiritual history primarily meant for them, as it means for us, the emergence of this transcendental sense; its capture of the field of consciousness, and the opening up of those paths which permit the inflow of a larger spiritual life, the perception of a higher reality. This, in so far as it was an isolated act, was "contemplation." When it was part of the general life process, and had permanent results, they called it the New Birth, which "maketh alive." The faculty or personality concerned in the "New Birth"—the "spiritual man," capable of the spiritual vision and life, which was dissociated from the "earthly man" adapted only to the natural life—was always sharply distinguished by them from the total personality, conscious or unconscious. It was something definite; a bit or spot of man which, belonging not to Time but to Eternity, was different in kind from the rest of his human nature, framed in all respects to meet the demands of the merely natural world. The business of the mystic in the eyes of these old specialists was to remake, transmute, his total personality in the interest of his spiritual self; to bring it out of the hiddenness, and unify himself about it as a centre, thus "putting on divine humanity."

The divine nucleus, the point of contact between man's life and the divine life in which it is immersed and sustained, has been given many names in course of the development of mystical doctrine. All clearly mean the same thing, though emphasizing different aspects of its life. Sometimes it is called the Synteresis, the keeper or preserver of his being: sometimes the Spark of the Soul, the *Fünklein* of the German mystics: sometimes its Apex the point at which it touches the heavens. Then, with a sudden flight to the other end of the symbolic scale, and in order to emphasize its participation in pure Being, rather than its difference from mere nature, it is called the Ground of the Soul, the foundation or basal stuff indwelt by God, whence springs all spiritual life. Clearly all these guesses and suggestions aim at one goal and are all to be understood in a symbolic sense; for, as Malaval observed in answer to his disciples' anxious inquiries on this subject, "since the soul of man is a spiritual thing and thus cannot have divisions or parts, consequently it cannot have height or depth, summit or surface. But because we judge spiritual things by the help of material things, since we know these better and they are more familiar to us, we call the highest of all forms of conception the summit, and the easier way of comprehending things the surface, of the understanding."

Here at any rate, whatever name we may choose to give it, is the organ of man's spiritual consciousness; the place where he meets the Absolute, the germ of his real life. Here is the seat of that deep "Transcendental Feeling," the "beginning and end of metaphysics" which is, says Professor Stewart, "at once the solemn sense of Timeless Being—of 'That which was and is and ever shall be' overshadowing us—and the conviction that Life is good." "I hold," says the same writer, "that it is in Transcendental Feeling, manifested normally as Faith in the Value of Life, and ecstatically as sense of Timeless Being, and not in Thought proceeding by way of speculative construction, that Consciousness comes nearest to the object of metaphysics, Ultimate Reality."

The existence of such a "sense," such an integral part or function of the complete human being, has been affirmed and dwelt upon not only by the mystics, but by seers and teachers of all times and creeds: by Egypt, Greece, and India, the poets, the fakirs, the philosophers, and the saints. A belief in its actuality is the pivot of the Christian position; indeed of every religion worthy of the name. It is the justification of mysticism, asceticism, the whole machinery of the self-renouncing life. That there is an extreme point at which man's nature touches the Absolute: that his ground, or substance, his true being, is penetrated by the Divine Life which constitutes the underlying reality of things; this is the basis on which the whole mystic claim of possible union with God must rest. Here, they say, is our link with reality and in this place alone can be celebrated the "marriage from which the Lord comes." To use another of their diagrams, it is thanks to the existence within him of this immortal spark from the central fire, that man is implicitly a "child of the infinite." The mystic way must therefore be a life, a discipline, which will so alter the constituents of his mental life as to include this spark within the conscious field; bring it out of the hiddenness, from those deep levels where it sustains and guides his normal existence, and make it the dominant element round which his personality is arranged.

It is clear that under ordinary conditions, and save for sudden gusts of "Transcendental Feeling" induced by some saving madness such as Religion, Art, or Love, the superficial self knows nothing of the attitude of this silent watcher—this "Dweller in the Innermost"—towards the incoming messages of the external world: nor of the activities which they awake in it. Concentrated on the sense-world, and the messages she receives from it, she knows nothing of the relations which exist between this subject and the unattainable Object of all thought. But by a deliberate inattention to the messages of the senses, such as that which is induced by contemplation, the mystic can bring the ground of the soul, the seat of "Transcendental Feeling," within the area of consciousness, making it amenable to the activity of the will. Thus becoming unaware of his usual and largely fictitious "external world," another and more substantial set of perceptions, which never have their chance under normal conditions, rise to the surface. Sometimes these unite with the normal reasoning faculties. More often, they supersede them. Some such exchange, such "losing to find," appears to be necessary, if man's transcendental powers are to have their full chance.

"The two eyes of the soul of man," says the "Theologia Germanica," here developing a profound Platonic image, "cannot both perform their work at once: but if the soul shall see with the right eye into eternity, then the left eye must close itself and refrain from working, and be as though it were dead. For if the left eye be fulfilling its office toward outward things, that is holding converse with time and the creatures; then must the right eye be hindered in its working; that is, in its contemplation. Therefore, whosoever will have the one must let the other go; for 'no man can serve two masters.'

There is within us an immense capacity for perception, for the receiving of messages from outside; and a very little consciousness which deals with them. It is as if one telegraph operator were placed in charge of a multitude of lines: all may be in action, but he can only attend to one at a time. In popular language, there is not enough consciousness to go round. Even upon the sensual plane, no one can be aware of more than a few things at once. These fill the centre of our field of consciousness as the object on which we happen to have focussed our vision dominates our field of sight. The other matters within that field retreat to the margin. We know, dimly, that they are there; but we pay them no attention and should hardly miss them if they ceased to exist.

Transcendental matters are, for most of us, always beyond the margin because most of us have given up our whole consciousness to the occupation of the senses, and permitted them to construct there a universe in which we are contented to remain. Only in certain states—recollection, contemplation, ecstasy and their allied conditions—does the self contrive to turn out the usual tenants, shut the "gateways of the flesh," and let those submerged powers which are capable of picking up messages from another plane of being have their turn. Then it is the sense-world which retreats beyond the margin, and another landscape that rushes in. At last, then, we begin to see something of what contemplation does for its initiates. It is one of the many names applied to that chain of processes which have for their object this alteration of the mental equilibrium: the putting to sleep of that "Normal Self" which usually wakes, and the awakening of that "Transcendental Self" which usually sleeps. To man, "meeting-point of various stages of reality," is given—though he seldom considers it—this unique power of choosing his universe.

The phenomenon known as double or disintegrated personality may perhaps give us a hint as to the mechanical nature of the change which contemplation effects. In this psychic malady the total character of the patient is split up; a certain group of qualities are, as it were, abstracted from the surface-consciousness and so closely associated as to form in themselves a complete "character" or "personality"—necessarily poles asunder from the "character" which the self usually shows to the world, since it consists exclusively of those elements which are omitted from it. Thus in the classical case of Miss Beauchamp, the investigator, Dr. Morton Prince, called the three chief "personalities," from their ruling characteristics, "the Saint," "the Woman," and "the Devil." The totality of character which composed the "real Miss Beauchamp" had split up into these contrasting types; each of which was excessive, because withdrawn from the control of the rest. When, voluntarily or involuntarily, the personality which had possession of the field of consciousness was lulled to sleep, one of the others emerged. Hypnotism was one of the means which most easily effected this change.

Now in persons of mystical genius, the qualities which the stress of normal life tends to keep below the threshold of consciousness are of enormous strength. In these natural explorers of Eternity the "transcendental faculty," the "eye of the soul," is not merely present in embryo, but is highly developed and is combined with great emotional and volitional power. The result of the segregation of such qualities below the threshold of consciousness is to remove from them the friction of those counterbalancing traits in the surface mind with which they might collide. They are "in the hiddenness," as Jacob Boehme would say. There they develop unchecked, until a point is reached at which their strength is such that they break their bounds and emerge into the conscious field: either temporarily dominating the subject as in ecstasy, or permanently transmuting the old self, as in the "unitive life." The attainment of this point may be accelerated by processes which have always been known and valued by the mystics; and which tend to produce a state of consciousness classed by psychologists with dreams, reverie, and the results of hypnosis. In all these the normal surface-consciousness is deliberately or involuntarily lulled, the images and ideas connected with normal life are excluded, and images or faculties from "beyond the threshold" are able to take their place.

Of course these images or faculties may or may not be more valuable than those already present in the surface-consciousness. In the ordinary subject, often enough, they are but the odds and ends for which the superficial mind has found no use. In the mystic, they are of a very different order: and this fact justifies the means which he instinctively employs to secure their emergence. Indian mysticism founds its external system almost wholly on (*a*) Asceticism, the domination of the senses, and (*b*) the deliberate practice of self-hypnotization; either by fixing the eyes on a near object, or by the rhythmic repetition of the *mantra* or sacred word. By these complementary forms of discipline, the pull of the phenomenal world is diminished and the mind is placed at the disposal of the subconscious powers. Dancing, music, and other exaggerations of natural rhythm have been pressed into the same service by the Greek initiates of Dionysus, by the Gnostics, by innumerable other mystic cults. That these proceedings do effect a remarkable change in the human consciousness is proved by experience: though how and why they do it is as yet little understood. Such artificial and deliberate production of ecstasy is against the whole instinct of the Christian contemplatives; but here and there amongst them also we find instances in which ecstatic trance or lucidity, the liberation of the "transcendental sense," was inadvertently produced by purely physical means. Thus Jacob Boehme, the "Teutonic theosopher," having one day as he sat in his room "gazed fixedly upon a burnished pewter dish which reflected the sunshine with great brilliance," fell into an inward ecstasy, and it seemed to him as if he could look into the principles and deepest foundations of things. The contemplation of running water had the same effect on St. Ignatius Loyola. Sitting on the bank of a river one day, and facing the stream, which was running deep, "the eyes of his mind were opened, not so as to see any kind of vision, but so as to understand and comprehend spiritual things... and this with such clearness that for him all these things were made new." This method of attaining to mental lucidity by a narrowing and simplification of the conscious field, finds an apt parallel in the practice of Immanuel Kant, who "found that he could better engage in philosophical thought while *gazing steadily* at a neighbouring church steeple."

It need hardly be said that rationalistic writers, ignoring the parallels offered by the artistic and philosophic temperaments, have seized eagerly upon the evidence afforded by such instances of apparent mono-ideism and self-hypnotization in the lives of the mystics, and by the physical disturbances which accompany the ecstatic trance, and sought by its application to attribute all the abnormal perceptions of contemplative genius to hysteria or other disease. They have not hesitated to call St. Paul an epileptic. St. Teresa the "patron saint of hysterics"; and have found room for most of their spiritual kindred in various departments of the pathological museum. They have been helped in this grateful task by the acknowledged fact that the great contemplatives, though almost always persons of robust intelligence and marked practical or intellectual ability—Plotinus, St. Bernard, the two Ss. Catherine, St. Teresa, St. John of the Cross, and the Sufi poets Jàmi and Jalalu 'ddin are cases in point—have often suffered from bad physical health. More, their mystical activities have generally reacted upon their bodies in a definite and special way; producing in several cases a particular kind of illness and of physical disability, accompanied by pains and functional disturbances for which no organic cause could be discovered, unless that cause were the immense strain which exalted spirit puts upon a body which is adapted to a very different form of life.

It is certain that the abnormal and highly sensitized type of mind which we call mystical does frequently, but not always, produce or accompany strange and inexplicable modifications of the physical organism with which it is linked. The supernatural is not here in question, except in so far as we are inclined to give that name to natural phenomena which we do not understand. Such instances of psycho-physical parallelism as the stigmatizations of the saints—and indeed of other suggestible subjects hardly to be ranked as saints—will occur to anyone. I here offer to the reader another less discussed and more extraordinary example of the modifying influence of the spirit on the supposed "laws" of bodily life.

We know, as a historical fact, unusually well attested by contemporary evidence and quite outside the sphere of hagiographic romance, that both St. Catherine of Siena and her namesake St. Catherine of Genoa—active women as well as ecstatics, the first a philanthropist, reformer, and politician, the second an original theologian and for many years the highly efficient matron of a large hospital—lived, in the first case for years, in the second for constantly repeated periods of many weeks, without other food than the consecrated Host which they received at Holy Communion. They did this, not by way of difficult obedience to a pious vow, but because they could not live, in any other way. Whilst fasting, they were well and active, capable of dealing with the innumerable responsibilities which filled their lives. But the attempt to eat even a few mouthfuls—and this attempt was constantly repeated, for, like all true saints, they detested eccentricity —at once made them ill and had to be abandoned as useless.

In spite of the researches of Murisier, Janet, Ribot, and other psychologists, and their persevering attempts to find a pathological explanation which will fit all mystic facts, this and other marked physical peculiarities which accompany the mystical temperament belong as yet to the unsolved problems of humanity. They need to be removed both from the sphere of marvel and from that of disease—into which enthusiastic friends and foes force them by turn—to the sphere of pure psychology; and there studied dispassionately with the attention which we so willingly bestow on the less interesting eccentricities of degeneracy and vice. Their existence no more discredits the sanity of mysticism or the validity of its results than the unstable nervous condition usually noticed in artists—who share to some extent the mystic's apprehension of the Real—discredits art. "In such cases as Kant and Beethoven," says Von Hügel justly, "a classifier of humanity according to its psycho-physical phenomena alone would put these great discoverers and creators, without hesitation, amongst hopeless and useless hypochondriacs."

In the case of the mystics the disease of hysteria, with its astounding variety of mental symptoms, its strange power of disintegrating, rearranging and enhancing the elements of consciousness, its tendencies to automatism and ecstasy, has been most often invoked to provide an explanation of the observed phenomena. This is as if one sought the source of the genius of Taglioni in the symptoms of St. Vitus's dance. Both the art and the disease have to do with bodily movements. So too both mysticism and hysteria have to do with the domination of consciousness by one fixed and intense idea or intuition, which rules the life and is able to produce amazing physical and psychical results. In the hysteric patient this idea is often trivial or morbid but has become—thanks to the self's unstable mental condition—an obsession. In the mystic the dominant idea is a great one: so great in fact, that when it is received in its completeness by the human consciousness, almost of necessity it ousts all else. It is nothing less than the idea or perception of the transcendent reality and presence of God. Hence the mono-ideism of the mystic is rational, whilst that of the hysteric patient is invariably irrational.

On the whole then, whilst psycho-physical relations remain so little understood, it would seem more prudent, and certainly more scientific, to withhold our judgment on the meaning of the psychophysical phenomena which accompany the mystic life; instead of basing destructive criticism on facts which are avowedly mysterious and at least capable of more than one interpretation. To deduce the nature of a compound from the character of its byproducts is notoriously unsafe.

Our bodies are animal things, made for animal activities. When a spirit of unusual ardour insists on using its nerve-cells for other activities, they kick against the pricks; and inflict, as the mystics themselves acknowledge, the penalty of "mystical ill-health." "Believe me, children," says Tauler, "one who would know much about these high matters would often have to keep his bed, for his bodily frame could not support it." "I cause thee extreme pain of body," says the voice of Love to Mechthild of Magdeburg. "If I gave myself to thee as often as thou wouldst have me, I should deprive myself of the sweet shelter I have of thee in this world, for a thousand bodies could not protect a loving soul from her desire. Therefore the higher the love the greater the pain." On the other hand the exalted personality of the mystic—his self-discipline, his heroic acceptance of labour and suffering, and his inflexible will—raises to a higher term that normal power of mind over body which all possess. Also the contemplative state—like the hypnotic state in a healthy person—seems to enhance life by throwing open deeper levels of personality. The self then drinks at a fountain which is fed by the Universal Life. True ecstasy is notoriously life-enhancing. In it a bracing contact with Reality seems to take place, and as a result the subject is himself more real. Often, says St. Teresa, even the sick come forth from ecstasy healthy and with new strength; for something great is then given to the soul. Contact has been set up with levels of being which the daily routine of existence leaves untouched. Hence the extraordinary powers of endurance, and independence of external conditions, which the great ecstatics so often display.

If we see in the mystics, as some have done, the sporadic beginning of a power, a higher consciousness, towards which the race slowly tends; then it seems likely enough that where it appears nerves and organs should suffer under a stress to which they have not yet become adapted, and that a spirit more highly organized than its bodily home should be able to impose strange conditions on the flesh. When man first stood upright, a body long accustomed to go on all fours, legs which had adjusted themselves to bearing but half his weight, must have rebelled against this unnatural proceeding; inflicting upon its author much pain and discomfort if not absolute illness. It is at least permissible to look upon the strange "psycho-physical" state common amongst the mystics as just such a rebellion on the part of a normal nervous and vascular system against the exigencies of a way of life to which it has not yet adjusted itself.

In spite of such rebellion, and of the tortures to which it has subjected them, the mystics, oddly enough, are a long-lived race: an awkward fact for critics of the physiological school. To take only a few instances from amongst marked ecstatics, St. Hildegarde lived to be eighty-one, Mechthild of Magdeburg to eighty-seven, Ruysbroeck to eighty-eight, Suso to seventy, St. Teresa to sixty-seven, St. Catherine of Genoa and St. Peter of Alcantara to sixty-three. It seems as though that enhanced life which is the reward of mystical surrender enabled them to triumph over their bodily disabilities and to live and do the work demanded of them under conditions which would have incapacitated ordinary men.

Such triumphs, which take heroic rank in the history of the human mind, have been accomplished as a rule in the same way. Like all intuitive persons, all possessors of genius, all potential artists—with whom in fact they are closely related—the mystics have, in psychological language, "thresholds of exceptional mobility." That is to say, a slight effort, a slight departure from normal conditions, will permit their latent or "subliminal" powers to emerge and occupy the mental field. A "mobile threshold" may make a man a genius, a lunatic, or a saint. All depends upon the character of the emerging powers. In the great mystic, these powers, these tracts of personality lying below the level of normal consciousness, are of unusual richness; and cannot be accounted for in terms of pathology. "If it be true," says Delacroix, "that the great mystics have not wholly escaped those nervous blemishes which mark nearly all exceptional organizations, there is in them a vital and creative power, a constructive logic, an extended scale of realization—in a word, a genius—which is, in truth, their essential quality.... The great mystics, creators and inventors who have found a new form of life and have justified it... join, upon the highest summits of the human spirit, the great simplifiers of the world."

The truth, then, so far as we know it at present, seems to be that those powers which are in contact with the Transcendental Order, and which constitute at the lowest estimate half the self, are dormant in ordinary men; whose time and interest are wholly occupied in responding to the stimuli of the world of sense. With those latent powers sleeps the landscape which they alone can apprehend. In mystics none of the self is always dormant. They have roused the Dweller in the Innermost from its slumbers, and round it have unified their life. Heart, Reason, Will are there in full action, drawing their incentive not from the shadow-show of sense, but from the deeps of true Being; where a lamp is lit, and a consciousness awake, of which the sleepy crowd remains oblivious. He who says the mystic is but half a man, states the exact opposite of the truth. Only the mystic can be called a whole man, since in others half the powers of the self always sleep. This wholeness of experience is much insisted on by the mystics. Thus the Divine Voice says to St. Catherine of Siena, "I have also shown thee the Bridge and the three general steps, placed there for the three powers of the soul; and I have told thee how no one can attain to the life of grace unless he has mounted all three steps, that is, gathered together all the three powers of the soul in My Name."

In those abnormal types of personality to which we give the name of genius, we seem to detect a hint of the relations which may exist between these deep levels of being and the crust of consciousness. In the poet, the musician, the great mathematician or inventor, powers lying below the threshold, and hardly controllable by their owner's conscious will, clearly take a major part in the business of perception and conception. In all creative acts, the larger share of the work is done subconsciously: its emergence is in a sense automatic. This is equally true of mystics, artists, philosophers, discoverers, and rulers of men. The great religion, invention, work of art, always owes its inception to some sudden uprush of intuitions or ideas for which the superficial self cannot account; its execution to powers so far beyond the control of that self, that they seem, as their owner sometimes says, to "come from beyond." This is "inspiration"; the opening of the sluices, so that those waters of truth in which all life is bathed may rise to the level of consciousness.

The great teacher, poet, artist, inventor, never aims deliberately at his effects. He obtains them he knows not how: perhaps from a contact of which he is unconscious with that creative plane of being which the Sufis call the Constructive Spirit, and the Kabalists Yesod, and which both postulate as lying next behind the world of sense. "Sometimes," said the great Alexandrian Jew Philo, "when I have come to my work empty, I have suddenly become full; ideas being in an invisible manner showered upon me, and implanted in me from on high; so that through the influence of divine inspiration, I have become greatly excited, and have known neither the place in which I was, nor those who were present, nor myself, nor what I was saying, nor what I was writing; for then I have been conscious of a richness of interpretation, an enjoyment of light, a most penetrating insight, a most manifest energy in all that was to be done; having such an effect on my mind as the clearest ocular demonstration would have on the eyes." This is a true creative ecstasy, strictly parallel to the state in which the mystic performs his mighty works.

To let oneself go, be quiet, receptive, appears to be the condition under which such contact with the Cosmic Life may be obtained. "I have noticed that when one paints one should think of nothing: everything then comes better," says the young Raphael to Leonardo da Vinci. The superficial self must here acknowledge its own insufficiency, must become the humble servant of a more profound and vital consciousness. The mystics are of the same opinion. "Let the will quietly and wisely understand," says St. Teresa, "that it is not by dint of labour on our part that we can converse to any good purpose with God." "The best and noblest way in which thou mayst come into this Life," says Eckhart, "is by keeping silence and letting God work and speak. Where all the powers are withdrawn from their work and images, there is this word spoken... the more thou canst draw in all thy powers and forget the creature the nearer art thou to this, and the more receptive."

Thus Boehme says to the neophyte, "When both thy intellect and will are quiet and passive to the expressions of the eternal Word and Spirit, and when thy soul is winged up above that which is temporal, the outward senses and the imagination being locked up by holy abstraction, *then* the eternal Hearing, Seeing, and Speaking will be revealed in thee. Blessed art thou therefore if thou canst stand still from self thinking and self willing, and canst stop the wheel of thy imagination and senses." Then, the conscious mind being passive, the more divine mind below the threshold—organ of our free creative life—can emerge and present its reports. In the words of an older mystic, "The soul, leaving all things and forgetting herself, is immersed in the ocean of Divine Splendour, and illuminated by the Sublime Abyss of the Unfathomable Wisdom."

The "passivity" of contemplation, then, is a necessary preliminary of spiritual energy: an essential clearing of the ground. It withdraws the tide of consciousness from the shores of sense, stops the "wheel of the imagination." "The Soul," says Eckhart again, "is created in a place between Time and Eternity: with its highest powers it touches Eternity, with its lower Time." These, the worlds of Being and Becoming, are the two "stages of reality" which meet in the spirit of man. By cutting us off from the temporal plane, the lower kind of reality, Contemplation gives the eternal plane, and the powers which can communicate with that plane, their chance. In the born mystic these powers are great, and lie very near the normal threshold of consciousness. He has a genius for transcendental—or as he would say, divine—discovery in much the same way as his cousins, the born musician and poet, have a genius for musical or poetic discovery. In all three cases, the emergence of these higher powers is mysterious, and not least so to those who experience it. Psychology on the one hand, theology on the other, may offer us diagrams and theories of this proceeding: of the strange oscillations of the developing consciousness, the fitful visitations of a lucidity and creative power over which the self has little or no control, the raptures and griefs of a vision by turns granted and withdrawn. But the secret of genius still eludes us, as the secret of life eludes the biologist.

The utmost we can say of such persons is, that reality presents itself to them under abnormal conditions and in abnormal terms, and that subject to these conditions and in these terms they are bound to deal with it. Thanks to their peculiar mental make up, one aspect of the universe is for them focussed so sharply that in comparison with it all other images are blurred, vague, and unreal. Hence the sacrifice which men of genius—mystics, artists, inventors—make of their whole lives to this one Object, this one vision of truth, is not self-denial, but rather self-fulfilment. They gather themselves up from the unreal, in order to concentrate on the real. The whole personality then absorbs or enters into communion with certain rhythms or harmonies existent in the universe, which the receiving apparatus of other selves cannot take up. "Here is the finger of God, a flash of the Will that can!" exclaims Abt Vogler, as the sounds grow under his hand. "The numbers *came!*" says the poet. He knows not how, certainly not by deliberate intellection.

So it is with the mystic. Madame Guyon states in her autobiography, that when she was composing her works she would experience a sudden and irresistible inclination to take up her pen; though feeling wholly incapable of literary composition, and not even knowing the subject on which she would be impelled to write. If she resisted this impulse it was at the cost of the most intense discomfort. She would then begin to write with extraordinary swiftness; words, elaborate arguments, and appropriate quotations coming to her without reflection, and so quickly that one of her longest books was written in one and a half days. "In writing I saw that I was writing of things which I had never seen: and during the time of this manifestation, I was given light to perceive that I had in me treasures of knowledge and understanding which I did not know that I possessed."

Similar statements are made of St. Teresa, who declared that in writing her books she was powerless to set down anything but that which her Master put into her mind. So Blake said of "Milton" and "Jerusalem," "I have written the poems from immediate dictation, twelve or sometimes twenty or thirty lines at a time, without premeditation and even against my will. The time it has taken in writing was thus rendered non-existent, and an immense poem exists which seems to be the labour of a long life, all produced without labour or study."

These are, of course, extreme forms of that strange power of automatic composition, in which words and characters arrive and arrange themselves in defiance of their authors' will, of which most poets and novelists possess a trace. Such composition is probably related to the automatic writing of "mediums" and other sensitives; in which the often disorderly and incoherent subliminal mind seizes upon this channel of expression. The subliminal mind of the great mystic, however, is not disorderly. It is abnormally sensitive, richly endowed and keenly observant—a treasure house, not a lumber room—and becomes in the course of its education, a highly disciplined and skilled instrument of knowledge. When, therefore, its contents emerge, and are presented to the normal consciousness in the form of lucidity, "auditions," visions, automatic writing, or any other translations of the supersensible into the terms of sensible perception, they cannot be discredited because the worthless unconscious region of feebler natures sometimes manifests itself in the same way. Idiots are often voluble but many orators are sane.

Now, to sum up: what are the chief characteristics which we have found to concern us in this sketch-map of the mental life of man?

(1) We have divided that life, arbitrarily enough, along the fluctuating line which psychologists call the "threshold of his consciousness" into the surface life and the unconscious deeps.

(2) In the surface life, though we recognized its essential wholeness, we distinguished three outstanding and ever-present aspects: the Trinity in Unity of feeling, thought, and will. Amongst these we were obliged to give the primacy to feeling, as the power which set the machinery of thought and will to work.

(3) We have seen that the expression of this life takes the two complementary forms of *conation,* or outgoing action and *cognition,* or indwelling knowledge; and that the first, which is dynamic in type, is largely the work of the will stimulated by the emotions; whilst the second, which is passive in type, is the business of the intellect. They answer to the two main aspects which man discerns in the universal life: Being and Becoming.

(4) Neither conation nor cognition—action nor thought—as performed by this surface mind, concerned as it is with natural existence and dominated by spatial conceptions, is able to set up any relations with the Absolute or transcendental world. Such action and thought deal wholly with material supplied directly or indirectly by the world of sense. The testimony of the mystics, however, and of all persons possessing an "instinct for the Absolute," points to the existence of a further faculty—indeed, a deeper self—in man; a self which the circumstances of diurnal life usually keep "below the threshold" of his consciousness, and which thus becomes one of the factors of his "subliminal life." This hidden self is the primary agent of mysticism, and lives a "substantial" life in touch with the real or transcendental world.

(5) Certain processes, of which contemplation has been taken as a type, can so alter the state of consciousness as to permit the emergence of this deeper self; which, according as it enters more or less into the conscious life, makes man more or less a mystic.

The mystic life, therefore, involves the emergence from deep levels of man's transcendental self; its capture of the field of consciousness; and the "conversion" or rearrangement of his feeling, thought, and will—his character—about this new centre of life.

We state, that the object of the mystic's adventure, seen from within, is the apprehension of, or direct communion with, that transcendental Reality to define from without. Here, as in the fulfilment of the highest earthly love, knowledge and communion are the same thing; we must be "oned with bliss" if we are to be aware of it. That aspect of our being by which we may attain this communion—that "marrow of the Soul," as Ruysbroeck calls it—usually lies below the threshold of our consciousness but in certain natures of abnormal richness and vitality, and under certain favourable conditions, it may be liberated by various devices, such as contemplation. Once it has emerged, however, it takes up, to help it in the work, aspects of the conscious self. The surface must co-operate with the deeps, and at last merge with those deeps to produce that unification of consciousness upon high levels which alone can put a term to man's unrest. The heart that longs for the All, the mind that conceives it, the will that concentrates the whole self upon it, must all be called into play. The self must be surrendered but it must not be annihilated, as some Quietists have supposed. It only dies that it may live again. Supreme success,—the permanent assurance of the mystic that "we are more verily in heaven than in earth,"—says the Lady Julian, in a passage which anticipates the classification of modern psychology, "cometh of the natural Love of our soul, and of the clear light of our Reason, and of the steadfast Mind."

But what is the order of precedence which these three activities are to assume in the work which is *one*? All, as we have seen, must do their part; for we are concerned with the response of man in his wholeness to the overwhelming attraction of God. But which shall predominate? The ultimate nature of the self's experience of reality will depend on the answer she gives to this question. What, here, are the relative values of Mind and Heart? Which will bring her closest to the Thought of God; the real life in which she is bathed? Which, fostered and made dominant, is most likely to put her in harmony with the Absolute? The Love of God, which is ever in the heart and often on the lips of the Saints, is the passionate desire for this harmony; the "malady of thought" is its intellectual equivalent. Though we may seem to escape God, we cannot escape some form of this craving except at the price of utter stagnation. We see them now as representing the cravings of the intellect and the emotions for the only end of all quests. The disciplined will—the "conative power"—with all the dormant faculties which it can wake and utilize, can come to the assistance of one of them. Which? The question is a crucial one, for the destiny of the self depends on the partner which the will selects.

5

MYSTICISM AND SYMBOLISM

In our study of theology we saw the Christian mystic adopting, as chart and pilot book of his voyages and adventures, the scheme of faith, and diagram of the spiritual world, which is accepted by ordinary Christian men. We saw that he found in it a depth and richness of content which the conventional believer in that theology, the "good churchman," seldom suspects and that which is true of the Christian mystic is also true in its measure and as regards their respective theologies, of the Pagan, the Mahommedan and the Buddhist.

But since the spiritual adventures of the mystic are not those of ordinary men, it will follow that this map, though always true for him, is not complete. He can press forward to countries which unmystical piety must mark as unexplored, Pushing out from harbour to "the vast and stormy sea of the divine," he can take soundings, and mark dangers the existence of which such piety never needs to prove. Hence it is not strange that certain maps, artistic representations or symbolic schemes, should have come into being which describe or suggest the special experiences of the mystical consciousness, and the doctrines to which these experiences have given birth. Many of these maps have an uncouth, even an impious appearance in the eyes of those unacquainted with the facts which they attempt to translate as the charts of the deep-sea sailor seem ugly and unintelligible things to those who have never been out of sight of land. Others—and these the most pleasing, most easily understood—have already been made familiar, perhaps tiresomely familiar, to us by the poets who, intuitively recognizing their suggestive qualities, their links with truth, have borrowed and adapted them to their own business of translating Reality into terms of rhythm and speech. Ultimately, however, they owe their origin to the mystics, or to that mystical sense which is innate in all true poets: and in the last resort it is the mystic's kingdom, and the mystic's experience, which they affect to describe.

These special mystical diagrams, these symbolic and artistic descriptions of man's inward history—his secret adventures with God—are almost endless in their variety since in each we have a picture of the country of the soul seen through a different temperament. To describe all would be to analyse the whole field of mystical literature, and indeed much other literature as well; to epitomize in fact all that has been dreamed and written concerning the so-called "inner life"—a dreary and a lengthy task. But the majority of them, I think, express a comparatively small number of essential doctrines or fundamental ways of seeing things; and as regards their imagery, they fall into three great classes, representative of the three principal ways in which man's spiritual consciousness reacts to the touch of Reality, the three primary if paradoxical facts of which that consciousness must be aware. Hence a consideration of mystic symbols drawn from each of these groups may give us a key with which to unlock some at least of the verbal riddles of the individual adventurer.

Thanks to the spatial imagery inseparable from human thinking and human expression, no direct description of spiritual experience is or can be possible to man. It must always be symbolic, allusive, oblique: always suggest, but never tell, the truth and in this respect there is not much to choose between the fluid and artistic language of vision and the arid technicalities of philosophy. In another respect, however, there is a great deal to choose between them and here the visionary, not the philosopher, receives the palm. The greater the suggestive quality of the symbol used, the more answering emotion it evokes in those to whom it is addressed, the more truth it will convey. A good symbolism, therefore, will be more than mere diagram or mere allegory: it will use to the utmost the resources of beauty and of passion, will bring with it hints of mystery and wonder, bewitch with dreamy periods the mind to which it is addressed. Its appeal will not be to the clever brain, but to the desirous heart, the intuitive sense, of man.

The three great classes of symbols which I propose to consider, appeal to three deep cravings of the self, three great expressions of man's restlessness, which only mystic truth can fully satisfy. The first is the craving which makes him a pilgrim and wanderer. It is the longing to go out from his normal world in search of a lost home, a "better country"; an Eldorado, a Sarras, a Heavenly Syon. The next is that craving of heart for heart, of the soul for its perfect mate, which makes him a lover. The third is the craving for inward purity and perfection, which makes him an ascetic, and in the last resort a saint.

These three cravings, I think, answer to three ways in which mystics of different temperaments attack the problem of the Absolute: three different formulae under which their transcendence of the sense-world can be described. In describing this transcendence, and the special adventures involved in it, they are describing a change from the state of ordinary men, in touch with the sense-world, responding to its rhythms, to the state of spiritual consciousness in which, as they say, they are "in union" with Divine Reality, with God. Whatever be the theological creed of the mystic, he never varies in declaring this close, definite, and actual intimacy to be the end of his quest. "Mark me like the tulip with Thine own streaks," says the Sufi. "I would fain be to the Eternal Goodness what his own hand is to a man," says the German contemplative. "My *me* is God, nor do I know my self-hood save in Him," says the Italian saint.

But, since this Absolute God is for him substance, ground or underlying Reality of all that *is* : present yet absent, near yet far: He is already as truly immanent in the human soul as in the Universe. The seeker for the Real may therefore objectify his quest in two apparently contradictory, yet really mutually explanatory ways. First he may see it as an outgoing journey from the world of illusion to the real or transcendental world: a leaving of the visible for the invisible. Secondly, it may appear to him as an inward alteration, remaking or regeneration, by which his personality or character is so changed as to be able to enter into communion with that Fontal Being which he loves and desires; is united with and dominated by the indwelling God who is the fount of his spiritual life. In the first case, the objective idea "God" is the pivot of his symbolism: the Blazing Star, or Magnet of the Universe which he has seen far off, and seeing, has worshipped and desired. In the second case, the emphasis falls on the subjective idea "Sanctity," with its accompanying consciousness of a disharmony to be abolished. The Mystic Way will then be described, not as a journey, but as an alteration of personality, the transmuting of "earthly" into "heavenly" man. Plainly these two aspects are obverse and reverse of one whole. They represent that mighty pair of opposites, Infinite and Finite, God and Self, which it is the business of mysticism to carry up into a higher synthesis. Whether the process be considered as outward search or inward change, its object and its end are the same. Man enters into that Order of Reality for which he was made, and which is indeed the inciting cause of his pilgrimage and his purification: for however great the demand on the soul's own effort may be, the initiative always lies with the living Divine World itself. Man's small desire is evoked, met, and fulfilled by the Divine Desire, his "separated will" or life becomes one with the great Life of the All.

It will be clear that the symbolism of outward search and of inward change will be adopted respectively by the two groups of selves whose experience of "union with the Divine" leans (1) to the Transcendent or external, (2) to the Immanent or internal way of apprehending Reality. A third or intermediate group of images will be necessary to express the experience of those to whom mystic feeling—the satisfaction of love—is the supreme factor in the mystic life. According, then, to whether man's instinct prompts him to describe the Absolute Reality which he knows and craves for as a Place, a Person, or a State—all three of course but partial and inadequate translations of the one

Indescribable Truth—so will he tend to adopt a symbolism of one or other of these three types.

(a) Those who conceive the Perfect as a beatific vision exterior to them and very far off, who find in the doctrine of Emanations something which answers to their inward experience, will feel the process of their entrance into reality to be a quest, an arduous journey from the material to the spiritual world. They move away from, rather than transmute to another form, the life of sense. The ecstasies of such mystics will answer to the root-meaning of that much perverted word, as a "standing out" from themselves; a flight to happier countries far away. For them, the soul is outward bound towards its home.

(b) Those for whom mysticism is above all things an intimate and personal relation, the satisfaction of a deep desire—who can say with Gertrude More, "never was there or can there be imagined such a love, as is between an humble soul and Thee"—will fall back upon imagery drawn largely from the language of earthly passion. Since the Christian religion insists upon the personal aspect of the Godhead, and provides in Christ an object of such intimacy, devotion and desire, an enormous number of Christian mystics inevitably describe their experiences under symbolism of this kind.

(c) Those who are conscious rather of the Divine as a Transcendent Life immanent in the world and the self, and of a strange spiritual seed within them by whose development man, moving to higher levels of character and consciousness, attains his end, will see the mystic life as involving inward change rather than outgoing search. Regeneration is their watchword, and they will choose symbols of growth or transmutation: saying with St. Catherine of Genoa, "my Being is God, not by simple participation, but by a true transformation of my Being."

These three groups of mystics, then, stand for three kinds of temperament and we may fairly take as their characteristic forms of symbolic expression the Mystic Quest, the Marriage of the Soul, and the "Great Work" of the Spiritual Alchemists.

The pilgrimage idea, the outgoing quest, appears in mystical literature under two different aspects. One is the search for the "Hidden Treasure which desires to be found." Such is the "quest of the Grail" when regarded in its mystic aspect as an allegory of the adventures of the soul. The other is the long, hard journey towards a known and definite goal or state. Such are Dante's "Divine Comedy" and Bunyan's "Pilgrim's Progress"; each in their manner faithful descriptions of the Mystic Way. The goal of the quest—the Empyrean of Dante, the Beatific Vision or fulfilment of love—is often called Jerusalem by the Christian mystics: naturally enough since that city was for the mediaeval mind the supreme end of pilgrimage. By Jerusalem they mean not only the celestial country

Heaven, but also the spiritual life, which is "itself a heaven." "Right as a true pilgrim going to Jerusalem," says Hilton, "leaveth behind him house and land, wife and child, and maketh himself poor and bare from all that he hath, that he may go lightly without letting: right so, if thou wilt be a ghostly pilgrim, thou shalt make thyself naked from all that thou hast... then shalt thou set in thy heart wholly and fully that thou wouldst be at Jerusalem, and at none other place but there." "Jerusalem," "is as much as to say a sight of peace; and betokeneth contemplation in perfect love of God."

Under this image of a pilgrimage—an image as concrete and practical, as remote from the romantic and picturesque, for the mediaeval writers who used it, as a symbolism of hotel and railway train would be to us—the mystics contrived to summarize and suggest much of the life history of the ascending soul; the developing spiritual consciousness. The necessary freedom and detachment of the traveller, his departure from his normal life and interests, the difficulties, enemies, and hardships encountered on the road—the length of the journey, the variety of the country, the dark night which overtakes him, the glimpses of destination far away—all these are seen more and more as we advance in knowledge to constitute a transparent allegory of the incidents of man's progress from the unreal to the real. Bunyan was but the last of a long series of minds which grasped this fact.

The Traveller, says the Sufi 'Aziz bin Mahommed Nafasi, in whose book, "The Remotest Aim," the pilgrimage-symbolism is developed in great detail, is the Perceptive or Intuitive Sense of Man. The goal to which he journeys is Knowledge of God. This mysterious traveller towards the only country of the soul may be known of other men by his detachment, charity, humility, and patience. These primary virtues, however—belonging to ethical rather than to spiritual life—are not enough to bring his quest to a successful termination. They make him, say the Sufis, "perfect in knowledge of his goal but deficient in the power of reaching it." Though he has fraternal love for his fellow-pilgrims, detachment from wayside allurements, untiring perseverance on the road, he is still encumbered and weakened by unnecessary luggage. The second stage of his journey, therefore, is initiated like that of Christian by a casting off of his burden: a total self-renouncement, the attainment of a Franciscan poverty of spirit whereby he becomes "Perfectly Free."

Having got rid of all impediments to the spiritual quest, he must now acquire or develop in their stead the characteristic mystical qualities, or Three Aids of the Pilgrim; which are called in this system Attraction, Devotion, and Elevation. Attraction is consciousness of the mutual desire existing between man's spirit and the Divine Spirit: of the link of love which knits up reality and draws all things to their home in God. This is the universal law on which all mysticism is based. It is St. Augustine's "Thou hast made us for Thyself and our hearts can find no rest except in Thee." This "natural magnetism," then, once he is aware of it, will draw the pilgrim irresistibly along the road from the Many to the One. His second aid, Devotion, says the "Remotest Aim" in a phrase of great depth and beauty, is "the prosecution of the journey *to* God and *in* God." It embraces, in fact, the whole contemplative life. It is the next degree of spiritual consciousness after the blind yielding to the attraction of the Real, and the setting in order of man's relation to his source.

The Traveller's journey *to* God is complete when he attains knowledge of Him—"Illumination," in the language of European mystics. The point at which this is reached is called the Tavern or resting-place upon the road, where he is fed with the Divine Mysteries. There are also "Wine Shops" upon the way, where the weary pilgrim is cheered and refreshed by a draught of the wine of Divine Love. Only when the journey *to* God is completed begins the "Journey *in* God"—that which the Christian mystics call the Unitive Way—and this, since it is the essence of Eternal Life, can have no end. Elevation, the pilgrim's third aid, is the exalted or ecstatic form of consciousness peculiar to the contemplative, and which allows the traveller a glimpse of the spiritual city towards which he goes.

The Sufi poet 'Attar, in his mystical poem, "The Colloquy of the Birds," has described the stages of this same spiritual pilgrimage with greater psychological insight, as the journey through "Seven Valleys." The lapwing, having been asked by other birds what is the length of the road which leads to the hidden Palace of the King, replies that there are Seven Valleys through which every traveller must pass but since none who attain the End ever come back to describe their adventures, no one knows the length of the way.

(1) The first valley, says the lapwing, is the Valley of the Quest. It is long and toilsome and there the traveller must strip himself of all earthly things, becoming poor, bare, and desolate: and so stay till the Supernal Light casts a ray on his desolation. It is in fact, Dante's Purgatorio, the Christian Way of Purgation: the period of self-stripping and purification which no mystic system omits.

(2) When the ray of Supernal Light has touched the pilgrim he enters the limitless Valley of Love: begins, that is to say, the mystic life. It is Dante's "Earthly Paradise," or, in the traditional system of the mystics, the onset of Illumination.

(3) Hence he passes to the Valley of Knowledge or Enlightenment—the contemplative state—where each finds in communion with Truth the place that belongs to him. No Dante student will fail to see here a striking parallel with those planetary heavens where each soul partakes of the Divine, "not supremely in the absolute sense," as St. Bonaventura has it, but "supremely in respect of *himself.*" The mystery of Being is now revealed to the traveller. He sees Nature's secret, and God in all things. It is the height of illumination.

(4) The next stage is the Valley of Detachment, of utter absorption in Divine Love—the Stellar Heaven of the Saints—where Duty is seen to be all in all. This leads to—

(5) The Valley of the Unity, where the naked Godhead is the one object of contemplation. This is the stage of ecstasy, or the Beatific Vision: Dante's condition in the last canto of the "Paradiso." It is transient, however, and leads to—

(6) The Valley of Amazement; where the Vision, far transcending the pilgrim's receptive power, appears to be taken from him and he is plunged in darkness and bewilderment. This is the state which Dionysius the Areopagite, and after him many mediaeval mystics, called the Divine Dark, and described as the truest and closest of all our apprehensions of the Godhead. It is the Cloud of Unknowing, "dark from excessive bright." The final stage is—

(7) The Valley of Annihilation of Self: the supreme degree of union or theopathetic state, in which the self is utterly merged "like a fish in the sea" in the ocean of Divine Love.

Through all these metaphors of pilgrimage to a goal—of a road followed, distance overpassed, fatigue endured—there runs the definite idea that the travelling self in undertaking the journey is fulfilling a destiny, a law of the transcendental life; obeying an imperative need. The chosen Knights are destined or *called* to the quest of the Grail. "All men are *called* to their origin," says Rulman Merswin, and the fishes which he sees in his Vision of Nine Rocks are impelled to struggle, as it were "against nature," uphill from pool to pool towards their source.

All mystical thinkers agree in declaring that there is a mutual attraction between the Spark of the Soul, the free divine germ in man, and the Fount from which it came forth. "We long for the Absolute," says Royce, "only in so far as in us the Absolute also longs, and seeks, through our very temporal striving, the peace that is nowhere in Time, but only, and yet Absolutely, in Eternity." So, many centuries before the birth of American philosophy, Hilton put the same truth of experience in lovelier words. "He it is that desireth in thee, and He it is that is desired. He is all and He doth all if thou might see Him."

The homeward journey of man's spirit, then, may be thought of as due to the push of a divine life within, answering to the pull of a divine life without. It is only possible because there is already in that spirit a certain kinship with the Divine, a capacity for Eternal Life; and the mystics, in undertaking it, are humanity's pioneers on the only road to rest. Hence that attraction which the Moslem mystic discerned as the traveller's necessary aid, is a fundamental doctrine of all mysticism: and as a consequence, the symbolism of mutual desire is here inextricably mingled with that of pilgrimage. The spiritual pilgrim goes because he is called; because he wants to go, must go, if he is to find rest and peace. "God *needs* man," says Eckhart. It is Love calling to love: and the journey, though in one sense a hard pilgrimage, up and out, by the terraced mount and the ten heavens to God, in another is the inevitable rush of the roving comet, caught at last, to the Central Sun. "My weight is my love," said St. Augustine. Like gravitation, it inevitably compels, for good or evil, every spirit to its own place. According to another range of symbols, that love flings open a door, in order that the larger Life may rush in and it and the soul be "one thing."

Here, then, we run through the whole gamut of symbolic expression; through Transcendence, Desire, and Immanence. All are seen to point to one consummation, diversely and always allusively expressed: the need of union between man's separated spirit and the Real, his remaking in the interests of transcendent life, his establishment in that Kingdom which is both "near and far."

"In the book of Hidden Things it is written," says Eckhart, "'I stand at the door and knock and wait'... thou needst not seek Him here or there: He is no farther off than the door of the heart. There He stands and waits and waits until He finds thee ready to open and let Him in. Thou needst not call Him from a distance; to wait until thou openest is harder for Him than for thee. He needs thee a thousand times more than thou canst need Him. *Thy opening and His entering are but one moment*." "God," he says in another place, "can as little do without us, as we without Him." Our attainment of the Absolute is not a one-sided ambition, but the fulfilment of a mutual desire. "For our natural Will," says Lady Julian, "is to have God, and the Good will of God is to have us; and we may never cease from longing till we have Him in fullness of joy."

So, in the beautiful poem or ritual called the "Hymn of Jesus," contained in the apocryphal "Acts of John" and dating from primitive Christian times, the Logos, or Eternal Christ, is thus represented as matching with His own transcendent, self-giving desire every need of the soul.

The Soul says:

"'I would be saved.'"

Christ replies:

"'And I would save.' Amen."

The Dialogue continues:

"'I would be loosed.'
'And I would loose.' Amen.
'I would be pierced.'
'And I would pierce.' Amen.
'I would be born.'

'And I would bear.' Amen.
'I would eat.'
'And I would be eaten.' Amen.
'I would hear.'
'And I would be heard.' Amen."
"'I am a Lamp to thee who beholdest Me,
I am a Mirror to thee who perceivest Me,
I am a Door to thee, who knockest at Me,
I am a Way to thee a wayfarer.'"

The same fundamental idea of the mutual quest of the Soul and the Absolute is expressed in the terms of another symbolism by the great Mahommedan mystic:

"No lover ever seeks union with his beloved,
But his beloved is also seeking union with him.
But the lover's love makes his body lean
While the beloved's love makes her fair and lusty.
When in *this* heart the lightning spark of love arises,
Be sure this love is reciprocated in *that* heart.
When the love of God arises in thy heart,
Without doubt God also feels love for thee."

The mystic vision, then, is of a spiritual universe held within the bonds of love: and of the free and restless human soul, having within it the spark of divine desire, the "tendency to the Absolute," only finding satisfaction and true life when united with this Life of God. Then, in Patmore's lovely image, "the babe is at its mother's breast," "the lover has returned to the beloved."

Whatever their outward sense, all true mystic symbols express aspects of this "secret of the world," this primal verity. But whereas such great visionary schemes as those of 'Attar and of Dante show it in its cosmic form, in many symbolic descriptions—particularly those which we meet in the writings of the ecstatic saints—the personal subjective note, the consciousness of an individual relation between that one self and the Supernal Self, overpowers all general applications. Then philosophy and formal allegory must step aside: the sacramental language of exalted emotion, of profoundly felt experience, takes its place. The phases of mutual love, of wooing and combat, awe and delight—the fevers of desire, the ecstasy of surrender—are drawn upon and made to contribute something to the description of the great and secret drama of the soul.

To such symbolic transcripts of intimate experience belongs one amazing episode of the spiritual life-history which, because it has been given immortal expression by the greatest mystical poet of modern times, is familiar to thousands of readers who know little or nothing of the more normal adventures incidental to man's attainment of the Absolute. In "The Hound of Heaven" Francis Thompson described with an almost terrible power, not the self's quest of adored Reality, but Reality's quest of the unwilling self. He shows to us the remorseless, untiring seeking and following of the soul by the Divine Life to which it will not surrender: the inexorable onward sweep of "this tremendous Lover," hunting the separated spirit, "strange piteous futile thing" that flees Him "down the nights and down the days." This idea of the love-chase, of the spirit rushing in terror from the overpowering presence of God, but followed, sought, conquered in the end, is common to all the mediaeval mystics: it is the obverse of their general doctrine of the necessary fusion of human and divine life, "escape from the flame of separation."

"I chased thee, for in this was my pleasure," says the voice of Love to Mechthild of Magdeburg; "I captured thee, for this was my desire; I bound thee, and I rejoice in thy bonds; I have wounded thee, that thou mayst be united to me. If I gave thee blows, it was that I might be possessed of thee."

So in the beautiful Middle English poem of "Quia amore langueo,"—

"I am true love that fals was nevere,
Mi sistyr, mannis soule, I loved hir thus;
Bicause we wolde in no wise discevere
I lefte my Kyngdom glorious.
I purveyde for hir a paleis precious;
She fleyth, I folowe, I sought hir so.
I suffride this peyne piteous
Quia amore langueo,"

Meister Eckhart has the same idea of the inexorable Following Love, impossible to escape, expressed under less personal images. "Earth," he says, "cannot escape the sky; let it flee up or down, the sky flows into it, and makes it fruitful whether it will or no. So God does to man. He who will escape Him only runs to His bosom; for all corners are open to Him."

We find in all the mystics this strong sense of a mysterious spiritual life—a Reality—over against man, seeking him and compelling him to Its will. It is not for him, they think, to say that he will or will not aspire to the transcendental world. Hence sometimes this inversion of man's long quest of God. The self resists the pull of spiritual gravitation, flees from the touch of Eternity; and the Eternal seeks it, tracks it ruthlessly down. The Following Love, the mystics say, is a fact of experience, not a poetic idea. "Those strong feet that follow, follow after," once set upon the chase, are bound to win. Man, once conscious of Reality, cannot evade it. For a time his separated spirit, his disordered loves, may wilfully frustrate the scheme of things: but he must be conquered in the end. Then the mystic process unfolds itself: Love triumphs: the "purpose of the worlds" fulfils itself in the individual life.

It was natural and inevitable that the imagery of human love and marriage should have seemed to the mystic the best of all images of his own "fulfilment of life"; his soul's surrender, first to the call, finally to the embrace of Perfect Love. It lay ready to his hand: it was understood of all men: and moreover, it certainly does offer, upon lower levels, a strangely exact parallel to the sequence of states in which man's spiritual consciousness unfolds itself, and which form the consummation of the mystic life.

It has been said that the constant use of such imagery by Christian mystics of the mediaeval period is traceable to the popularity of the Song of Songs, regarded as an allegory of the spiritual life. I think that the truth lies rather in the opposite statement: namely, that the mystic loved the Song of Songs because he there saw reflected, as in a mirror, the most secret experiences of his soul. The sense of a desire that was insatiable, of a personal fellowship so real, inward, and intense that it could only be compared with the closest link of human love, of an intercourse that was no mere spiritual self-indulgence, but was rooted in the primal duties and necessities of life—more, those deepest, most intimate secrets of communion, those self-giving ecstasies which all mystics know, but of which we, who are not mystics, may not speak—all these he found symbolized and suggested, their unendurable glories veiled in a merciful mist, in the poetry which man has invented to honour that august passion in which the merely human draws nearest to the divine.

The great saints who adopted and elaborated this symbolism, applying it to their pure and ardent passion for the Absolute, were destitute of the prurient imagination which their modern commentators too often possess. They were essentially pure of heart; and when they "saw God" they were so far from confusing that unearthly vision with the products of morbid sexuality, that the dangerous nature of the imagery which they employed did not occur to them. They knew by experience the unique nature of spiritual love and no one can know anything about it in any other way.

Thus for St. Bernard, throughout his deeply mystical sermons on the Song of Songs, the Divine Word is the Bridegroom, the human soul is the Bride but how different is the effect produced by his use of these symbols from that with which he has been charged by hostile critics! In the place of that "sensuous imagery" which is so often and so earnestly deplored by those who have hardly a nodding acquaintance with the writings of the saints, we find images which indeed have once been sensuous; but which are here anointed and ordained to a holy office, carried up, transmuted, and endowed with a radiant purity, an intense and spiritual life.

"*'Let Him kiss me with the kisses of His mouth.'* Who is it speaks these words? It is the Bride. Who is the Bride? It is the Soul thirsting for God.... She who asks this is held by the bond of love to him from whom she asks it. Of all the sentiments of nature, this of love is the most excellent, especially when it is rendered back to Him who is the principle and fountain of it—that is, God. Nor are there found any expressions equally sweet to signify the mutual affection between the Word of God and the soul, as those of Bridegroom and of Bride; inasmuch as between individuals who stand in such relation to each other all things are in common, and they possess nothing separate or divided. They have one inheritance, one dwelling-place, one table, and they are in fact one flesh. If, then, mutual love is especially befitting to a bride and bridegroom, it is not unfitting that the name of Bride is given to a soul which loves."

To women mystics of the Catholic Church, familiar with the antique and poetic metaphor which called every cloistered nun the Bride of Christ, that crisis in their spiritual history in which they definitely vowed themselves to the service of Transcendent Reality seemed, naturally enough, the veritable betrothal of the soul. Often, in a dynamic vision, they saw as in a picture the binding vows exchanged between their spirits and their God. That further progress on the mystic way which brought with it a sharp and permanent consciousness of union with the Divine Will, the constant sustaining presence of a Divine Companion, became, by an extension of the original simile, Spiritual Marriage. The elements of duty, constancy, irrevocableness, and loving obedience involved in the mediaeval conception of the marriage tie, made it an apt image of a spiritual state in which humility, intimacy, and love were the dominant characteristics. There is really no need to seek a pathological explanation of these simple facts. Moreover with few exceptions, the descriptions of spiritual marriage which the great mystics have left are singularly free from physical imagery. "So mysterious is the secret," says St. Teresa, "and so sublime the favour that God thus bestows instantaneously on the soul, that it feels a supreme delight, only to be described by saying that our Lord vouchsafes for the moment to reveal to it His own heavenly glory in a far more subtle way than by any vision or spiritual delight. As far as can be understood, the soul, I mean the spirit of this soul, is made one with God, who is Himself a spirit, and Who has been pleased to show certain persons how far His love for us extends in order that we may praise His greatness. He has thus deigned to unite Himself to His creature: He has bound Himself to her as firmly as two human beings are joined in wedlock and will never separate Himself from her."

The great Richard of St. Victor, in one of his most splendid mystical treatises, has given us perhaps the most daring and detailed application of the symbolism of marriage to the adventures of the spirit of man. He divides the "steep stairway of love," by which the contemplative ascends to union with the Absolute, into four stages. These he calls the betrothal, the marriage, the wedlock, and the fruitfulness of the soul. In the betrothal, he says, the soul "thirsts for the Beloved"; that is to say, it longs to experience the delights of Reality. "The Spirit comes to the Soul, and seems sweeter than honey." It is conversion, the awakening to mystical truth; the kindling of the passion for the Absolute. "Then the Soul with pertinacity demands more": and because of her burning desire she attains to pure contemplation, and so passes to the second degree of love. In this she is "led in bridal" by the Beloved.

Ascending "above herself" in contemplation, she "sees the Sun of Righteousness." She is now confirmed in the mystic life; the irrevocable marriage vows are made between her spirit and her God. At this point she can "see the Beloved," but "cannot yet come in to Him," says Richard. This degree, answers more or less to that which other mystics call the Illuminative Way: but any attempt to press these poetic symbols into a cast-iron series, and establish exact parallels, is foredoomed to failure, and will merely succeed in robbing them of their fragrance and suggestive power. In Richard's "third stage," however, that of union, or wedlock, it is clear that the soul enters upon the "Unitive Way." She has passed the stages of ecstatic and significant events, and is initiated into the Life. She is "deified," "passes utterly *into* God, and is glorified in Him": is transfigured, he says, by immediate contact with the Divine Substance, into an utterly different quality of being. "Thus," says St. John of the Cross, "the soul, when it shall have driven away from itself all that is contrary to the divine will, becomes transformed in God by love.

"The Soul," says Richard again, "is utterly concentrated on the One." She is "caught up to the divine light." The expression of the personal passion, the intimate relation, here rises to its height. But this is not enough. Where most mystical diagrams leave off, Richard of St. Victor's "steep stairway of Love" goes on with the result that this is almost the only symbolic system bequeathed to us by the great contemplatives in which all the implications contained in the idea of the spiritual marriage have been worked out to their term. He saw clearly that the union of the soul with its Source could not be a barren ecstasy. That was to mistake a means for an end; and to frustrate the whole intention of life, which is, on all levels, fruitful and creative. Therefore he says that in the fourth degree, the Bride who has been so greatly honoured, caught up to such unspeakable delight, sinks her own will and "is humiliated below herself." She accepts the pains and duties in the place of the raptures of love; and becomes a source, a "parent" of fresh spiritual life. The *Sponsa Dei* develops into the *Mater Divinae gratiae.* That imperative need of life, to push on, to create, to spread, is here seen operating in the spiritual sphere. This forms that rare and final stage in the evolution of the great mystics, in which they return to the world which they forsook; and there live, as it were, as centres of transcendental energy, the creators of spiritual families, the partners and fellow-labourers with the Divine Life.

We come now to the symbols which have been adopted by those mystics in whom temperamental consciousness of their own imperfection, and of the unutterable perfection of the Absolute Life for which they longed, has overpowered all other aspects of man's quest of reality. The "seek, and ye shall find" of the pilgrim, the "by Love shall He be gotten and holden" of the bride, can never seem an adequate description of experience to minds of this type. They are intent on the inexorable truth which must be accepted in some form by both these classes: the crucial fact that "we behold that which we are," or, in other words, that "only the Real can know Reality." Hence the state of the inward man, the "unrealness" of him when judged by any transcendental standard, is their centre of interest. His remaking or regeneration appears to them as the primal necessity, if he is ever to obtain rights of citizenship in the "country of the soul."

We have seen that this idea of the New Birth, the remaking or transmutation of the self, clothed in many different symbols, runs through the whole of mysticism and much of theology. It is the mystic's subjective reading of those necessary psychological and moral changes which he observes within himself as his spiritual consciousness grows. His hard work of renunciation, of detachment from the things which that consciousness points out as illusory or impure, his purifications and trials, all form part of it. If that which is whole or perfect is to come, then that which is in part must be done away: "for in what measure we put off the creature, in the same measure are we able to put on the Creator: neither more nor less."

Of all the symbolic systems in which this truth has been enshrined none is so complete, so picturesque, and now so little understood as that of the "Hermetic Philosophers" or Spiritual Alchemists. This fact would itself be sufficient to justify us in examining some of the chief features of their symbolism. There is a further excuse for this apparently eccentric proceeding, however, in the fact that the language of alchemy was largely—though not always accurately and consistently—used by the great mystic Jacob Boehme, and after him by his English disciple, William Law. Without, then, some knowledge of the terms which they employed, but seldom explained, the writings of this important school can hardly be understood.

The alchemic symbols, especially as applied to the mystic life, are full of an often deliberate obscurity; which makes their exact interpretation a controversial matter at the best. Moreover, the authors of the various Hermetic writings do not always use them in the same sense, and whilst many of these writings are undoubtedly mystical, others clearly deal with the physical quest of gold: nor have we any sure standard by which to divide class from class. The elements from which the spiritual alchemists built up their allegories of the mystic life are, however, easily grasped and these elements, with the significance generally attributed to them, are as much as those who are not specialists can hope to unravel from this very tangled skein. First, there are the metals; of course the obvious materials of physical alchemy. These are usually called by the names of their presiding planets: thus in Hermetic language Luna means silver, Sol gold, etc. Then there is the Vessel, or Athanor, in which the transmutation of base metal to gold took place: an object whose exact nature is veiled in much mystery. The Fire, and various solvents and waters, peculiar to the different alchemistic recipes, complete the apparatus necessary to the "Great Work."

The process of this work, sometimes described in chemical, and sometimes in astrological terms, is more often than not disguised in a strange heraldic and zoological symbolism dealing with Lions, Dragons, Eagles, Vultures, Ravens and Doves: which, delightful in its picturesqueness, is unequalled in its power of confusing the anxious and unwary inquirer. It is also the subject of innumerable and deliberate allegories, which were supposed to convey its secrets to the elect, whilst most certainly concealing them from the crowd. Hence it is that the author of "A Short Enquiry concerning the Hermetic Art" speaks for all investigators of this subject when he describes the "Hermetic science" as a "great Labyrinth, in which are abundance of enquirers rambling to this day, many of them undiscerned by one another." Like him, I too "have taken several Turns in it myself, wherein one shall meet with very few; for 'tis so large, and almost every one taking a different Path, that they seldom meet. But finding it a very melancholy place, I resolved to get out of it, and rather content myself to walk in the little garden before the entrance, where many things, though not all, were orderly to be seen. Choosing rather to stay there, and contemplate on the Metaphor set up, than venture again into the wilderness."

Coming, then, to the "contemplation of the Metaphor set up,"—by far the most judicious course for modern students of the Hermetic art—we observe first that the prime object of alchemy was held to be the production of the Philosopher's Stone, that perfect and incorrupt substance or "noble Tincture," never found upon our imperfect earth in its natural state, which could purge all baser metals of their dross, and turn them to pure gold. The quest of the Stone, in fact, was but one aspect of man's everlasting quest of perfection, his hunger for the Absolute and hence an appropriate symbol of the mystic life. But this quest was not conducted in some far off transcendental kingdom. It was prosecuted in the Here and Now within the physical world.

Gold, the Crowned King, or Sol, as it is called in the planetary symbolism of the alchemists, was their standard of perfection, the "Perfect Metal." Towards it, as the Christian towards sanctity, their wills were set. It had for them a value not sordid but ideal. Nature, they thought, is always trying to make gold, this incorruptible and perfect thing; and the other metals are merely the results of the frustration of her original design. Nor is this aiming at perfection and achieving of imperfection limited to the physical world. *Quod superius, sicut quod inferius.* Upon the spiritual plane also they held that the Divine Idea is always aiming at "Spiritual Gold"—divine humanity, the New Man, citizen of the transcendental world—and "natural man" as we ordinarily know him is a lower metal, silver at best. He is a departure from the "plan," who yet bears within himself, if we could find it, the spark or seed of absolute perfection: the "tincture" which makes gold. "The smattering I have of the Philosopher's Stone," says Sir Thomas Browne, "(which is something more than the perfect exaltation of gold) hath taught me a great deal of divinity, and instructed my belief how that immortal spirit and incorruptible substance of my soul may lie obscure, and sleep awhile within this house of flesh." This "incorruptible substance" is man's goldness, his perfect principle: for "the highest mineral virtue resides in Man," says Albertus Magnus, "and God may be found everywhere." Hence the prosecution of a spiritual chemistry is a proper part of the true Hermetic science.

The art of the alchemist, whether spiritual or physical, consists in completing the work of perfection, bringing forth and making dominant, as it were, the "latent goldness" which "lies obscure" in metal or man. The ideal adept of alchemy was therefore an "auxiliary of the Eternal Goodness." By his search for the "Noble Tincture" which should restore an imperfect world, he became a partner in the business of creation, assisting the Cosmic Plan. Thus the proper art of the Spiritual Alchemist, with whom alone we are here concerned, was the production of the spiritual and only valid tincture or Philosopher's Stone; the mystic seed of transcendental life which should invade, tinge, and wholly transmute the imperfect self into spiritual gold. That this was no fancy of seventeenth-century allegorists, but an idea familiar to many of the oldest writers upon alchemy—whose quest was truly a spiritual search into the deepest secrets of the soul—is proved by the words which bring to an end the first part of the antique "Golden Treatise upon the Making of the Stone," sometimes attributed to Hermes Trismegistus. "This, O Son," says that remarkable tract, "is the Concealed Stone of Many Colours, which is born and brought forth in one colour; know this and conceal it... it leads from darkness into light, from this desert wilderness to a secure habitation, and from poverty and straits to a free and ample fortune."

Man, then, was for the alchemists "the true laboratory of the Hermetic art" which concealed in an entanglement of vague and contradictory symbols the life-process of his ascension to that perfect state in which he was able to meet God. This state must not be confused with a merely moral purity, but is to be understood as involving utter transmutation into a "new form." It naturally followed from this that the indwelling Christ, the "Corner Stone," the Sun of Righteousness, became, for many of the Christian alchemists, identified with the *Lapis Philosophorum* and with Sol: and was regarded both as the image and as the earnest of this "great work." His spirit was the "noble tincture" which "can bring that which is lowest in the death to its highest ornament or glory;" transmuting the natural to the supernatural, operating the "New Birth." "This," says Boehme, "is the noble precious Stone *(Lapis Philosophorum),* the Philosopher's Stone, which the Magi (or wise men) find which *tinctureth nature,* and generateth a new son in the old. He who findeth that, esteemeth more highly of it than of this (outward) world. For the Son is many thousand times greater than the Father." Again, "If you take the *spirit* of the tincture, then indeed you go on a way in which *many have found* Sol; but they have followed on the way to *the heart* of Sol, where the spirit of the heavenly tincture hath laid hold on *them,* and brought them into the liberty, into the Majesty, where they have *Known* the Noble Stone, *Lapis Philosophorum,* the Philosopher's Stone, and have stood amazed at man's blindness, and seen his labouring in vain. Would you fain find the Noble Stone? Behold, we will show it you plain enough, if you be a *Magus,* and worthy, else you shall remain blind still: therefore fall to work thus: for it hath no more but *three numbers.* First tell from *one* till you come to the Cross, which is ten (X)... and *there* lieth the *Stone* without any great painstaking, for it is pure and not defiled with any earthly nature."

"In this stone there lieth hidden, whatsoever God and the Eternity, also heaven, the stars and elements contain and are able to do. There never was from eternity anything better or more precious than this, and it is offered by God and bestowed upon man; every one may have it... it is in a simple form, and hath the power of the whole Deity in it."

Boehme is here using alchemic symbols, according to his custom, in a loose and artistic manner; for the true Hermetic Philosopher's Stone is not something which can be found but something which must be made. The alchemists, whether their search be for a physical or a spiritual "tincture," say always that this tincture is the product of the furnace and Athanor: and further that it is composed of "three numbers" or elements, which they call Sulphur, Salt, and Mercury. These, when found, and forced into the proper combination, form the "Azoth" or "Philosopher's Egg"—the stuff or First Matter of the Great Work. Sulphur, Salt, and Mercury, however, must not be understood in too literal a sense. "You need not look for our metallic seed among the elements," says Basil the Monk, "it need not be sought so far back. If you can only rectify the Mercury, Sulphur, and Salt (understand *those of the sages)* until the metallic spirit and body are inseparably joined together by means of the metallic soul, you thereby firmly rivet the chain of love and prepare the palace for the Coronation."

Of these three ingredients, the important one is the spiritual principle, the unseizable Mercury; which is far from being the metal which we ordinarily know by that name. The Mercury which the alchemists sought—often in strange places—is a hidden and powerful substance. They call it "Mercury of the Wise"; and he who can discover it, they say, is on the way towards success. The reader in search of mystical wisdom already begins to be bewildered; but if he persevere in this labyrinth of symbolism, he presently discovers—as Basil the Monk indeed hints—that the Sulphur and the Salt, or "metallic soul and body" of the spiritual chemistry, represent something analogous to the body and mind of man—Sulphur his earthly nature, seasoned with intellectual Salt. The Mercury is Spirit in its most mystic sense, the Synteresis or holy Dweller in the Innermost, the immanent spark or Divine Principle of his life. Only the "wise," the mystically awakened, can know this Mercury, the agent of man's transmutation and until it has been discovered, brought out of the hiddenness, nothing can be done. "This Mercury or Snowy Splendour, is a Celestial Body drawn from the beams of the Sun and the Moon. It is the only Agent in the world for this art." It is the divine-human "spark of the soul," the bridge between Gold and Silver, God and man.

The Three Principles being enclosed in the vessel, or Athanor, which is man himself, and subjected to a gentle fire—the *Incendium Amoris* —the process of the Great Work, the mystic transmutation of natural into spiritual man, can begin. This work, like the ingredients which compose it, has "three numbers" and the first matter, in the course of its transmutation, assumes three successive colours: the Black, the White, and the Red. These three colours are clearly analogous to the three traditional stages of the Mystic Way: Purgation, Illumination, Union.

The alchemists call the first stage, or Blackness, Putrefaction. In it the three principles which compose the "whole man" of body, soul and spirit, are "sublimated" till they appear as a black powder full of corruption, and the imperfect body is "dissolved and purified by subtle Mercury"; as man is purified by the darkness, misery, and despair which follows the emergence of his spiritual consciousness. As psychic uproar and disorder seems part of the process of mental growth, so " *Solve et coagula* "—break down that you may build up—is the watchword of the spiritual alchemist. The "black beast," the passional element, of the lower nature must emerge and be dealt with before anything further can be done. "There is a black beast in our forest," says the highly allegorical "Book of Lambspring," "his name is Putrefaction, his blackness is called the Head of the Raven; when it is cut off, Whiteness appears." This Whiteness, the state of Luna, or Silver, the "chaste and immaculate Queen," is the equivalent of the Illuminative Way: the highest point which the mystic can attain short of union with the Absolute. This White Stone is pure, and precious but in it the Great Work of man's spiritual evolution has not yet reached its term. That term is the attainment of the Red, the colour of Perfection or alchemic gold; a process sometimes called the "Marriage of Luna and Sol"—the fusion of the human and divine spirit. Under this image is concealed the final secret of the mystic life: that ineffable union of finite and infinite—that loving reception of the inflowing vitality of God—from which comes forth the *Magnum Opus:* deified or spiritual man.

"This," says the author of "A Suggestive Enquiry," "is the union supersentient, the nuptials sublime, *Mentis et Universi*.... Lo! behold I will open to thee a mystery, cries the Adept, the bridegroom crowneth the bride of the north [*i.e.*, she who comes out of the cold and darkness of the lower nature]. In the darkness of the north, out of the crucifixion of the cerebral life, when the sensual dominant is occultated in the Divine Fiat, and subdued, there arises a Light wonderfully about the summit, which wisely returned and multiplied according to the Divine Blessing, is made substantial in life."

I have said, that side by side with the metallic and planetary language of the alchemists, runs a strange heraldic symbolism in which they take refuge when they fear—generally without reason—that they are telling their secrets too plainly to an unregenerate world. Many of these heraldic emblems are used in an utterly irresponsible manner; and whilst doubtless conveying a meaning to the individual alchemist and the disciples for whom he wrote, are, and must ever be, unintelligible to other men. But others are of a more general application; and appear so frequently in seventeenth-century literature, whether mystical or non-mystical, that some discussion of them may well be of use.

Perhaps the quaintest and most celebrated of all these allegories is that which describes the quest of the Philosopher's Stone as "the hunting of the Green Lion." The Green Lion, though few would divine it, is the First Matter of the Great Work: hence, in spiritual alchemy, natural man in his wholeness—Salt, Sulphur, and Mercury in their crude state. He is called green because, seen from the transcendent standpoint, he is still unripe, his latent powers undeveloped; and a Lion, because of his strength, fierceness, and virility. Here the common opinion that a pious effeminacy, a diluted and amiable spirituality, is the proper raw material of the mystic life, is emphatically contradicted. It is not by the education of the lamb, but by the hunting and taming of the wild intractable lion, instinct with vitality, full of ardour and courage, exhibiting heroic qualities on the sensual plane, that the Great Work is achieved. The lives of the saints enforce the same law.

"Our lyon wanting maturitie
Is called greene for his unripeness trust me:
And yet full quickly he can run,
And soon can overtake the Sun."

The Green Lion, then, in his strength and wholeness is the only creature potentially able to attain Perfection. It needs the adoption and purification of all the wealth and resources of man's nature, not merely the encouragement of his transcendental tastes, if he is to "overtake the Sun" and achieve the Great Work. The Kingdom of Heaven is taken by violence, not by amiable aspiration. "The Green Lion," says one alchemist, "is the priest by whom Sol and Luna are wed." In other words, the raw stuff of indomitable human nature is the means by which man is to attain union with the Absolute. The duty of the alchemist, the transmuting process, is therefore described as the hunting of the Green Lion through the forest of the sensual world. He, like the Hound of Heaven, is on a love chase down the nights and down the days.

When the lion is caught, when Destiny overtakes it, its head must be cut off as the preliminary to the necessary taming process. This is called by the alchemists "the head of the Raven," the Crow, or the Vulture, "for its blackness." It represents the fierce and corrupt life of the passions and its removal is that "death of the lower nature" which is the object of all asceticism— *i.e.*, Purgation. The lion, the whole man, Humanity in its strength, is as it were "slain to the world," and then resuscitated; but in a very different shape. By its passage through this mystic death or the "putrefaction of the Three Principles" the "colour of unripeness" is taken away. Its taming completed, it receives wings, wherewith it may fly up to Sol, the Perfect or Divine; and is transmuted, say the alchemists, into the Red Dragon. This is to us a hopelessly grotesque image but to the Hermetic philosophers, whose sense of wonder was uncorrupt, it was the deeply mystical emblem of a new, strange, and transcendental life, powerful alike in earth and in heaven. As the angel to the man, so was the dragon to the world of beasts: a creature of splendour and terror, a super-brute, veritably existent if seldom seen. We realize something of the significance of this symbol for the alchemic writers, if we remember how sacred a meaning it has for the Chinese: to whom the dragon is the traditional emblem of free spiritual life, as the tiger represents the life of the material plane in its intensest form. Since it is from China that alchemy is supposed to have reached the European world, it may yet be found that the Red Dragon is one of the most antique and significant symbols of the Hermetic Art.

For the Spiritual Chemistry, then, the Red Dragon represents Deified Man; whose emergence must always seem like the birth of some monstrous and amazing creature when seen from the standpoint of the merely natural world. With his coming forth, the business of the alchemist, in so far as he be a mystic, is done. Man has transcended his lower nature, has received wings wherewith to live on higher levels of reality. The Tincture, the latent goldness, has been found and made dominant, the *Magnum Opus* achieved. That the trite and inward business of that Work, when stripped of its many emblematic veils, was indeed the reordering of spiritual rather than material elements, is an opinion which rests on a more solid foundation than personal interpretations of old allegories and alchemic-tracts. The Norwich physician—himself deeply read in the Hermetic science—has declared to us his own certainty concerning it in few but lovely words. In them is contained the true mystery of man's eternal and interior quest of the Stone: its reconciliation with that other, outgoing quest of "the Hidden Treasure that desires to be found."

"Do but extract from the corpulency of bodies, or resolve things beyond their First Matter, and you discover the habitation of Angels: which, if I call it the ubiquitary and omnipresent Essence of God, I hope I shall not offend Divinity."

6

MYSTICISM AND MAGIC

It is unnecessary to examine in detail the mistakes—in ecclesiastical language, the heresies—into which men have been led by a feeble, a deformed, or an arrogant mystical sense. The number of these mistakes is countless; their wildness almost inconceivable to those who have not been forced to study them. Too often the loud voices and strange declarations of their apostles have drowned the quieter accents of the orthodox.

It seems as though the moment of puberty were far more critical in the spiritual than it is in the physical life: the ordinary dangers of adolescence being intensified when they appear upon the higher levels of consciousness. In the condition of psychic instability which is characteristic of his movement to new states, man is unusually at the mercy of the suggestions and impressions which he receives. Hence in every period of true mystical activity we find an outbreak of occultism, illuminism, or other perverted spirituality and—even more dangerous and confusing for the student—a borderland region where the mystical and psychical meet. In the youth of the Christian Church, side by side with genuine mysticism descending from the Johannine writings or brought in by the Christian Neoplatonists, we have the arrogant and disorderly transcendentalism of the Gnostics: their attempted fusion of the ideals of mysticism and magic. During the Middle Ages and the Renaissance there are the spurious mysticism of the Brethren of the Free Spirit, the occult propaganda of Paracelsus, the Rosicrucians, the Christian Kabalists and the innumerable pantheistic, Manichean, mystery-making, and Quietist heresies which made war upon Catholic tradition. In the modern world, Theosophy in its various forms is probably the most widespread and respectable representative of the occult tradition.

The root idea from which these varied beliefs and practices develop is always the same and, since right doctrine is often most easily defined by contrast with its opposite, its study is likely to help us to fix more precisely the true characters of mysticism.

Leaving therefore the specifically mystical error of Quietism until we come to the detailed discussion of the contemplative states, we will consider here some of those other supernormal activities of the self which we have already agreed to classify as magic and learn through them more of those hidden and half-comprehended forces which she has at her command.

The word "magic" is out of fashion, though its spirit was never more widely diffused than at the present time. Thanks to the gradual debasement of the verbal currency, it suggests to the ordinary reader the production of optical illusions and other parlour tricks. It has dragged with it in its fall the terrific verb "to conjure," which, forgetting that it once undertook to compel the spirits of men and angels, is now content to produce rabbits from top-hats. These facts would have little importance, were it not that modern occultists—annoyed, one supposes, by this abuse of their ancient title—constantly arrogate to their tenets and practices the name of "Mystical Science." Vaughan, in his rather supercilious survey of the mystics, classed all forms of white magic, alchemy, and occult philosophy as "theurgic mysticism," and, on the other side of the shield, the occultists display an increasing eagerness to claim the mystics as masters in their school. Even the "three-fold way" of mysticism has been adopted by them and relabelled "Probation, Enlightenment, Initiation."

In our search for the characteristics of mysticism we have already marked the boundary which separates it from magic and tried to define the true nature and intention of occult philosophy. We saw that it represented the instinctive human "desire to know more" applied to suprasensible things. For good or ill this desire, and the occult sciences and magic arts which express it, have haunted humanity from the earliest times. No student of man can neglect their investigation, however distasteful to his intelligence their superficial absurdities may be. The starting-point of all magic, and of all magical religion—the best and purest of occult activities—is, as in mysticism, man's inextinguishable conviction that there are other planes of being than those which his senses report to him; and its proceedings represent the intellectual and individualistic results of this conviction—his craving for the hidden knowledge. It is, in the eyes of those who really practise it, a *moyen de parvenir*: not the performance of illicit tricks, but a serious attempt to solve the riddle of the world. Its result, according to a modern writer upon occult philosophy, "comprises an actual, positive, and realizable knowledge concerning the worlds which we denominate invisible, because they transcend the imperfect and rudimentary faculties of a partially developed humanity, and concerning the latent potentialities which constitute—by the fact of their latency—the interior man. In more strictly philosophical language, the Hermetic science is a method of transcending the phenomenal world and attaining to the reality which is behind phenomena."

Though fragments of this enormous claim seem able to justify themselves in experience, the whole of it cannot be admitted. The last phrase in particular is identical with the promise which we have seen to be characteristic of mysticism. It presents magic as a pathway to reality; a promise which it cannot fulfil, for the mere transcending of phenomena does not entail the attainment of the Absolute. Magic even at its best extends rather than escapes the boundaries of the phenomenal world. It stands, where genuine, for that form of transcendentalism which does abnormal things, but does not lead anywhere and we are likely to fall victims to some kind of magic the moment that the declaration "I want to know" ousts the declaration "I want to be" from the chief place in our consciousness. The true "science of ultimates" must be a science of pure Being, for reasons which the reader is now in a position to discover for himself. But magic is merely a system whereby the self tries to assuage its transcendental curiosity by extending the activities of the will beyond their usual limits; sometimes, according to its own account, obtaining by this means an experimental knowledge of planes of existence usually—but inaccurately—regarded as "supernatural."

Even this modified claim needs justification. For most persons who do not specialize in the eccentric sciences the occultist can only be said to exist in either the commercial or the academic sense. The fortune-teller represents one class; the annotator of improper *grimoires* the other. In neither department is the thing supposed to be taken seriously, it is merely the means of obtaining money, or of assuaging a rather morbid curiosity.

Such a view is far from accurate. In magic, whether regarded as a superstition or a science, we have at any rate the survival of a great and ancient tradition, the true meaning of whose title should hardly have been lost in a Christian country; for it claims to be the science of those Magi whose quest of the symbolic Blazing Star brought them once, at least, to the cradle of the Incarnate God. Its laws, and the ceremonial rites which express those laws, have come down from immemorial antiquity. They appear to enshrine a certain definite knowledge, and a large number of less definite theories, concerning the sensual and supersensual worlds, and concerning powers which man, according to occult thinkers, may develop if he will. Orthodox persons should be careful how they condemn the laws of magic: for they unwittingly conform to many of them whenever they go to church. All ceremonial religion contains some elements of magic. The art of medicine will never wholly cast it off, many centuries ago it gave birth to that which we now call modern science. It seems to possess inextinguishable life. This is not surprising when we perceive how firmly occultism is rooted in psychology: how perfectly it is adapted to certain perennial characteristics of the human mind—its curiosity, its arrogance, its love of mystery.

Magic, in its uncorrupted form, claims to be a practical, intellectual, highly individualistic science; working towards the declared end of enlarging the sphere on which the human will can work, and obtaining experimental knowledge of planes of being usually regarded as transcendental. It is the last descendant of a long line of teaching—the whole teaching, in fact, of the mysteries of Egypt and Greece—which offered to initiate man into a certain secret knowledge and understanding of things. "In every man," says a modern occultist, "there are latent faculties by means of which he can acquire for himself knowledge of the higher worlds... as long as the human race has existed there have always been schools in which those who possessed these higher faculties gave instruction to those who were in search of them. Such are called the occult schools, and the instruction which is imparted therein is called esoteric science or the occult teaching."

These occult schools, as they exist in the present day, state their doctrine in terms which seem distressingly prosaic to the romantic inquirer; borrowing from physics and psychology theories of vibration, attraction, mental suggestion and subconscious activity which can be reapplied for their own purposes. According to its modern teachers, magic is simply an extension of the theory and practice of volition beyond the usual limits. The will, says the occultist, is king, not only of the House of Life, but of the universe outside the gates of sense. It is the key to "man limitless" the true "ring of Gyges," which can control the forces of nature known and unknown. This aspect of occult philosophy informs much of the cheap American transcendentalism which is so lightly miscalled mystical by its teachers and converts; Menticulture, "New" or "Higher Thought," and the scriptures of the so-called "New Consciousness." The ingenious authors of "Volo," "The Will to be Well," and "Just How to Wake the Solar Plexus," the seers who assure their eager disciples that by "Concentration" they may acquire not only health, but also that wealth which is "health of circumstance," are no mystics. They are magicians and teach, though they know it not, little else but the cardinal doctrines of Hermetic science, omitting only their picturesque ceremonial accompaniments.

These cardinal doctrines, in fact, have varied little since their first appearance early in the world's history: though, like the doctrines of theology, they have needed re-statement from time to time. In discussing them I shall quote chiefly from the works of Eliphas Lévi; the pseudonym under which Alphonse Louis Constant, the most readable occult philosopher of the nineteenth century, offered his conclusions to the world.

The tradition of magic, like most other ways of escape which man has offered to his own soul, appears to have originated in the East. It was formulated, developed, and preserved by the religion of Egypt. It made an early appearance in that of Greece. It has its legendary grand master in Hermes Trismegistus, who gave to it its official name of Hermetic Science, and whose status in occultism is much the same as that occupied by Moses in the tradition of the Jews. Fragmentary writings attributed to this personage and said to be derived from the Hermetic books, are the primitive scriptures of occultism and the probably spurious Table of Emerald, which is said to have been discovered in his tomb, ranks as the magician's Table of Stone. In Gnosticism, in the allegories of the Kabalah, in theosophy, in secret associations which still exist in England, France, and Germany—and even in certain practices embedded in the ceremonial of the Christian Church—the main conceptions which constitute the "secret wisdom" of magical tradition have wandered down the centuries. The baser off-shoots of that tradition are but too well known, and need not be particularized.

Like the world which it professes to interpret, magic has a body and a soul: an outward vesture of words and ceremonies and an inner doctrine. The outward vesture, which is all that the uninitiated are permitted to perceive, consists of a series of confusing and often ridiculous symbolic veils: of strange words and numbers, grotesque laws and ritual acts, personifications and mystifications. The outward vestures of our religious, political, and social systems—which would probably appear equally irrational to a wholly ignorant yet critical observer—offer an instructive parallel to this aspect of occult philosophy. Stripped of these archaic formulae, symbols, and mystery-mongerings, however, magic as described by its apologists, is found to rest upon three fundamental axioms which can hardly be dismissed as ridiculous by those who listen respectfully to the ever-shifting hypotheses of psychology and physics.

(1) The first axiom declares the existence of an imponderable "medium" or "universal agent," which is described as beyond the plane of our normal sensual perceptions yet interpenetrating and binding up the material world. This agent, which is not luminous and has nothing to do with the stars, is known to the occultists by the unfortunate name of "Astral Light": a term originally borrowed from the Martinists by Eliphas Lévi. To live in conscious communication with the "Astral Light" is to live upon the "Astral Plane," or in the Astral World: to have achieved, that is to say, a new level of consciousness. The education of the occultist is directed towards this end.

This doctrine of the Astral Plane, like most of our other diagrams of the transcendent, possesses a respectable ancestry, and many prosperous relations in the world of philosophic thought. Traces of it may even be detected under veils in the speculations of orthodox physics. It is really identical with the "Archetypal World" or *Yesod* of the Kabalah—the "Perfect Land" of old Egyptian religion—in which the true or spirit forms of all created things are held to exist. It may be connected with the "real world" described by such visionaries as Boehme and Blake, many of whose experiences are far more occult than mystical in character. A persistent tradition as to the existence of such a plane of being or of consciousness is found all over the world: in Indian, Greek Egyptian, Celtic, and Jewish thought. "Above this visible nature there exists another, unseen and eternal, which, when all things created perish, does not perish," says the Bhagavad Gita. According to the Kabalists it is "the seat of life and vitality, and the nourishment of all the world." Vitalism might accept it as one of those aspects of the universe which can be perceived by a more extended rhythm than that of normal consciousness. Various aspects of the Astral have been identified with the "Burning Body of the Holy Ghost" of Christian Gnosticism and with the Odic force of the old-fashioned spiritualists.

Further, the Astral Plane is regarded as constituting the "Cosmic Memory," where the images of all beings and events are preserved, as they are preserved in the memory of man.

> "The high that proved too high, the heroic for earth too hard
> The passion that left the ground to lose itself in the sky"—

all are living in the Astral World. There too the concepts of future creation are present in their completeness in the Eternal Now before being brought to birth in the material sphere. On this theory prophecy, and also clairvoyance—one of the great objects of occult education—consist in opening the eyes of the mind upon this timeless Astral World and spiritualists, evoking the phantoms of the dead, merely call them up from the recesses of universal instead of individual remembrance. The reader who feels his brain to be whirling amidst this medley of solemn statement and unproven fairy tale must remember that the dogmatic part of the occult tradition can only represent the attempt of an extended or otherwise abnormal consciousness to find an explanation of its own experiences.

Further, our whole selves—not merely our sentient selves—are regarded as being bathed in the Astral Light, as in the ether of physics. Hence in occult language it is a "universal agent" connecting soul with soul, and becomes the possible vehicle of hypnotism, telepathy, clairvoyance, and all those supernormal phenomena which are the subject-matter of "psychical research." This hypothesis also accounts for the confusing fact of an initial similarity of experience in many of the proceedings of mystic and occultist. Both must pass through the plane of consciousness which the concept of the "Astral" represents, because this plane of perception is the one which lies "next beyond" our normal life. The transcendental faculties may become aware of this world; only, in the case of the mystic, to pass through it as quickly as they can. But the occultist, the medium, the psychic, rest in the "Astral" and develop their perceptions of this aspect of the world. It is the medium in which they work.

From earliest times, occult philosophy has insisted on the existence of this medium: as a scientific fact, outside the range of our normal senses, but susceptible of verification by the trained powers of the "initiate." The possessor of such trained powers, not the wizard or the fortune-teller, is regarded as the true magician and it is the declared object of occult education, or initiation, to actualize this supersensual plane of experience, to give the student the power of entering into conscious communion with it, and teach him to impose upon its forces the directive force of his own will, as easily as he imposes that will upon the "material" things of senses.

(2) This brings us to the second axiom of magic, which also has a curiously modern air: for it postulates simply the limitless power of the disciplined human will. This dogma has been "taken over" without acknowledgment from occult philosophy to become the trump card of menticulture, "Christian Science," and "New Thought." The preachers of "Joy Philosophy" and other dilute forms of mental discipline, the Liberal Catholic "priest" producing "a vast bubble of etheric astromental matter, a thought-edifice, ethereal, diaphanous, a bubble which just includes the congregation—"these are the true hierophants of magic in the modern world.

The first lesson of the would-be magus is self-mastery. "By means of persevering and gradual athletics," says Eliphas Lévi, "the powers of the body can be developed to an amazing extent. It is the same with the powers of the soul. Would you govern yourself and others? Learn how to will. How may one learn how to will? This is the first secret of magical initiation; and it was to make the foundations of this secret thoroughly understood that the antique keepers of the mysteries surrounded the approach to the sanctuary with so many terrors and illusions. They did not believe in a will until it had given its proofs; and they were right. Strength cannot prove itself except by conquest. Idleness and negligence are the enemies of the will, and this is the reason why all religions have multiplied their practices and made their cults difficult and minute. The more trouble one gives oneself for an idea, the more power one acquires in regard to that idea.... Hence the power of religions resides entirely in the inflexible will of those who practise them."

This last sentence alone is enough to define the distinction between mysticism and magic, and clear the minds of those who tend to confuse the mystical and magical elements of religion. In accordance with it, real "magical initiation" is in essence a form of mental discipline, strengthening and focussing the will. This discipline, like that of the religious life, consists partly in physical austerities and a deliberate divorce from the world, partly in the cultivation of will-power but largely in a yielding of the mind to the influence of suggestions which have been selected and accumulated in the course of ages because of their power over that imagination which Eliphas Lévi calls "The eye of the soul." There is nothing supernatural about it. Like the more arduous, more disinterested self-training of the mystic, it is character-building with an object, conducted upon an heroic scale. In magic the "will to know" is the centre round which the personality is rearranged. As in mysticism, unconscious factors are dragged from the hiddenness to form part of that personality. The uprushes of thought, the abrupt intuitions which reach us from the subliminal region, are developed, ordered, and controlled by rhythms and symbols which have become traditional because the experience of centuries has proved, though it cannot explain, their efficacy and powers of apprehension which normally lie below the threshold may thus be liberated and enabled to report their discoveries.

"The fundamental principle," says A. E. Waite, speaking of occult evocations, "was in the exercise of a certain occult force resident in the magus, and strenuously exerted for the establishment of such a correspondence between two planes of nature as would effect his desired end. This exertion was termed the evocation, conjuration, or calling of the spirit, but *that which in reality was raised was the energy of the inner man;* tremendously developed and exalted by combined will and aspiration, this energy germinated by sheer force a new intellectual faculty of sensible psychological perception. To assist and stimulate this energy into the most powerful possible operation, artificial means were almost invariably used.... The synthesis of these methods and processes was called Ceremonial Magic, which in effect was a tremendous forcing-house of the latent faculties of man's spiritual nature."

This is the psychological explanation of those apparently absurd rituals of preparation, doctrines of signs and numbers, pentacles, charms, angelical names, the "power of the word" which made up ceremonial magic. The power of such artifices is known amongst the Indian mystics; who, recognizing in the *Mantra,* or occult and rhythmic formula, consciously held and repeated, an invaluable help to the attainment of the true ecstatic state, are not ashamed to borrow from the magicians. So, too, the modern American schools of mental healing and New Thought recommend concentration upon a carefully selected word as the starting-point of efficacious meditation. This fact of the psychical effect of certain verbal combinations, when allowed to dominate the field of consciousness, may have some bearing upon that need of a formal liturgy which is felt by nearly every great religion; for religion, on its ceremonial side, has certain affinities with magic. It, too, seeks by sensible means to stimulate supra-sensible energies. The true magic "word" or spell is untranslatable; because its power resides only partially in that outward sense which is apprehended by the reason, but chiefly in the rhythm, which is addressed to the subliminal mind. Symbols, religious and other, and symbolic acts which appear meaningless when judged by the intellect alone, perform a similar office. They express the deep-seated instinct of the human mind that it must have a focus on which to concentrate its volitional powers, if those powers are to be brought to their highest state of efficiency. The nature of the focus matters little: its office matters much.

"... All these figures, and acts analogous to them," says Lévi, "all these dispositions of numbers and of characters [*i.e.* sacred words, charms, pentacles, etc.] are, as we have said, but instruments for the education of the will, of which they fix and determine the habits. They serve also to concentrate in action all the powers of the human soul, and to strengthen the creative power of the imagination.... A practice, even though it be superstitious and foolish, may be efficacious because it is a realization of the will.... We laugh at the poor woman who denies herself a ha'porth of milk in the morning, that she may take a little candle to burn upon the magic triangle in some chapel. But those who laugh are ignorant, and the poor woman does not pay too dearly for the courage and resignation which she thus obtains.

Magic symbols, therefore, from penny candles to Solomon's seal, fall in modern technical language into two classes. The first contains instruments of self-suggestion, exaltation, and will direction. To this belong all spells, charms, rituals, perfumes from the magician's vervain wreath to the "Youth! Health! Strength!" which the student of New Thought repeats when she is brushing her hair in the morning. The second class contains *autoscopes: i.e.,* material objects which focus and express the subconscious perceptions of the operator. The dowser's divining rod, fortuneteller's cards, and crystal-gazer's ball, are characteristic examples. Both kinds are rendered necessary rather by the disabilities of the human than by the peculiarities of the superhuman plane and the great adept may attain heights at which he dispenses with these "outward and visible signs." "Ceremonies being, as we have said, artificial methods of creating certain habits of the will, they cease to be necessary when these habits have become fixed." These facts, now commonplaces of psychology, have long been known and used by students of magic. Those who judge the philosophy by the apparent absurdity of its symbols and ceremonies should remember that the embraces, gestures, grimaces, and other ritual acts by which we all concentrate, liberate, or express love, wrath, or enthusiasm, will ill endure the cold revealing light of a strictly rational inquiry.

(3) The dogmas of the "Astral Light" or universal agent and the "power of the will" are completed by a third: the doctrine of Analogy, of an implicit correspondence between appearance and reality, the microcosm of man and the macrocosm of the universe the seen and the unseen worlds. In this, occultism finds the basis of its transcendental speculations. *Quod superius sicut quod inferius* —the first words of that Emerald Table which was once attributed to Hermes Trismegistus himself—is an axiom which must be agreeable to all Platonists. It plays a great part in the theory of mysticism; which, whilst maintaining an awed sense of the total "otherness" and incomprehensibility of the Divine, has always assumed that the path of the individual soul towards loving union with the Absolute is somehow analogous with the path on which the universe moves to its consummation in God.

The notion of analogy ultimately determines the religious concepts of every race, and resembles the verities of faith in the breadth of its application. It embraces alike the appearances of the visible world—which thus become the mirrors of the invisible—the symbols of religion, the tiresome arguments of Butler's "Analogy," the allegories of the Kabalah and the spiritual alchemists, and that childish "doctrine of signatures" on which much of mediaeval science was built. "Analogy," says Lévi, "is the last word of science and the first word of faith... the *sole possible mediator* between the visible and the invisible, between the finite and the infinite." Here Magic clearly defines her own limitations; stepping incautiously from the useful to the universal, and laying down a doctrine which no mystic could accept—which, carried to its logical conclusion, would turn the adventure of the infinite into a guessing game.

The argument by analogy is carried by the occultists to lengths which cannot be described here. Armed with this torch, they explore the darkest, most terrible mysteries of life and do not hesitate to cast the grotesque shadows of these mysteries upon the unseen world. The principle of correspondence is no doubt sound so long as it works within reasonable limits. It was admitted into the system of the Kabalah, though that profound and astute philosophy was far from giving to it the importance which it assumes in Hermetic "science." It has been eagerly accepted by many of the mystics. Boehme and Swedenborg availed themselves of its method in presenting their intuitions to the world. It is implicitly acknowledged by thinkers of many other schools: its influence permeates the best periods of literature. Sir Thomas Browne spoke for more than himself when he said, in a well-known passage of the "Religio Medici": "The severe schools shall never laugh me out of the philosophy of Hermes that this visible world is but a picture of the invisible, wherein, as in a portrait, things are not truly but in equivocal shapes, and as they counterfeit some real substance in that invisible framework." Such a sense of analogy, whatever the "severe schools" may say, is indeed the foundation of every perfect work of art. "Intuitive perception of the hidden analogies of things," says Hazlitt in "English Novelists," "or, as it may be called, his *instinct of the imagination,* is perhaps what stamps the character of genius on the productions of art more than any other circumstance."

The central doctrine of magic may now be summed up thus:

(1) That a supersensible and real "cosmic medium" exists, which interpenetrates, influences, and supports the tangible and apparent world, and is amenable to the categories both of philosophy and of physics.

(2) That there is an established analogy and equilibrium between the real and unseen world, and the illusory manifestations which we call the world of sense.

(3) That this analogy may be discerned, and this equilibrium controlled, by the disciplined will of man, which thus becomes master of itself and of fate.

We must now examine in more detail the third of these propositions—that which ascribes abnormal powers to the educated and disciplined will—for this assumption lies at the root of all magical practices, old and new. "Magical operations," says Eliphas Lévi, "are the exercise of a power which is natural, but superior to the ordinary powers of nature. They are the result of a science, and of habits, which exalt the human will above its usual limits." This power of the will is now recognized as playing an important part both in the healing of the body and the healing of the soul; for our most advanced theories on these subjects are little more than the old wine of magic in new bottles. The ancient occultists owed much of their power, and also of their evil reputation, to the fact that they were psychologists before their time. Effective methods of suggestion, recipes for the alteration and exaltation of personality and enhancement of will-power, the artificial production of hypnotic states, photisms, automatism and ecstasy, with the opening up of the subliminal field which accompanies these phenomena—concealed from the profane by a mass of confusing allegories and verbiage—form the backbone of all genuine occult rituals. Their authors were aware that ceremonial magic has no objective importance, but depends solely on its effect upon the operator's mind. That this effect might be enhanced, it was given an atmosphere of sanctity and mystery; its rules were strict, its higher rites difficult of attainment. These rules and rites constituted at once a test of the student's earnestness and a veil guarding the sanctuary from the profane. The long and difficult preparations, majestic phrases, and strange ceremonies of an evocation had power, not over the spirit of the dead, but over the consciousness of the living; who was thus caught up from the world of sense to a new plane of perception. Thus, according to its apologists, the education of the genuine occult student tends to awaken in him a new view and a new attitude. It adjusts the machinery of his cinematograph to the registering of new intervals in the stream of things, which passed it by before; and thus introduces new elements into that picture by which ordinary men are content to know and judge the—or rather *their*— universe.

So much for the principles which govern occult education. Magic therapeutics, or as it is now called, "mental healing," is but the application of these principles upon another plane. It results, first, from a view of humanity which sees a difference only of degree between diseases of body and of soul, and can state seriously and in good faith that "moral maladies are more contagious than physical, and there are some triumphs of infatuation and fashion which are comparable to leprosy or cholera." Secondly, it is worked by that enhancement of will power, that ability to alter and control weaker forms of life, which is claimed as the reward of the occult discipline. "All the power of the occult healer lies in his conscious will and all his art consists in producing faith in the patient."

This simple truth was in the possession of occult thinkers at a time when Church and State saw no third course between the burning or beatification of its practitioners. Now, under the polite names of mental hygiene, suggestion, and psycho-therapeutics, it is steadily advancing to the front rank of medical shibboleths. Yet it is still the same "magic art" which has been employed for centuries, with varying ritual accompaniments, by the adepts of occult science. The methods of Brother Hilarian Tissot, who is described as curing lunacy and crime by "the unconscious use of the magnetism of Paracelsus," who attributed his cases "either to disorder of the will or to the perverse influence of external wills," and would "regard all crimes as acts of madness and treat the wicked as diseased," anticipated in many respects those of the most modern psychologists.

The doctrine of magic which has here been described shows us the "Secret Wisdom" at its best and sanest. But even on these levels, it is dogged by the defects which so decisively separate the occultist from the mystic. The chief of these is the peculiar temper of mind, the cold intellectual arrogance, the intensely individual point of view which occult studies seem to induce by their conscious quest of exclusive power and knowledge, their implicit neglect of love. At bottom, every student of occultism is striving towards a point at which he may be able to "touch the button" and rely on the transcendental world "springing to do the rest." In this hard-earned acquirement of power over the Many, he tends to forget the One. In Levi's words, "Too deep a study of the mysteries of nature may estrange from God the careless investigator, in whom mental fatigue paralyses the ardours of the heart." When he wrote this sentence Lévi stood, as the greater occultists have often done, at the frontiers of mysticism. The best of the Hermetic philosophers, indeed, are hardly ever without such mystical hankerings, such flashes of illumination; as if the transcendental powers of man, once roused from sleep, cannot wholly ignore the true end for which they were made.

In Levi's case, as is well known, the discord between the occult and mystical ideals was resolved by his return to the Catholic Church. Characteristically, he "read into" Catholicism much that the orthodox would hardly allow; so that it became for him, as it were, a romantic gloss on the occult tradition. He held that the Christian Church, nursing mother of the mystics, was also the heir of the magi; and that popular piety and popular magic veiled the same ineffable truths. He had more justification than at first appears probable for this apparently wild and certainly heretical statement. Religion, as we have seen, can never entirely divorce herself from magic: for her rituals and sacraments must have, if they are to be successful in their appeal to the mind, a certain magical character. All persons who are naturally drawn towards the ceremonial aspect of religion are acknowledging the strange power of subtle rhythms, symbolic words and movements, over the human will. An "impressive service" conforms exactly to the description which I have already quoted of a magical rite: it is "a tremendous forcing-house of the latent faculties of man's spiritual nature." Sacraments, too, however simple their beginnings, always tend, as they evolve, to assume upon the phenomenal plane a magical aspect—a fact which does not invalidate their claim to be the vehicles of supernatural grace. Those who have observed with understanding, for instance, the Roman rite of baptism, with its spells and exorcisms, its truly Hermetic employment of salt, anointing chrism and ceremonial lights, must have seen in it a ceremony far nearer to the operations of white magic than to the simple lustrations practiced by St. John the Baptist.

There are obvious objections to the full working out of this subject in a book which is addressed to readers of all shades of belief; but any student who is interested in this branch of religious psychology may easily discover for himself the occult elements in the liturgies of the Christian—or indeed of any other—Church. There are invocative arrangements of the Names of God which appear alike in *grimoire* and in Missal. Sacred numbers, ritual actions, perfumes, purifications, words of power, are all used, and rightly used by institutional religion in her work of opening up the human mind to the messages of the suprasensible world. In certain minor observances, and charm-like prayers, we seem to stand on the very borderland between magician and priest.

It is surely inevitable that this should be so. The business of the Church is to appeal to the whole man, as she finds him living in the world of sense. She would hardly be adequate to this task did she neglect the powerful weapons which the occultist has developed for his own ends. She, who takes the simplest and most common gifts of nature and transmutes them into heavenly food, takes also every discovery which the self has made concerning its own potentialities, and turns them to her own high purposes. Founding her external system on sacraments and symbols, on rhythmic invocations and ceremonial acts of praise, insisting on the power of the pure and self-denying will and the "magic chain" of congregational worship, she does but join hands with those Magi whose gold, frankincense, and myrrh were the first gifts that she received.

But she pays for this, sharing some of the limitations of the system which her Catholic nature has compelled her to absorb. It is true, of course, that she purges it of all its baser elements—its arrogance, its curiosity—true also that she is bound to adopt it, because it is the highest common measure which she can apply to the spirituality of that world to which she is sent. But she cannot—and her great teachers have always known that she cannot—extract finality from a method which does not really seek after ultimate things. This method may and does teach men goodness, gives them happiness and health. It can even induce in them a certain exaltation in which they become aware, at any rate for a moment, of the existence of the supernatural world—a stupendous accomplishment. But it will not of itself make them citizens of that world, give to them the freedom of Reality.

"The work of the Church in the world," says Patmore, "is not to teach the mysteries of life, so much as to persuade the soul to that arduous degree of purity at which God Himself becomes her teacher. The work of the Church ends when the knowledge of God begins."

7

MYSTICISM AND VITALISM

We glanced, at the universes which result from the various forms of credulity practised by the materialist, the idealist, and the sceptic. We saw the mystic denying by word and act the validity of the foundations on which those universes are built, substituting his living experience for their conceptual schemes. But there is another way of seeing reality or, more correctly, one aspect of reality. This scheme of things possesses the merit of accepting and harmonizing many different forms of experience; even those supreme experiences and intuitions peculiar to the mystics. The first distinct contribution of the twentieth century to man's quest of the Real, it entered the philosophic arena from several different directions; penetrating and modifying current conceptions not only of philosophy but of religion, science, art and practical life. It was applied by Driesch and other biologists in the sphere of organic life. Bergson, starting from psychology, developed its intellectual and metaphysical implications; whilst Rudolph Eucken constructed from, or beside it, a philosophy of the Spirit, of man's relations to the Real.

In all these we find the same principle; the principle of a free spontaneous and creative life as the essence of Reality. Not law but aliveness, incalculable and indomitable, is their subject-matter: not human logic, but actual living experience is their criterion of truth. Vitalists, whether the sphere of their explorations be biology, psychology or ethics, see the whole Cosmos, the physical and spiritual worlds, as instinct with initiative and spontaneity: as above all things free. For them, nature, though conditioned by the matter with which she works, is stronger than her chains. Pushing out from within, ever seeking expression, she buds and breaks forth into original creation. The iron "laws" of the determinists are merely her observed habits, not her fetters and man, seeing nature in the terms of "cause and effect," has been the dupe of his own limitations and prejudices.

Bergson, Nietzsche, Eucken, differing in their opinion as to life's meaning, are alike in this vision: in the stress which they lay on the supreme importance and value of life—a great Cosmic life transcending and including our own. This is materialism inside out: for here what we call the universe is presented as an expression of life, not life as an expression or by-product of the universe. The strange passionate philosophy of Nietzsche is really built upon an intense belief in this supernal nature and value of Life, Action and Strength and spoilt by the one-sided individualism which prevented him from holding a just balance between the great and significant life of the Ego and the greater and more significant life of the All.

Obviously, the merit of vitalistic philosophy lies in its ability to satisfy so many different thinkers, starting from such diverse points in our common experience. On the phenomenal side it can accept and transfigure the statements of physical science. In its metaphysical aspect it leaves place for those ontological speculations which seem to take their rise in psychology. It is friendly to those who demand an important place for moral and spiritual activity in the universe. Finally—though here we must be content with deduction rather than declaration—it leaves in the hands of the mystics that power of attaining to Absolute Reality which they have always claimed, shows them as the true possessors of freedom, the torch-bearers of the race.

Did it acknowledge its ancestors with that reverence which is their due, Vitalism would identify itself with the mystic philosopher, Heracleitus; who, in the fifth century B.C., introduced its central idea to the European world: for his "Logos" or Energizing Fire is but another symbol for that free and living Spirit of Becoming, that indwelling creative power, which Vitalism acknowledges as the very soul or immanent reality of things. It is in essence both a Hellenic and a Christian system of thought. In its view of the proper function of the intellect it has some unexpected affinities with Aristotle, and after him with St. Thomas Aquinas; regarding it as a departmental affair, not the organ of ultimate knowledge. Its theory of knowledge is close to that of the mystics: or would be, if those gazers on reality had interested themselves in any psychological theory of their own experiences.

A philosophy which can harmonize such diverse elements as these, and make its influence felt in so many fields of thought, may be useful in our present attempt towards an understanding of mysticism: for it illustrates certain aspects of perceived reality which other systems ignore. It has the further recommendation of involving not a mere diagram of metaphysical possibilities, but a genuine theory of knowledge. Its scope includes psychology as well as philosophy: the consideration, not only of the nature of Reality but also of the self's power of knowing it—the machinery of contact between the mind and the flux of things. Thus it has an inclusive quality lacking in the tidy ring-fenced systems of other schools of thought. It has no edges, and if it be true to itself should have no negations. It is a vision, not a map.

The primary difference between Vitalism and the classic philosophic schools is this. Its focal point is not Being but Becoming. Translated into Platonic language, not the changeless One, the Absolute, transcending all succession, but rather His energizing Thought—the Son, the Creative Logos—is the supreme reality which it proposes as accessible to human consciousness.

"All things," said Heracleitus, "are in a state of flux." "Everything happens through strife." "Reality is a condition of unrest." Such is also the opinion of Bergson and Alexander; who, agreeing in this with the conclusions of physical science, look upon the Real as dynamic rather than static, as *becoming* rather than *being* perfect, and invite us to see in Time—the precession or flux of things—the very stuff of reality—

"From the fixed lull of Heaven she saw
Time like a pulse shake fierce
Through all the worlds"—

said Rossetti of the Blessed Damozel. So Bergson, while ignoring if he does not deny the existence of the "fixed lull," the still Eternity, the point of rest, finds everywhere the pulse of Time, the vast unending storm of life and love. Reality, says Bergson, is pure creative Life; a definition which excludes those ideas of perfection and finality involved in the idealist's concept of Pure Being as the Absolute and Unchanging One. This life, as he sees it, is fed from within rather than upheld from without. It evolves by means of its own inherent and spontaneous creative power. The biologist's Nature "so careful of the type"; the theologian's Creator transcending His universe, and "holding all things in the hollow of His hand": these are gone, and in their place we have a universe teeming with free individuals, each self-creative, each evolving eternally, yet towards no term.

Here, then, the deep instinct of the human mind that there must be a unity, an orderly plan in the universe, that the strung-along beads of experience do really form a rosary, though it be one which we cannot repeat, is deliberately thwarted. Creation, Activity, Movement; this, says Vitalism, rather than any merely apparent law and order, any wholeness, is the essential quality of the Realms the Real: and life is an eternal Becoming, a ceaseless changefulness. At its highest it may be conceived as "the universe flowering into deity," As the Hermetic philosophers found in the principle of analogy, "*Quod inferius sicut quod superius,*" the Key of Creation, so we are invited to see in that uninterrupted change which is the condition of our normal consciousness, a true image, a microcosm of the living universe as a part of which that consciousness has been evolved.

If we accept this theory, we must then impute to life in its fullness—the huge, many levelled, many coloured life, the innumerable worlds which escape the rhythm of our senses; not merely that patch of physical life which those senses perceive—a divinity, a greatness of destiny far beyond that with which it is credited by those who hold to a physico-chemical theory of the universe. We must perceive in it, as some mystics have done, "the beating of the Heart of God"; and agree with Heracleitus that "there is but one wisdom, to understand the knowledge by which all things are steered through the All." Union with reality—apprehension of it—will upon this hypothesis be union with life at its most intense point: in its most dynamic aspect. It will be a deliberate harmony set up with the Logos which that same philosopher described as "man's most constant companion." *Ergo,* says the mystic, union with a Personal and Conscious spiritual existence, immanent in the world—one form, one half of the union which I have always sought, since this is clearly life in its highest manifestation. Beauty, Goodness, Splendour, Love, all those shining words which exhilarate the soul, are but the names of aspects or qualities picked out by human intuition as characteristic of this intense and eternal Life in which is the life of men.

How, then, may we knew this Life, this creative and original soul of things, in which we are bathed; in which, as in a river, swept along? Not, says Bergson bluntly, by any intellectual means. The mind which thinks it knows Reality because it has made a diagram of Reality, is merely the dupe of its own categories. The intellect is a specialized aspect of the self, a form of consciousness: but specialized for very different purposes than those of metaphysical speculation. Life has evolved it in the interests of life; has made it capable of dealing with "solids," with concrete things. With these it is at home. Outside of them it becomes dazed, uncertain of itself; for it is no longer doing its natural work, which is to *help* life, not to *know* it.

In the interests of experience, and in order to grasp perceptions, the intellect breaks up experience, which is in reality a continuous stream, an incessant process of change and response with no separate parts, into purely conventional "moments," "periods," or psychic "states." It picks out from the flow of reality those bits which are significant for human life; which "interest" it, catch its attention. From these it makes up a mechanical world in which it dwells, and which seems quite real until it is subjected to criticism. It does, says Bergson, the work of a cinematograph: takes snapshots of something which is always moving, and by means of these successive static representations—none of which are real, because Life, the object photographed, never was at rest—it recreates a picture of life, of motion. This rather jerky representation of divine harmony, from which innumerable moments are left out, is useful for practical purposes: but it is not reality, because it is not alive.

This "real world," then, is the result of your selective activity, and the nature of your selection is largely outside your control. Your cinematograph machine goes at a certain pace, takes its snapshots at certain intervals. Anything which goes too quickly for these intervals, it either fails to catch, or merges with preceding and succeeding movements to form a picture with which it can deal. Thus we treat, for instance, the storm of vibrations which we convert into "sound" and "light." Slacken or accelerate its clock-time, change its rhythmic activity, and at once you take a different series of snapshots, and have as a result a different picture of the world. Thanks to the time at which the normal human machine is set, it registers for us what we call, in our simple way, "the natural world." A slight accession of humility or common sense might teach us that a better title would be " *our* natural world."

Let human consciousness change or transcend its rhythm, and any other aspect of any other world may be ours as a result. Hence the mystics' claim that in their ecstasies they change the conditions of consciousness, and apprehend a deeper reality which is unrelated to human speech, cannot be dismissed as unreasonable. Do not then confuse that surface-consciousness which man has trained to be an organ of utility and nothing more—and which therefore can only deal adequately with the "given" world of sense—with that mysterious something in you, that ground of personality, inarticulate but inextinguishable, by which you are aware that a greater truth exists. This truth, whose neighbourhood you feel, and for which you long, is Life. You are in it all the while, "like a fish in the sea, like a bird in the air," as St. Mechthild of Hackborn said many centuries ago.

Give yourself, then, to this divine and infinite life, this mysterious Cosmic activity in which you are immersed, of which you are born. Trust it. Let it surge in on you. Cast off, as the mystics are always begging you to do, the fetters of the senses, the "remora of desire"; and making your interests identical with those of the All, rise to freedom, to that spontaneous, creative life which, inherent in every individual self, is our share of the life of the Universe. You are yourself *vital* —a free centre of energy—did you but know it. You can move to higher levels, to greater reality, truer self-fulfilment, if you will. Though you be, as Plato said, like an oyster in your shell, you can open that shell to the living waters without, draw from the "Immortal Vitality." Thus only—by contact with the real—shall you *know* reality. *Cot ad cot loquitur.*

The Indian mystics declare substantially the same truth when they say that the illusion of finitude is only to be escaped by relapsing into the substantial and universal life, abolishing individuality. So too, by a deliberate self-abandonment to that which Plato calls the "saving madness" of ecstasy, did the initiates of Dionysus "draw near to God." So their Christian cousins assert that "self-surrender" is the only way: that they must die to live, must lose to find: that knowing implies being: that the method and secret which they have always practiced consists merely in a meek and loving union—the synthesis of passion and self-sacrifice—with that divine and unseparated life, that larger consciousness in which the soul is grounded, and which they hold to be an aspect of the life of God. In their hours of contemplation, they deliberately empty themselves of the false images of the intellect, neglect the cinematograph of sense. Then only are they capable of transcending the merely intellectual levels of consciousness, and perceiving that Reality which "hath no image."

"Pilgrimage to the place of the wise," said Jalalu 'ddin, "is to find escape from the flame of separation." It is the mystics' secret in a nutshell. "When I stand empty *in* God's will and empty *of* God's will and of all His works and of God Himself," cries Eckhart with his usual violence of language, "*then* am I above all creatures and am neither God nor creature, but I am what I was and evermore shall be." He attains, that is to say, by this escape from a narrow selfhood, not to identity with God—that were only conceivable upon a basis of pantheism—but to an identity with his own substantial life, and through it with the life of a real and living universe; in symbolic language, with "the thought of the Divine Mind" whereby union with that Mind in the essence or ground of the soul becomes possible. The first great message of Vitalistic philosophy is then seen to be—Cease to identify your intellect and your self: a primary lesson which none who purpose the study of mysticism may neglect. Become at least aware of, if you cannot "know," the larger, truer self: that root and depth of spirit, as St. Francois de Sales calls it, from which intellect and feeling grow as fingers from the palm of the hand—that free creative self which constitutes your true life, as distinguished from the scrap of consciousness which is its servant.

How then, asks the small consciously-seeking personality of the normal man, am I to become aware of this, my larger self, and of the free, eternal, spiritual life which it lives?

Here philosophy, emerging from the water-tight compartment in which metaphysics have lived too long retired, calls in psychology; and tells us that in intuition, in a bold reliance on contact between the totality of the self and the external world—perhaps too in those strange states of lucidity which accompany great emotion and defy analysis—lies the normal man's best chance of attaining, as it were, a swift and sidelong knowledge of this real. Smothered in daily life by the fretful activities of our surface-mind, reality emerges in our great moments; and, seeing ourselves in its radiance, we know, for good or evil, what we are. "We are not pure intellects... around our conceptional and logical thought there remains a vague, nebulous Somewhat, the substance at whose expense the luminous nucleus we call the intellect is formed." In this aura, this diffused sensitiveness, we are asked to find man's medium of communication with the Universal Life.

Such fragmentary, dim and unverifiable perceptions of the Real, however, such "excursions into the Absolute," cannot be looked upon as a satisfaction of man's hunger for Truth. He does not want to peep, but to live. Hence he cannot be satisfied with anything less than a total and permanent adjustment of his being to the greater life of reality. This alone can resolve the disharmonies between the self and the world, and give meaning and value to human life. The possibility of this adjustment—of union between man's life and that "independent spiritual life" which is the stuff of reality—is the theme alike of mysticism and of Eucken's spiritual vitalism or Activistic Philosophy. Reality, says Eucken, is an independent spiritual world, unconditioned by the apparent world of sense. To know it and to live in it is man's true destiny. His point of contact with it is personality: the inward fount of his being: his heart, not his head. Man is real, and in the deepest sense alive, in virtue of this free personal life-principle within him; but he is bound and blinded by the ties set up between his surface-intelligence and the sense-world.

The struggle for reality must be a struggle on man's part to transcend the sense-world, escape its bondage. He must renounce it, and be "re-born" to a higher level of consciousness; shifting his centre of interest from the natural to the spiritual plane. According to the thoroughness with which he does this, will be the amount of real life he enjoys. The initial break with the "world," the refusal to spend one's life communing with one's own cinematograph picture, is essential if the freedom of the infinite is to be attained. We are amphibious creatures: our life moves upon two levels at once—the natural and the spiritual. The key to the puzzle of man lies in the fact that he is "the meeting point of various stages of Reality." All his difficulties and triumphs are grounded in this. The whole question for him is, which world shall be central for him—the real, vital, all-embracing life we call spirit, or the lower life of sense? Shall "Existence," the superficial obvious thing, or "Substance," the underlying verity, be his home? Shall he remain the slave of the senses with their habits and customs, or rise to a plane of consciousness, of heroic endeavour, in which—participating in the life of spirit—he knows reality because he is real?

The mystics, one and all, have answered this question in the same sense, and proved in their own experience that the premises of "Activism" are true. This application of the vitalistic idea to the transcendental world, does in fact fit the observed facts of mysticism far more closely even than it fits the observed facts of man's ordinary mental life.

(1) The primary break with the sense-world.

(2) The "new" birth and development of the spiritual consciousness on high levels—in Eucken's eyes an essential factor in the attainment of reality.

(3) That ever closer and deeper dependence on and appropriation of the fullness of the Divine Life; a conscious participation, and active union with the infinite and eternal.

These three imperatives, form an exact description of the psychological process through which the mystics pass. If then this transcendence is the highest destiny of the race, mysticism becomes the crown of man's ascent towards Reality; the orderly completion of the universal plan.

The mystics show us this independent spiritual life, this fruition of the Absolute, enjoyed with a fullness to which others cannot attain. They are the heroic examples of the life of spirit; as the great artists, the great discoverers, are the heroic examples of the life of beauty and the life of truth. Directly participating, like all artists, in the Divine Life, they are usually persons of great vitality but this vitality expresses itself in unusual forms, hard of understanding for ordinary men. When we see a picture or a poem, hear a musical composition, we accept it as an expression of life, an earnest of the power which brought it forth. But the deep contemplations of the great mystic, his visionary reconstructions of reality, and the fragments of them which he is able to report, do not seem to us—as they are—the equivalents, or more often the superiors of the artistic and scientific achievements of other great men.

Mysticism, then, offers us the history, as old as civilization, of a race of adventurers who have carried to its term the process of a deliberate and active return to the divine fount of things. They have surrendered themselves to the life-movement of the universe, hence have lived with an intenser life than other men can ever know; have transcended the "sense-world" in order to live on high levels the spiritual life. Therefore they witness to all that our latent spiritual consciousness, which shows itself in the "hunger for the Absolute," can be made to mean to us if we develop it; and have in this respect a unique importance for the race. It is the mystics, too, who have perfected that method of intuition, that knowledge by union, the existence of which philosophy has been driven to acknowledge. But where the metaphysician obtains at best a sidelong glance at that Being "unchanging yet elusive," whom he has so often defined but never discovered, the artist a brief and dazzling vision of the Beauty which is Truth, they gaze with confidence into the very eyes of the Beloved.

The mystics, again, are, by their very constitution, acutely conscious of the free and active "World of Becoming," the Divine Immanence and its travail. It is in them and they are in it or, as they put it in their blunt theological way, "the Spirit of God is within you." But they are not satisfied with this statement and this knowledge; and here it is that they part company with vitalism. It is, they think, but half a truth. To know Reality in this way, to know it in its dynamic aspect, enter into "the great life of the All": this is indeed, in the last resort, to know it supremely from the point of view of man—to liberate from selfhood the human consciousness—but it is not to know it from the point of view of God. There are planes of being beyond this; countries dark to the intellect, deeps into which only the very greatest contemplatives have looked. These, coming forth, have declared with Ruysbroeck that "God according to the Persons is Eternal Work, but according to the Essence and Its perpetual stillness He is Eternal Rest."

The full spiritual consciousness of the true mystic is developed not in one, but in two apparently opposite but really complementary directions. On the one hand he is intensely aware of, and knows himself to be at one with that active World of Becoming, that immanent Life, from which his own life takes its rise. Hence, though he has broken for ever with the bondage of the senses, he perceives in every manifestation of life a sacramental meaning; a loveliness, a wonder, a heightened significance, which is hidden from other men. He may, with St. Francis, call the Sun and the Moon, Water and Fire, his brothers and his sisters: or receive, with Blake, the message of the trees. Because of his cultivation of disinterested love, because his outlook is not conditioned by "the exclusive action of the will-to-live," he has attained the power of communion with the living reality of the universe; and in this respect can truly say that he finds "God in all and all in God." Thus, the skilled spiritual vision of Lady Julian, transcending the limitations of human perception, entering into harmony with a larger world whose rhythms cannot be received by common men, *saw* the all-enfolding Divine Life, the mesh of reality. "For as the body is clad in the cloth," she said, "and the flesh in the skin and the bones in the flesh and the heart in the whole, so are we, soul and body, clad in the Goodness of God and enclosed. Yea, and more homely: for all these may waste and wear away, but the Goodness of God is ever whole." Many mystical poets and pantheistic mystics never pass beyond this degree of lucidity.

On the other hand, the full mystic consciousness also attains to what is, I think, its really characteristic quality. It develops the power of apprehending the Absolute, Pure Being, the utterly Transcendent or, as its possessor would say, can experience "passive union with God." This all-round expansion of consciousness, with its dual power of knowing by communion the temporal and eternal, immanent and transcendent aspects of reality—the life of the All, vivid, flowing and changing, and the changeless, conditionless life of the One—is the peculiar mark, the *ultimo sigillo* of the great mystic, and must never be forgotten in studying his life and work.

As the ordinary man is the meeting-place between two stages of reality—the sense-world and the world of spiritual life—so the mystic, standing head and shoulders above ordinary men, is again the meeting-place between two orders. Or, if you like it better, he is able to perceive and react to reality under two modes. On the one hand he knows, and rests in, the eternal world of Pure Being, the "Sea Pacific" of the Godhead, indubitably present to him in his ecstasies, attained by him in the union of love. On the other, he knows—and works in—that "stormy sea," the vital World of Becoming which is the expression of Its will. "Illuminated men," says Ruysbroeck, "are caught up, above the reason, into naked vision. There the Divine Unity dwells and calls them. Hence their bare vision, cleansed and free, penetrates the activity of all created things, and pursues it to search it out even to its height."

Though philosophy has striven since thought began—and striven in vain—to resolve the paradox of Being and Becoming, of Eternity and Time, she has failed strangely enough to perceive that a certain type of personality has substituted experience for her guesses at truth; and achieved its solution, not by the dubious processes of thought, but by direct perception. To the great mystic the "problem of the Absolute" presents itself in terms of life, not in terms of dialectic. He solves it in terms of life: by a change or growth of consciousness which—thanks to his peculiar genius—enables him to apprehend that two-fold Vision of Reality which eludes the perceptive powers of other men. It is extraordinary that this fact of experience a central fact for the understanding of the contemplative type—has received so little attention from writers upon mysticism. As we proceed with our inquiry, its importance, its far-reaching implications in the domains of psychology, of theology, of action, will become more and more evident. It provides the reason why the mystics could never accept the diagram of the Vitalists or Evolutionists as a complete statement of the nature of Reality. "Whatever be the limits of your knowledge, we know"—they would say—"that the world has another aspect than this: the aspect which is present to the Mind of God." "Tranquillity according to His essence, activity according to His nature: perfect stillness, perfect fecundity," says Ruysbroeck again, this is the two-fold character of the Absolute. That which to us is action, to Him, they declare, is rest, "His very peace and stillness coming from the brimming fullness of His infinite life."

The evolution of the mystic consciousness, then, brings its possessors to this transcendent point of view: their secret is this unity in diversity, this stillness in strife. Here they are in harmony with Heracleitus rather than with his modern interpreters. That most mystical of philosophers discerned a hidden unity beneath the battle, transcending all created opposites, and taught his disciples that "Having hearkened not unto me but unto the Logos, it is wise to confess that all things are *one.*" This is the secret at which the idealists' and concept of Pure Being has tried, so timidly, to hint and which the Vitalists' more intimate, more actual concept of Becoming has tried, so unnecessarily, to destroy. We shall see the glorious raiment in which the Christian mystics deck it when we come to consider their theological map of the quest.

If it be objected—and this objection has been made by advocates of each school of thought—that the existence of the idealists' and mystics' "Absolute" is utterly inconsistent with the deeply alive, striving life which the Vitalists identify with reality, I reply that both concepts at bottom are but symbols of realities which the human mind can never reach and that the idea of stillness, unity and peace is and has ever been humanity's best translation of its intuition of the achieved Perfection of God. "In the midst of silence a hidden word was spoken to me." Where is this Silence, and where is the place in which this word is spoken? It is in the purest that the soul can produce, in her noblest part, in the Ground, even the Being of the Soul." So Eckhart: and here he does but subscribe to a universal tradition. The mystics have always insisted that "Be still, be still, and *know*" is the condition of man's purest and most direct apprehensions of reality: that he experiences in quiet the truest and deepest activity and Christianity when she formulated her philosophy made haste to adopt and express this paradox.

It has been said that "Whatever we may do, our hunger for the Absolute will never cease." This hunger—that innate craving for, and intuition of, a final Unity, an unchanging good—will go on, however heartily we may feed on those fashionable systems which offer us a dynamic or empirical universe. If, now, we admit in all living creatures—as Vitalists must do—an instinct of self-preservation, a free directive force which may be trusted and which makes for life: is it just to deny such an instinct to the human soul? The "entelechy" of the Vitalists, the "hidden steersman," drives the phenomenal world on and up. What about that other sure instinct embedded in the race, breaking out again and again, which drives the spirit on and up; spurs it eternally towards an end which it feels to be definite yet cannot define? Shall we distrust this instinct for the Absolute, as living and ineradicable as any other of our powers, merely because philosophy finds it difficult to accommodate and to describe?

"We must," says Plato in the "Timaeus," "make a distinction of the two great forms of being, and ask, 'What is that which Is and has no Becoming, and what is that which is always becoming and never Is?' "Without necessarily subscribing to the Platonic answer to this question, we may surely acknowledge that the question itself is sound and worth asking; that it expresses a perennial demand of human nature; and that the analogy of man's other instincts and cravings assures us that these his fundamental demands always indicate the existence of a supply. The great defect of Vitalism, considered as a system, is that it only answers half the question; the half which Absolute Idealism disdained to answer at all.

We have seen that the mystical experience, the fullest all-round experience in regard to the transcendental world which humanity has attained, declares that there are two aspects, two planes of discoverable Reality. We have seen also that hints of these two planes—often clear statements concerning them—abound in mystical literature of the personal first-hand type. Pure Being, says Boutroux in the course of his exposition of Boehme, has two characteristic manifestations. It shows itself to us as Power, by means of strife, of the struggle and opposition of its own qualities. But it shows itself to us as Reality, in harmonizing and reconciling within itself these discordant opposites.

Its manifestation as Power, then, is for us in the dynamic World of Becoming, amidst the thud and surge of that life which is compounded of paradox, of good and evil, joy and sorrow, life and death. Here, Boehme declares that the Absolute God is voluntarily self-revealing. But each revelation has as its condition the appearance of its opposite: light can only be recognized at the price of knowing darkness, life needs death, love needs wrath. Hence if Pure Being—the Good, Beautiful and True—is to reveal itself, it must do so by evoking and opposing its contrary: as in the Hegelian dialectic no idea is complete without its negative. Such a revelation by strife, however, is rightly felt by man to be incomplete. Absolute Reality, the Player whose sublime music is expressed at the cost of this everlasting friction between bow and lyre, is present, it is true, in His music. But He is best known in that "light behind," that unity where all these opposites are lifted up into harmony, into a higher synthesis; and the melody is perceived, not as a difficult progress of sound, but as a whole.

We have, then, (*a*) The achieved Reality which the Greeks, and every one after them, meant by that seemingly chill abstraction which they called Pure Being: that Absolute One, unconditioned and undiscoverable, in Whom all is resumed. In the undifferentiated Godhead of Eckhart, the Transcendent Father of orthodox Christian theology, we see the mind's attempt to conceive that "wholly other" Reality, unchanging yet changer of all. It is the great contribution of the mystics to humanity's knowledge of the real that they find in this Absolute, in defiance of the metaphysicians, a personal object of love, the goal of their quest, a "Living One who lives first and lives perfectly, and Who, touching me, the inferior, derivative life, can cause me to live by Him and for His sake".

(*b*) But, contradicting the nihilism of Eastern contemplatives, they see also a reality in the dynamic side of things: in the seething pot of appearance. They are aware of an eternal Becoming, a striving, free, evolving life; not merely as a shadow-show, but as an implicit of their Cosmos felt also in the travail of their own souls—God's manifestation or showing, in which He is immanent, in which His Spirit truly works and strives. It is in *this* plane of reality that all individual life is immersed: this is the stream which set out from the Heart of God and "turns again home."

The mystic knows his task to be the attainment of Being, Eternal Life, union with the One, the "return to the Father's heart": for the parable of the Prodigal Son is to him the history of the universe. This union is to be attained, first by cooperation in that Life which bears him up, in which he is immersed. He must become conscious of this "great life of the All," merge himself in it, if he would find his way back whence he came. *Vae soli*. Hence there are really two distinct acts of "divine union," two distinct kinds of illumination involved in the Mystic Way: the dual character of the spiritual consciousness brings a dual responsibility in its train. First, there is the union with Life, with the World of Becoming and parallel with it, the illumination by which the mystic "gazes upon a more veritable world." Secondly, there is the union with Being, with the One and that final, ineffable illumination of pure love which is called the "knowledge of God." It is through the development of the third factor, the free, creative "spirit," the scrap of Absolute Life which is the ground of his soul, that the mystic can (a) conceive and (b) accomplish these transcendent acts. Only Being can know Being: we "behold that which we are, and are that which we behold." But there is a spark in man's soul, say the mystics, which is real—which in fact is—and by its cultivation we may know reality. "Thus," says Von Hügel "a real succession, real efforts, and the continuous sense of limitation and inadequacy are the very means in and through which man apprehends increasingly (if only he thus loves and wills) the contrasting yet sustaining Simultaneity, Spontaneity, Infinity, and pure action of the Eternal Life of God."

Over and over again—as Being and Becoming, as Eternity and Time, as Transcendence and Immanence, Reality and Appearance, the One and the Many—these two dominant ideas, demands, imperious instincts of man's self will reappear; the warp and woof of his completed universe. On the one hand is his intuition of a remote, unchanging Somewhat calling him: on the other there is his longing for and as clear intuition of an intimate, adorable Somewhat, companioning him. Man's true Real, his only adequate God, must be great enough to embrace this sublime paradox, to take up these apparent negations into a higher synthesis. Neither the utter transcendence of extreme Absolutism, nor the utter immanence of the Vitalists will do. Both these, taken alone, are declared by the mystics to be incomplete. They conceive that Absolute Being who is the goal of their quest as manifesting Himself in a World of Becoming: working in it, at one with it yet though *semper agens,* also *semper quietus.*The Divine spirit which they know to be immanent in the heart and in the universe comes forth from and returns to the Transcendent One; and this division of persons in unity of substance completes the "Eternal Circle, from Goodness, through Goodness, to Goodness."

Absolute Being and Becoming, the All and the One, are found to be alike inadequate to their definition of this discovered Real; the "triple star of Goodness, Truth, and Beauty." Speaking always from experience—the most complete experience achieved by man—they assure us of an Absolute which overpasses and includes the Absolute of philosophy, far transcends that Cosmic life which it fills and sustains, and is best defined in terms of Transcendent Personality; which because of its unspeakable richness and of the poverty of human speech, they have sometimes been driven to define only by negations. At once static and dynamic, above life and in it, "all love yet all law," eternal in essence though working in time, this vision resolves the contraries which tease those who study it from without, and swallows up whilst it kindles to life all the partial interpretations of metaphysics and of science.

Here then stands the mystic. By the help of two types of philosophy, eked out by the resources of symbolic expression and suggestion, he has contrived to tell us something of his vision and his claim. Confronted by that vision—that sublime intuition of eternity—we may surely ask, indeed are bound to ask, "What is the machinery by which this self, akin to the imprisoned and sense-fed self of our daily experience, has contrived to slip its fetters and rise to those levels of spiritual perception on which alone such vision can be possible to man? How has it brought within the field of consciousness those deep intuitions which fringe upon Absolute Life; how developed powers by which it is enabled to arrive at this amazing, this superhuman concept of the nature of Reality?" Psychology will do something, perhaps, to help us to an answer to this question; and it is her evidence which we must examine next. But for the fullest and most satisfying answer we must go to the mystics; and they reply to our questions, when we ask them, in the direct and uncompromising terms of action, not in the refined and elusive periods of speculative thought.

"Come with us," they say to the bewildered and entangled self, craving for finality and peace, "and we will show you a way out that shall not only be an issue from your prison, but also a pathway to your Home. True, you are immersed, fold upon fold, in the World of Becoming; worse, you are besieged on all sides by the persistent illusions of sense. But you too are a child of the Absolute. You bear within you the earnest of your inheritance. At the apex of your spirit there is a little door, so high up that only by hard climbing can you reach it. There the Object of your craving stands and knocks; thence came those persistent messages—faint echoes from the Truth eternally hammering at your gates—which disturbed the comfortable life of sense. Come up then by this pathway, to those higher levels of reality to which, in virtue of the eternal spark in you, you belong. Leave your ignoble ease, your clever prattle, your absurd attempts to solve the apparent contradictions of a Whole too great for your useful little mind to grasp. Trust your deep instincts: use your latent powers. Appropriate that divine, creative life which is the very substance of your being. Remake yourself in its interest, if you would know its beauty and its truth. You can only behold that which you *are*. Only the Real can know Reality."

8

THE MYSTIC WAY

We are now to turn from general principles and study those principles in action: to describe the psychological process, or "Mystic Way," by which that peculiar type of personality which is able to set up direct relations with the Absolute is usually developed. The difficulty of this description will lie in the fact that all mystics differ one from another; as all the individual objects of our perception, "living" and "not living," do. The creative impulse in the world, so far as we are aware of it, appears upon ultimate analysis to be free and original not bound and mechanical: to express itself, in defiance of the determinists, with a certain artistic spontaneity. Man, when he picks out some point of likeness as a basis on which to arrange its productions in groups, is not discovering its methods; but merely making for his own convenience an arbitrary choice of one or two—not necessarily characteristic—qualities, which happen to appear in a certain number of different persons or things. Hence the most scientific classification is a rough-and-ready business at the best.

When we come to apply such classification to so delicate and elusive a series of psychological states as those which accompany the "contemplative life," all the usual difficulties are increased. No one mystic can be discovered in whom all the observed characteristics of the transcendental consciousness are resumed, and who can on that account be treated as typical. Mental states which are distinct and mutually exclusive in one case, exist simultaneously in another. In some, stages which have been regarded as essential are entirely omitted: in others, their order appears to be reversed. We seem at first to be confronted by a group of selves which arrive at the same end without obeying any general law.

Take, however, a number of such definitely mystical selves and make of them, so to speak, a "composite portrait": as anthropologists do when they wish to discover the character of a race. From this portrait we may expect a type to emerge, in which all the outstanding characteristics contributed by the individual examples are present together, and minor variations are suppressed. Such a portrait will of course be conventional but it will be useful as a standard, which can be constantly compared with, and corrected by, isolated specimens.

The first thing we notice about this composite portrait is that the typical mystic seems to move towards his goal through a series of strongly marked oscillations between "states of pleasure" and "states of pain." The existence and succession of these states—sometimes broken and confused, sometimes crisply defined—can be traced, to a greater or less degree, in almost every case of which we possess anything like a detailed record. *Gyrans gyrando radii spiritus.* The soul, as it treads the ascending spiral of its road towards reality, experiences alternately the sunshine and the shade. These experiences are "constants" of the transcendental life. "The Spiritual States of the Soul are all Eternal," said Blake, with the true mystical genius for psychology.

The complete series of these states—and it must not be forgotten that few individuals present them all in perfection, whilst in many instances several are blurred or appear to be completely suppressed—will be, I think, most conveniently arranged under five heads. This method of grouping means, of course, the abandonment of the time-honoured threefold division of the Mystic Way, and the apparent neglect of St. Teresa's equally celebrated Seven Degrees of Contemplation, but I think that we shall gain more than we lose by adopting it. The groups, however, must be looked upon throughout as diagrammatic, and only as answering loosely and generally to experiences which seldom present themselves in so rigid and unmixed a form. These experiences, largely conditioned as they are by surroundings and by temperament, exhibit all the variety and spontaneity which are characteristic of life in its highest manifestations and, like biological specimens, they lose something of their essential reality in being prepared for scientific investigation. Taken all together, they constitute phases in a single process of growth; involving the movement of consciousness from lower to higher levels of reality, the steady remaking of character in accordance with the "independent spiritual world." But as the study of physical life is made easier for us by an artificial division into infancy, adolescence, maturity, and old age, so a discreet indulgence of the human passion for map-making will increase our chances of understanding the nature of the Mystic Way.

Here, then, is the classification under which we shall study the phases of the mystical life.

(1) The awakening of the Self to consciousness of Divine Reality. This experience, usually abrupt and well-marked, is accompanied by intense feelings of joy and exaltation.

(2) The Self, aware for the first time of Divine Beauty, realizes by contrast its own finiteness and imperfection, the manifold illusions in which it is immersed, the

immense distance which separates it from the One. Its attempts to eliminate by discipline and mortification all that stands in the way of its progress towards union with God constitute *Purgation:* a state of pain and effort.

(3) When by Purgation the Self has become detached from the "things of sense," and acquired those virtues which are the "ornaments of the spiritual marriage," its joyful consciousness of the Transcendent Order returns in an enhanced form. Like the prisoners in Plato's "Cave of Illusion," it has awakened to knowledge of Reality, has struggled up the harsh and difficult path to the mouth of the cave. Now it looks upon the sun. This is *Illumination:* a state which includes in itself many of the stages of contemplation, "degrees of orison," visions and adventures of the soul described by St. Teresa and other mystical writers. These form, as it were, a way within the Way: a *moyen de parvenir*, a training devised by experts which will strengthen and assist the mounting soul. They stand, so to speak, for education; whilst the Way proper represents organic growth. Illumination is the "contemplative state" *par excellence.* It forms, with the two preceding states, the "first mystic life." Many mystics never go beyond it; and, on the other hand, many seers and artists not usually classed amongst them, have shared, to some extent, the experiences of the illuminated state. Illumination brings a certain apprehension of the Absolute, a sense of the Divine Presence but not true union with it. It is a state of happiness.

(4) In the development of the great and strenuous seekers after God, this is followed—or sometimes intermittently accompanied—by the most terrible of all the experiences of the Mystic Way: the final and complete purification of the Self, which is called by some contemplatives the "mystic pain" or "mystic death," by others the Purification of the Spirit or *Dark Night of the Soul.* The consciousness which had, in Illumination, sunned itself in the sense of the Divine Presence, now suffers under an equally intense sense of the Divine Absence: learning to dissociate the personal satisfaction of mystical vision from the reality of mystical life. As in Purgation the senses were cleansed and humbled, and the energies and interests of the Self were concentrated upon transcendental things: so now the purifying process is extended to the very centre of I-hood, the will. The human instinct for personal happiness must be killed. This is the "spiritual crucifixion" so often described by the mystics: the great desolation in which the soul seems abandoned by the Divine. The Self now surrenders itself, its individuality, and its will, completely. It desires nothing, asks nothing, is utterly passive.

(5) *Union:* the true goal of the mystic quest. In this state the Absolute Life is not merely perceived and enjoyed by the Self, as in Illumination: but is *one* with it.

This is the end towards which all the previous oscillations of consciousness have tended. It is a state of equilibrium, of purely spiritual life; characterized by peaceful joy, by enhanced powers, by intense certitude. To call this state, as some authorities do, by the name of Ecstasy, is inaccurate and confusing: since the term Ecstasy has long been used both by psychologists and ascetic writers to define that short and rapturous trance—a state with well-marked physical and psychical accompaniments—in which the contemplative, losing all consciousness of the phenomenal world, is caught up to a brief and immediate enjoyment of the Divine Vision. Ecstasies of this kind are often experienced by the mystic in Illumination, or even on his first conversion. They cannot therefore be regarded as exclusively characteristic of the Unitive Way. In some of the greatest mystics—St. Teresa is an example—the ecstatic trance seems to diminish rather than increase in frequency after the state of union has been attained: whilst others achieve the heights by a path which leaves on one side all abnormal phenomena.

Union must be looked upon as the true goal of mystical growth; that permanent establishment of life upon transcendent levels of reality, of which ecstasies give a foretaste to the soul. Intense forms of it, described by individual mystics, under symbols such as those of Mystical Marriage, Deification, or Divine Fecundity, all prove on examination to be aspects of this same experience "seen through a temperament."

It is right, however, to state here that Oriental Mysticism insists upon a further stage beyond that of union, which stage it regards as the real goal of the spiritual life. This is the total annihilation or reabsorption of the individual soul in the Infinite. Such an annihilation is said by the Sufis to constitute the "Eighth Stage of Progress," in which alone they truly attain to God. Thus stated, it appears to differ little from the Buddhist's Nirvana, and is the logical corollary of that pantheism to which the Oriental mystic always tends. Thus Jalalu d'Din:

"O, let me not exist! for Non-Existence
Proclaims in organ tones, 'To Him we shall return.'"

It is at least doubtful, however, whether the interpretation which has been put by European students upon such passages as this be correct. The language in which Al Ghazzali attempts to describe the Eighth Stage is certainly more applicable to the Unitive Life as understood by Christian contemplatives, than to the Buddhistic annihilation of personality. "The end of Sufi-ism," he says, "is total absorption in God. This is at least the relative end to that part of their doctrine which I am free to reveal and describe. But *in reality it is but the beginning* of the Sufi life, for those intuitions and other things which precede it are, so to speak, but the porch by which they enter.... In this state some have imagined themselves to be amalgamated with God, others to be identical with Him, others again to be associated with Him: but *all this is sin*."

The doctrine of annihilation as the end of the soul's ascent, whatever the truth may be as to the Moslem attitude concerning it, is decisively rejected by all European mystics, though a belief in it is constantly imputed to them by their enemies: for their aim is not the suppression of life, but its intensification, a change in its form. This change, they say in a paradox which is generally misunderstood, consists in the perfecting of personality by the utter surrender of self. It is true that the more Orientally-minded amongst them, such as Dionysius the Areopagite, do use language of a negative kind which seems almost to involve a belief in the annihilation rather than the transformation of the self in God but this is because they are trying to describe a condition of supersensible vitality from the point of view of the normal consciousness to which it can only seem a Nothing, a Dark, a Self-loss. Further it will be found that this language is often an attempt to describe the conditions of transitory perception, not those of permanent existence: the characteristics, that is to say, of the Ecstatic Trance, in which for a short time the whole self is lifted to transcendent levels, and the Absolute is apprehended by a total suspension of the surface consciousness. Hence the Divine Dark, the Nothing, is not a state of non-being to which the mystic aspires to attain: it is rather a paradoxical description of his experience of that Undifferentiated Godhead, that Supernal Light whence he may, in his ecstasies, bring down fire from heaven to light the world.

In the mystics of the West, the highest forms of Divine Union impel the self to some sort of active, rather than of passive life and this is now recognized by the best authorities as the true distinction between Christian and non-Christian mysticism. "The Christian mystics," says Delacroix, "move from the Infinite to the Definite; they aspire to infinitize life and to define Infinity; they go from the conscious to the subconscious, and from the subconscious to the conscious. The obstacle in their path is not consciousness in general, but self-consciousness, the consciousness of the Ego. The Ego is the limitation, that which opposes itself to the Infinite: the states of consciousness free from self, lost in a vaster consciousness, may become modes of the Infinite, and states of the Divine Consciousness." So Starbuck: "The individual learns to transfer himself from a centre of self-activity into an organ of revelation of universal being, and to live a life of affection for and one-ness with, the larger life outside."

Hence, the ideal of the great contemplatives, the end of their long education, is to become "modes of the Infinite." Filled with an abounding sense of the Divine Life, of ultimate and adorable reality, sustaining and urging them on, they wish to communicate the revelation, the more abundant life, which they have received. Not spiritual marriage, but divine fecundity is to be their final state. In a sense St. Teresa in the Seventh Habitation, Suso when his great renunciation is made, have achieved the quest, yet there is nothing passive in the condition to which they have come. Not Galahad, but the Grail-bearer is now their type and in their life, words or works they are impelled to exhibit that "Hidden Treasure which desires to be found."

"You may think, my daughters," says St. Teresa, "that the soul in this state [of union] should be so absorbed that she can occupy herself with nothing. You deceive yourselves. She turns with greater ease and ardour than before to all that which belongs to the service of God, and when these occupations leave her free again, she remains in the enjoyment of that companionship."

No temperament is less slothful than the mystical one; and the "quiet" to which the mystics must school themselves in the early stages of contemplation is often the hardest of their tasks. The abandonment of bodily and intellectual activity is only undertaken in order that they may, in the words of Plotinus, "energize enthusiastically" upon another plane. Work they must but this work may take many forms—forms which are sometimes so wholly spiritual that they are not perceptible to practical minds. Much of the misunderstanding and consequent contempt of the contemplative life comes from the narrow and superficial definition of "work" which is set up by a muscular and wage-earning community.

All records of mysticism in the West, then, are also the records of supreme human activity. Not only of "wrestlers in the spirit" but also of great organizers, such as St. Teresa and St. John of the Cross; of missionaries preaching life to the spiritually dead, such as St. Francis of Assisi, St. Ignatius Loyola, Eckhart, Suso Tauler, Fox; of philanthropists, such as St. Catherine of Genoa or St. Vincent de Paul; poets and prophets, such as Mechthild of Magdeburg, Jacopone da Todi and Blake, finally, of some immensely virile souls whose participation in the Absolute Life has seemed to force on them a national destiny. Of this St. Bernard, St. Catherine of Siena, and Saint Joan of Arc are the supreme examples. "The soul enamoured of My Truth," said God's voice to St. Catherine of Siena, "never ceases to serve the whole world in general."

Utterly remade in the interests of Reality, exhibiting that dual condition of fruition and activity which Ruysbroeck described as the crowning stage of human evolution, the "Supreme summit of the Inner Life," all these lived, as it were, with both hands towards the finite and towards the Infinite, towards God and man. It is true that in nearly every case such "great actives" have first left the world, as a necessary condition of establishing communion with that Absolute Life which reinforced their own: for a mind distracted by the many cannot apprehend the One. Hence something equivalent to the solitude of the wilderness is an essential part of mystical education. But, having established that communion, re-ordered their inner lives upon transcendent levels—being united with their Source not merely in temporary ecstasies, but in virtue of a permanent condition of the soul, they were impelled to abandon their solitude; and resumed, in some way, their contact with the world in order to become the medium whereby that Life flowed out to other men. To go up alone into the mountain and come back as an ambassador to the world, has ever been the method of humanity's best friends. This systole-and-diastole motion of retreat as the preliminary to a return remains the true ideal of Christian Mysticism in its highest development. Those in whom it is not found, however great in other respects they may be, must be considered as having stopped short of the final stage.

Thus St. Catherine of Siena spent three years in hermit-like seclusion in the little room which we still see in her house in the Via Benincasa, entirely cut off from the ordinary life of her family. "Within her own house," says her legend, "she found the desert; and a solitude in the midst of people." There Catherine endured many mortifications, was visited by ecstasies and visions: passed, in fact, through the states of Purgation and Illumination, which existed in her case side by side. This life of solitude was brought to an abrupt end by the experience which is symbolized in the vision of the Mystic Marriage, and the Voice which then said to her, "Now will I wed thy soul, which shall ever be conjoined and united to Me!" Catherine, who had during her long retreat enjoyed illumination to a high degree, now entered upon the Unitive State, in which the whole of her public life was passed. Its effect was immediately noticeable.

She abandoned her solitude, joined in the family life, went out into the city to serve the poor and sick, attracted and taught disciples, converted sinners, and began that career of varied and boundless activity which has made her name one of the greatest in the history of the fourteenth century. Nor does this mean that she ceased to live the sort of life which is characteristic of mystical consciousness: to experience direct contact with the Transcendental World, to gaze into "the Abyss of Love Divine." On the contrary, her practical genius for affairs, her immense power of ruling men, drew its strength from the long series of visions and ecstasies which accompanied and supported her labours in the world. She "descended into the valley of lilies to make herself more fruitful," says her legend. The conscious vehicle of some "power not herself," she spoke and acted with an authority which might have seemed strange enough in an uneducated daughter of the people, were it not justified by the fact that all who came into contact with her submitted to its influence.

Our business, then, is to trace from its beginning a gradual and complete change in the equilibrium of the self. It is a change whereby that self turns from the unreal world of sense in which it is normally immersed, first to apprehend, then to unite itself with Absolute Reality: finally, possessed by and wholly surrendered to this Transcendent Life, becomes a medium whereby the spiritual world is seen in a unique degree operating directly in the world of sense. In other words, we are to see the human mind advance from the mere perception of phenomena, through the intuition—with occasional contact—of the Absolute under its aspect of Divine Transcendence, to the entire realization of, and union with, Absolute Life under its aspect of Divine Immanence.

The completed mystical life, then, is more than intuitional: it is theopathetic. In the old, frank language of the mystics, it is the *deified life*.

THE AWAKENING OF THE SELF

First in the sequence of the mystic states, we must consider that decisive event, the awakening of the transcendental consciousness. This awakening, from the psychological point of view, appears to be an intense form of the phenomenon of "conversion"; and closely akin to those deep and permanent conversions of the adult type which some religious psychologists call "sanctification." It is a disturbance of the equilibrium of the self, which results in the shifting of the field of consciousness from lower to higher levels, with a consequent removal of the centre of interest from the subject to an object now brought into view: the necessary beginning of any process of transcendence. It must not, however, be confused or identified with religious conversion as ordinarily understood: the sudden and emotional acceptance of theological beliefs which the self had previously either rejected or treated as conventions dwelling upon the margin of consciousness and having no meaning for her actual life. The mechanical process may be much the same; but the material involved, the results attained, belong to a higher order of reality.

"Conversion," says Starbuck, in words which are really far more descriptive of mystical awakening than of the revivalistic phenomena encouraged by American Protestantism, "is primarily an unselfing. The first birth of the individual is into his own little world. He is controlled by the deep-seated instincts of self-preservation and self-enlargement—instincts which are, doubtless, a direct inheritance from his brute ancestry. The universe is organized around his own personality as a centre." Conversion, then, is "the larger world-consciousness now pressing in on the individual consciousness. Often it breaks in suddenly and becomes a great new revelation. This is the first aspect of conversion: the person emerges from a smaller limited world of existence into a larger world of being. His life becomes swallowed up in a larger whole."

All conversion entails the abrupt or gradual emergence of intuitions from below the threshold, the consequent remaking of the field of consciousness, an alteration in the self's attitude to the world. "It is," says Pratt, "a change of taste—the most momentous one that ever occurs in human experience." But in the mystic this process is raised to the nth degree of intensity, for in him it means the first emergence of that passion for the Absolute which is to constitute his distinctive character: an emergence crucial in its effect on every department of his life. Those to whom it happens, often enough, are already "religious": sometimes deeply and earnestly so. Rulman Merswin, St. Catherine of Genoa, George Fox, Lucie-Christine—all these had been bred up in piety, and accepted in its entirety the Christian tradition. They were none the less conscious of an utter change in their world when this opening of the soul's eye took place.

Sometimes the emergence of the mystical consciousness is gradual, unmarked by any definite crisis. The self slides gently, almost imperceptibly, from the old universe to the new. The records of mysticism, however, suggest that this is exceptional: that travail is the normal accompaniment of birth. In another type, of which George Fox is a typical example, there is no conversion in the ordinary sense; but a gradual and increasing lucidity, of which the beginning has hardly been noticed by the self, intermittently accompanies the pain, misery of mind, and inward struggles characteristic of the entrance upon the Way of Purgation. Conversion and purification then go hand in hand, finally shading off into the serenity of the Illuminated State. Fox's "Journal" for the year 1647 contains a vivid account of these "showings" or growing transcendental perceptions of a mind not yet at one with itself, and struggling towards clearness of sight. "Though my exercises and troubles," he says, "were very great, yet were they not so continual but I had some intermissions, and was sometimes brought into such a heavenly joy that I thought I had been in Abraham's bosom.... Thus in the deepest miseries, and in the greatest sorrows and temptations that many times beset me, the Lord in His mercy did keep me. I found that there were two thirsts in me, the one after the creatures to get help and strength there; and the other after the Lord, the Creator.... It was so with me, that there seemed to be two pleadings in me.... One day when I had been walking solitarily abroad and was come home, I was wrapped up in the love of God, so that I could not but admire the greatness of his love. While I was in that condition it was opened unto me by the eternal Light and Power, and I saw clearly therein. But O! then did I see my troubles, trials, and temptations more clearly than ever I had done."

The great oscillations of the typical mystic between joy and pain are here replaced by a number of little ones. The "two thirsts" of the superficial and spiritual consciousness assert themselves by turns. Each step towards the vision of the Real brings with it a reaction. The nascent transcendental powers are easily fatigued, and the pendulum of self takes a shorter swing. "I was swept up to Thee by Thy Beauty, and torn away from Thee by my own weight," says St. Augustine, crystallizing the secret of this experience in an unforgettable phrase.

Commonly, however, if we may judge from those first-hand accounts which we possess, mystic conversion is a single and abrupt experience, sharply marked off from the long, dim struggles which precede and succeed it. It usually involves a sudden and acute realization of a splendour and adorable reality in the world—or sometimes of its obverse, the divine sorrow at the heart of things—never before perceived. In so far as I am acquainted with the resources of language, there are no words in which this realization can be described. It is of so actual a nature that in comparison the normal world of past perception seems but twilit at the best. Consciousness has suddenly changed its rhythm and a new aspect of the universe rushes in. The teasing mists are swept away, and reveal, if only for an instant, the sharp outline of the Everlasting Hills. "He who knows this will know what I say, and will be convinced that the soul has then another life."

In most cases, the onset of this new consciousness seems to the self so sudden, so clearly imposed from without rather than developed from within, as to have a supernatural character. The typical case is, of course, that of St. Paul: the sudden light, the voice, the ecstasy, the complete alteration of life. We shall see, however, when we come to study the evidence of those mystics who have left a detailed record of their preconverted state, that the apparently abrupt conversion is really, as a rule, the sequel and the result of a long period of restlessness, uncertainty, and mental stress. The deeper mind stirs uneasily in its prison, and its emergence is but the last of many efforts to escape. The temperament of the subject, his surroundings, the vague but persistent apprehensions of a supersensual reality which he could not find yet could not forget; all these have prepared him for it.

When, however, the subconscious intuitions, long ago quickened, are at last brought to birth and the eyes are opened on new light—and it is significant that an actual sense of blinding radiance is a constant accompaniment of this state of consciousness—the storm and stress, the vague cravings and oscillations of the past life are forgotten. In this abrupt recognition of reality "all things are made new": from this point the life of the mystic begins. Conversion of this sort has, says De Sanctis, three marked characteristics: a sense of liberation and victory: a conviction of the nearness of God: a sentiment of love towards God. We might describe it as a sudden, intense, and joyous perception of God immanent in the universe; of the divine beauty and unutterable power and splendour of that larger life in which the individual is immersed, and of a new life to be lived by the self in correspondence with this now dominant fact of existence. "Suddenly," says the French contemplative Lucie-Christine of the beginning of her mystical life, "I saw before my inward eyes these words— *God only...* they were at the same time a Light, an Attraction and a Power. A Light which showed me how I could belong completely to God alone in this world, and I saw that hitherto I had not well understood this; an Attraction by which my heart was subdued and delighted; a Power which inspired me with a generous resolution and somehow placed in my hands the means of carrying it out."

I will here set down for comparison a few instances of such mystical conversion; quoting, where this is available, the actual description left by the subject of his own experience, or in default of it, the earliest authentic account. In these cases, when grouped together, we shall see certain constant characteristics, from which it may be possible to deduce the psychological law to which they owe their peculiar form.

First in point of time, and perhaps also in importance, amongst those I have chosen, is the case of that great poet and contemplative, that impassioned lover of the Absolute, St. Francis of Assisi. The fact that St. Francis wrote little and lived much, that his actions were of unequalled simplicity and directness, long blinded his admirers to the fact that he is a typical mystic: the only one, perhaps, who forced the most trivial and sordid circumstances of sensual life to become perfect expressions of Reality.

Now the opening of St. Francis's eyes, which took place in A.D. 1206 when he was twenty-four years old, had been preceded by a long, hard struggle between the life of the world and the persistent call of the spirit. His mind, in modern language, had not unified itself. He was a high-spirited boy, full of vitality: a natural artist, with all the fastidiousness which the artistic temperament involves. War and pleasure both attracted him, and upon them, says his legend, he "miserably squandered and wasted his time." Nevertheless, he was vaguely dissatisfied. In the midst of festivities, he would have sudden fits of abstraction: abortive attempts of the growing transcendental consciousness, still imprisoned below the threshold but aware of and in touch with the Real, to force itself to the surface and seize the reins. "Even in ignorance," says Thomas of Celano again, "he was being led to perfect knowledge." He loved beauty, for he was by nature a poet and a musician, and shrank instinctively from contact with ugliness and disease. But something within ran counter to this temperamental bias, and sometimes conquered it. He would then associate with beggars, tend the leprous, perform impulsive acts of charity and self-humiliation.

When this divided state, described by the legend as "the attempt to flee God's hand," had lasted for some years, it happened one day that he was walking in the country outside the gates of Assisi, and passed the little church of S. Damiano, "the which" (I again quote from Thomas of Celano's "Second Life") "was almost ruinous and forsaken of all men. And, being led by the Spirit, he went in to pray; and he fell down before the Crucifix in devout supplication, and *having been smitten by unwonted visitations, found himself another man than he who had gone in.*"

Here, then, is the first stage of conversion. The struggle between two discrepant ideals of life has attained its term. A sudden and apparently "irrational" impulse to some decisive act reaches the surface-consciousness from the seething deeps. The impulse is followed; and the swift emergence of the transcendental sense results. This "unwonted visitation" effects an abrupt and involuntary alteration in the subject's consciousness: whereby he literally "finds himself another man." He is as one who has slept and now awakes. The crystallization of this new, at first fluid apprehension of Reality in the form of vision and audition: the pointing of the moral, the direct application of truth to the awakened self, follow. "And whilst he was thus moved, straightway—a thing unheard of for long ages!—the painted image of Christ Crucified spoke to him from out its pictured lips. And, calling him by his name, "Francis," it said, "go, repair My house, the which as thou seest is falling into decay." And Francis trembled, being utterly amazed, and almost as it were carried away by these words. And he prepared to obey, for he was wholly set on the fulfilling of this commandment. But *forasmuch as he felt that the change he had undergone was ineffable,* it becomes us to be silent concerning it...." From this time he "gave untiring toil to the repair of that Church. For though the words which were said to him concerned that divine Church which Christ bought with His own Blood, he would not hasten to such heights, but little by little from things of the flesh would pass to those of the Spirit."

In a moment of time, Francis's whole universe has suffered complete rearrangement. There are no hesitations, no uncertainties. The change, which he cannot describe, he knows to be central for life. Not for a moment does he think of disobeying the imperative voice which speaks to him from a higher plane of reality and demands the sacrifice of his career.

Compare now with the experience of St. Francis that of another great saint and mystic, who combined, as he did, the active with the contemplative life. Catherine of Genoa, who seems to have possessed from childhood a religious nature, was prepared for the remaking of her consciousness by years of loneliness and depression, the result of an unhappy marriage. She, like St. Francis—but in sorrow rather than in joy—had oscillated between the world, which did not soothe her, and religion, which helped her no more. At last, she had sunk into a state of dull wretchedness, a hatred alike of herself and of life.

Her emancipation was equally abrupt. In the year 1474, she being twenty-six years old, "The day after the feast of St. Benedict (at the instance of her sister that was a nun), Catherine went to make her confession to the confessor of that nunnery; but she was not disposed to do it. Then said her sister, 'At least go and recommend yourself to him, because he is a most worthy religious'; and in fact he was a very holy man. And suddenly, as she knelt before him, she received in her heart the wound of the unmeasured Love of God, with so clear a vision of her own misery and her faults, and of the goodness of God, that she almost fell upon the ground. And by these sensations of infinite love, and of the offenses that had been done against this most sweet God, she was so greatly drawn by purifying affection away from the poor things of this world that she was almost beside herself, and for this she cried inwardly with ardent love, 'No more world! no more sin!' And at this point if she had possessed a thousand worlds, she would have thrown all of them away.... And she returned home, kindled and deeply wounded with so great a love of God, the which had been shown her inwardly, with the sight of her own wretchedness, that she seemed beside herself. And she shut herself in a chamber, the most secluded she could find, with burning sighs. And in this moment she was inwardly taught the whole practice of orison: but her tongue could say naught but this—'O Love, can it be that thou has called me with so great a love, and made me to know in one instant that which worlds cannot express?'" This intuition of the Absolute was followed by an interior vision of Christ bearing the Cross, which further increased her love and self-abasement. "And she cried again, 'O Love, no more sins! no more sins!' And her hatred of herself was more than she could endure."

Of this experience Von Hügel says, "If the tests of reality in such things are their persistence and large and rich spiritual applicability and fruitfulness, then something profoundly real and important took place in the soul of that sad and weary woman of six-and-twenty, within that convent-chapel, at that Annunciation-tide." It is certain that for St. Catherine, as for St. Francis, an utterly new life did, literally, begin at this point. The centre of interest was shifted and the field of consciousness remade. She "knew in an instant that which words cannot express." Some veil about her heart was torn away; so abruptly, that it left a wound behind. For the first time she saw and knew the Love in which life is bathed; and all the energy and passion of a strong nature responded to its call.

The conversion of Madame Guyon to the mystic life, of her Autobiography—"How a holy Religious caused her to find God within her heart, with Admirable Results," is its characteristic title—is curiously like a dilute version of this experience of St. Catherine's. It, too, followed upon a period of mental distress; also the result of an uncongenial marriage. But since Madame Guyon's unbalanced, diffuse, and sentimental character entirely lacks the richness and dignity, the repressed ardours and exquisite delicacy of St. Catherine's mind, so, too, her account of her own interior processes is marred by a terrible and unctuous interest in the peculiar graces vouchsafed to her.

Madame Guyon's value to the student of mysticism partly consists in this feeble quality of her surface-intelligence, which hence had little or no modifying or contributory effect upon her spiritual life and makes her an ideal "laboratory specimen" for the religious psychologist. True to her great principle of passivity or "quiet," it lets the uncriticized interior impulses have their way; thus we are able to observe their workings uncomplicated by the presence of a vigorous intellect or a disciplined will. The wind that bloweth where it listeth whistles through her soul: and the response which she makes is that of a weathercock rather than a windmill. She moves to every current; she often mistakes a draught for the divine breath; she feels her gyrations to be of enormous importance. But in the description of her awakening to the deeper life, even her effusive style acquires a certain dignity.

Madame Guyon had from her childhood exhibited an almost tiresome taste for pious observances. At twelve years old she studied St. François de Sales and St. Jeanne Françoise de Chantal; begged her confessor to teach her the art of mental prayer; and when he omitted to do so, tried to teach herself, but without result. She wished at this time to become a nun of the Visitation, as St. Catherine at the same age wanted to be an Augustinian canoness; but as the longings of little girls of twelve for the cloister are seldom taken seriously, we are not surprised to find the refusal of her parents' consent chronicled in the chapter which is headed *"Diverses croix chez M. son pèr."* Growing up into an unusually beautiful young woman, she went into society, and for a short time enjoyed life in an almost worldly way. Her marriage with Jacques Guyon, however—a marriage of which she signed the articles without even being told the bridegroom's name—put an end to her gaiety. "The whole town was pleased by this marriage; and in all this rejoicing only I was sad... hardly was I married, when the remembrance of my old desire to be a nun overcame me."

Her early married life was excessively unhappy. She was soon driven to look for comfort in the practices of religion. "Made to love much, and finding nothing to love around her, she gave her love to God", says Guerrier tersely. But she was not satisfied: like most of her fellow-contemplatives, she was already vaguely conscious of something that she missed, some vital power unused, and identified this something with the "orison of quiet," the "practice of the presence of God" which mystically minded friends had described to her. She tried to attain to it deliberately, and naturally failed. "I could not give myself by multiplicity that which Thou Thyself givest, and which is only experienced in simplicity."

When these interior struggles had lasted for nearly two years, and Madame Guyon was nineteen, the long desired, almost despaired of, apprehension came—as it did to St. Catherine—suddenly, magically almost; and under curiously parallel conditions. It was the result of a few words spoken by a Franciscan friar whom a "secret force" acting in her interest had brought into the neighbourhood, and whom she had been advised to consult. He was a recluse, who disliked hearing the confessions of women, and appears to have been far from pleased by her visit; an annoyance which he afterwards attributed to her fashionable appearance, "which filled him with apprehension." "He hardly came forward, and was a long time without speaking to me. I, however, did not fail to speak to him and to tell him in a few words my difficulties on the subject of orison. He at once replied, 'Madame, you are seeking without that which you have within. Accustom yourself to seek God in your own heart, and you will find him.'

Having said this, he left me. The next morning he was greatly astonished when I again visited him and told him the effect which these words had had upon my soul:

for, indeed, they were as an arrow, which pierced my heart through and through. I felt in this moment a *profound wound,* which was full of delight and of love—a wound so sweet that I desired that it might never heal. These words had put into my heart that which I sought for so many years, or, rather, they caused me to find that which was there. O, my Lord, you were within my heart, and you asked of me only that I should return within, in order that I might feel your presence. O, Infinite Goodness, you were so near, and I running here and there to seek you, found you not!" She, too, like St. Catherine, learned in this instant the long-sought practice of orison, or contemplation. "From the moment of which I have spoken, my orison was emptied of all form, species, and images; nothing of my orison passed through the mind; but it was an orison of joyous possession in the Will, where the taste for God was so great, pure, and simple that it attracted and absorbed the two other powers of the soul in a profound recollection without action or speech."

Take now the case of a less eminent mystic, who has also left behind him a vivid personal description of his entrance upon the Mystic Way. Rulman Merswin was a wealthy, pious, and respected merchant of Strassburg. In the year 1347, when he was about thirty-six years old, he retired from business in order that he might wholly devote himself to religious matters. It was the time of that spiritual revival within the Catholic Church in Germany which, largely influenced by the great Rhenish mystics Suso and Tauler, is identified with the "Friends of God"; and Merswin himself was one of Tauler's disciples.

One evening, in the autumn which followed his retirement, "about the time of Martinmas," he was strolling in his garden alone. Meditating as he walked, a picture of the Crucifix suddenly presented itself to his mind. In such an imaginary vision as this there is nothing, of course, that we can call abnormal. The thoughts of a devout Catholic, influenced by Tauler and his school, must often have taken such a direction during his solitary strolls. This time, however, the mental image of the Cross seems to have released subconscious forces which had long been gathering way. Merswin was abruptly filled with a violent hatred of the world and of his own free-will. "Lifting his eyes to heaven he solemnly swore that he would utterly surrender his own will, person, and goods to the service of God."

This act of complete surrender, releasing as it were the earthbound self, was at once followed by the onset of pure mystical perception. "The reply from on high came quickly. A brilliant light shone about him: he heard in his ears a divine voice of adorable sweetness; he felt as if he were lifted from the ground and carried several times completely round his garden." Optical disturbance, auditions, and the sense of levitation, are of course frequent physical accompaniments of these shiftings of the level of consciousness. There are few cases in which one or other is not present and in some we find all. Coming to himself after this experience, Merswin's heart was filled by a new consciousness of the Divine; and by a transport of intense love towards God which made him undertake with great energy the acts of mortification which he believed necessary to the purification of his soul. From this time onwards, his mystical consciousness steadily developed. That it was a consciousness wholly different in kind from the sincere piety which had previously caused him to retire from business in order to devote himself to religious truth, is proved by the name of *Conversion* which he applies to the vision of the garden; and by the fact that he dates from this point the beginning of his real life.

The conversion of Merswin's greater contemporary, Suso, seems to have been less abrupt. Of its first stage he speaks vaguely at the beginning of his autobiography, wherein he says that "he began to be converted when in the eighteenth year of his age." He was at this time, as St. Francis had been, restless, dissatisfied; vaguely conscious of something essential to his peace, as yet unfound. His temperament, at once deeply human and ardently spiritual, passionately appreciative of sensuous beauty yet unable to rest in it, had not "unified itself": nor did it do so completely until after a period of purgation which is probably unequalled for its austerity in the history of the mysticism of the West. "He was kept of God in this, that when he turned to those things that most enticed him he found neither happiness nor peace therein. He was restless, and-it seemed to him that something which was as yet unknown could alone give peace to his heart. And he suffered greatly of this restlessness.... God at last delivered him by a complete conversion. His brothers in religion were astonished by so quick a change: for the event took them unawares. Some said of it one thing, and some another but none could know the reason of his conversion. It was God Who, *by a hidden light,* had caused this return to Himself."

This secret conversion was completed by a more violent uprush of the now awakened and active transcendental powers. Suso, whom one can imagine as a great and highly nervous artist if his genius had not taken the channel of sanctity instead, was subject all his life to visions of peculiar richness and beauty. Often these visions seem to have floated up, as it were, from the subliminal region without disturbing the course of his conscious life; and to be little more than pictorial images of his ardour towards and intuition of, divine realities. The great ecstatic vision—or rather apprehension—with which the series opens, however, is of a very different kind; and represents the characteristic experience of Ecstasy in its fullest form. It is described with a detail and intensity which make it a particularly valuable document of the mystical life. It is doubtful whether Suso ever *saw* more than this: the course of his long education rather consisted in an adjustment of his nature to the Reality which he then perceived.

"In the first days of his conversion it happened upon the Feast of St. Agnes, when the Convent had breakfasted at midday, that the Servitor went into the choir. He was alone, and he placed himself in the last stall on the prior's side. And he was in much suffering, for a heavy trouble weighed upon his heart. And being there alone, and devoid of all consolations—no one by his side, no one near him—of a sudden his soul was rapt in his body, or out of his body. Then did he see and hear that which no tongue can express.

"That which the Servitor saw had no form neither any manner of being; yet he had of it a joy such as he might have known in the seeing of the shapes and substances of all joyful things. His heart was hungry, yet satisfied, his soul was full of contentment and joy: his prayers and hopes were all fulfilled. And the Friar could do naught but contemplate this Shining Brightness, and he altogether forgot himself and all other things. Was it day or night? He knew not. It was, as it were, a manifestation of the sweetness of Eternal Life in the sensations of silence and of rest. Then he said, 'If that which I see and feel be not the Kingdom of Heaven, I know not what it can be: for it is very sure that the endurance of all possible pains were but a poor price to pay for the eternal possession of so great a joy.'"

The physical accompaniments of ecstasy were also present. "This ecstasy lasted from half an hour to an hour, and whether his soul were in the body or out of the body he could not tell. But when he came to his senses it seemed to him that he returned from another world. And so greatly did his body suffer in this short rapture that it seemed to him that none, even in dying, could suffer so greatly in so short a time. The Servitor came to himself moaning, and he fell down upon the ground like a man who swoons. And he cried inwardly, heaving great sighs from the depth of his soul and saying, 'Oh, my God, where was I and where am I?' And again, 'Oh, my heart's joy, never shall my soul forget this hour!' He walked, but it was but his body that walked, as a machine might do. None knew from his demeanour that which was taking place within. But his soul and his spirit were full of marvels; heavenly lightnings passed and repassed in the deeps of his being, and it seemed to him that he walked on air. And all the powers of his soul were full of these heavenly delights. He was like a vase from which one has taken a precious ointment, but in which the perfume long remains."

Finally, the last phrases seem to suggest the true position of this exalted pleasure-state as a first link in the long chain of mystical development. "This foretaste of the happiness of heaven," he says, "the which the Servitor enjoyed for many days, excited in him a most lively desire for God."

Mystical activity, then, like all other activities of the self, opens with that sharp stimulation of the will, which can only be obtained through the emotional life.

Suso was a scholar, and an embryo ecclesiastic. During the period which elapsed between his conversion and his description of it, he was a disciple of Meister Eckhart, a student of Dionysius and St. Thomas Aquinas. His writings show familiarity with the categories of mystical theology and naturally enough this circumstance, and also the fact that they were written for purposes of edification, may have dictated to some extent the language in which his conversion-ecstasy is described. As against this, I will give two first-hand descriptions of mystical conversion in which it is obvious that theological learning plays little or no part. Both written in France within a few years of one another, they represent the impact of Reality on two minds of very different calibre. One is the secret document in which a great genius set down, in words intended only for his own eyes, the record of a two hours' ecstasy. The other is the plain, unvarnished statement of an uneducated man of the peasant class. The first is, of course, the celebrated Memorial, or Amulet, of Pascal; the second is the Relation of Brother Lawrence.

The Memorial of Pascal is a scrap of parchment on which, round a rough drawing of the Flaming Cross, there are written a few strange phrases, abrupt and broken words; all we know about one of the strangest ecstatic revelations chronicled in the history of the mystic type. After Pascal's death a servant found a copy of this little document, now lost, sewn up in his doublet. He seems always to have worn it upon his person: a perpetual memorial of the supernal experience, the initiation into Reality, which it describes. Though Bremand has shown that the opening of Pascal's spiritual eyes had begun, on his own declaration, eleven months earlier, "d'une manière douce et obligeante," the conversion thus prepared was only made actual by this abrupt illumination; ending a long period of spiritual stress, in which indifference to his ordinary interests was counterbalanced by an utter inability to feel the attractive force of that Divine Reality which his great mind discerned as the only adequate object of desire.

The Memorial opens thus:

"L'an de grace 1654
lundi, 23 novembre, jour de Saint Clément, pape
et martyr, et autres au martyrologe,
veille de Saint Chrysogone, martyr et autres
depuis environ dix heures et demie du soir jusques
environ minuit et demie,
Feu."

"From half-past ten till half-past twelve, Fire!" That is all, so far as description is concerned; but enough, apparently, to remind the initiate of all that passed. The rest tells us only the passion of joy and conviction which this nameless revelation—this long, blazing vision of Reality—brought in its train. It is but a series of amazed exclamations, crude, breathless words, placed there helter-skelter, the artist in him utterly in abeyance; the names of the overpowering emotions which swept him, one after the other, as the Fire of Love disclosed its secrets, evoked an answering flame of humility and rapture in his soul.

"Dieu d'Abraham, Dieu d'Isaac, Dieu de Jacob,
Non des philosophes et des savants.
Certitude. Certitude. Sentiment. Joie. Paix".

"Not the God of philosophers and of scholars!" cries in amazement this great scholar and philosopher abruptly turned from knowledge to love.

"Oubli du monde et de tout hormis Dieu," he says again, seeing his universe suddenly swept clean of all but this Transcendent Fact. Then, "Le monde ne t'a point connu, *mais je t'ai connu.* Joie! joie joie! pleurs de joie!" Compare with the classic style, the sharp and lucid definition of the "Pensées," the irony and glitter of the "Provinciales," these little broken phrases—this child-like stammering speech—in which a supreme master of language has tried to tell his wonder and his delight. I know few things in the history of mysticism at once more convincing, more poignant than this hidden talisman; upon which the brilliant scholar and stylist, the merciless disputant, has jotted down in hard, crude words, which yet seem charged with passion—the inarticulate language of love—a memorial of the certitude, the peace, the joy, above all, the reiterated, all-surpassing joy, which accompanied his ecstatic apprehension of God.

" Mon Dieu, me quitterez vous?" he says again; the fire apparently beginning to die down, the ecstasy drawing to an end. " Que je n'en sois pas séparé éternellement!" "Are you going to leave me? Oh, let me not be separated from you for ever!—the one unendurable thought which would, said Aquinas, rob the Beatific Vision of its glory, were we not sure that it can never fade. But the rhapsody is over, the vision of the Fire has gone; and the rest of the Memorial clearly contains Pascal's meditations upon his experience, rather than a transcript of the experience itself. It ends with the watchword of all mysticism, Surrender—" Renonciation, totale et douce" in Pascal's words—the only way, he thinks, in which he can avoid continued separation from Reality.

Pascal's vision of Light, Life, and Love was highly ecstatic; an indescribable, incommunicable experience, which can only be suggested by his broken words of certitude and joy. By his simple contemporary, Brother Lawrence, that Transcendent Reality Who "is not the God of philosophers and scholars," was perceived in a moment of abrupt intuition, peculiarly direct, unecstatic and untheological in type, but absolutely enduring in its results. Lawrence was an uneducated young man of the peasant class; who first served as a soldier, and afterwards as a footman in a great French family, where he annoyed his masters by breaking everything. When he was between fifty and sixty years of age, he entered the Carmelite Order as a lay brother; and the letters, "spiritual maxims," and conversations belonging to this period of his life were published after his death in 1691. "He told me," says the anonymous reporter of the conversations, supposed to be M. Beaufort, who was about 1660 Grand Vicar to the Cardinal de Noailles, "that God had done him a singular favour in his conversion at the age of eighteen. That in the winter, seeing a tree stripped of its leaves, and considering that within a little time the leaves would be renewed, and after that the flowers and fruit appear, he received a high view of the Providence and Power of God, which has never since been effaced from his soul. That this view had set him perfectly loose from the world and kindled in him such a love for God that he could not tell whether it had increased in above forty years that he had lived since."

Such use of visible nature as the stuff of ontological perceptions, the medium whereby the self reaches out to the Absolute, is not rare in the history of mysticism. The mysterious vitality of trees, the silent magic of the forest, the strange and steady cycle of its life, possess in a peculiar degree this power of unleashing the human soul: are curiously friendly to its cravings, minister to its inarticulate needs. Unsullied by the corroding touch of consciousness, that life can make a contact with the "great life of the All"; and through its mighty rhythms man can receive a message concerning the true and timeless World of "all that is, and was, and evermore shall be." Plant life of all kinds, indeed, from the "flower in the crannied wall" to the "Woods of Westermain" can easily become, for selves of a certain type, a "mode of the Infinite." So obvious does this appear when we study the history of the mystics, that Steiner has drawn from it the hardly warrantable inference that "plants are just those natural phenomena whose qualities in the higher world are similar to their qualities in the physical world."

Though the conclusion be not convincing, the fact remains. The flowery garment of the world is for some mystics a medium of ineffable perception, a source of exalted joy, the veritable clothing of God. I need hardly add that such a state of things has always been found incredible by common sense. "The tree which moves some to tears of joy," says Blake, who possessed in an eminent degree this form of sacramental perception, "is in the Eyes of others only a green thing that stands in the Way."

Such a perception of the Divine in Nature, of the true and holy meaning of that rich, unresting life in which we are immersed, is really a more usual feature of Illumination than of Conversion. All the most marked examples of it must be referred to that state; and will be discussed when we come to its consideration. Sometimes, however, as in the case of Brother Lawrence, the first awakening of the self to consciousness of Reality does take this form. The Uncreated Light manifests Itself in and through created things. This characteristically immanental discovery of the Absolute occurs chiefly in two classes: in unlettered men who have lived close to Nature, and to whom her symbols are more familiar than those of the Churches or the schools, and in temperaments of the mixed or mystical type, who are nearer to the poet than to the true contemplative, for whom as a rule the Absolute "hath no image." "It was like entering into another world, a new state of existence," says a witness quoted by Starbuck, speaking of his own conversion. "Natural objects were glorified. My spiritual vision was so clarified that I saw beauty in every material object in the universe. The woods were vocal with heavenly music." "Oh, how I was changed! Everything became new. My horses and hogs and everybody became changed!" exclaims with naive astonishment another in the same collection. "When I went in the morning into the fields to work," says a third, "the glory of God appeared in all His visible creation. I well remember we reaped oats, and how every straw and head of the oats seemed, as it were, arrayed in a kind of rainbow glory, or to glow, if I may so express it, in the glory of God."

Amongst modern men, Walt Whitman possessed in a supreme degree the permanent sense of this glory, the "light rare, untellable, lighting the very light." But evidences of its existence, and the sporadic power of apprehending it, are scattered up and down the literature of the world. Its discovery constitutes the awakening of the mystical consciousness in respect of the World of Becoming: a sharp and sudden break with the old and obvious way of seeing things. The human cinematograph has somehow changed its rhythm, and begins to register new and more real aspects of the external world. With this, the self's first escape from the limitations of its conventional universe, it receives an immense assurance of a great and veritable life surrounding, sustaining, explaining its own. Thus Richard Jefferies says, of the same age as that at which Suso and Brother Lawrence awoke to sudden consciousness of Reality, "I was not more than eighteen when an inner and esoteric meaning began to come to me from all the visible universe." "I now became lost, and absorbed into the being or existence of the universe... and losing thus my separateness of being, came to seem like a part of the whole." "I feel on the margin of a life unknown, very near, almost touching it—on the verge of powers which, if I could grasp, would give men an immense breadth of existence."

What was this "life unknown" but the Life known to the great mystics, which Richard Jefferies apprehended in these moments of insight, yet somehow contrived to miss?

Such participation in the deep realities of the World of Becoming, the boundless existence of a divine whole—which a modern psychologist has labelled and described as "Cosmic Consciousness" —whilst it is not the final object of the mystic's journey, is a constant feature of it. It may represent one-half of his characteristic consciousness: an entrance into communion with the second of the Triune Powers of God, the Word which "is through all things everlastingly." Jefferies stood, as so many mystically minded men have done, upon the verge of such a transcendental life. The "heavenly door," as Rolle calls it, was ajar but not pushed wide. He peeped through it to the greater world beyond; but, unable to escape from the bonds of his selfhood, he did not pass through to live upon the independent spiritual plane.

Rolle, Jefferies's fellow countryman, and his predecessor by close upon six hundred years in the ecstatic love and understanding of natural things, shall be our last example of the mystical awakening. He, like his spiritual brother St. Francis, and other typical cases, had passed through a preliminary period of struggle and oscillation between worldly life and a vague but growing spirituality: between the superficial and the deeper self. "My youth was fond, my childhood vain, my young age unclean," but "when I should flourish unhappily, and youth of wakeful age was now come, the grace of my Maker was near, the which lust of temporal shape restrained, and unto ghostly supplications turned my desires, and the soul, from low things lifted, to heaven has borne."

The real "life-changing," however, was sharply and characteristically marked off from this preparatory state. Rolle associates it with the state which he calls "Heat": the form in which his ardour of soul was translated to the surface consciousness. "Heat soothly I call when the mind truly is kindled in Love Everlasting, and the heart on the same manner to burn not hopingly but verily is felt. The heart truly turned into fire, gives feeling of burning love." This burning heat is not merely a mental experience. In it we seem to have an unusual but not unique form of psychophysical parallelism: a bodily expression of the psychic travail and distress accompanying the "New Birth." "More have I marvelled than I show, forsooth," he says in his prologue, "when I first felt my heart wax warm, and truly, *not imaginingly, but as it were with a sensible fire,* burned. I was forsooth marvelled, as this burning burst up in my soul, and of an unwonted solace; for in my ignorance of such healing abundance, oft have I groped my breast, seeing whether this burning were of any bodily cause outwardly. But when I knew that only it was kindled of ghostly cause inwardly, and this burning was naught of fleshly love or desire, in this I conceived it was the gift of my Maker." Further on, he gives another and more detailed account. "From the beginning, forsooth, of my life-changing and of my mind, to the opening of the heavenly door which Thy Face showed, that the heart might behold heavenly things and see by what way its Love it might seek and busily desire, three years are run except three months or four. The door, forsooth, biding open, a year near-by I passed unto the time in which the heat of Love Everlasting was verily felt in heart. I sat forsooth in a chapel and whilst with sweetness of prayer and meditation greatly I was delighted, suddenly in me I felt a merry heat and unknown. But at first I wondered, doubting of whom it should be; but a long time I am assured that not of the Creature but of my Maker it was, for more hot and gladder I found it."

To this we must add a passage which I cannot but think one of the most beautiful expressions of spiritual joy to be found in mystical literature. Based though it certainly is upon a passage in St. Augustine—for the nightingale is not a Yorkshire bird—its sketch of the ideal mystic life, to the cultivation of which he then set himself, reveals in a few lines the most charming aspect of Rolle's spirituality, its poetic fervour, its capacity for ardent love.

"In the beginning truly of my conversion and singular purpose, I though I would be like the little bird that for love of her lover longs, but in her longing she is gladdened when he comes that she loves. And joying she sings, and singing she longs, but in sweetness and heat. It is said the nightingale to song and melody all night is given, that she may please him to whom she is joined. How muckle more with greatest sweetness to Christ my Jesu should I sing, that is spouse of my soul by all this present life, that is night in regard of clearness to come."

Glancing back at the few cases here brought together, we can see in them, I think, certain similarities and diversities which are often of great psychological interest and importance and have their influence upon the subsequent development of the mystic life. We see in particular at this point—before purification, or the remaking of character, begins—the reaction of the natural self, its heart and its mind, upon that uprush of new truth which operates "mystical conversion." This reaction is highly significant, and gives us a clue not only to the future development of the mystic, but to the general nature of man's spiritual consciousness.

We have said that this consciousness in its full development seems to be extended not in one but in two directions. These directions, these two fundamental ways of apprehending Reality may be called the eternal and temporal, transcendent and immanent, absolute and dynamic aspects of Truth. They comprise the twofold knowledge of a God Who is both Being and Becoming near and far: pairs of opposites which the developed mystical experience will carry up into a higher synthesis. But the first awakening of the mystic sense, the first breaking in of the suprasensible upon the soul, commonly involves the emergence of one only of these complementary forms of perception. One side always wakes first: the incoming message always choosing the path of least resistance. Hence mystical conversion tends to belong to one of two distinctive types: tends also, as regards its expression, to follow that temperamental inclination to objectivize Reality as a Place, a Person, or a State which we found to govern the symbolic systems of the mystics.

There is first, then, the apprehension of a splendour without: an expansive, formless, ineffable vision, a snatching up of the self, as it were, from knowledge of this world to some vague yet veritable knowledge of the next. The veil parts, and the Godhead is perceived as transcendent to, yet immanent in, the created universe. Not the personal touch of love transfiguring the soul, but the impersonal glory of a transfigured world, is the dominant note of this experience and the reaction of the self takes the form of awe and rapture rather than of intimate affection. Of such a kind was the conversion of Suso, and in a less degree of Brother Lawrence. Of this kind also were the Light which Rulman Merswin saw, and the mystical perception of the Being of the universe reported by Richard Jefferies and countless others.

This experience, if it is to be complete, if it is to involve the definite emergence of the self from "the prison of I-hood," its setting out upon the Mystic Way, requires an act of concentration on the self's part as the complement of its initial act of expansion. It must pass beyond the stage of metaphysical rapture or fluid splendour, and crystallize into a willed response to the Reality perceived; a definite and personal relation must be set up between the self and the Absolute Life. To be a spectator of Reality is not enough. The awakened subject is not merely to perceive transcendent life, but to participate therein; and for this, a drastic and costly life-changing is required. In Jefferies's case this crystallization, this heroic effort towards participation did not take place, and he never therefore laid hold of "the glory that has been revealed." In Suso's it did, "exciting in him a most lively desire for God."

In most cases this crystallization, the personal and imperative concept which the mind constructs from the general and ineffable intuition of Reality, assumes a theological character. Often it presents itself to the consciousness in the form of visions or voices: objective, as the Crucifix which spoke to St. Francis, or mental, as the visions of the Cross experienced by Rulman Merswin and St. Catherine of Genoa. Nearly always, this concept, this intimate realization of the divine, has reference to the love and sorrow at the heart of things, the discord between Perfect Love and an imperfect world; whereas the complementary vision of Transcendence strikes a note of rapturous joy. "The beatings of the Heart of God sounded like so many invitations which thus spake: Come and do penance, come and be reconciled, come and be consoled, come and be blessed; come, My love, and receive all that the Beloved can give to His beloved.... Come, My bride, and enjoy My Godhead."

It is to this personal touch, to the individual appeal of an immediate Presence, not to the great light and the Beatific Vision, that the awakened self makes its most ardent, most heroic response. Not because he was rapt from himself, but because the figure on the Cross called him by name, saying, "Repair My Church" did St. Francis, with that simplicity, that disregard of worldly values which constituted his strength, accept the message in a literal sense and set himself instantly to the work demanded; bringing stones, and, in defiance alike of comfort and convention, building up with his own hands the crumbling walls.

In many conversions to the mystic life, the revelation of an external splendour, the shining vision of the transcendent spiritual world, is wholly absent. The self awakes to that which is within, rather than to that which is without: to the immanent not the transcendent God, to the personal not the cosmic relation. Where those who look out receive the revelation of Divine Beauty, those who look in receive rather the wound of Divine Love: another aspect of the "triple star." Emotional mystics such as Richard Rolle and Madame Guyon give us this experience in an extreme form. We find in St. Catherine of Genoa a nobler example of the same type of response. That inward revelation in its anguish and abruptness, its rending apart of the hard tissues of I-hood and vivid disclosures of the poverty of the finite self, seemed, says the legend of St. Catherine "the wound of Unmeasured Love," an image in which we seem to hear the very accents of the saint. "A wound full of delight," says the effusive Madame Guyon, "I wished that it might never heal." Rolle calls this piercing rapture a great heat: the heat which is to light the Fire of Love. "As it were if the finger were put in fire, it should be clad with feeling of burning so the soul with love (as aforesaid) set afire, truly feels most very heat."

Love, passionate and all-dominant, here takes the place of that joyous awe which we noticed as the characteristic reaction upon reality in conversions of the Transcendent type. In the deep and strong temperaments of the great mystics this love passes quickly—sometimes instantly—from the emotional to the volitional stage. Their response to the voice of the Absolute is not merely an effusion of sentiment, but an act of will: an act often of so deep and comprehensive a kind as to involve the complete change of the outward no less than of the inward life. "Divine love," says Dionysius "draws those whom it seizes beyond themselves and this so greatly that they belong no longer to themselves but wholly to the Object loved."

Merswin's oath of self-surrender: St. Catherine of Genoa's passionate and decisive "No more world! no more sins!": St. Francis's naive and instant devotion to church-restoration in its most literal sense: these things are earnests of the reality of the change. They represent—symbolize as well as they can upon the sensual plane—the spontaneous response of the living organism to a fresh external stimulus: its first effort of adjustment to the new conditions which that stimulus represents. They complete the process of conversion; which is not one-sided, not merely an infusion into the surface-consciousness of new truth, but rather the beginning of a life-process, a breaking down of the old and building up of the new. A never to be ended give-and-take is set up between the individual and the Absolute. The Spirit of Life has been born and the first word it learns to say is *Abba,* Father. It aspires to its origin, to Life in its most intense manifestation, hence all its instincts urge it to that activity which it feels to be inseparable from life. It knows itself a member of that mighty family in which the stars are numbered, the family of the sons of God, who, free and creative, sharing the rapture of a living, striving Cosmos, "shout for joy."

So, even in its very beginning, we see how active, how profoundly organic, how deeply and widely alive is the true contemplative life; how truly on the transcendent as on the phenomenal plane, the law of living things is action and reaction, force and energy. The awakening of the self is to a new and more active plane of being, new and more personal relations with Reality; hence to a new and more real work which it must do.

THE PURIFICATION OF THE SHELF

Here, then, stands the newly awakened self: aware, for the first time, of reality, responding to that reality by deep movements of love and of awe. She sees herself, however, not merely to be thrust into a new world, but set at the beginning of a new road. Activity is now to be her watchword, pilgrimage the business of her life. "That a quest there is, and an end, is the single secret spoken." Under one symbol or another, the need of that long slow process of transcendence, of character building, whereby she is to attain freedom, become capable of living upon high levels of reality, is present in her consciousness. Those in whom this growth is not set going are no mystics, in the exact sense in which that word is here used; however great their temporary illumination may have been.

What must be the first step of the self upon this road to perfect union with the Absolute? Clearly, a getting rid of all those elements of normal experience which are not in harmony with reality: of illusion, evil, imperfection of every kind. By false desires and false thoughts man has built up for himself a false universe: as a mollusk by the deliberate and persistent absorption of lime and rejection of all else, can build up for itself a hard shell which shuts it from the external world, and only represents in 199 a distorted and unrecognisable form the ocean from which it was obtained. This hard and wholly unnutritious shell, this one-sided secretion of the surface-consciousness, makes as it were a little cave of illusion for each separate soul. A literal and deliberate getting out of the cave must be for every mystic, as it was for Plato's prisoners, the first step in the individual hunt for reality.

In the plain language of old-fashioned theology "man's sin is stamped upon man's universe." We see a sham world because we live a sham life. We do not know ourselves, hence do not know the true character of our senses and instincts; hence attribute wrong values to their suggestions and declarations concerning our relation to the external world. That world, which we have distorted by identifying it with our own self-regarding arrangements of its elements, has got to reassume for us the character of Reality, of God. In the purified sight of the great mystics it did reassume this character: their shells were opened wide, they knew the tides of the Eternal Sea. This lucid apprehension of the True is what we mean when we speak of the Illumination which results from a faithful acceptance of the trials of the Purgative Way.

That which we call the "natural" self as it exists in the "natural" world—the "old Adam" of St. Paul—is wholly incapable of supersensual adventure. All its activities are grouped about a centre of consciousness whose correspondences are with the material world. In the moment of its awakening, it is abruptly made aware of this disability. It knows itself finite. It now aspires to the infinite. It is encased in the hard crust of individuality: it aspires to union with a larger self. It is fettered: it longs for freedom. Its every sense is attuned to illusion: it craves for harmony with the Absolute Truth. "God is the only Reality," says Patmore, "and we are real only as far as we are in His order and He is in us." Whatever form, then, the mystical adventure may take it, must begin with a change in the attitude of the subject; a change which will introduce it into the order of Reality, and enable it to set up permanent relations with an Object which is not normally part of its universe. Therefore, though the end of mysticism is not adequately defined as goodness, it entails the acquirement of goodness. The virtues are the "ornaments of the spiritual marriage" because that marriage is union with the Good no less than with the Beautiful and the True.

Primarily, then, the self must be purged of all that stands between it and goodness: putting on the character of reality instead of the character of illusion or "sin." It longs ardently to do this from the first moment in which it sees itself in the all-revealing radiance of the Uncreated Light. "When love 200 openeth the inner eyes of the soul for to see this truth," says Hilton, "with other circumstances that come withal then beginneth the soul for sooth to be vastly meek. For then by the sight of God it feeleth and seeth itself as it is, and then doth the soul forsake the beholding and leaning to itself."

So, with Dante, the first terrace of the Mount of Purgatory is devoted to the cleansing of pride and the production of humility: the inevitable—one might almost say mechanical—result of a vision, however fleeting, of Reality, and an undistorted sight of the earthbound self. All its life that self has been measuring its candlelight by other candles. Now for the first time it is out in the open air and sees the sun. "This is the way," said the voice of God to St. Catherine of Siena in ecstasy. "If thou wilt arrive at a perfect knowledge and enjoyment of Me, the Eternal Truth, thou shouldst never go outside the knowledge of thyself; and by humbling thyself in the valley of humility thou wilt know Me and thyself, from which knowledge thou wilt draw all that is necessary.... In self knowledge, then, thou wilt humble thyself; seeing that, in thyself, thou dost not even exist."

The first thing that the self observes, when it turns back upon itself in that awful moment of lucidity—enters, as St. Catherine says, into "the cell of self-knowledge,"—is the horrible contrast between its clouded contours and the pure sharp radiance of the Real; between its muddled faulty life, its perverse self-centred drifting, and the clear onward sweep of that Becoming in which it is immersed. It is then that the outlook of rapture and awe receives the countersign of repentance. The harbinger of that new self which must be born appears under the aspect of a desire: a passionate longing to escape from the suddenly perceived hatefulness of selfhood, and to conform to Reality, the Perfect which it has seen under its aspect of Goodness, of Beauty, or of Love—to be worthy of it, in fact to be *real*. "This showing," says Gerlac Petersen of that experience, "is so vehement and so strong that the whole of the interior man, not only of his heart but of his body, is marvellously moved and shaken, and faints within itself, unable to endure it. And by this means, his interior aspect is made clear without any cloud, and conformable in its own measure to Him whom he seeks."

The lives of the mystics abound in instances of the "vehemence of this showing": of the deep-seated sense of necessity which urges the newly awakened self to a life of discomfort and conflict, often to intense poverty and pain, as the only way of replacing false experience by true. Here the transcendental consciousness, exalted by a clear intuition of its goal, and not merely "counting" but *perceiving* the world to be obviously well lost for such a prize, takes the reins. It forces on the unwilling surface mind a sharp vision of its own disabilities, its ugly and imperfect life and the thirst for Perfection which is closely bound up with the mystic temperament makes instant response. "No more sins!" was the first cry of St. Catherine of Genoa in that crucial hour in which she saw by the light of love her own self-centred and distorted past. She entered forthwith upon the Purgative Way, in which for four years she suffered under a profound sense of imperfection, endured fasting, solitude and mortification and imposed upon herself the most repulsive duties in her efforts towards that self-conquest which should make her "conformable in her own measure" to the dictates of that Pure Love which was the aspect of reality that she had seen. It is the inner conviction that this conformity—this transcendence of the unreal—is possible and indeed normal which upholds the mystic during the terrible years of Purgation, so that "not only without heaviness, but with a joy unmeasured he casts back all thing that may him let."

To the true lover of the Absolute, Purgation no less than Illumination is a privilege, a dreadful joy. It is an earnest of increasing life. "Let me suffer or die!" said St. Teresa: a strange alternative in the ears of common sense, but a forced option in the spiritual sphere. However harsh its form, however painful the activities to which it spurs him, the mystic recognizes in this breakup of his old universe an essential part of the Great Work and the act in which he turns to it is an act of loving desire, no less than an act of will. "Burning of love into a soul truly taken all vices purgeth:... for whilst the true lover with strong and fervent desire into God is borne, all things him displease that from the sight of God withdrawn." His eyes once opened, he is eager for that costly ordering of his disordered loves which alone can establish his correspondences with Transcendental Life. "Teach me, my only joy," cries Suso, "the way in which I may bear upon my body the marks of Thy Love." "Come, my soul, depart from outward things and gather thyself together into a true interior silence, that thou mayst set out with all thy courage and bury and lose thyself in the desert of a deep contrition."

It is in this torment of contrition, this acute consciousness of unworthiness, that we have the first swing back of the oscillating self from the initial state of mystic pleasure to the complementary state of pain. It is, so to speak, on its transcendental side, the reflex

202 action which follows the first touch of God. Thus, we read that Rulman Merswin, "swept away by the transports of Divine Love," did not surrender himself to the passive enjoyment of this first taste of Absolute Being, but was impelled by it to diligent and instant self-criticism. He was "seized with a hatred of his body, and inflicted on himself such hard mortifications that he fell ill." It is useless for lovers of healthy-mindedness to resent this and similar examples of self-examination and penance: to label them morbid or mediaeval. The fact remains that only such bitter knowledge of wrongness of relation, seen by the light of ardent love, can spur the will of man to the hard task of readjustment.

"I saw full surely," says Julian of Norwich, "that it behoveth needs to be that we should be in longing and in penance, until the time that we be led so deep into God that we verily and truly know our own soul."

Dante's whole journey up the Mount of Purgation is the dramatic presentation of this one truth. So, too, the celebrated description of Purgatory attributed to St. Catherine of Genoa is obviously founded upon its author's inward experience of this Purgative Way. In it, she applies to the souls of the dead her personal consciousness of the necessity of purification; its place in the organic process of spiritual growth. It is, as she acknowledges at the beginning, the projection of her own psychological adventures upon the background of the spiritual world: its substance being simply the repetition after death of that eager and heroic acceptance of suffering, those drastic acts of purification, which she has herself been compelled to undertake under the whip of the same psychic necessity—that of removing the rust of illusion, cleansing the mirror in order that it may receive the divine light. "It is," she says, "as with a covered object, the object cannot respond to the rays of the sun, not because the sun ceases to shine—for it shines without intermission—but because the covering intervenes. Let the covering be destroyed, and again the object will be exposed to the sun, and will answer to the rays which beat against it in proportion as the work of destruction advances. Thus the souls are covered by a rust—that is, by sin—which is gradually consumed away by the fire of purgatory. The more it is consumed, the more they respond to God their true Sun. Their happiness increases as the rust falls off and lays them open to the divine ray... the instinctive tendency to seek happiness in God develops itself, and goes on increasing through the fire of love which draws it to its end with such impetuosity and vehemence that any obstacle seems intolerable; and the more clear its vision, the more extreme its pain."

"Mostratene la via di gire al monte!" cry the souls of the newly-dead in Dante's vision, pushed by that "instinctive tendency" towards the purifying flames. Such a tendency, such a passionate desire, the aspiring self must have. No cool, well-balanced knowledge of the need of new adjustments will avail to set it on the Purgative Way. This is a heroic act, and demands heroic passions in the soul.

"In order to overcome our desires," says St. John of the Cross, who is the classic authority upon this portion of the mystic quest, "and to renounce all those things, our love and inclination for which are wont so to inflame the will that it delights therein, we require a more ardent fire and a nobler love—that of the Bridegroom. Finding her delight and strength in Him, the soul gains the vigour and confidence which enable her easily to abandon all other affections. It was necessary, in her struggle with the attractive force of her sensual desires, not only to have this love for the Bridegroom, but also to be filled with a burning fervour, full of anguish... if our spiritual nature were not on fire with other and nobler passions we should never cast off the yoke of the senses, nor be able to enter on their night, neither should we have the courage to remain in the darkness of all things, and in denial of every desire."

"We must be filled with a burning fervour full of anguish." Only this deep and ardent passion for a perceived Object of Love can persuade the mystic to those unnatural acts of abnegation by which he kills his lesser love of the world of sense, frees himself from the "remora of desire," unifies all his energies about the new and higher centre of his life. His business, I have said, is transcendence: a mounting up, an attainment of a higher order of reality. Once his eyes have been opened on Eternity, his instinct for the Absolute roused from its sleep, he sees union with that Reality as his duty no less than his joy: sees too, that this union can only be consummated on a plane where illusion and selfhood have no place.

The inward voice says to him perpetually, at the least seasonable moments, "Dimitte omnia transitoria, quaere aeterna." Hence the purgation of the senses, and of the character which they have helped to build is always placed first in order in the Mystic Way; though sporadic flashes of illumination and ecstasy may, and often do, precede and accompany it. Since spiritual no less than physical existence, as we know it, is an endless Becoming, it too has no end. In a sense the whole of the mystical experience in this life consists in a series of purifications, whereby the Finite slowly approaches the nature of its Infinite Source: climbing up the cleansing mountain pool by pool, like the industrious fish in Rulman Merswin's vision, until it reaches its Origin. The greatest of the contemplative saints, far from leaving purgation behind them in their progress, were increasingly aware of their own inadequateness, the nearer they approached to the unitive state: for the true lover of the Absolute, like every other lover, is alternately abased and exalted by his unworthiness and his good fortune. There are moments of high rapture when he knows only that the banner over him is Love: but there are others in which he remains bitterly conscious that in spite of his uttermost surrender there is within him an ineradicable residuum of selfhood, which "stains the white radiance of eternity."

In this sense, then, purification is a perpetual process. That which mystical writers mean, however, when they speak of the Way of Purgation, is rather the slow and painful completion of Conversion. It is the drastic turning of the self from the unreal to the real life: a setting of her house in order, an orientation of the mind to Truth. Its business is the getting rid, first of self-love; and secondly of all those foolish interests in which the surface-consciousness is steeped.

"The essence of purgation," says Richard of St. Victor, "is self-simplification." Nothing can happen until this has proceeded a certain distance: till the involved interests and tangled motives of the self are simplified, and the false complications of temporal life are recognized and cast away.

"No one," says another authority in this matter, "can be enlightened unless he be first cleansed or purified and stripped." Purgation, which is the remaking of character in conformity with perceived reality, consists in these two essential acts: the cleansing of that which is to remain, the stripping of that which is to be done away. It may best be studied, therefore, in two parts: and I think that it will be in the reader's interest if we reverse the order which the "Theologia Germanica" adopts, and first consider Negative Purification, or self-stripping, and next Positive Purification, or character-adjustment. These, then, are the branches into which this subject will here be split.

(1) The Negative aspect, the stripping or purging away of those superfluous, unreal, and harmful things which dissipate the precious energies of the self. This is the business of Poverty, or *Detachment*.

(2) The Positive aspect: a raising to their highest term, their purest state, of all that remains—the permanent elements of character. This is brought about by *Mortification*, the gymnastic of the soul: a deliberate recourse to painful experiences and difficult tasks.

Detachment

Apart from the plain necessity of casting out imperfection and sin, what is the type of "good character" which will best serve the self in its journey towards union with the Absolute?

The mystics of all ages and all faiths agree in their answer. Those three virtues which the instinct of the Catholic Church fixed upon as the necessities of the cloistered life—the great Evangelical counsel of voluntary Poverty with its departments, Chastity, the poverty of the senses, and Obedience, the poverty of the will—are also, when raised to their highest term and transmuted by the Fire of Love, the essential virtues of the mystical quest.

By *Poverty* the mystic means an utter self-stripping, the casting off of immaterial as well as material wealth, a complete detachment from all finite things. By *Chastity* he means an extreme and limpid purity of soul, cleansed from personal desire and virgin to all but God: by *Obedience*, that abnegation of selfhood, that mortification of the will, which results in a complete self-abandonment, a "holy indifference" to the accidents of life. These three aspects of perfection are really one: linked together as irrevocably as the three aspects of the self. Their common characteristic is this: they tend to make the subject regard itself, not as an isolated and interesting individual, possessing desires and rights, but as a scrap of the Cosmos, an ordinary bit of the Universal Life, only important as a part of the All, an expression of the Will Divine. Detachment and purity go hand in hand, for purity is but detachment of the heart; and where these are present they bring with them that humble spirit of obedience which expresses detachment of will. We may therefore treat them as three manifestations of one thing: which thing is Inward Poverty. "Blessed are the poor in spirit, for theirs is the Kingdom of Heaven," is the motto of all pilgrims on this road.

"God is pure Good in Himself," says Eckhart, "therefore will He dwell nowhere but in a pure soul. There He can pour Himself out: into that He can wholly flow. What is Purity? It is that a man should have turned himself away from all creatures and have set his heart so entirely on the Pure Good that no creature is to him a comfort, that he has no desire for aught creaturely, save so far as he may apprehend therein the Pure Good, which is God. And as little as the bright eye can endure aught foreign in it, so little can the pure soul bear anything in it, any stain on it, that comes between it and God. To it all creatures are pure to enjoy; for it enjoyeth all creatures in God, and God in all creatures."

"To it all creatures are pure to enjoy!" This is hardly the popular concept of the mystic; which credits him, in the teeth of such examples as St. Francis, St. Mechthild of Magdeburg, Rolle, Suso, and countless others, with a hearty dread of natural things. Too many examples of an exaggerated asceticism—such as the unfortunate story told of the holy Curé d'Ars, who refused to smell a rose for fear of sin—have supported in this respect the vulgar belief; for it is generally forgotten that though most mystics have practised asceticism as a means to an end, all ascetics are not mystics. Whatever may be the case with other deniers of the senses, it is true that the soul of the great mystic, dwelling on high levels of reality, his eyes set on the Transcendental World, is capable of combining with the perfection of detachment that intense and innocent joy in natural things, as veils and vessels of the divine, which results from seeing "all creatures in God and God in all creatures." "Who so knows and loves the nobleness of My Freedom," said the voice of God to Mechthild of Magdeburg, "cannot bear to love Me alone, he must love also Me in the creatures." That all-embracing love is characteristic of the illumination which results from a faithful endurance of the Purgative Way; for the corollary of "blessed are the pure in heart" is not merely a poetic statement. The annals of mysticism prove it to be a psychological law.

How then is this contradiction to be resolved: that the mystic who has declared the fundamental necessity of "leaving all creatures" yet finds them pure to enjoy? The answer to the riddle lies in the ancient paradox of Poverty: that we only enjoy true liberty in respect of such things as we neither possess nor desire. "That thou mayest have pleasure in everything, seek pleasure in nothing. That thou mayest know everything, seek to know nothing. That thou mayest possess all things, seek to possess nothing.... In detachment the spirit finds quiet and repose, for coveting nothing, nothing wearies it by elation, and nothing oppresses it by dejection, because it stands in the centre of its own humility. For as soon as it covets anything, it is immediately fatigued thereby."

It is not love but lust—the possessive case, the very food of selfhood—which poisons the relation between the self and the external world and "immediately fatigues" the soul. Divide the world into "mine" and "not mine," and unreal standards are set up, claims and cravings begin to fret the mind. We are the slaves of our own property. We drag with us not a treasure, but a chain. "Behold," says the "Theologia Germanica," "on this sort must we cast all things from us and strip ourselves of them: we must refrain from claiming anything for our own. When we do this, we shall have the best, fullest, clearest, and noblest knowledge that a man can have, and also the noblest and purest love and desire." "Some there are," says Plotinus, "that for all their effort have not attained the Vision.... They have received the authentic Light, all their soul has gleamed as they have drawn near, but they come with a load on their shoulders which holds them back from the place of Vision. They have not ascended in the pure integrity of their being, but are burdened with that which keeps them apart. They are not yet made one within." Accept Poverty, however, demolish ownership, the verb "to have" in every mood and tense, and this downward drag is at an end. At once the Cosmos belongs to you, and you to it. You escape the heresy of separateness, are "made one," and merged in "the greater life of the All." Then, a free spirit in a free world, the self moves upon its true orbit; undistracted by the largely self-imposed needs and demands of ordinary earthly existence.

This was the truth which St. Francis of Assisi grasped, and applied with the energy of a reformer and the delicate originality of a poet to every circumstance of the inner and the outer life. This noble liberty it is which is extolled by his spiritual descendant, Jacopone da Todi, in one of his most magnificent odes:

"Povertá, alto sapere,
a nulla cosa sojacere,
en desprezo possedere
tutte le cose create....
Dio non alberga en core stretto,
tant'é grande quant' hai affetto,

povertate ha si gran petto
che ci alberga deitate....
Povertate è nulla avere
e nulla cosa poi volere;
ad omne cosa possedere
en spirito de libertate."

"My little sisters the birds," said St. Francis, greatest adept of that high wisdom, "Brother Sun, Sister Water, Mother Earth." Not my servants, but my kindred and fellow-citizens; who may safely be loved so long as they are not desired. So, in almost identical terms, the dying Hindu ascetic:

"Oh Mother Earth, Father Sky,
Brother Wind, Friend Light, Sweetheart Water,
Here take my last salutation with folded hands!
For to-day I am melting away into the Supreme
Because my heart became pure,
And all delusion vanished,
Through the power of your good company."

It is the business of Lady Poverty to confer on her lovers this freedom of the Universe, to eradicate delusion, cut out the spreading growth of claimfulness, purify the heart, and initiate them into the "great life of the All." Well might St. Francis desire marriage with that enchantress, who gives back ten-fold all that she takes away. "Holy poverty," he said, "is a treasure so high excelling and so divine that we be not worthy to lay it up in our vile vessels; since this is that celestial virtue whereby all earthly things and fleeting are trodden underfoot, and whereby all hindrances are lifted from the soul, so that freely she may join herself to God Eternal."

Poverty, then, prepares man's spirit for that union with God to which it aspires. She strips off the clothing which he so often mistakes for himself, transvaluates all his values, and shows him things as they are. "There are," says Eckhart, "four ascending degrees of such spiritual poverty. 1. The soul's contempt of all things that are not God. 2. Contempt of herself and her own works. 3. Utter self-abandonment. 4. Self-loss in the incomprehensible Being of God." So, in the "Sacrum Commercium," when the friars, climbing "the steeps of the hill," found Lady Poverty at the summit "enthroned only in her nakedness," she "preventing them with the blessings of sweetness," said, "Why hasten ye so from the vale of tears to the mount of light? If, peradventure, it is me that ye seek, lo, I am but as you behold, a little poor one, stricken with storms and far from any consolation." Whereto the brothers answer, " *Only admit us to thy peace; and we shall be saved.*"

The same truth: the saving peace of utter detachment from everything but Divine Reality—a detachment which makes those who have it the citizens of the world, and enabled the friars to say to Lady Poverty as they showed her from the hill of Assisi the whole countryside at her feet, "Hoc est claustrum nostrum, Domina,"—is taught by Meister Eckhart in a more homely parable.

There was a learned man who, eight years long, desired that God would show him a man who would teach him the truth. And once when he felt a very great longing, a voice from God came to him and said, 'Go to the church, and there shalt thou find a man who shalt show thee the way to blessedness.' And he went thence and found a poor man whose feet were torn and covered with dust and dirt: and all his clothes were hardly worth three farthings. And he greeted him, saying:

'God give you good day!'
He answered: 'I have never had a bad day.'
'God give you good luck.'
'I have never had ill luck.'
'May you be happy! but why do you answer me thus?'
'I have never been unhappy.'
'Pray explain this to me, for I cannot understand it.'

The poor man answered, 'Willingly. You wished me good day. I never had a bad day; for if I am hungry I praise God; if it freezes, hails, snows, rains, if the weather is fair or foul, still I praise God; am I wretched and despised, I praise God, and so I have never had an evil day. You wished that God would send me luck. But I never had ill luck, for I know how to live with God, and I know that what He does is best; and what God gives me or ordains for me, be it good or ill, I take it cheerfully from God as the best that can be, and so I have never had ill luck. You wished that God would make me happy. I was never unhappy; for my only desire is to live in God's will, and I have so entirely yielded my will to God's, that what God wills, I will.'

'But if God should will to cast you into hell,' said the learned man, 'what would you do then?'

'Cast me into hell? His goodness forbids! But if He did cast me into hell, I should have two arms to embrace Him. One arm is true humility, that I should lay beneath Him, and be thereby united to His holy humanity. And with the right arm of love, which is united with His holy divinity, I should so embrace Him that He would have to go to hell with me. And I would rather be in hell and have God, then in heaven and not have God.'

Then the Master understood that true abandonment with utter humility is the nearest way to God.

The Master asked further: 'Whence are you come?'

'From God.'

'Where did you find God?'

'When I forsook all creatures.'

'Where have you left God?'

'In pure hearts, and in men of good will.'

The Master asked: 'What sort of man are you?'

'I am a king.'

'Where is your kingdom?'

'My soul is my kingdom, for I can so rule my senses inward and outward, that all the desires and power of my soul are in subjection, and this kingdom is greater than a kingdom on earth.'

'What brought you to this perfection?'

'My silence, my high thoughts, and my union with God. For I could not rest in anything that was less than God. Now I have found God; and in God have eternal rest and peace.'

Poverty, then, consists in a breaking down of man's inveterate habit of trying to rest in, or take seriously, things which are "less than God": *i.e.,* which do not possess the character of reality. Such a habit is the most fertile of all causes of "world-weariness," disillusion and unrest: faults, or rather spiritual diseases, which the mystics never exhibit, but which few who are without all mystic feeling can hope to escape. Hence the sharpened perceptions of the contemplatives have always seen poverty as a counsel of prudence, a higher form of common sense. It was not with St. Francis, or any other great mystic, a first principle, an end in itself. It was rather a logical deduction from the first principle of their science—the paramount importance to the soul of an undistracted vision of reality.

Here East and West are in agreement: "Their science," says Al Ghazzali of the Sufis, who practised, like the early Franciscans, a complete renunciation of worldly goods, "has for its object the uprooting from the soul of all violent passions, the extirpation from it of vicious desires and evil qualities; so that the heart may become detached from all that is not God, and give itself for its only occupation meditation upon the Divine Being."

All those who have felt themselves urged towards the attainment of this transcendental vision, have found that possessions interrupt the view; that claims, desires, attachments become centres of conflicting interest in the mind. They assume a false air of importance, force themselves upon the attention, and complicate life. Hence, in the interest of self-simplification, they must be cleared away: a removal which involves for the real enthusiast little more sacrifice than the weekly visit of the dustman. "Having entirely surrendered my own free-will," says Al Ghazzali of his personal experience," my heart no longer felt any distress in renouncing fame, wealth, or the society of my children."

Others have reconciled self-surrender with a more moderate abandonment of outward things; for possessions take different rank for almost every human soul. The true rule of poverty consists in giving up those things which enchain the spirit, divide its interests, and deflect it on its road to God—whether these things be riches, habits, religious observances, friends, interests, distastes, or desires—not in mere outward destitution for its own sake. It is attitude, not act, that matters; self-denudation would be unnecessary were it not for our inveterate tendency to attribute false value to things the moment they become our own. "What is poverty of spirit but meekness of mind, by which a man knows his own infirmity?" says Rolle, "seeing that to perfect stableness he may not come but by the grace of God, all thing that him might let from that grace he forsakes, and only in joy of his Maker he sets his desire. And as of one root spring many branches, so of wilful poverty on this wise taken proceed virtues and marvels untrowed. Not as some, that change their clothes and not their souls; riches soothly it seems these forsake, and vices innumerable they cease not to gather.... If thou truly all thing for God forsake, *see more what thou despised than what thou forsaketh.* "

The Poverty of the mystics, then, is a mental rather than a material state. Detachment of the will from all desire of possessions is the inner reality, of which Franciscan poverty is a sacrament to the world. It is the poor in spirit, not the poor in substance, who are to be spiritually blessed. "Let all things be forsaken of me," says Gerlac Petersen, "so that being poor I may be able in great inward spaciousness, and without any hurt, to suffer want of all those things which the mind of man can desire; out of or excepting God Himself."

"The soul," says St. John of the Cross, "is not empty, so long as the desire for sensible things remains. But the absence of this desire for things produces emptiness and liberty of soul; even when there is an abundance of possessions."

Every person in whom the mystical instinct awakes soon discovers in himself certain tastes or qualities which interrupt the development of that instinct. Often these tastes and qualities are legitimate enough upon their own plane; but they are a drain upon the energy of the self, preventing her from attaining that intenser life for which she was made and which demands her undivided zest. They distract her attention, fill the field of perception, stimulate her instinctive life: making of the surface-consciousness so active a thing that it can hardly be put to sleep. "Where can he have that pure and naked vision of unchangeable Truth whereby he see into all things," says Petersen again, "who is so busied in other things, not perhaps evil, which operate... upon his thoughts and imagination and confuse and enchain his mind... that his sight of that unique One in Whom all things are is overclouded?"

The nature of these distracting factors which "confuse and enchain the mind" will vary with almost every individual. It is impossible to predict what those things will be which a self must give up, in order that the transcendental consciousness may grow. "It makes little difference whether a bird be held by a slender thread or by a rope; the bird is bound, and cannot fly until the cord that holds it is broken. It is true that a slender thread is more easily broken; still notwithstanding, if it is not broken the bird cannot fly. This is the state of a soul with particular attachments: it never can attain to the liberty of the divine union, whatever virtues it may possess. Desires and attachments affect the soul as the remora is said to affect a ship; that is but a little fish, yet when it clings to the vessel it effectually hinders its progress."

Thus each adventurer must discover and extirpate all those interests which nourish selfhood, however innocent or even useful these interests may seem in the eyes of the world. The only rule is the ruthless abandonment of everything which is in the way. "When any man God perfectly desires to love, all things as well inward as outward that to God's love are contrary and from His love do let, he studies to do away." This may mean the prompt and utter self-stripping of St. Francis of Assisi, who cast off his actual clothing in his relentless determination to have nothing of his own: the reluctant bit-by-bit renunciations which at last set his follower Angela of Foligno free, or the drastic proceedings of Antoinette Bourignan, who found that a penny was enough to keep her from God.

"Being one night in a most profound Penitence," says the biographer of this extraordinary woman, "she said from the bottom of her Heart, 'O my Lord! what must I do to please Thee? For I have nobody to teach me. Speak to my soul and it will hear Thee.'" At that instant she heard, as if another had spoken within her "Forsake all earthly things. Separate thyself from the love of the creatures. Deny thyself." From this time, the more she entered into herself the more she was inclined to abandon all. But she had not the courage necessary for the complete renunciation towards which her transcendental consciousness was pressing her. She struggled to adjust herself to the inner and the outer life, but without success. For such a character as hers, compromise was impossible. "She asked always earnestly, When shall I be perfectly thine, O my God? and she thought He still answered her, *When thou shalt no longer possess anything, and shalt die to thyself.* And where shall I do that, Lord? He answered, *In the Desert.*" At last the discord between her deeper and her superficial self became intolerable.

Reinforced by the miseries of an unsympathetic home, still more by a threat of approaching marriage, the impulse to renunciation got its way. She disguised herself in a hermit's dress—she was only eighteen, and had no one to help or advise her—and "went out of her chamber about Four in the Morning, taking nothing but one Penny to buy Bread for that Day and it being said to her in the going out, *Where is thy Faith? In a Penny?* she threw it away.... Thus she went away wholly delivered from the heavy burthen of the Cares and Good Things of this World."

An admirable example of the mystic's attitude towards the soul-destroying division of interests, the natural but hopeless human struggle to make the best of both worlds, which sucks at its transcendental vitality, occurs in St. Teresa's purgative period. In her case this war between the real and the superficial self extended over many years; running side by side with the state of Illumination, and a fully developed contemplative life. At last it was brought to an end by a "Second Conversion" which unified her scattered interests and set her firmly and for ever on the Unitive Way. The virile strength of Teresa's character, which afterwards contributed to the greatness of her achievement, opposed the invading transcendental consciousness; disputed every inch of territory; resisted every demand made upon it by the growing spiritual self. Bit by bit it was conquered, the sphere of her deeper life enlarged; until the moment came in which she surrendered, once for all, to her true destiny.

During the years of inward stress, of penance and growing knowledge of the Infinite, which she spent in the Convent of the Incarnation, and which accompanied this slow remaking of character, Teresa's only self-indulgence—as it seems, a sufficiently innocent one—was talking to the friends who came down from Avila to the convent-parlour, and spoke to her through the *grille.* Her confessors, unaccustomed to the education of mystical genius, saw nothing incompatible between this practice and the pursuit of a high contemplative life. But as her transcendental consciousness, her states of orison grew stronger, Teresa felt more and more the distracting influence of these glimpses of the outer world. They were a drain upon the energy which ought to be wholly given to that new, deep, more real life which she felt stirring within her, and which could only hope to achieve its mighty destiny by complete concentration upon the business in hand. No genius can afford to dissipate his energies: the mystic genius least of all. Teresa knew that so long as she retained these personal satisfactions, her life had more than one focus; she was not whole-hearted in her surrender to the Absolute. But though her inward voices, her deepest instincts, urged her to give them up, for years she felt herself incapable of such a sacrifice. It was round the question of their retention or surrender that the decisive battle of her life was fought.

"The devil," says her great Augustinian eulogist, Fray Luis de Leon, in his vivid account of these long interior struggles, "put before her those persons most sympathetic by nature; and God came, and in the midst of the conversation discovered Himself aggrieved and sorrowful. The devil delighted in the conversation and pastime, but when she turned her back on them and betook herself to prayer, God redoubled the delight and favours, as if to show her how false was the lure which charmed her at the grating, and that His sweetness was the veritable sweetness.... So that these two inclinations warred with each other in the breast of this blessed woman, and the authors who inspired them each did his utmost to inflame her most, and the oratory blotted out what the grating wrote, and at times the grating vanquished and diminished the good fruit produced by prayer, causing agony and grief which disquieted and perplexed her soul: for though she was resolved to belong entirely to God, she knew not how to shake herself free from the world: and at times she persuaded herself that she could enjoy both, which ended mostly, as she says, in complete enjoyment of neither. For the amusements of the locutorio were embittered and turned into wormwood by the memory of the secret and sweet intimacy with God; and in the same way when she retired to be with God, and commenced to speak with Him, the affections and thoughts which she carried with her from the grating took possession of her."

Compare with these violent oscillations between the superficial and mystical consciousness—characteristic of Teresa's strong volitional nature, which only came to rest after psychic convulsions which left no corner of its being unexplored—the symbolic act of renunciation under which Antoinette Bourignan's "interior self" vanquished the surface intelligence and asserted its supremacy. Teresa must give up her passionate delight in human friendship. Antoinette, never much tempted in that direction, must give up her last penny. What society was to Teresa's generous, energetic nature, prudence was to the temperamentally shrewd and narrow Antoinette: a distraction, a check on the development of the all-demanding transcendental genius, an unconquered relic of the "lower life."

Many a mystic, however, has found the perfection of detachment to be consistent with a far less drastic renunciation of external things than that which these women felt to be essential to their peace. The test, as we have seen, does not lie in the nature of the things which are retained, but in the reaction which they stimulate in the self. "Absolute poverty is thine," says Tauler, "when thou canst not remember whether anybody has ever owed thee or been indebted to thee for anything; just as all things will be forgotten by thee in the last journey of death." Poverty, in this sense, may be consistent with the habitual and automatic use of luxuries which the abstracted self never even perceives. Thus we are told that St. Bernard was reproached by his enemies with the inconsistency of preaching evangelical poverty whilst making his journeys from place to place on a magnificently caparisoned mule, which had been lent to him by the Cluniac monks. He expressed great contrition but said that he had never noticed what it was that he rode upon.

Sometimes, the very activity which one self has rejected as an impediment becomes for another the channel of spiritual perception. I have mentioned the Curé d'Ars, who, among other inhibitions, refused to allow himself to smell a rose. Yet St. Francis preached to the flowers, and ordered a plot to be set aside for their cultivation when the convent garden was made, "in order that all who saw them might remember the Eternal Sweetness." So, too, we are told of his spiritual daughter, St. Douceline, that "out of doors one day with her sisters, she heard a bird's note. 'What a lovely song!' she said: and the song drew her straight way to God. Did they bring her a flower, *its beauty had a like effect*." "To look on trees, water, and flowers," says St. Teresa of her own beginnings of contemplation, "helped her to recollect the Presence of God." Here we are reminded of Plato. "The true order of going is to use the beauties of Earth as steps along which one mounts upwards for the sake of that other Beauty." This, too, is the true order of Holy Poverty: the selfless use, not the selfish abuse of lovely and natural things.

To say that some have fallen short of this difficult ideal and taken refuge in mere abnegation is but to say that asceticism is a human, not a superhuman art, and is subject to "the frailty of the creature." But on the whole, these excesses are mainly found amongst saintly types who have not exhibited true mystic intuition. This intuition, entailing as it does communion with intensest Life, gives to its possessors a sweet sanity, a delicate balance, which guards them, as a rule, from such conceptions of chastity as that of the youthful saint who shut himself in a cupboard for fear he should see his mother pass by: from the obedience which identifies the voice of the director with the voice of God; from detachment such as that exhibited by the Blessed Angela of Foligno, who, though a true mystic, viewed with almost murderous satisfaction the deaths of relatives who were "impediments." The detachment of the mystic is just a restoration to the liberty in which the soul was made: it is a state of joyous humility in which he cries, "Nought I am, nought I have, nought I lack." To have arrived at this is to have escaped from the tyranny of selfhood: to be initiated into the purer air of that universe which knows but one rule of action—that which was laid down once for all by St. Augustine when he said, in the most memorable and misquoted of epigrams: "Love, and do what you like."

Mortification

By mortification, I have said, is to be understood the positive aspect of purification: the remaking in relation to reality of the permanent elements of character. These elements, so far, have subserved the interests of the old self, worked for it in the world of sense. Now they must be adjusted to the needs of the new self and to the transcendent world in which it moves. Their focal point is the old self; the "natural man" and his self-regarding instincts and desires. The object of mortification is to kill that old self, break up his egoistic attachments and cravings, in order that the higher centre, the "new man," may live and breathe. As St. Teresa discovered when she tried to reconcile the claims of worldly friendships and contemplation, one or other must go: a house divided against itself cannot stand. "Who hinders thee more," says Thomas a Kempis, "than the unmortified affections of thy own heart?... if we were perfectly dead unto ourselves, and not entangled within our own breasts, then should we be able to taste Divine things, and to have some experience of heavenly contemplation."

In psychological language, the process of mortification is the process of setting up "new paths of neural discharge." That is to say, the mystic life has got to express itself in action and for this new paths must be cut and new habits formed—all, in spite of the new self's enthusiasm, "against the grain"—resulting in a complete sublimation of personality. The energy which wells up incessantly in every living being must abandon the old road of least resistance and discharge itself in a new and more difficult way. In the terms of the hormic psychology, the conative drive of the psyche must be concentrated on new objectives; and the old paths, left to themselves, must fade and die. When they are dead, and the new life has triumphed, Mortification is at an end. The mystics always know when this moment comes. Often an inner voice then warns them to lay their active penances aside.

Since the greater and stronger the mystic, the stronger and more stubborn his character tends to be, this change of life and turning of energy from the old and easy channels to the new is often a stormy matter. It is a period of actual battle between the inharmonious elements of the self, its lower and higher springs of action: of toil, fatigue, bitter suffering, and many disappointments. Nevertheless, in spite of its etymological associations, the object of mortification is not death but life: the production of health and strength, the health and strength of the human consciousness viewed *sub specie aeternitatis*. "In the truest death of all created things, the sweetest and most natural life is hidden."

"This dying," says Tauler again, "has many degrees, and so has this life. A man might die a thousand deaths in one day and find at once a joyful life corresponding to each of them. This is as it must be: God cannot deny or refuse this to death. The stronger the death the more powerful and thorough is the corresponding life; the more intimate the death, the more inward is the life. Each life brings strength, and strengthens to a harder death. When a man dies to a scornful word, bearing it in God's name, or to some inclination inward or outward, acting or not acting against his own will, be it in love or grief, in word or act, in going or staying; or if he denies his desires of taste or sight, or makes no excuses when wrongfully accused; or anything else, whatever it may be, to which he has not yet died, it is harder at first to one who is unaccustomed to it and unmortified than to him who is mortified.... A great life makes reply to him who dies in earnest even in the least things, a life which strengthens him immediately to die a greater death; a death so long and strong, that it seems to him hereafter more joyful, good and pleasant to die than to live, for he finds life in death and light shining in darkness."

No more than detachment, then, is mortification an end in itself. It is a process, an education directed towards the production of a definite kind of efficiency, the adjustment of human nature to the demands of its new life. Severe, and to the outsider apparently unmeaning—like their physical parallels the exercises of the gymnasium—its disciplines, faithfully accepted, do release the self from the pull of the lower nature, establish it on new levels of freedom and power. "Mortification," says the Benedictine contemplative Augustine Baker, "tends to subject the body to the spirit and the spirit to God. And this it does by crossing the inclinations of sense, which are quite contrary to those of the Divine Spirit... by such crossing and afflicting of the body, self-love and self-will (the poison of our spirits) are abated, and in time in a sort destroyed; and instead of them there enter into the soul the Divine love and Divine will, and take possession thereof." This transformation accomplished, mortification may end, and often does, with startling abruptness. After a martyrdom which lasted sixteen years, says Suso—speaking as usual in the third person—of his own experience, "On a certain Whitsun Day a heavenly messenger appeared to him, and ordered him in God's name to continue it no more. He at once ceased, and threw all the instruments of his sufferings [irons, nails, hair-shirt, etc.] into a river." From this time onward, austerities of this sort had no part in Suso's life.

The Franco-Flemish mystic who wrote, and the English contemplative who translated, "The Mirror of Simple Souls," have between them described and explained in bold and accurate language the conditions under which the soul is enabled to abandon that "hard service of the virtues" which has absorbed it during the Purgative Way. The statement of the "French Book" is direct and uncompromising: well calculated to startle timid piety. "Virtues, I take leave of you for evermore!" exclaims the Soul. "Now shall mine heart be more free and more in peace than it hath been before. I wot well your service is too travaillous.... Some time I laid mine heart in you without any dissevering: ye wot well this: I was in all things to you obedient. O I was then your servant, but now I am delivered out of your thraldom."

To this astounding utterance the English translator has added a singularly illuminating gloss. "I am stirred here," he says, "to say more to the matter, as thus: First: when a soul giveth her to perfection, she laboureth busily day and night to get virtues, by counsel of reason, and striveth with vices at every thought, at every word and deed that she perceiveth cometh of them, and busily searcheth vices, them to destroy. Thus the virtues be mistresses, and every virtue maketh her to war with its contrary, the which be vices. Many sharp pains and bitterness of conscience feeleth the soul in this war.... But so long one may bite on the bitter bark of the nut, that at last he shall come to the sweet kernel. Right so, ghostly to understand, it fareth by these souls that be come to peace. They have so long striven with vices and wrought by virtues, that they be come to the nut kernel, that is, to the love of God, which is sweetness. And when the soul hath deeply tasted this love, so that this love of God worketh and hath his usages in her soul, then the soul is wondrous light and gladsome.... Then is she mistress and lady over the virtues, for she hath them all within herself.... And then this soul taketh leave of virtues, as of the thraldom and painful travail of them that she had before, and now she is lady and sovereign, and they be subjects."

Jacopone da Todi speaks to the same effect:

"La guerra è terminata
de le virtu battaglia,
de la mente travaglia
cosa nulla contende".

Thus, St. Catherine of Genoa, after a penitential period of four years, during which she was haunted by a constant sense of sin, and occupied by incessant mortifications, found that "all thought of such mortifications was *in an instant* taken from her mind: in such a manner that, had she even wished to continue such mortifications, she would have been unable to do so... the sight of her sins was now taken from her mind, so that henceforth she did not catch a glimpse of them: it was as though they had all been cast into the depths of the sea." In other words, the new and higher centre of consciousness, finally established, asserted itself and annihilated the old. "La guerra e teminata,"all the energy of a strong nature flows freely in the new channels; and mortification ceases, mechanically, to be possible to the now unified, sublimated, or "regenerated" self.

Mortification takes its name from the reiterated statement of all ascetic writers that the senses, or "body of desire," with the cravings which are excited by different aspects of the phenomenal world, must be mortified or killed; which is, of course, a description of psychological necessities from their special point of view. All those self-regarding instincts—so ingrained that they have become automatic—which impel the self to choose the more comfortable part, are seen by the awakened intuition of the embryo mystic as gross infringements of the law of love. "This is the travail that a man behoveth, to draw out his heart and his mind from the fleshly love and the liking of all earthly creatures, from vain thoughts and from fleshly imaginations, and out from the love and the vicious feeling of himself, that his soul should find no rest in no fleshly thought, nor earthly affection." The rule of Poverty must be applied to the temper of normal consciousness as well as to the tastes and possessions of the self. Under this tonic influence, real life will thrive, unreal life will wither and die.

This mortifying process is necessary, not because the legitimate exercise of the senses is opposed to Divine Reality, but because those senses have usurped a place beyond their station; become the focus of energy, steadily drained the vitality of the self. "The dogs have taken the children's meat." The senses have grown stronger than their masters, monopolized the field of perception, dominated an organism which was made for greater activities, and built up those barriers of individuality which must be done away if true personality is to be achieved, and with it some share in the boundless life of the One. It is thanks to this wrong distribution of energy, this sedulous feeding of the cuckoo in the nest, that "in order to approach the Absolute, mystics must withdraw from everything, even themselves." "The soul is plunged in utter ignorance, when she supposes that she can attain to the high estate of union with God before she casts away the desire of all things, natural and supernatural, which she may possess," says St. John of the Cross, "because the distance between them and that which takes place in the state of pure transformation in God is infinite." Again, "until the desires be lulled to sleep by the mortification of sensuality, and sensuality itself be mortified in them, so that it shall war against the spirit no more, the soul cannot go forth in perfect liberty to union with the Beloved."

The death of selfhood in its narrow individualistic sense is, then, the primary object of mortification. All the twisted elements of character which foster the existence of this unreal yet complex creature are to be pruned away. Then, as with the trees of the forest, so with the spirit of man, strong new branches will spring into being, grow towards air and light. "I live, yet not I" is to be the declaration of the mystic who has endured this "bodily death." The self-that-is-to-be will live upon a plane where her own prejudices and preferences are so uninteresting as to be imperceptible. She must be weaned from these nursery toys: and weaning is a disagreeable process. The mystic, however, undertakes it as a rule without reluctance: pushed by his vivid consciousness of imperfection, his intuition of a more perfect state, necessary to the fulfilment of his love. Often his entrance upon the torments of the Purgative Way, his taking up of the spiritual or material instruments of mortification, resembles in ardour and abruptness that "heroic plunge into Purgatory" of the newly dead when it perceives itself in the light of Love Divine, which is described in the "Treatise" of St. Catherine of Genoa as its nearest equivalent. "As she, plunged in the divine furnace of purifying love, was united to the Object of her love, and satisfied with all he wrought in her, so she understood it to be with the souls in Purgatory."

This "divine furnace of purifying love" demands from the ardent soul a complete self-surrender, and voluntary turning from all impurity, a humility of the most far-reaching kind: and this means the deliberate embrace of active suffering, a self-discipline in dreadful tasks. As gold in the refiner's fire, so "burning of love into a soul truly taken all vices purgeth." Detachment may be a counsel of prudence, a practical result of seeing the true values of things; but the pain of mortification is seized as a splendid opportunity, a love token, timidly offered by the awakened spirit to that all-demanding Lover from Whom St. Catherine of Siena heard the terrible words "I, Fire, the Acceptor of sacrifices, ravishing away from them their darkness, give the light." "Suffering is the ancient law of love," says the Eternal Wisdom to Suso, "there is no quest without pain, there is no lover who is not also a martyr. Hence it is inevitable that he who would love so high a thing as Wisdom should sometimes suffer hindrances and griefs."

The mystics have a profound conviction that Creation, Becoming, Transcendence, is a painful process at the best. Those who are Christians point to the Passion of Christ as a proof that the cosmic journey to perfection, the path of the Eternal Wisdom, follows of necessity the Way of the Cross. That law of the inner life, which sounds so fantastic and yet is so bitterly true—"No progress without pain"—asserts itself. It declares that birth pangs must be endured in the spiritual as well as in the material world: that adequate training must always hurt the athlete. Hence the mystics' quest of the Absolute drives them to an eager and heroic union with the reality of suffering, as well as with the reality of joy.

This divine necessity of pain, this necessary sharing in the travail of a World of Becoming, is beautifully described by Tauler in one of those "internal conversations" between the contemplative soul and its God, which abound in the works of the mystics and are familiar to all readers of "The Imitation of Christ." "A man once thought," says Tauler, "that God drew some men even by pleasant paths, while other were drawn by the path of pain. Our Lord answered him thus, 'What think ye can be pleasanter or nobler than to be made most like unto Me? that is by suffering. Mark, to whom was ever offered such a troubled life as to Me? And in whom can I better work in accordance with My true nobility than in those who are most like Me? They are the men who suffer.... Learn that My divine nature never worked so nobly in human nature as by suffering; and because suffering is so efficacious, it is sent out of great love. I understand the weakness of human nature at all times, and out of love and righteousness I lay no heavier load on man than he can bear. The crown must be firmly pressed down that is to bud and blossom in the Eternal Presence of of My Heavenly Father. He who desires to be wholly immersed in the fathomless sea of My Godhead must also be deeply immersed in the deep sea of bitter sorrow. I am exalted far above all things, and work supernatural and wonderful works in Myself: the deeper and more supernaturally a man crushes himself beneath all things the more supernaturally will he be drawn far above all things.'"

Pain, therefore, the mystics always welcome and often court: sometimes in the crudely physical form which Suso describes so vividly and horribly in the sixteenth chapter of his Life, more frequently in those refinements of torture which a sensitive spirit can extract from loneliness, injustice, misunderstanding—above all, from deliberate contact with the repulsive accidents of life. It would seem from a collation of the evidence that the typical mystical temperament is by nature highly fastidious. Its passionate apprehension of spiritual beauty, its intuitive perception of divine harmony, is counterbalanced by an instinctive loathing of ugliness, a shrinking from the disharmonies of squalor and disease. Often its ideal of refinement is far beyond the contemporary standards of decency: a circumstance which is alone enough to provide ample opportunity of wretchedness. This extreme sensitiveness, which forms part of the normal psychophysical make-up of the mystic, as it often does of the equally highly-strung artistic type, is one of the first things to be seized upon by the awakened self as a disciplinary instrument. Then humility's axiom, "Naught is too low for love" is forced to bear the less lovely gloss, "Naught must be too disgusting."

Two reasons at once appear for this. One is the contempt for phenomena, nasty as well as nice—the longing to be free from all the fetters of sense—which often goes with the passion for invisible things. Those mystics to whom the attractions of earth are only illusion, are inconsistent if they attribute a greater reality to the revolting and squalid incidents of life. St. Francis did but carry his own principles to their logical conclusion, when he insisted that the vermin were as much his brothers as the birds. Real detachment means the death of preferences of all kinds: even of those which seem to other men the very proofs of virtue and fine taste.

The second reason is nobler. It is bound up with that principle of self-surrender which is the mainspring of the mystic life. To the contemplative mind, which is keenly conscious of unity in multiplicity—of Gods in the world—all disinterested service is service of the Absolute which he loves: and the harder it is, the more opposed to his self-regarding and aesthetic instincts, the more nearly it approaches his ideal. The point to which he aspires—though he does not always know it—is that in which all disharmony, all appearance of vileness, is resolved in the concrete reality which he calls the Love of God. Then, he feels dimly, everything will be seen under the aspect of a cosmic and charitable beauty; exhibiting through the woof of corruption the web of eternal life.

It is told of St. Francis of Assisi, in whom the love of lovely things was always paramount, how he forced himself to visit the lepers whose sight and smell disgusted him: how he served them and even kissed them. "Then as he departed, in very truth that which had aforetime been bitter unto him, to wit, the sight and touch of lepers, now changed into sweetness. For, as he confessed, the sight of lepers had been so grievous unto him that he had been minded to avoid not only seeing them, but even going nigh their dwelling. And if at any time he chanced to pass their abodes, or to see them, albeit he were moved by compassion to do them an alms through another person, yet alway would he turn aside his face, stopping his nostrils with his hand. But through the grace of God he became so intimate a friend of the lepers that, even as he recorded in his will, he did sojourn with them and did humbly serve them."

Also, after his great renunciation of all property, he, once a prosperous young man who had been "dainty in his father's home," accustomed himself to take a bowl and beg scraps of food from door to door: and here too, as in the case of the lepers, that which at first seemed revolting became to him sweet. "And when he would have eaten that medley of various meats," says the legend, "at first he shrank back, for that he had never been used willingly even to see, much less to eat, such scraps. At length, conquering himself, he began to eat; and it seemed to him that in eating no rich syrup had he ever tasted aught so delightsome."

The object, then, of this self-discipline is, like the object of all purgation, freedom: freedom from the fetters of the senses, the "remora of desire," from the results of environment and worldly education, from pride and prejudice, preferences and distaste: from selfhood in every form. Its effect is a sharp reaction to the joy of self-conquest. The very act that had once caused in the enchained self a movement of loathing becomes not merely indifferent, but an occasion of happiness. So Margery Kempe "had great mourning and sorrowing if she might not kiss a leper when she met them in the way for the love of our Lord, *which was all contrary to her disposition* in the years of her youth and prosperity, for then she abhorred them most."

I spare the sensitive reader a detailed account of the loathsome ordeals by which St. Catherine of Genoa and Madame Guyon strove to cure themselves of squeamishness and acquire this liberty of spirit. They, like St. Francis, St. Elizabeth of Hungary, and countless other seekers for the Real, sought out and served with humility and love the sick and the unclean; deliberately associated themselves with life in its meanest forms; compelled themselves to contact with the most revolting substances; and mortified the senses by the traditional ascetic expedient of deliberately opposing all—even their most natural and harmless—inclinations. "In the first four years after she received the sweet wound from her Lord," says the Life of St. Catherine of Genoa, she "made great penances: so that all her senses were mortified. And first, so soon as she perceived that her nature desired anything at once she deprived it thereof, and did so that it should receive all those things that it abhorred. She wore harsh hair, ate no meat nor any other thing that she liked; ate no fruit, neither fresh nor dried... and she lived greatly submitted to all persons, and always sought to do all those things which were contrary to her own will; in such a way that she was always inclined to do more promptly the will of others than her own."... "And while she worked such and so many mortifications of all her senses it was several times asked of her 'Why do you do this?' And she answered 'I do not know, but I feel myself drawn inwardly to do this... and I think it is God's will.'"

St. Ignatius Loyola, in the world a highly bred Spanish gentleman of refined personal habits, found in those habits an excellent opportunity of mortification. "As he was somewhat nice about the arrangement of his hair, as was the fashion of those days and became him not ill, he allowed it to grow naturally, and neither combed it nor trimmed it nor wore any head covering by day or night. For the same reason he did not pare his finger or toe nails; for on these points he had been fastidious to an extreme."

Madame Guyon, a delicate girl of the leisured class, accustomed to the ordinary comforts of her station, characteristically chose the most crude and immoderate forms of mortification in her efforts towards the acquirement of "indifference." But the peculiar psychic constitution which afterwards showed itself in the forms of automatism and clairvoyance, seems to have produced a partial anesthesia. "Although I had a very delicate body, the instruments of penitence tore my flesh without, as it seemed to me, causing pain. I wore girdles of hair and of sharp iron, I often held wormwood in my mouth." "If I walked, I put stones in my shoes. These things, my God, Thou didst first inspire me to do, in order that I might be deprived even of the most innocent satisfactions."

In the earlier stages of their education, a constant *agere contra*, even in apparently indifferent things, seems essential to the mystics; till the point is reached at which the changes and chances of mortal life are accepted with a true indifference and do not trouble the life of the soul. This established ascendancy of the "interior man," the transcendental consciousness, over "sensitive nature"—the self in its reactions to the ups and downs and manifold illusions of daily life—is the very object of Purgation. It is, then, almost impossible that any mystic, whatever his religion, character or race, should escape its battles: for none at the beginning of their growth are in a position to dispense with its good offices. Neoplatonists and Mahommedans, no less than the Christian ascetics, are acquainted with the Purgative Way. All realize the first law of Spiritual Alchemy, that you must tame the Green Lion before you give him wings. Thus in 'Attar's allegory of the Valleys, the valley of self-stripping and renunciation comes first. So too Al Ghazzali, the Persian contemplative, says of the period immediately following his acceptance of the principles of Sufi-ism and consequent renunciation of property, "I went to Syria, where I remained more than two years; without any other object than that of living in seclusion and solitude, conquering my desires, struggling with my passions, striving to purify my soul, to perfect my character, and to prepare my heart to meditate upon God." At the end of this period of pure purgation circumstances forced him to return to the world; much to his regret, since he "had not yet attained to the perfect ecstatic state, unless it were in one or two isolated moments."

Such gleams of ecstatic vision, distributed through the later stages of purification, seem to be normal features of mystical development. Increasing control of the lower centres, of the surface intelligence and its scattered desires, permits the emergence of the transcendental perceptions. We have seen that Fox in his early stages displayed just such an alternation between the light and shade of the mystic way. So too did that least ascetic of visionaries, Jacob Boehme. "Finding within myself a powerful contrarium, namely the desires that belong to the flesh and blood," he says, "I began to fight a hard battle against my corrupted nature, and with the aid of God I made up my mind to overcome the inherited evil will, to break it, and to enter wholly into the Love of God.... This, however, was not possible for me to accomplish, but I stood firmly by my earnest resolution, and fought a hard battle with myself. Now while I was wrestling and battling, being aided by God, a wonderful light arose within my soul. It was a light entirely foreign to my unruly nature, but in it I recognized the true nature of God and man, and the relation existing between them, a thing which heretofore I had never understood, and for which I would never have sought."

In these words Boehme bridges the gap between Purgation and Illumination: showing these two states or ways as coexisting and complementary one to another, the light and dark sides of a developing mystic consciousness. As a fact, they do often exist side by side in the individual experience and any treatment which exhibits them as sharply and completely separated may be convenient for purposes of study, but becomes at best diagrammatic if considered as a representation of the mystic life. The mystical consciousness, as we have seen, belongs—from the psychological point of view—to that mobile or "unstable" type in which the artistic temperament also finds a place. It sways easily between the extremes of pleasure and pain in its gropings after transcendental reality. It often attains for a moment to heights in which it is not able to rest: is often flung from some rapturous vision of the Perfect to the deeps of contrition and despair.

The mystics have a vivid metaphor by which to describe that alternation between the onset and the absence of the joyous transcendental consciousness which forms as it were the characteristic intermediate stage between the bitter struggles of pure Purgation, and the peace and radiance of the Illuminative Life. They call it *Ludus Amoris*, the "Game of Love" which God plays with the desirous soul. It is the "game of chess," says St. Teresa, "in which game Humility is the Queen without whom none can checkmate the Divine King." "Here," says Martensen, "God plays a blest game with the soul." The "Game of Love" is a reflection in consciousness of that state of struggle, oscillation and unrest which precedes the first unification of the self. It ceases when this has taken place and the new level of reality has been attained. Thus St. Catherine of Siena, that inspired psychologist, was told in ecstasy, "With the souls who have arrived at perfection,

I play no more the Game of Love, which consists in leaving and returning again to the soul; though thou must understand that it is not, properly speaking, I, the immovable GOD, Who thus elude them, but rather the sentiment that My charity gives them of Me." In other terms, it is the imperfectly developed spiritual perception which becomes tired and fails, throwing the self back into the darkness and aridity whence it has emerged. So we are told of Rulman Merswin that after the period of harsh physical mortification which succeeded his conversion came a year of "delirious joy alternating with the most bitter physical and moral sufferings."

It is, he says, "the Game of Love which the Lord plays with His poor sinful creature." Memories of all his old sins still drove him to exaggerated penances: morbid temptations "made me so ill that I feared I should lose my reason." These psychic storms reacted upon the physical organism. He had a paralytic seizure, lost the use of his lower limbs, and believed himself to be at the point of death. When he was at his worst, however, and all hope seemed at an end, an inward voice told him to rise from his bed. He obeyed, and found himself cured. Ecstasies were frequent during the whole of this period. In these moments of exaltation he felt his mind to be irradiated by a new light, so that he knew, intuitively, the direction which his life was bound to take, and recognized the inevitable and salutary nature of his trials. "God showed Himself by turns harsh and gentle: to each access of misery succeeded the rapture of supernatural grace." In this intermittent style, torn by these constant fluctuations between depression and delight, did Merswin, in whom the psychic instability of the artistic and mystic types is present in excess, pass through the purgative and illuminated states. They appear to have coexisted in his consciousness, first one and then the other emerging and taking control. Hence he did not attain the peaceful condition which is characteristic of full illumination, and normally closes the "First Mystic Life"; but passed direct from these violent alternations of mystical pleasure and mystical pain to the state which he calls "the school of suffering love." This, when we come to its consideration, is strictly analogous to that which other mystics have called the "Dark Night of the Soul," and opens the "Second Mystic Life" or Unitive Way.

Such prolonged coexistence of alternating pain and pleasure states in the developing soul, such delay in the attainment of equilibrium, is not infrequent, and must be taken into account in all analyses of the mystic type. Though it is convenient for purposes of study to practise a certain dissection, and treat as separate states which are, in the living subject, closely intertwined, we should constantly remind ourselves that such a proceeding is artificial. The struggle of the self to disentangle itself from illusion and attain the Absolute is a life-struggle. Hence, it will and must exhibit the freedom and originality of life: will, as a process, obey artistic rather than scientific laws. It will sway now to the light and now to the shade of experience: its oscillations will sometimes be great, sometimes small. Mood and environment, inspiration and information, will all play their part.

There are in this struggle three factors.

(1) The unchanging light of Eternal Reality: that Pure Being "which ever shines and nought shall ever dim."

(2) The web of illusion, here thick, there thin; which hems in, confuses, and allures the sentient self.

(3) That self, always changing, moving, struggling—always, in fact, *becoming*—alive in every fibre, related at once to the unreal and to the real; and, with its growth in true being, ever more conscious of the contrast between them.

In the ever-shifting relations between these three factors, the consequent energy engendered, the work done, we may find a cause of the innumerable forms of stress and travail which are called in their objective form the Purgative Way. One only of the three is constant: the Absolute to which the soul aspires. Though all else may fluctuate, that goal is changeless. That Beauty so old and so new, "with whom is no variableness, neither shadow of turning," which is the One of Plotinus, the All of Eckhart and St. John of the Cross, the Eternal Wisdom of Suso, the Unplumbed Abyss of Ruysbroeck, the Pure Love of St. Catherine of Genoa, awaits yesterday, to-day, and for ever the opening of Its creature's eyes.

In the moment of conversion those eyes were opened for an instant: obtained, as it were, a dazzling and unforgettable glimpse of the Uncreated Light. They must learn to stay open: to look steadfastly into the eyes of Love: so that, in the beautiful imagery of the mystics, the "faithful servant" may become the "secret friend." Then it is, says Boehme, that "the divine glimpse and beam of joy ariseth in the soul, being a new eye, in which the dark, fiery soul conceiveth the Ens and Essence of the divine light." So hard an art is not at once acquired in its perfection. It is in accordance with all that we know of the conditions of development that a partial achievement should come first; bewildering moments of lucidity, splendid glimpses, whose brevity is due to the weakness of the newly opened and unpractised "eye which looks upon Eternity," the yet undisciplined strength of the "eye which looks upon Time." Such is that play of light and dark, of exaltation and contrition, which often bridges the gap between the Purgative and the Illuminative states. Each by turn takes the field and ousts the other; for "these two eyes of the soul of man cannot both perform their work at once."

To use another and more domestic metaphor, that Divine Child which was, in the hour of the mystic conversion, born in the spark of the soul, must learn like other children to walk. Though it is true that the spiritual self must never lose its sense of utter dependence on the Invisible; yet within that supporting atmosphere, and fed by its gifts, it must "find its feet." Each effort to stand brings first a glorious sense of growth, and then a fall: each fall means another struggle to obtain the difficult balance which comes when infancy is past. There are many eager trials, many hopes, many disappointments. At last, as it seems suddenly, the moment comes: tottering is over, the muscles have learnt their lesson, they adjust themselves automatically, and the new self suddenly finds itself—it knows not how—standing upright and secure. That is the moment which marks the boundary between the purgative and the illuminative states.

The process of this passage of the "new" or spiritual man from his awakening to the illuminated life, has been set out by Jacob Boehme in language which is at once poetic and precise. "When Christ the Corner-Stone [*i.e.*, the divine principle latent in man] stirreth himself in the extinguished Image of Man in his hearty Conversion and Repentance," he says, "then Virgin Sophia appeareth in the stirring of the Spirit of Christ in the extinguished Image, in her Virgin's attire before the Soul; at which the Soul is so amazed and astonished in its Uncleanness that all its Sins immediately awake in it, and it trembleth before her; for then the judgment passeth upon the Sins of the Soul, so that it even goeth back in its unworthiness, being ashamed in the Presence of its fair Love, and entereth into itself, feeling and acknowledging itself utterly unworthy to receive such a Jewel. This is understood by those who are of our tribe and have tasted of this heavenly Gift, and by none else. But the noble Sophia draweth near in the Essence of the Soul, and kisseth it in friendly Manner, and tinctureth its dark Fire with her Rays of Love, and shineth through it with her bright and powerful Influence. Penetrated with the strong Sense and Feeling of which, the Soul skippeth in its Body for great Joy, and in the strength of this Virgin Love exulteth, and praiseth the great God for his blest Gift of Grace. I will set down here a short description how it is when the Bride thus embraceth the Bridegroom, for the consideration of the Reader, who perhaps hath not yet been in this wedding chamber. It may be he will be desirous to follow us, and to enter into the Inner Choir, where the Soul joineth hands and danceth with Sophia, or the Divine Wisdom."

THE ILLUMINATION OF THE SELF

In illumination we come to that state of consciousness which is popularly supposed to be peculiar to the mystic: a form of mental life, a kind of perception, radically different from that of "normal" men. His preceding adventures and experiences cannot be allowed this quality. His awakening to consciousness of the Absolute—though often marked by a splendour and intensity which seem to distinguish it from other psychic upheavals of that kind—does but reproduce upon higher levels those characteristic processes of conversion and falling in love which give depth and actuality to the religious and personal life. The purification to which he then sets himself—though this possesses as a rule certain features peculiar to mystical development—is again closely related to the disciplines and mortifications of ascetic, but not necessarily mystical, piety. It is the most exalted form with which we are acquainted of that *catharsis*— that pruning and training of the human plant—which is the essence of all education, and a necessary stage in every kind of transcendence. Here, the mystic does but adopt in a more drastic form the principles which all who would live with an intense life, all seekers after freedom, all true lovers must accept: though he may justly claim with Ophelia that these wear their rue with a difference.

But in the great swing back into sunshine which is the reward of that painful descent into the "cell of self-knowledge," he parts company with these other pilgrims. Those who still go with him a little way—certain prophets, poets, artists, dreamers do so in virtue of that mystical genius, that instinct for transcendental reality, of which all seers and creators have some trace. The initiates of beauty or of wisdom, as the great mystic is the initiate of love, they share in some degree the experiences of the way of illumination. But the mystic has now a veritable foothold in that transcendental world into which they penetrate now and again: enjoys a certain fellowship—not yet union—with the "great life of the All," and thence draws strength and peace. Really and actually, as one whose noviciate is finished, he has "entered the Inner Choir, where the Soul joineth hands and danceth with Sophia, the Divine Wisdom": and, keeping time with the great rhythms of the spiritual universe, feels that he has found his place.

This change of consciousness, however abrupt and amazing it may seem to the self which experiences it, seems to the psychologist a normal phase in that organic process of development which was initiated by the awakening of the transcendental sense. Responding to the intimations received in that awakening, ordering itself in their interest, concentrating its scattered energies on this one thing, the self emerges from long and varied acts of purification to find that it is able to apprehend another order of reality. It has achieved consciousness of a world that was always there, and wherein its substantial being—that Ground which is of God—has always stood. Such a consciousness is "Transcendental Feeling" *in excelsis:* a deep, intuitional knowledge of the "secret plan."

"We are like a choir who stand round the conductor," says Plotinus, "but do not always sing in tune, because their attention is diverted by looking at external things. So we always move round the One—if we did not, we should dissolve and cease to exist—but we do not always look towards the One." Hence, instead of that free and conscious co-operation in the great life of the All which alone can make personal life worth living, we move like slaves or marionettes, and, oblivious of the whole to which our little steps contribute, fail to observe the measure "whereto the worlds keep time." Our minds being distracted from the Corypheus in the midst the "energetic Word" who sets the rhythm, we do not behold Him. We are absorbed in the illusions of sense; the "eye which looks on Eternity" is idle. "But when we *do* behold Him," says Plotinus again, "we attain the end of our existence and our rest. Then we no longer sing out of tune, but form a truly divine chorus about Him; in the which chorus dance the soul beholds the Fountain of life the Fountain of intellect, the Principle of Being, the cause of good the root of soul." Such a beholding, such a lifting of consciousness from a self-centred to a God-centred world, is of the essence of illumination.

It will be observed that in these passages the claim of the mystic is not yet to supreme communion; the "Spiritual Marriage" of the Christian mystic, or that "flight of the Alone to the Alone" which is the Plotinian image for the utmost bliss of the emancipated soul. He has now got through preliminaries; detached himself from his chief entanglements; re-orientated his instinctive life. The result is a new and solid certitude about God, and his own soul's relation to God: an "enlightenment" in which he is adjusted to new standards of conduct and thought. In the traditional language of asceticism he is "proficient" but not yet perfect. He achieves a real vision and knowledge, a conscious harmony with the divine World of Becoming: not yet self-loss in the Principle of Life, but rather a willing and harmonious revolution about Him, that "in dancing he may know what is done." This character distinguishes almost every first-hand description of illumination and it is this which marks it off from mystic union in all its forms. All pleasurable and exalted states of mystic consciousness in which the sense of I-hood persists, in which there is a loving and joyous relation between the Absolute as object and the self as subject, fall under the head of Illumination which is really an enormous development of the intuitional life at high levels. All veritable and first-hand apprehensions of the Divine obtained by the use of symbols, as in the religious life; all the degrees of prayer lying between meditation and the prayer of union; many phases of poetic inspiration and "glimpses of truth," are activities of the illuminated mind.

To "see God in nature," to attain a radiant consciousness of the "otherness" of natural things, is the simplest and commonest form of illumination. Most people, under the spell of emotion or of beauty, have known flashes of rudimentary vision of this kind. Where such a consciousness is recurrent, as it is in many poets, there results that partial yet often overpowering apprehension of the Infinite Life immanent in all living things, which some modern writers have dignified by the name of "nature-mysticism." Where it is raised to its highest denomination, till the veil is obliterated by the light behind, and "faith has vanished into sight," as sometimes happened to Blake, we reach the point at which the mystic swallows up the poet.

"Dear Sir," says that great genius in one of his most characteristic letters, written immediately after an onset of the illuminated vision which he had lost for many years, "excuse my enthusiasm, or rather madness, for I am really drunk with intellectual vision whenever I take a pencil or graver into my hand." Many a great painter, philosopher, or poet, perhaps every inspired musician, has known this indescribable inebriation of Reality in those moments of transcendence in which his masterpieces were conceived. This is the "saving madness" of which Plato speaks in the "Phaedrus"; the ecstasy of the "God-intoxicated man," the lover, the prophet, and the poet "drunk with life." When the Christian mystic, eager for his birthright, says "Sanguis Christi, inebria me!" he is asking for just such a gift of supernal vitality, a draught of that Wine of Absolute Life which runs in the arteries of the world. Those to whom that cup is given attain to an intenser degree of vitality, hence to a more acute degree of perception, a more vivid consciousness, than that which is enjoyed by other men. For though, as Ruysbroeck warns us, this "is not God," yet it is for many selves "the Light in which we see Him."

Blake conceived that it was his vocation to bring this mystical illumination, this heightened vision of reality, within the range of ordinary men: to "cleanse the doors of perception" of the race. They thought him a madman for his pains.

"... I rest not upon my great task
To open the Eternal Worlds, to open the immortal Eyes
Of Man inwards into the Worlds of Thought: into Eternity
Ever expanding in the Bosom of God, the Human Imagination.
O Saviour, pour upon me thy Spirit of meekness and love,
Annihilate the Selfhood in me: be thou all my life."

The Mysteries of the antique world appear to have been attempts—often by way of a merely magical initiation—to "open the immortal eyes of man inwards": exalt his powers of perception until they could receive the messages of a higher degree of reality. In spite of much eager theorizing, it is impossible to tell how far they succeeded in this task. To those who had a natural genius for the Infinite, symbols and rituals which were doubtless charged with ecstatic suggestions, and often dramatized the actual course of the Mystic Way, may well have brought some enhancement of consciousness: though hardly that complete rearrangement of character which is an essential of the mystic's entrance on the true Illuminated State. Hence Plato only claims that "he whose initiation is recent" can see Immortal Beauty under mortal veils.

"O blessèd he in all wise,
Who hath drunk the Living Fountain
Whose life no folly staineth

And whose soul is near to God:
Whose sins are lifted pall-wise
As he worships on the Mountain."

Thus sang the initiates of Dionysus; that mystery-cult in which the Greeks seem to have expressed all they knew of the possible movement of consciousness through rites of purification to the ecstasy of the Illuminated Life. The mere crude rapture of illumination has seldom been more vividly expressed. With its half-Oriental fervours, its self-regarding glory in personal purification achieved, and the spiritual superiority conferred by adeptship, may be compared the deeper and lovelier experience of the Catholic poet and saint, who represents the spirit of Western mysticism at its best. His sins, too, had been "lifted pall-wise" as a cloud melts in the sunshine of Divine Love but here the centre of interest is not the little self which has been exalted, but the greater Self which deigns thus to exalt.

"O burn that burns to heal!
O more than pleasant wound!
And O soft hand, O touch most delicate
That dost new life reveal
That dost in grace abound
And, slaying, dost from death to life translate."

Here the joy is as passionate, the consciousness of an exalted life as intense but it is dominated by the distinctive Christian concepts of humility, surrender, and intimate love.

We have seen that all real artists, as well as all pure mystics, are sharers to some degree in the Illuminated Life. They have drunk, with Blake, from that cup of intellectual vision which is the chalice of the Spirit of Life: know something of its divine inebriation whenever Beauty inspires them to create. Some have only sipped it. Some, like John of Parma, have drunk deep, accepting in that act the mystic heritage with all its obligations. But to all who have seen Beauty face to face, the Grail has been administered; and through that sacramental communion they are made participants in the mystery of the world.

In one of the most beautiful passages of the "Fioretti" it is told how Brother Jacques of la Massa, "unto whom God opened the door of His secrets," saw in a vision this Chalice of the Spirit of Life delivered by Christ into the hands of St. Francis, that he might give his brothers to drink thereof.

"Then came St. Francis to give the chalice of life to his brothers. And he gave it first to Brother John of Parma: who, taking it drank it all in haste, devoutly; and straightway he became all shining like the sun. And after him St. Francis gave it to all the other brothers in order and there were but few among them that took it with due reverence and devotion and drank it all. Those that took it devoutly and drank it all, became straightway shining like the sun; but those that spilled it all and took it not devoutly, became black, and dark, and misshapen and horrible to see; but those that drank part and spilled part, became partly shining and partly dark, and more so or less according to the measure of their drinking or spilling thereof. But the aforesaid Brother John was resplendent above all the rest; the which had more completely drunk the chalice of life, *whereby he had the more deeply gazed into the abyss of the infinite light divine.*"

No image, perhaps, could suggest so accurately as this divine picture the conditions of perfect illumination: the drinking deeply, devoutly, and in haste—that is, without prudent and self-regarding hesitation—of the heavenly Wine of Life; that wine of which Rolle says that it "fulfils the soul with a great gladness through a sweet contemplation." John of Parma, the hero of those Spiritual Franciscans in whose interest this exquisite allegory was composed, stands for all the mystics, who, "having completely drunk," have attained the power of gazing into the abyss of the infinite light divine. In those imperfect brothers who dared not drink the cup of sacrifice to the dregs, but took part and spilled part, so that they became partly shining and partly dark, "according to the measure of their drinking or spilling thereof," we may see an image of the artist, musician, prophet, poet, dreamer, more or less illuminated according to the measure of courage and self-abandonment in which he has drunk the cup of ecstasy but always in comparison with the radiance of the pure contemplative, "partly shining and partly dark." "Hinder me not," says the soul to the senses in Mechthild of Magdeburg's vision, "I would drink for a space of the unmingled wine." In the artist, the senses have somewhat hindered the perfect inebriation of the soul.

We have seen that a vast tract of experience—all the experience which results from contact between a purged and heightened consciousness and the World of Becoming in which it is immersed; and much, too, of that which results from contact set up between such a consciousness and the Absolute Itself—is included in that stage of growth which the mystics call the Illuminative Way. This is the largest and most densely populated province of the mystic kingdom. Such different visionaries as Suso and Blake, Boehme and Angela of Foligno, Mechthild of Magdeburg, Fox, Rolle, St. Teresa, and countless others have left us the record of their sojourn therein. Amongst those who cannot be called pure mystics we can detect in the works of Plato and Heracleitus, Wordsworth, Tennyson, and Walt Whitman indications that they too were acquainted, beyond most poets and seers, with the phenomena of the illuminated life. In studying it then, we shall be confronted by a mass of apparently irreconcilable material: the results of the relation set up between every degree of lucidity, every kind of character, and the suprasensible world.

To say that God is Infinite is to say that He may be apprehended and described in an infinity of ways. That Circle whose centre is everywhere and whose circumference is nowhere, may be approached from every angle with a certainty of being found. Mystical history, particularly that which deals with the Illuminative Way, is a demonstration of this fact. Here, in the establishment of the "first mystic life," of conscious correspondence with Reality, the self which has oscillated between two forms of consciousness, has alternately opposed and embraced its growing intuitions of the Absolute, comes for a time to rest. To a large extent, the discordant elements of character have been purged away. Temporally at least the mind has "unified itself" upon high levels, and attained, as it believes, a genuine consciousness of the divine and veritable world. The depth and richness of its own nature will determine how intense that consciousness shall be.

Whatever its scope, however, this new apprehension of reality generally appears to the illuminated Self as final and complete. As the true lover is always convinced that he has found in his bride the one Rose of the World, so the mystic, in the first glow of his initiation, is sure that his quest is now fulfilled. Ignorant as yet of that consummation of love which overpasses the proceedings of the inward eye and ear, he exclaims with entire assurance "Beati oculi qui exterioribus clausi, interioribus autem sunt intenti," and, absorbed in this new blissful act of vision, forgets that it belongs to those who are still *in via*. He has yet to pass through that "night of the senses" in which he learns to distinguish the substance of Reality from the accidents under which it is perceived; to discover that the heavenly food here given cannot satisfy his "hunger for the Absolute." His true goal lies far beyond this joyful basking in the sunbeams of the Uncreated Light. Only the greatest souls learn this lesson, and tread the whole of that "King's Highway" which leads man back to his Source. "For the many that come to Bethlehem, there be few that will go on to Calvary." The rest stay here, in this Earthly Paradise, these flowery fields; where the liberated self wanders at will, describing to us as well as it can now this corner, now that of the Country of the Soul.

It is in these descriptions of the joy of illumination—in the outpourings of love and rapture belonging to this state—that we find the most lyrical passages of mystical literature. Here poet, mystic, and musician are on common ground: for it is only by the oblique methods of the artist, by the use of aesthetic suggestion and musical rhythm, that the wonder of that vision can be expressed. When essential goodness, truth, and beauty—Light, Life, and Love—are apprehended by the heart, whether the heart be that of poet, painter, lover, or saint, that apprehension can only be communicated in a living, that is to say, an artistic form. The natural mind is conscious only of succession: the special *differentia* of the mystic is the power of apprehending simultaneity. In the peculiarities of the illuminated consciousness we recognize the effort of the mind to bridge the gap between Simultaneity and Succession: the characters of Creator and Creation. Here the successive is called upon to carry the values of the Eternal.

Here, then, genius and sanctity kiss one another; and each, in that sublime encounter, looks for an instant through the other's eyes. Hence it is natural and inevitable that the mystic should here call into play all the resources of artistic expression: the lovely imagery of Julian and Mechthild of Magdeburg, Suso's poetic visions, St. Augustine's fire and light, the heavenly harmonies of St. Francis and Richard Rolle. Symbols, too, play a major part, not only in the description, but also in the machinery of illumination: the intuitions of many mystics presenting themselves directly to the surface-mind in a symbolic form. We must therefore be prepared for a great variety and fluidity of expression, a constant and not always conscious recourse to symbol and image, in those who try to communicate the secret of this state of consciousness. We must examine, and even classify so far as possible, a wide variety of experience—some which is recognized by friends and foes alike as purely "mystical," some in which the operation of poetic imagination is clearly discernible, some which involves "psychic phenomena" and other abnormal activities of the mind—refusing to be frightened away from investigation by the strange, and apparently irreconcilable character of our material.

There are three main types of experience which appear again and again in the history of mysticism; nearly always in connection with illumination, rather than any other phase of mystical development. I think that they may fairly be regarded as its main characteristics, though the discussion of them cannot cover all the ground. In few forms of spiritual life is the spontaneity of the individual so clearly seen as here and in few is the ever-deadly process of classification attended with so many risks.

These three characteristics are:

1. A joyous apprehension of the Absolute: that which many ascetic writers call "the practice of the Presence of God." This, however, is not to be confused with that unique consciousness of union with the divine which is peculiar to a later stage of mystical development. The self, though purified, still realizes itself as a separate entity over against God. It is not immersed in its Origin, but contemplates it. This is the "betrothal" rather than the "marriage" of the soul.
2. This clarity of vision may also be enjoyed in regard to the phenomenal world. The actual physical perceptions seem to be strangely heightened, so that the self perceives an added significance and reality in all natural things: is often convinced that it knows at last "the secret of the world." In Blake's words "the doors of perception are cleansed" so that "everything appears to man as it *is*, infinite." In these two forms of perception we see the growing consciousness of the mystic stretching in two directions, until it includes in its span both the World of Being

and the World of Becoming; that dual apprehension of reality as transcendent yet immanent which we found to be one of the distinguishing marks of the mystic type.

3. Along with this two-fold extension of consciousness, the energy of the intuitional or transcendental self may be enormously increased. The psychic upheavals of the Purgative Way have tended to make it central for life: to eliminate from the character all those elements which checked its activity. Now it seizes upon the ordinary channels of expression; and may show itself in such forms as (a) auditions, (b) dialogues between the surface consciousness and another intelligence which purports to be divine, (c) visions, and sometimes (d) in automatic writings. In many selves this automatic activity of those growing but still largely subconscious powers which constitute the "New Man," increases steadily during the whole of the mystic life.

Illumination, then, tends to appear mainly under one or all of these three forms. Often all are present; though, as a rule, one is dominant. The balance of characteristics will be conditioned in each case by the self's psychic make-up; its temperamental leaning towards "pure contemplation," "lucid vision," or automatic expression; emanation or immanence, the metaphysical, artistic, or intimate aspects of truth. The possible combinations between these various factors are as innumerable as the possible creations of Life itself.

In the wonderful rhapsodies of St. Augustine, in St. Bernard's converse with the Word, in Angela of Foligno's apprehensions of Deity, in Richard Rolle's "state of song," when "sweetest heavenly melody he took, with him dwelling in mind," or in Brother Lawrence's "practice of the Presence of God," we may see varied expressions of the first type of illuminated consciousness. Jacob Boehme is rightly looked upon as a classic example of the second; which is also found in one of its most attractive forms in St. Francis of Assisi. Suso and St. Teresa, perhaps, may stand for the third, since in them the visionary and auditory phenomena were peculiarly well marked. A further study of each characteristic in order, will help us to disentangle the many threads which go to the psychical make-up of these great and complex mystic types.

The Consciousness of the Absolute, or "Sense of the Presence of God"

This consciousness, in its various forms and degrees, is perhaps the most constant characteristic of Illumination; and makes it, for the mystic soul, a pleasure-state of the intensest kind. I do not mean by this that the subject passes months or years in a continuous ecstasy of communion with the Divine. Intermittent periods of spiritual fatigue or "aridity"—renewals of the temperamental conflicts experienced in purgation—the oncoming gloom of the Dark Night—all these may be, and often are, experienced at intervals during the Illuminated Life; as flashes of insight, indistinguishable from illumination, constantly break the monotony of the Purgative Way. But a deep certitude of the Personal Life omnipresent in the universe has been achieved; and this can never be forgotten, even though it be withdrawn. The "spirit stretching towards God" declares that it has touched Him; and its normal condition henceforth is joyous consciousness of His Presence with "many privy touchings of sweet spiritual sights and feeling, measured to us as our simpleness may bear it." Where he prefers less definite or more pantheistic language, the mystic's perceptions may take the form of "harmony with the Infinite"—the same divine music transposed to a lower key.

This "sense of God" is not a metaphor. Innumerable declarations prove it to be a consciousness as sharp as that which other men have, or think they have, of colour, heat, or light. It is a well-known though usually transitory experience in the religious life: like the homing instinct of birds, a fact which can neither be denied nor explained. "How that presence is felt, it may better be known by experience than by any writing," says Hilton, "for it is the life and the love, the might and the light, the joy and the rest of a chosen soul. And therefore he that hath soothfastly once felt it he may not forbear it without pain; he may not undesire it, it is so good in itself and so comfortable.... He cometh privily sometimes when thou art least aware of Him, but thou shalt well know Him or He go; for wonderfully He stirreth and mightily He turneth thy heart into beholding of His goodness, and doth thine heart melt delectably as wax against the fire into softness of His love."

Modern psychologists have struggled hard to discredit this "sense of the presence"; sometimes attributing it to the psychic mechanism of projection, sometimes to "wish-fulfilments" of a more unpleasant origin. The mystics, however, who discriminate so much more delicately than their critics between true and false transcendental experience, never feel any doubt about its validity. Even when their experience seems inconsistent with their theology, they refuse to be disturbed.

Thus St. Teresa writes of her own experience, with her usual simplicity and directness, "In the beginning it happened to me that I was ignorant of one thing—I did not know that God was in all things: and when He seemed to me to be so near, I thought it impossible. Not to believe that He was present was not in my power; for it seemed to me, as it were, evident that I felt there His very presence. Some unlearned men used to say to me, that He was present only by His grace. *I could not believe that,* because, as I am saying, He seemed to me to be present Himself: so I was distressed. A most learned man, of the Order of the glorious Patriarch St. Dominic, delivered me from this doubt, for he told me that He was present, and how He communed with us: this was a great comfort to me."

Again, "An interior peace, and the little strength which either pleasures or displeasures have to remove this presence (during the time it lasts) of the Three Persons, and that without power to doubt of it, continue in such a manner that I clearly seem to experience what St. John says, *That He will dwell in the soul,* and this not only by grace, but that He will also make her perceive this presence." St. Teresa's strong "immanental" bent comes out well in this passage.

Such a sense of the divine presence may go side by side with the daily life and normal mental activities of its possessor; who is not necessarily an ecstatic or an abstracted visionary, remote from the work of the world. It is true that the transcendental consciousness has now become, once for all, his centre of interest, its perceptions and admonitions dominate and light up his daily life. The object of education, in the Platonic sense, has been achieved, his soul has "wheeled round from the perishing world" to "the contemplation of the real world and the brightest part thereof." But where vocation and circumstances require it, the duties of a busy outward life continue to be fulfilled with steadiness and success and this without detriment to the soul's contemplation of the Real.

In many temperaments of the unstable or artistic type, however, this intuitional consciousness of the Absolute becomes ungovernable: it constantly breaks through, obtaining forcible possession of the mental field and expressing itself in the "psychic" phenomena of ecstasy and rapture. In others, less mobile, it wells up into an impassioned apprehension, a "flame of love" in which the self seems to "meet God in the ground of the soul." This is "pure contemplation": that state of deep orison in which the subject seems to be "seeing, feeling and thinking all at once." By this spontaneous exercise of all his powers under the dominion of love, the mystic attains that "Vision of the Heart" which, "more interior, perhaps, than the visions of dream or ecstasy," stretches to the full those very faculties which it seems to be holding in suspense; as a top "sleeps" when it is spinning fast. *Ego dormio et cor meum vigilat*. This act of contemplation, this glad surrender to an overwhelming consciousness of the Presence of God, leaves no sharp image on the mind, only a knowledge that we have been lifted up, to a veritable gazing upon that which eye hath not seen.

St. Bernard gives in one of his sermons a simple, ingenuous and obviously personal account of such "privy touchings," such convincing but elusive contacts of the soul with the Absolute. "Now bear with my foolishness for a little," he says, "for I wish to tell you, as I have promised, how such events have taken place in me. It is, indeed, a matter of no importance. But I put myself forward only that I may be of service to you; and if you derive any benefit I am consoled for my egotism. If not, I shall but have displayed my foolishness. I confess, then, though I say it in my foolishness, that the Word has visited me, and even very often. But, though He has frequently entered into my soul, I have never at any time been sensible of the precise moment of His coming. I have felt that He was present, I remember that He has been with me; I have sometimes been able even to have a presentiment that He would come: but never to feel His coming nor His departure. For whence He came to enter my soul, or whither He went on quitting it, by what means He has made entrance or departure, I confess that I know not even to this day; according to that which is said, *Nescis unde veniat aut quo vadat*. Nor is this strange, because it is to Him that the psalmist has said in another place, *Vestigia tua non cognoscentur*.

"It is not by the eyes that He enters, for He is without form or colour that they can discern; nor by the ears, for His coming is without sound; nor by the nostrils, for it is not with the air but with the mind that He is blended.... By what avenue then has He entered? Or perhaps the fact may be that He has not entered at all, nor indeed come at all from outside: for not one of these things belongs to outside. Yet it has not come from within me, for it is good, and I know that in me dwelleth no good thing. I have ascended higher than myself, and lo! I have found the Word above me still. My curiosity has led me to descend below myself also, and yet I have found Him still at a lower depth. If I have looked without myself, I have found that He is beyond that which is outside of me, and if within, He was at an inner depth still. And thus have I learned the truth of the words I have read, *In ipso enim vivimus et movemur et sumus*."

Such a lifting up, such a condition of consciousness as that which St. Bernard is here trying to describe, seems to snatch the spirit for a moment into a state which it is hard to distinguish from that of true "union." This is what the contemplatives call passive or infused contemplation, or sometimes the "orison of union": a brief foretaste of the Unitive State, often enjoyed for short periods in the Illuminative Way, which reinforces their conviction that they have now truly attained the Absolute. It is but a foretaste, however, of that attainment: the precocious effort of a soul still in that stage of "Enlightening" which the "Theologia Germanica" declares to be "belonging to such as are growing."

This distinction between the temporary experience of union and the achievement of the Unitive Life is well brought out in a fragment of dialogue between Soul and Self in Hugh of St. Victor's mystical tract, "De Arrha Animae."

The Soul says, "Tell me, what can be this thing of delight that merely by its memory touches and moves me with such sweetness and violence that I am drawn out of myself and carried away, I know not how? I am suddenly renewed: I am changed: I am plunged into an ineffable peace. My mind is full of gladness, all my past wretchedness and pain is forgot. My soul exults: my intellect is illuminated: my heart is afire: my desires have become kindly and gentle: I know not where I am, because my Love has embraced me. Also, because my Love has embraced me I seem to have become possessed of something, and I know not what it is; but I try to keep it, that I may never lose it. My soul strives in gladness that she may not be separated from That which she desires to hold fast for ever: as if she had found in it the goal of all her desires. She exults in a sovereign and ineffable manner, seeking nought, desiring nought, but to rest in this. Is *this,* then, my Beloved? Tell me that I may know Him, and that if He come again I may entreat Him to leave me not, but to stay with me for ever."

Man says, "It is indeed thy Beloved who visits thee; but He comes in an invisible shape, He comes disguised, He comes incomprehensibly. He comes to touch thee, not to be seen of thee: to arouse thee, not to be comprehended of thee. He comes not to give Himself wholly, but to be tasted by thee: not to fulfil thy desire, but to lead upwards thy affection. He gives a foretaste of His delights, brings not the plenitude of a perfect satisfaction: and the earnest of thy betrothal consists chiefly in this, that He who shall afterwards give Himself to be seen and possessed by thee perpetually, now permits Himself to be sometimes tasted, that thou mayest learn how sweet He is. This shall console thee for His absence: and the savour of this gift shall keep thee from all despair."

The real distinction between the Illuminative and the Unitive Life is that in Illumination the individuality of the subject—however profound his spiritual consciousness, however close his apparent communion with the Infinite—remains separate and intact. His heightened apprehension of reality lights up rather than obliterates the rest of his life and may even increase his power of dealing adequately with the accidents of normal existence. Thus Brother Lawrence found that his acute sense of reality, his apprehension of the Presence of God, and the resulting detachment and consciousness of liberty in regard to mundane things, upheld and assisted him in the most unlikely tasks; as, for instance, when he was sent into Burgundy to buy wine for his convent, "which was a very unwelcome task to him, because he had no turn for business, and because he was lame, and could not go about the boat but by rolling himself over the casks. That, however, he gave himself no uneasiness about it, nor about the purchase of the wine. That he said to God, *It was His business he was about:* and that he afterwards found it very well performed.... So likewise in his business in the kitchen, to which he had naturally a great aversion."

The mind, concentrated upon a higher object of interest, is undistracted by its own anxieties, likes, or dislikes; and hence performs the more efficiently the work that is given it to do. Where it does not do so, then the normal make-up or imperfect discipline of the subject, rather than its mystical proclivities, must be blamed. St. Catherine of Genoa found in this divine companionship the power which made her hospital a success. St. Teresa was an administrator of genius and an admirable housewife, and declared that she found her God very easily amongst the pots and pans. Appearances notwithstanding, Mary would probably have been a better cook than Martha, had circumstances required of her this form of activity.

In persons of feeble or diffuse intelligence, however, and above all in victims of a self-regarding spirituality, this deep absorption in the sense of Divine Reality may easily degenerate into monoideism. Then the "shady side" of Illumination, a selfish preoccupation with transcendental joys, the "spiritual gluttony" condemned by St. John of the Cross, comes out. "I made many mistakes," says Madame Guyon pathetically, "through allowing myself to be too much taken up by my interior joys.... I used to sit in a corner and work, but I could hardly do anything, because the strength of this attraction made me let the work fall out of my hands. I spent hours in this way without being able to open my eyes or to know what was happening to me: so simply, so peacefully, so gently that sometimes I said to myself, 'Can heaven itself be more peaceful than I?'"

Here we see Madame Guyon basking like a pious tabby cat in the beams of the Uncreated Light, and already leaning to the extravagances of Quietism, with its dangerous "double character of passivity and beatitude." The heroic aspect of the mystic vocation is in abeyance. Those mystical impressions which her peculiar psychic make-up permitted her to receive, have been treated as a source of personal and placid satisfactions; not as a well-spring, whence new vitality might be drawn for great and self-giving activities.

It has been claimed by the early biographers of St. Catherine of Genoa, that she passed in the crisis of her conversion directly through the Purgative to the Unitive Life; and never exhibited the characteristics of the Illuminative Way. This has been effectually disproved by Baron von Hügel, though he too is inclined in her case to reject the usual sequence of the mystic states. Yet the description of Catherine's condition after her four great penitential years were ended, as given in cap. vi. of the "Vita e Dottrina," is an almost perfect picture of healthy illumination of the inward or "immanental" type; and makes an effective foil to the passage which I have quoted from Madame Guyon's life.

No doubt there were hours in which St. Catherine's experience, as it were, ran ahead; and she felt herself not merely lit up by the Indwelling Light, but temporally merged in it. These moments are responsible for such passages as the beautiful fragment in cap. v.; which does, when taken alone, seem to describe the true unitive state. "Sometimes," she said, "I do not see or feel myself to have either soul, body, heart, will or taste, or any other thing except Pure Love." Her normal condition of consciousness, however, was clearly not yet that which Julian of Norwich calls being "oned with bliss"; but rather an intense and continuous communion with an objective Reality which was clearly realized as distinct from herself. "After the aforesaid four years," says the next chapter of the "Vita," "there was given unto her a purified mind, free, and filled with God: insomuch that no other thing could enter into it. Thus, when she heard sermons or Mass, so much was she absorbed in her interior feelings, that she neither heard nor saw that which was said or done without. But within, in the sweet divine light, she saw and heard other things, being wholly absorbed by that interior light: and it was not in her power to act otherwise." St. Catherine, then, is still a spectator of the Absolute, does not feel herself to be *one* with it. "And it is a marvellous thing that with so great an interior recollection, the Lord never permitted her to go beyond control. But when she was needed, she always came to herself: so that she was able to reply to that which was asked of her: and the Lord so guided her, that none could complain of her. And she had her mind so filled by Love Divine, that conversation became hard to her: and by this continuous taste and sense of God, several times she was so greatly transported, that she was forced to hide herself, that she might not be seen." It is clear, however, that Catherine herself was aware of the transitory and imperfect nature of this intensely joyous state. Her growing transcendental self, unsatisfied with the sunshine of the Illuminative Way, the enjoyment of the riches of God, already aspired to union with the Divine. With her, as with all truly heroic souls, it was love for love, not love for joy. "She cried to God because He gave her so many consolations, *'Non voglio quello che esce da te, ma sol voglio te, O dolce Amore* !'"

"Non voglio quello che esce da te." When the growing soul has reached this level of desire, the Illuminative Way is nearly at an end. It has seen the goal, "that Country which is no mere vision, but a home," and is set upon the forward march. So Rabia, the Moslem saint: "O my God, my concern and my desire in this world, is that I should remember thee above all the things of this world, and in the next that out of all who are in that world, I should meet with thee alone." So Gertrude More: "No knowledge which we can here have of thee can satisfy my soul seeking and longing without ceasing after thee.... Alas, my Lord God, what is all thou canst give to a loving soul which sigheth and panteth after thee alone, and esteemeth all things as dung that she may gain thee? What is all I say, whilst thou givest not thyself, who art that one thing which is only necessary and which alone can satisfy our souls? Was it any comfort to St. Mary Magdalen, when she sought thee, to find two angels which presented themselves instead of thee? verily I cannot think it was any joy unto her. For that soul that hath set her whole love and desire on thee can never find any true satisfaction but only in thee."

What is the nature of this mysterious mystic illumination? Apart from the certitude it imparts, what is the form which it most usually assumes in the consciousness of the self? The illuminatives seem to assure us that its apparently symbolic name is really descriptive; that they do experience a kind of radiance, a flooding of the personality with new light. A new sun rises above the horizon, and transfigures their twilit world. Over and over again they return to light-imagery in this connection. Frequently, as in their first conversion, they report an actual and overpowering consciousness of radiant light, ineffable in its splendour, as an accompaniment of their inward adjustment.

"Sopr' onne lengua amore,
bontá senza figura,
lume fuor di mesura
resplende nel mio core,"

sang Jacopone da Todi. "Light rare, untellable!" said Whitman. "The flowing light of the Godhead," said Mechthild of Magdeburg, trying to describe *what* it was that made the difference between her universe and that of normal men. *"Lux vixens dicit,"* said St. Hildegarde of her revelations, which she described as appearing in a special light, more brilliant than the brightness round the sun. It is an "infused brightness," says St. Teresa, "a light which knows no night; but rather, as it is always light, nothing ever disturbs it."

"De subito parve giorno a giorno
essere aggiunto!"

exclaims Dante, initiated into the atmosphere of heaven; "Lume è lassù"is his constant declaration:

"Cio ch' io dico è un semplice lume,"

his last word, in the effort to describe the soul's apprehension of the Being of God.

It really seems as though the mystics' attainment of new levels of consciousness did bring with it the power of perceiving a splendour always there, but beyond the narrow range of our poor sight; to which it is only a "luminous darkness" at the best. "In Eternal Nature, or the kingdom of Heaven," said Law, "materiality stands in life and light." The cumulative testimony on this point is such as would be held to prove, in any other department of knowledge, that there is indeed an actual light, "lighting the very light" and awaiting the recognition of men.

Consider the accent of realism with which St. Augustine speaks of his own experience of Platonic contemplation; a passage in which we seem to see a born psychologist desperately struggling by means of negations to describe an intensely positive state. "I entered into the secret closet of my soul, led by Thee; and this I could do because Thou wast my helper. I entered, and beheld with the mysterious eye of my soul the Light that never changes, above the eye of my soul, above my intelligence. It was not the common light which all flesh can see, nor was it greater yet of the same kind, as if the light of day were to grow brighter and brighter and flood all space. It was not like this, but different: altogether different from all such things. Nor was it above my intelligence in the same way as oil is above water, or heaven above earth; but it was higher because it made me, and I was lower because made by it. He who knoweth the truth knoweth that Light: and who knoweth it, knoweth eternity. Love knoweth it."

Here, as in the cases of St. Teresa, St. Catherine of Genoa, and Jacopone da Todi, we have a characteristically "immanental" description of the illuminated state. The self, by the process which mystics call "introversion," the deliberate turning inwards of its attention, its conative powers, discerns Reality within the heart: "the rippling tide of love which flows secretly from God into the soul, and draws it mightily back into its source." But the opposite or transcendental tendency is not less frequent. The cosmic vision of Infinity, exterior to the subject—the expansive, outgoing movement towards a Divine Light,

"Che visible face
lo Creatore a quella creatura,
che solo in lui vedere ha la sua pace,"

wholly other than anything the earth-born creature can conceive—the strange, formless absorption in the Divine Dark to which the soul is destined to ascend—all these modes of perception are equally characteristic of the Illuminative Way. As in conversion, so here Reality may be apprehended in either transcendent or immanent, positive or negative terms. It is both near and far; "closer to us than our most inward part, and higher than our highest"; and for some selves that which is far is easiest to find. To a certain type of mind, the veritable practice of the Presence of God is not the intimate and adorable companionship of the personal Comrade or the Inward Light, but the awestruck contemplation of the Absolute, the "naked Godhead," source and origin of all that Is. It is an ascent to the supernal plane of perception, where "the simple, absolute and unchangeable mysteries of heavenly Truth lie hidden in the dazzling obscurity of the secret Silence, outshining all brilliance with the intensity of their darkness, and surcharging our blinded intellects with the utterly impalpable and invisible fairness of glories which exceed all beauty."

With such an experience of eternity, such a vision of the triune all-including Absolute which "binds the Universe with love," Dante ends his "Divine Comedy": and the mystic joy with which its memory fills him is his guarantee that he has really seen the Inviolate Rose, the flaming heart of things.

"O abbondante grazia, ond' io presunsi
ficcar lo viso per la luce eterna
tanto che la veduta vi consunsi!
Nel suo profondo vidi che s' interna,
legato con amore in un volume,
ciò che per l'universo si squaderna;
Sustanzia ed accidenti, e lor costume,
quasi conflati insieme per tal modo

che ciò ch' io dico è un semplice lume.
La forma universal di questo nodo
credo ch' io vidi, perchè più di largo,
dicendo questo, mi sento ch' io godo.
.....
O, quanto è corto il dire, e come fioco
al mio concetto! e questo, a quel ch' io vidi,
è tanto che non basta a dicer poco.
O luce eterna, che sola in te sidi,
sola t' intendi, e, da te intelletta
ed intendente te, ami ed arridi!"

In Dante, the transcendent and impersonal aspect of illumination is seen in its most exalted form. It seems at first sight almost impossible to find room within the same system for this expansive vision of the Undifferentiated Light and such intimate and personal apprehensions of Deity as Lady Julian's conversations with her "courteous and dearworthy Lord," or St. Catherine's companionship with Love Divine. Yet all these are really reports of the same psychological state: describe the attainment by selves of different types, of the same stage in the soul's progressive apprehension of reality.

In a wonderful passage, unique in the literature of mysticism, Angela of Foligno has reported the lucid vision in which she perceived this truth: the twofold revelation of an Absolute at once humble and omnipotent, personal and transcendent—the unimaginable synthesis of "unspeakable power" and "deep humility."

"The eyes of my soul were opened, and I beheld the plenitude of God, wherein I did comprehend the whole world, both here and beyond the sea, and the abyss and ocean and all things. In all these things I beheld naught save the divine power, in a manner assuredly indescribable; so that through excess of marvelling the soul cried with a loud voice, saying 'This whole world is full of God!' Wherefore I now comprehended how small a thing is the whole world, that is to say both here and beyond the seas, the abyss, the ocean, and all things; and that the Power of God exceeds and fills all. Then He said unto me: 'I have shown thee something of My Power,' and I understood, that after this I should better understand the rest. He then said 'Behold now My humility.' Then was I given an insight into the deep humility of God towards man. And comprehending that unspeakable power and beholding that deep humility, my soul marvelled greatly, and did esteem itself to be nothing at all."

It must never be forgotten that all apparently one-sided descriptions of illumination—more, all experiences of it—are governed by temperament. "That Light whose smile kindles the Universe" is ever the same; but the self through whom it passes, and by whom we must receive its report, has already submitted to the moulding influences of environment and heredity, Church and State. The very language of which that self avails itself in its struggle for expression, links it with half a hundred philosophies and creeds. The response which it makes to Divine Love will be the same in type as the response which its nature would make to earthly love: but raised to the *n* th degree. We, receiving the revelation, receive with it all those elements which the subject has contributed in spite of itself. Hence the soul's apprehension of Divine Reality may take almost any form, from the metaphysical ecstasies which we find in Dionysius, and to a less degree in St. Augustine, to the simple, almost "common-sense" statements of Brother Lawrence, the emotional ardours of St. Gertrude, or the lovely intimacies of Julian or Mechthild.

Sometimes—so rich and varied does the nature of the great mystic tend to be—the exalted and impersonal language of the Dionysian theology goes, with no sense of incongruity, side by side with homely parallels drawn from the most sweet and common incidents of daily life. Suso, in whom illumination and purgation existed side by side for sixteen years, alternately obtaining possession of the mental field, and whose oscillations between the harshest mortification and the most ecstatic pleasure-states were exceptionally violent and swift, is a characteristic instance of such an attitude of mind. His illumination was largely of the intimate and immanental type; but, as we might expect in a pupil of Eckhart, it was not without touches of mystical transcendence, which break out with sudden splendour side by side with those tender and charming passages in which the Servitor of the Eternal Wisdom tries to tell his love.

Thus, he describes of his life how "whilst he was thinking, according to his custom, of the most lovable Wisdom, he questioned himself, and interrogated his heart, which sought persistently for love, saying, 'O my heart, whence comes this love and grace, whence comes this gentleness and beauty, this joy and sweetness of the heart? Does not all this flow forth from the Godhead, as from its origin? Come! let my heart, my senses and my soul immerse themselves in the deep Abyss whence come these adorable things. What shall keep me back? To-day I will embrace you, even as my burning heart desires to do.' And at this moment there was within his heart as it were an emanation of all good, all that is beautiful, all that is lovable and desirable was there spiritually present, and this in a manner which cannot be expressed. Whence came the habit that every time he heard God's praises sung or said, he recollected himself in the depths of his heart and soul, and thought on that Beloved Object, whence comes all love. It is impossible to tell how often, with eyes filled with tears and open heart, he has embraced his sweet Friend, and pressed Him to a heart overflowing with love. He was like a baby which a mother holds upright on her knees, supporting it with her hands beneath its arms. The baby, by the movements of its little head, and all its little body, tries to get closer and closer to its dear mother, and shows by its little laughing gestures the gladness in its heart. Thus did the heart of the Servitor ever seek the sweet neighbourhood of the Divine Wisdom, and thus he was as it were altogether filled with delight."

The Illuminated Vision of the World

Closely connected with the sense of the "Presence of God," or power of perceiving the Absolute, is the complementary mark of the illuminated consciousness; the vision of "a new heaven and a new earth," or an added significance and reality in the phenomenal world. Such words as those of Julian, "God is all thing that is good as to my sight, and the goodness that all thing hath, it is He," seem to supply the link between the two. Here again we must distinguish carefully between vaguely poetic language—"the light that never was," "every common bush afire with God"—and descriptions which can be referred to a concrete and definite psychological experience. This experience, at its best, balances and completes the experience of the Presence of God at its best. That is to say, its "note" is sacramental, not ascetic. It entails the expansion rather than the concentration of consciousness; the discovery of the Perfect One self-revealed in the Many, not the forsaking of the Many in order to find the One. Its characteristic expression is—

"The World is charged with the grandeur of God;
It will flame out, like shining from shook foil,"

not "turn thy thoughts into thy own soul, where He is hid." It takes, as a rule, the form of an enhanced mental lucidity—an abnormal sharpening of the senses—whereby an ineffable radiance, a beauty and a reality never before suspected, are perceived by a sort of clairvoyance shining in the meanest things.

"From the moment in which the soul has received the impression of Deity in infused orison," says Malaval, "she sees Him everywhere, by one of love's secrets which is only known of those who have experienced it. The simple vision of pure love, which is marvellously penetrating, does not stop at the outer husk of creation: it penetrates to the divinity which is hidden within."

Thus Browning makes David declare—

"I but open my eyes,—and perfection, no more and no less
In the kind I imagined full-fronts me, and God is seen God
In the star, in the stone, in the flesh, in the soul and the clod."

Blake's "To see a world in a grain of sand," Tennyson's "Flower in the crannied wall," Vaughan's "Each bush and oak doth know I AM," and the like, are exact though over-quoted reports of "things seen" in this state of consciousness, this "simple vision of pure love": the value of which is summed up in Eckhart's profound saying, "The meanest thing that one knows in God—for instance if one could understand a flower as it has its Being in God—this would be a higher thing than the whole world!" Mystical poets of the type of Wordsworth and Walt Whitman seem to possess in a certain degree this form of illumination. It is this which Bucke, the American psychologist, analysed under the name of "Cosmic Consciousness." It is seen at its full development in the mystical experiences of Boehme, Fox, and Blake.

We will take first the experience of Jacob Boehme, a mystic who owed little or nothing to the influence of tradition, and who furnishes one of the best recorded all-round examples of mystical illumination; exhibiting, along with an acute consciousness of divine companionship, all those phenomena of visual lucidity, automatism, and enhanced intellectual powers which properly belong to it, but are seldom developed simultaneously in the same individual.

In Boehme's life, as described in the Introduction to the English translation of his collected works, there were three distinct onsets of illumination; all of the pantheistic and external type. In the first, which seems to have happened whilst he was very young, we are told that "he was surrounded by a divine Light for seven days, and stood in the highest contemplation and Kingdom of Joy." This we may perhaps identify with mystical awakening, of the kind experienced by Suso. About the year 1600 occurred the second illumination, initiated by a trance-like state of consciousness, the result of gazing at a polished disc. To this I have already referred. This experience brought with it that peculiar and lucid vision of the inner reality of the phenomenal world in which, as he says, "he looked into the deepest foundations of things." "He believed that it was only a fancy, and in order to banish it from his mind he went out upon the green. But here he remarked that he gazed into the very heart of things, the very herbs and grass, and that actual Nature harmonized with what he had inwardly seen." Of this same experience and the clairvoyance which accompanied it, another biographer says, "Going abroad in the fields to a green before Neys Gate, at Görlitz, he there sat down, and, viewing the herbs and grass of the field in his inward light, he saw into their essences, use and properties, which were discovered to him by their lineaments, figures and signatures.... In the unfolding of these mysteries before his understanding, he had a great measure of joy, yet returned home and took care of his family and lived in great peace and silence, scarce intimating to any these wonderful things that had befallen him."

So far as we can tell from his own scattered statements, from this time onwards Boehme must have enjoyed a frequent and growing consciousness of the transcendental world: though there is evidence that he, like all other mystics, knew seasons of darkness, "many a shrewd Repulse," and times of struggle with that "powerful contrarium" the lower consciousness. In 1610—perhaps as the result of such intermittent struggles—

the vivid illumination of ten years before was repeated in an enhanced form: and it was in consequence of this, and in order that there might be some record of the mysteries upon which he had gazed, that he wrote his first and most difficult book, the "Aurora," or "Morning Redness." The passage in which the "inspired shoemaker" has tried to tell us what his vision of Reality was like, to communicate something of the grave and enthusiastic travail of his being, the unspeakable knowledge of things which he attained, is one of those which arouse in all who have even the rudiments of mystical perception the sorrow and excitement of exiles who suddenly hear the accents of home. Like absolute music, it addresses itself to the whole being, not merely to the intellect. Those who will listen and be receptive will find themselves repaid by a strange sense of extended life, an exhilarating consciousness of truth. Here, if ever, is a man who is struggling to "speak as he saw" and it is plain that he saw much—as much, perhaps, as Dante, though he lacked the poetic genius which was needed to give his vision an intelligible form. The very strangeness of the phrasing, the unexpected harmonies and dissonances which worry polite and well-regulated minds, are earnests of the Spirit of Life crying out for expression from within. Boehme, like Blake, seems "drunk with intellectual vision"—"a God-intoxicated man."

"In this my earnest and Christian Seeking and Desire," he says, "(wherein I suffered many a shrewd Repulse, but at last resolved rather to put myself in Hazard, than give over and leave off) the Gate was opened to me, that in one Quarter of an Hour I saw and knew more than if I had been many years together at an University, at which I exceedingly admired, and thereupon turned my Praise to God for it. For I saw and knew the Being of all Beings, the Byss and the Abyss, and the Eternal Generation of the *Holy Trinity,* the Descent and Original of the World, and of all creatures through the Divine Wisdom: knew and saw in myself all the three Worlds, namely, *The Divine,* angelical and paradisical; and the *dark World,* the Original of the Nature to the Fire; and then, thirdly, the *external;* and *visible World,* being a Procreation or external Birth from both the internal and spiritual Worlds. And I saw and knew the whole working Essence in the Evil and the Good, and the Original and Existence of each of them; and likewise how the fruitful bearing Womb of Eternity brought forth.... Yet however I must begin to labour in these great mysteries, as a Child that goes to School. I saw it as in a great Deep in the Internal. For I had a thorough view of the Universe, as in a Chaos, wherein all things are couched and wrapped up, but it was impossible for me to explain the same. Yet it opened itself to me, from Time to Time, as in a Young Plant; though the same was with me for the space of twelve years, and as it was as it were breeding, and I found a powerful Instigation within me, before I could bring it forth into external Form of Writing and whatever I could apprehend with the external Principle of my mind, that I wrote down."

Close to this lucid vision of the reality of things—this sudden glimpse of the phenomenal in the light of the intelligible world—is George Fox's experience at the age of twenty-four, as recorded in his Journal. Here, as in Boehme's case, it is clear that a previous and regrettable acquaintance with the "doctrine of signatures" has to some extent determined the language and symbols under which he describes his intuitive vision of actuality as it exists in the Divine Mind.

"Now was I come up in spirit through the flaming sword into the Paradise of God. All things were new: and all the creation gave another smell unto me than before, beyond what words can utter.... The creation was opened to me; and it was showed me how all things had their names given them, according to their nature and virtue. And I was at a stand in my mind whether I should practise physic for the good of mankind, seeing the nature and virtue of the creatures were so opened to me by the Lord.... Great things did the Lord lead me unto, and wonderful depths were opened unto me beyond what can by words be declared; but as people come into subjection to the Spirit of God, and grow up in the image and power of the Almighty, they may receive the word of wisdom that opens all things, and come to know the *hidden unity in the Eternal Being."*

"To know the hidden unity in the Eternal Being"—know it with an invulnerable certainty, in the all-embracing act of consciousness with which we are aware of the personality of those we truly love—is to live at its fullest the Illuminated Life, enjoying "all creatures in God and God in all creatures." Lucidity of this sort seemes to be an enormously enhanced form of the poetic consciousness of "otherness" in natural things—the sense of a unity in separateness, a mighty and actual Life beyond that which eye can see, a glorious reality shining through the phenomenal veil—frequent in those temperaments which are at one with life. The self then becomes conscious of the living reality of that World of Becoming, the vast arena of the Divine creativity, in which the little individual life is immersed. Alike in howling gale and singing cricket it hears the crying aloud of that "Word which is through all things everlastingly." It participates, actively and open-eyed, in the mighty journey of the Son towards the Father's heart: and seeing with purged sight all things and creatures as they are in that transcendent order, detects in them too that striving of Creation to return to its centre which is the secret of the Universe.

A harmony is thus set up between the mystic and Life in all its forms. Undistracted by appearance, he sees, feels, and knows it in one piercing act of loving comprehension. "And the bodily sight stinted," says Julian, "but the spiritual sight dwelled in mine understanding, and I abode with reverent dread joying in that I saw." The heart outstrips the clumsy senses, and sees—perhaps for an instant, perhaps for long periods of bliss—an undistorted and more veritable world. All things are perceived in the light of charity, and hence under the aspect of beauty: for beauty is simply Reality seen with the eyes of love. As in the case of another and more beatific Vision, *essere in caritate è qui necesse.* For such a reverent and joyous sight the meanest accidents of life are radiant. The London streets are paths of loveliness; the very omnibuses look like coloured archangels, their laps filled full of little trustful souls.

Often when we blame our artists for painting ugly things, they are but striving to show us a beauty to which we are blind. They have gone on ahead of us, and attained that state of "fourfold vision to which Blake laid claim; in which the visionary sees the whole visible universe transfigured, because he has "put off the rotten rags of sense and memory," and "put on Imagination uncorrupt." In this state of lucidity symbol and reality, Nature and Imagination, are seen to be *One:* and in it are produced all the more sublime works of art, since these owe their greatness to the impact of Reality upon the artistic mind. "I know," says Blake again, "that this world is a world of imagination and vision. I see everything I paint in this world, but everybody does not see alike. To the eye of a miser a guinea is far more beautiful than the sun and a bag worn with the use of money has more beautiful proportions than a vine filled with grapes. The tree which moves some to tears of joy is in the eyes of others only a green thing which stands in the way. Some see Nature all ridicule and deformity, and by these I shall not regulate my proportions; and some scarce see Nature at all. But to the eyes of the man of imagination Nature is Imagination itself. As a man is, so he sees. As the eye is formed, such are its powers. You certainly mistake, when you say that the visions of fancy are not to be found in this world. To me this world is all one continued vision of fancy or imagination, and I feel flattered when I am told so."

If the Mystic Way be considered as an organic process of transcendence, this illuminated apprehension of things, this cleansing of the doors of perception, is surely what we might expect to occur as man moves towards higher centres of consciousness. It marks the self's growth towards free and conscious participation in the Absolute Life; its progressive appropriation of that life by means of the contact which exists in the deeps of man's being—the ground or spark of the soul—between the subject and the transcendental world. The surface intelligence, purified from the domination of the senses, is invaded more and more by the transcendent personality; the "New Man" who is by nature a denizen of the independent spiritual world, and whose destiny, in mystical language, is a "return to his Origin." Hence an inflow of new vitality, a deeper and wider apprehension of the mysterious world in which man finds himself, an exaltation of his intuitive powers.

In such moments of clear sight and enhanced perception as that which Blake and Boehme describe, the mystic and the artist do really see *sub specie aeternitatis* the Fourfold River of Life—that World of Becoming in which, as Erigena says, "Every visible and invisible creature is a theophany or appearance of God"— as all perhaps might see it, if prejudice, selfhood, or other illusion did not distort our sight. From this loving vision there comes very often that beautiful sympathy with, that abnormal power over, all living natural things, which crops up again and again in the lives of the mystical saints; to amaze the sluggish minds of common men, barred by "the torrent of Use and Wont" from all free and deep communion alike with their natural and supernatural origin.

Yet it is surely not very amazing that St. Francis of Assisi, feeling and knowing—not merely "believing"—that every living creature was veritably and actually a "theophany or appearance of God," should have been acutely conscious that he shared with these brothers and sisters of his the great and lovely life of the All. Nor, this being so, can we justly regard him as eccentric because he acted in accordance with his convictions, preached to his little sisters the birds, availed himself of the kindly offices of the falcon, enjoyed the friendship of the pheasant, soothed the captured turtledoves, his "simple-minded sisters, innocent and chaste," or persuaded his Brother Wolf to a better life.

The true mystic, so often taunted with "a denial of the world," does but deny the narrow and artificial world of self: and finds in exchange the secrets of that mighty universe which he shares with Nature and with God. Strange contacts, unknown to those who only lead the life of sense, are set up between his being and the being of all other things. In that remaking of his consciousness which follows upon the "mystical awakening," the deep and primal life which he shares with all creation has been roused from its sleep. Hence the barrier between human and non-human life, which makes man a stranger on earth as well as in heaven, is done away. Life now whispers to his life: all things are his intimates, and respond to his fraternal sympathy.

Thus it seems quite a simple and natural thing to the Little Poor Man of Assisi, whose friend the pheasant preferred his cell to "the haunts more natural to its state," that he should be ambassador from the terrified folk of Gubbio to his formidable brother the Wolf. The result of the interview, reduced to ordinary language, could be paralleled in the experience of many persons who have possessed this strange and incommunicable power over animal life.

"O wondrous thing! whereas St. Francis had made the sign of the Cross, right so the terrible wolf shut his jaws and stayed his running and when he was bid, came gently as a lamb and laid him down at the feet of St. Francis.... And St. Francis stretching forth his hand to take pledge of his troth, the wolf lifted up his right paw before him and laid it gently on the hand of St. Francis, giving thereby such sign of good faith as he was able. Then quoth St. Francis, 'Brother Wolf, I bid thee in the name of Jesu Christ come now with me, nothing doubting, and let us go stablish this peace in God's name.' And the wolf obedient set forth with him, in fashion as a gentle lamb; whereat the townsfolk made mighty marvel, beholding.... And thereafter this same wolf lived two years in Agobio; and went like a tame beast in and out the houses from door to door, without doing hurt to any, or any doing hurt to him, and was courteously nourished by the people; and as he passed thus wise through the country and the houses, never did any dog bark behind him. At length after a two years space, brother wolf died of old age: whereat the townsfolk sorely grieved, sith marking him pass so gently through the city, they minded them the better of the virtue and the sanctity of St. Francis."

In another mystic, less familiar than St. Francis to English readers—Rose of Lima, the Peruvian saint—this deep sympathy with natural things assumed a particularly lovely form. To St. Rose the whole world was a holy fairyland, in which it seemed to her that every living thing turned its face towards Eternity and joined in her adoration of God. It is said in her biography that "when at sunrise, she passed through the garden to go to her retreat, she called upon nature to praise with her the Author of all things. Then the trees were seen to bow as she passed by, and clasp their leaves together, making a harmonious sound. The flowers swayed upon their stalks, and opened their blossoms that they might scent the air; thus according to their manner praising God. At the same time the birds began to sing, and came and perched upon the hands and shoulders of Rose. The insects greeted her with a joyous murmur, and all which had life and movement joined in the concert of praise she addressed to the Lord."

Again—and here we catch an echo of the pure Franciscan spirit, the gaiety of the Troubadours of God—during her last Lent, "each evening at sunset a little bird with an enchanting voice came and perched upon a tree beside her window, and waited till she gave the sign to him to sing. Rose, as soon as she saw her little feathered chorister, made herself ready to sing the praises of God, and challenged the bird to this musical duel in a song which she had composed for this purpose. 'Begin, dear little bird,' she said, 'begin thy lovely song! Let thy little throat, so full of sweet melodies, pour them forth: that together we may praise the Lord. Thou dost praise thy Creator, I my sweet Saviour: thus we together bless the Deity. Open thy little beak, begin and I will follow thee: and our voices shall blend in a song of holy joy.'

"At once the little bird began to sing, running through his scale to the highest note. Then he ceased, that the saint might sing in her turn... thus did they celebrate the greatness of God, turn by turn, for a whole hour: and with such perfect order, that when the bird sang Rose said nothing, and when she sang in her turn the bird was silent, and listened to her with a marvellous attention. At last, towards the sixth hour, the saint dismissed him, saying, 'Go, my little chorister, go, fly far away. But blessed be my God who never leaves me!'"

The mystic whose illumination takes such forms as these, who feels with this intensity and closeness the bond of love which "binds in one book the scattered leaves of all the universe," dwells in a world unknown to other men. He pierces the veil of imperfection, and beholds Creation with the Creator's eye. The "Pattern is shown him in the Mount." "The whole consciousness," says Récéjac, "is flooded with light to unknown depths, under the gaze of love, from which nothing escapes. In this stage, intensity of vision and sureness of judgment are equal: and the things which the seer brings back with him when he returns to common life are not merely partial impressions, or the separate knowledge of 'science' or 'poetry.' They are rather truths which embrace the world, life and conduct: in a word, *the whole consciousness*."

It is curious to note in those diagrams of experience which we have inherited from the more clear-sighted philosophers and seers, indications that they have enjoyed prolonged or transitory periods of this higher consciousness; described by Récéjac as the marriage of imaginative vision with moral transcendence. I think it at least a reasonable supposition that Plato's doctrine of Ideas owed something to an intuition of this kind; for a philosophy, though it may claim to be the child of pure reason, is usually found to owe its distinctive character to the philosopher's psychological experience. The Platonic statements as to the veritable existence of the Idea of a house, a table, or a bed, and other such concrete and practical applications of the doctrine of the ideal, which have annoyed many metaphysicians, become explicable on such a psychological basis. That illuminated vision in which "all things are made new" can afford to embrace the homeliest as well as the sublimest things; and, as a matter of experience, it does do this, seeing all objects, as Monet saw the hayrick, as "modes of light." Blake said that his cottage at Felpham was a shadow of the angels' houses, and I have already referred to the converted Methodist who saw his horses and hogs on the ideal plane.

Again, when Plotinus, who is known to have experienced ecstatic states, speaks with the assurance of an explorer of an "intelligible world," and asks us, "What other fire could be a better image of the fire which is there, than the fire which is here? Or what other earth than this, of the earth which is there?" we seem to detect behind the language of Neoplatonic philosophy a hint of the same type of first-hand experience. The minds to whom we owe the Hebrew Kabalah found room for it too in their diagram of the soul's ascent towards Reality. The first "Sephira" above Malkuth, the World of Matter, or lowest plane upon that Tree of Life which is formed by the ten emanations of the Godhead is, they say, "Yesod," the "archetypal universe." In this are contained the realities, patterns, or Ideas, whose shadows constitute the world of appearance in which we dwell.

The path of the ascending soul upon the Tree of Life leads him first from Malkuth to Yesod: *i.e.*, human consciousness in the course of its transcendence passes from the normal illusions of men to a deeper perception of its environment—a perception which is symbolized by the "archetypal plane" or world of Platonic Ideas. "Everything in temporal nature," says William Law, "is descended out of that which is eternal, and stands as a palpable visible outbirth of it, so when we know how to separate the grossness, death, and darkness of time from it, we find what it is in its eternal state.... In Eternal Nature, or the Kingdom of Heaven, materiality stands in life and light; it is the light's glorious Body, or that garment wherewith light is clothed, and therefore has all the properties of light in it, and only differs from light as it is its brightness and beauty, as the holder and displayer of all its colours, powers, and virtues." When Law wrote this, he may have believed that he was interpreting to English readers the unique message of his master, Jacob Boehme. As a matter of fact he was reiterating truths which a long line of practical mystics had been crying for centuries into the deaf ears of mankind. He was saying in the eighteenth century what Gregory of Nyssa had said in the fourth and Erigena in the ninth; telling the secret of that "Inviolate Rose" which can never be profaned because it can only be seen with the eyes of love.

That serene and illuminated consciousness of the relation of things inward and outward—of the Hidden Treasure and its Casket, the energizing Absolute and its expression in Time and Space—which we have been studying here, is at its best a state of fine equilibrium; a sane adjustment of the inner and outer life. By that synthesis of love and will which is the secret of the heart, the mystic achieves a level of perception in which the whole world is seen and known in God, and God is seen and known in the whole world. It is a state of exalted emotion: being produced by love, of necessity it produces love in its turn. The sharp division between its inlooking and outlooking forms which I have adopted for convenience of description, is seldom present to the minds which achieve it. They, "cleansed, fed, and sanctified," are initiated into a spiritual universe where such clumsy distinctions have little meaning. All is alike part of the "new life" of peaceful charity: and that progressive abolition of selfhood which is of the essence of mystical development, is alone enough to prevent them from drawing a line between the inward personal companionship and outward impersonal apprehension of the Real. True Illumination, like all real and vital experience, consists rather in the breathing of a certain atmosphere, the living at certain levels of consciousness, than in the acquirement of specific information. It is, as it were, a resting-place upon "the steep stairway of love"; where the self turns and sees all about it a transfigured universe, radiant with that same Light Divine which nests in its own heart and leads it on.

"When man's desires are fixed immovably on his Maker as far as for deadliness and corruption of the flesh he is let," says Rolle of the purified soul which has attained the illuminated state, "then it is no marvel that his strength manly using, first as it were heaven being opened, with his understanding he beholds high heavenly citizens; and afterwards sweetest heat, as it were burning fire, he feels. Then with marvellous sweetness he is taught, and so forth in songful noise he is joyed. This, therefore, is perfect charity, which no man knows but he that hath it took. And he that it has taken, it never leaves: sweetly he lives and sickerly he shall die."

Sweetly, it is true, the illuminated mystic may live; but not, as some think, placidly. Enlightenment is a symptom of growth and growth is a living process, which knows no rest. The spirit, indeed, is invaded by a heavenly peace; but it is the peace, not of idleness, but of ordered activity. "A rest most busy," in Hilton's words: a progressive appropriation of the Divine. The urgent push of an indwelling spirit, aspiring to its home in the heart of Reality, is felt more and more, as the invasion of the normal consciousnesss by the transcendental personality—the growth of the New Man—proceeds towards its term.

Therefore the great seekers for reality are not as a rule long delayed by the exalted joys of Illumination. Intensely aware now of the Absolute Whom they adore, they are aware too that though known He is unachieved. Even whilst they enjoy the rapture of the Divine Presence—of life in a divine, ideal world—something, they feel, makes default. *Sol voglio Te, O dolce Amore*. Hence for them that which they now enjoy, and which passes the understanding of other men, is not a static condition; often it coexists with that travail of the heart which Tauler has called "stormy love." The greater the mystic, the sooner he realizes that the Heavenly Manna which has been administered to him is not yet That with which the angels are full fed. Nothing less will do: and for him the progress of illumination is a progressive consciousness that he is destined not for the sunny shores of the spiritual universe, but for "the vast and stormy sea of the divine."

"Here," says Ruysbroeck of the soul which has been lit by the Uncreated Light, "there begins an eternal hunger, which shall never more be satisfied. It is the inward craving and hankering of the affective power and created spirit after an Uncreated Good. And as the spirit longs for fruition, and is invited and urged thereto by God, she must always desire to attain it. Behold! here begin an eternal craving and continual yearning in eternal insatiableness! These men are poor indeed: for they are hungry and greedy, and their hunger is insatiable! Whatsoever they eat and drink they shall never be satisfied, for this hunger is eternal.... Here are great dishes of food and drink, of which none know but those who taste them; but full satisfaction in fruition is the one dish that lacks them, and this is why their hunger is ever renewed. Nevertheless in this contact rivers of honey full of all delight flow forth; for the spirit tastes these riches under every mode that it can conceive or apprehend. But all this is according to the manner of the creatures, and is below God: and hence there remains an eternal hunger and impatience. If God gave to such a man all the gifts which all the saints possess, and all that He is able to give, but without giving Himself, the craving desire of the spirit would remain hungry and unsatisfied."

9

HINDU MYSTICISM

The Hindus possess a body of sacred compositions called the Vedas. Of these there are four collections. Two of them comprise original hymns. The contents of the others consist largely of poems derived from the former two. The collections of original hymns, known as the Rig Veda and the Atharva Veda, include, respectively, 1028 original hymns of about 10600 stanzas and 731 hymns of about 6000 stanzas. All of these were kept in memory and transmitted by recitation and close memorizing on the part of teachers and pupils in an unbroken chain of early traditions from a time when writing was probably not known. The opinions of scholars vary greatly regarding the antiquity of this literature; some think that the hymns were composed about 6000 B. C. or at a still earlier date, while others think that they were composed about 1200 B. C. or 1000 B. C. The Vedic hymns are probably the earliest important religious documents of the human race.

The hymns of the Atharva Veda contain among other things descriptions of charms for curing diseases, prayers for long life and health, imprecations against demons, sorcerers and enemies, charms pertaining to women—to secure their love or arouse jealousy, and the like—charms for securing harmony and influence in an assembly, charms for securing the prosperity of household, fields, cattle, business, gambling, etc., charms in expiation of sins and defilement. The hymns of the Rig Veda, on the other hand, are often praises of various deities, who are frequently mere personifications of the different powers of nature, such as the rain-god, the wind-god, the fire-god, and the like. The prayers in these hymns are praises of the greatness and power, the mysterious nature, and the exploits of these deities, as well as prayers for various favors.

Often the favors sought are of the nature of material blessings, such as long life, vigorous offspring, cattle and horses, gold, etc. Prayers for the advancement of the inner spiritual achievements of man, for righteousness or moral greatness, prayers a passionate longing for the divine or a humble submission of the mind to the divine will are not so frequent. Most of these prayers were recited in the performance of certain prescribed rituals. Though from the praises of the gods one might infer that it was the gods who were supposed to bestow the benefits, it was in fact the complete set of ritualistic performances that was considered to be the cause of the showering of the benefits. It was supposed that these ritualistic performances when carried out in all their details, precisely and accurately, could by their joint and mysterious effect produce a mysterious something whereby the prayers were fulfilled.

I shall omit from my discussion the hymns of the Atharva Veda which deal only with spells, witchcraft and incantations. But while I take for examination those hymns of the Rig Veda which express beautiful ideas about the nature-deities and which voice personal requests for material comforts or for advantages, it should be understood that they also were chanted in connection with the performance of rituals and sacrifices. It is difficult to determine whether in the earliest period definite theories had been formulated regarding the intimate and indispensable connection between the chanting of these hymns of personal appeal and the performance of the rituals. But if we judge by the Vedic literature of the Brahmanas (probably composed shortly after the hymns, and later appended to them) which indicate authoritatively the place of these hymns in the ritualistic observances and specify what hymns were to be uttered under what ritualistic conditions and in what order or manner, it seems almost certain that the prevailing form of what is commonly called the Vedic religion may in strictness not be considered as a religion in the ordinarily accepted meaning of this term.

Many of the ritualistic observances, or *yajna,* required the help of a large number of priests, and large quantities of butter, rice, milk, animals, etc. They had to be performed with the most elaborate details from day to day, for months together and sometimes even for ten or twelve years; and it was enjoined that all the observances should be performed in exact accordance with the prescriptions laid down in the Brahmana literature. Even the slightest inaccuracy or the most trifling inexactness would be sufficient to spoil the entire effect of the sacrifice. But if the sacrifices were performed with the strictest accuracy, then the material advantages for which they were performed were bound to come regardless of the good will or the ill will of the gods to whom the prayers were offered. Tvashtar had performed a sacrifice for the birth of a son who might kill Indra, but owing to a slight error in pronunciation the meaning of the prayer was changed and the sacrifice produced a son who was not a killer of Indra but of whom Indra was the killer.

This idea of sacrifice is entirely different from anything found in other races. For with the Vedic people, the sacrifices were more powerful than the gods. The gods could be pleased or displeased; if the sacrifices were duly performed the prayers were bound to be fulfilled. The utterance or chanting of the stanzas of the Vedic hymns with specially prescribed accents and modulations, the pouring of the melted butter in the prescribed manner into the sacrificial fire, the husking of rice in a particular way, the making and exact placing of cakes, all the thousand details of rituals—often performed continuously for days, months and years with rigorous exactness—was called a *yajna* (frequently translated into English, "sacrifice"). All the good things that the people wanted, be it the birth of a son, a shower of rain, or a place of enjoyment in heaven, were believed to be secured through the performance of these sacrifices. It is possible that when these hymns were originally composed, they were but simple prayers to the deified powers of nature, or that they were only associated with some simple rituals.

But the evidence that is presented to us in the later Vedic and non-Vedic records containing descriptions of these sacrifices and discussions respecting their value, convinces us beyond doubt that it was the performance of these sacrifices, perfect in every detail in accordance with the dictates of the sacrificial manuals, the Brahmanas, that was believed to be capable of producing everything that a man could desire. A direct consequence of this apparently unmeaning necessity of strictest accuracy of ritualistic performances is a theory that came to be formulated and accepted in later periods, namely, that the sacrificial rites revealed such supernatural wisdom that they could not have been made by any one but were self-existent. It came to be held that the hymns of the Vedas, as well as the sacrificial manuals, were without authorship; that they existed eternally, prescribing certain courses of ritualistic procedure for the attainment of particular advantages and prohibiting certain undesirable courses of action. Consistently with the sacrificial theory it was also believed that the meanings of the hymns, so far as they described events or facts of nature or the exploits and the conduct of the gods were of a legendary character, that their true value consisted in the enjoining of particular courses of action or of dissuading people from other courses of action.

Religion in its ordinarily accepted sense means a personal relationship with some divine or transcendent person to whom we submit and to whom we pray for material advantages or for spiritual or moral enlightenment.

But here was a belief in the divinity or the uncreatedness of a literature—the Vedas—which was believed to contain within itself the secret laws of the universe. Here there was a conception of commands, categorical in nature and external in character, without the least suggestion of any commander. Though these commands were supposed not to have emanated from any person, they may nevertheless in some sense be described as transcendent, for they were regarded as far above human wisdom. No reason could be given why a particular sacrificial performance should produce any particular kind of material advantage. There stand the commands—commands which had revealed themselves to the minds of the various sages, which had no beginning in time, which do not imply any commander, and which are absolutely faultless and unerring in their directions.

The sacrifices, thus, were supposed to possess a mysterious power capable of regulating and modifying the workings of the universe for the advantage of individuals; and the Vedic commands were thought to embody omniscience respecting the ways of the world. Though the repository of omniscience, the Vedas were not conceived as divulging to us their secrets but merely as providing a body of directions which, if followed, would give whatever advantages one craved in this life or the next. The sacrifices (*yajna*) or their mysterious powers, are called *dharma*, a term which in Indian vernaculars is often used wrongly to translate the English word "religion." The Vedic hymns, the priests, and the sacrifices are also called "the great" by the application of the term *brahman*, which in later Indian philosophy and religion had such a momentous history.

What we have described is no ordinary magic of spells and incantations, but a repository of the cosmic secrets and cosmic forces. These impersonal commands unite in them the concepts of an unalterable law and perfect omniscience; they imply therefore the possibility of reaping all the comforts of this life and of the after-life by submission to them and compliance with them. But they involve no law-giver, no divine person, no author of the universe or of the destinies of human beings who must be pacified, obeyed or loved, and by whose grace we receive the blessings of life. We can control our own destinies, and have whatever we may want, if we only follow the commands. There is no other mystery of life save this great mystery of the Vedic commands, and these are absolutely inscrutable. These commands do not teach ordinary laws of social life or of behavior toward our fellow-beings, or anything that we could discover by our own intelligence and wisdom. Neither do they teach us anything that we could learn by experience or reason. They give direction for the attainment of the good things of this life or of the after-life only in so far as the means thereto are absolutely undiscoverable by us. They are not a body of facts, but a body of commands and prohibitions. Yet they do not represent commands of the inner conscience or of the spirit within us; they do not give us any food for the spirit.

They represent an objective and unalterable law realistically conceived, and they relate to desires for material comforts in this life or the life in heaven. This concept gives us all the principal elements of religion except that of a divine person. The acceptance of the blessings of this life as gifts from God, and a sense of our duty to please Him by submission and prayer are, therefore, not implied in this system of

Vedic sacrifices. What is implied is some great impersonal force which harmonises ourselves and our destinies with the happenings and events of the world of nature. Instead of God we find here a body of commands which demand our obedience and reverence; but the source of their power and the secret of their omniscient character and uncreatedness cannot be determined by us through reason or experience. But this ritualistic mysticism—if we may be permitted thus to call it—must be distinguished from the simple feelings and ideas that are found in the hymns themselves. In all probability the latter did not originally imply the complicated ritualistic hypotheses of the later period.

The forces of nature with their wonderful manifestations of inexplicable marvels appeared to the early sages like great beings endowed with life and personality. They were treated at times as friendly, but again as hostile. Sometimes the mystery of the natural phenomena seemed stupifying in its psychological effect. The laws of nature were at that time unknown, and there was no obstacle to the free flight of the imagination. When the Vedic sage saw the sun proceeding in his upward and downward course through the sky he cried out in his wonder:

"Undropped beneath, not fastened firm, how comes it
That downward turned he falls not downward?
The guide of his ascending path,—who saw it?"

The sage is full of wonder that "the sparkling waters of all rivers flow into one ocean without ever filling it." He perceives the unalterable course of the sun from day to day, and the succession of day and night, and he exclaims with delight: "Every day, in unceasing interchange with night and her dark wonders, comes the dawn with her beautiful ones to reanimate the worlds, never failing in her place, never in her time." Again, he is puzzled when thinking whither the shining ones of the sky disappear, and he cries forth in amazement:

"Who is it knows, and who can tell us surely
Where lies the path that leads to the Eternals?
Their deepest dwellings only we discover,
And hidden these in distant secret regions."

In how many hymns does the singer express his wonder that the rough red cow gives soft white milk. To the god Indra he cries:

"Grant me, O God, the highest, best of treasures,
A judging mind, prosperity abiding,
Riches abundant, lasting health of body,
The grace of eloquence, and days propitious."

To the God of the destroying storm he prays:

"Let me through thy best medicines, O Rudra,
My life on earth prolong a hundred winters.
From us dispel all hatred and oppression,
On every side calamity drive from us.
Where then, O Rudra, is thy hand of mercy,
The hand that healing brings and softens sorrow,
That takes away the ills which the gods send?
Let me, O mighty one, feel thy forgiveness.
The hero gladdened me amid tumult
With greater might when I his aid entreated;
Like some cool shade from the Sun's heat protected
May I attain to Rudra's grace and refuge."

Again when he is penitent he would ask forgiveness of the god Varuna, the personification of the all-embracing heaven, and say:

"If we to any dear and loved companion
Have evil done, to brother or to neighbour,
To our own countryman or to a stranger,
That sin do thou O Varuna forgive us."

Or,

"Forgive the wrongs, committed by our fathers,
What we ourselves have sinned in mercy pardon;
My own misdeeds do thou O God take from me,
And for another's sin let me not suffer."

Or, again,

"If ever we deceived like cheating players,
If consciously we have erred or all unconscious
According to our sin do not thou punish;
Be thou the singer's guardian in thy wisdom."

But besides these prayers, we sometimes find poems composed by the Vedic people, descriptive of their varied experiences of ordinary life. Thus a gambler gives his experience as follows:

"My wife has never angered me nor striven,
Was ever kind to me and my companions;
Though she was faithful to me, I have spurned her,
For love of dice, the only thing I value.
The gambler's wife deserted mourns; his mother

Laments her son, she knows not where he wanders
And he in debt and trouble, seeking money,
Remains at night beneath the roof of strangers.
And when I say that I will play no longer,
My friends abandon me and all desert me;
Yet then again I hear the brown dice rattling
I hasten, like a wanton to her lover."

Again we read:

"The gambler hurries to the gaming table,
'Today I'll win,' he thinks in his excitement.
The dice inflame his greed, his hopes mount higher;
He leaves his winnings all with his opponent."

When we read these hymns we see in them the simple prayers of a simple primitive people impressed with the inexplicable and varied phenomena of a tropical climate. They turn to the forces behind the latter as personified deities, describing the phenomena and offering their simple prayers. We find in these prayers experiences of simple wonder, of sufferings and of simple enjoyments. But when we come to the sacrificial stage of development we find a religious outlook in which the independent simple meanings of the hymns possess importance only for their sacrificial utterance in particular contexts. During the particular ritual observances the different verses were often torn out of their contexts and were combined with others which apparently had little or no relation with them and no conceivable bearing on the performances during which they were chanted or uttered.

They were simply the means for the performance of the sacrifices. Their simple meanings as descriptions of things or events or phenomena or ideas were dropped from consideration. The value attached to them centered about their being uttered or chanted in particular Vedic sacrifices in accordance with certain sacrificial canons of interpretation. The entire significance of these hymns consisted either in their use as directions for the performance of certain sacrificial duties or in their utterance in these sacrifices under prescribed conditions as found in the sacrificial manuals, the Brahmanas, which were considered as part of the Vedas. Thought and feeling were driven from their places of importance in human nature, and the whole emphasis was laid on the interpretation of the Vedic literature as a system of duties involving commands and prohibitions, and nothing else. Some of these duties were compulsory, while others were voluntary in the sense that they had to be performed only when one wanted to secure some desired end unattainable by any means discoverable by his reason or experience.

The authority which this system of Vedic injunctions and prohibitions was supposed to possess was so high as to demand the entire submission of one's will and thought.

Their claims did not stand in need of any justification by reason or logic, for they were supposed to be guides in a sphere where reason and experience were utterly helpless. The only fruitful way in which reason could be employed with regard to these Vedic commands was by accepting their authority and then trying to explain them in such a way that their mysterious nature might be reconciled to us. These Vedic commands cannot be described as "revelations" in the ordinary Christian sense of the term; for the latter presupposes the existence of a living God able and willing to bestow the body of truths that man requires, whereas the Vedic commands are devoid of any notion of a law-giver. This sacrificial mysticism, if it may be so called, does not recognize any God or supreme being from whom these commands emanate or who reveals them to man. The commands are taken as eternal truths, beginningless and immortal, revealing themselves to man and demanding man's submission to them. Nevertheless they are not spiritual or inner truths revealed from within man himself; they are external and impersonal commands which contain within themselves the inscrutable secrets of nature and of the happiness of man.

The fact that the Vedas were regarded as revelations of eternal truths, truths which no human reason could ever challenge, naturally divested reason of confidence in its ability to unravel the mysteries of man and of the world. Even in the somewhat later days of the evolution of Vedic culture, when there grew up a school of thinkers who disbelieved the claim that the whole of the Vedas were nothing but a body of commands and prohibitions and who held that there were at least some particular portions of the Vedas which dealt with the eternal truths of spiritual facts and experiences of reality, the belief remained unshaken that what the Vedas gave one as truths were unshakeable and unchallengeable by reason or by experience. This means a definite lowering or degradation of reason in its capacity as truth-finder. Reason calls for counter-reason and leads through an endless regressus without ever being able to lead to truth. The Vedas, then, are the only repository of the highest truths, and the function of reason is only to attempt to reconcile these truths with our experience and sense-observation. It is surprising that reason has continued to remain in this subordinate position throughout the development of Indian religious and philosophical thought almost to our own days. No change, no new idea could be considered to be right or could be believed by the people, unless it could also be shown that it had the sanction of the Vedas. Reason was never trusted as the only true and safe guide.

The word "mysticism" is a European word with a definite history. Most European writers have used it to denote an intuitive or ecstatic union with the deity, through contemplation, communion, or other mental experiences, or to denote the relationship and potential union of the human soul with ultimate reality. But I should for my present purposes like to give it a wider meaning which would include this and the other different types of mysticism. I should like to define mysticism as a theory, doctrine, or view that considers reason to be incapable of discovering or of realising the nature of ultimate truth, whatever be the nature of this ultimate truth, but at the same time believes in the certitude of some other means of arriving at it. If this definition be accepted, then this ritualistic philosophy of the Vedas is the earliest form of mysticism that is known to India or to the world. This Vedic mysticism prepared the way for the rise of the other forms of mysticism that sprang up in India.

The main elements of the sacrificial mysticism of the Vedas may be summarised as follows: First, a belief that the sacrifices when performed with perfect accuracy, possess a secret, mysterious power to bring about or produce as their effect whatever we may desire either in this life or in the hereafter. Second, the conception of an unalterable law—involved in such invariable and unfailing occurrences of effects consequent upon the performance of these sacrifices. Third, an acceptance of the impersonal nature of the Vedic literature, as having existed by itself from beginningless time and as not created or composed by any person, human or divine. Fourth, the view that the Vedic literature embodies nothing but a system of duties involving commands and prohibitions. Fifth, a recognition of the supreme authority of the Vedas as the only source of the knowledge of ultimate truths which are far beyond the powers of human reason. Sixth, the view that truth or reality, whether it be of the nature of commands or of facts (as was maintained by the later Vedic schools of thought, the Upanishads), could be found once for all in the words of the Vedas. Seventh, the belief that the Vedic system of duties demands unfailing obedience and submission. Two definite characteristics emerge from these: first, the transcendent, mysterious, and secret power of the sacrifices, replacing the natural forces personified as gods; second, the ultimate superiority of the Vedas as the source of all truths, and as the unchallengeable dictators of our duties, leading to our material well-being and happiness. The assumption of the mysterious omnipotence of sacrifices, performed by following the authoritative injunctions of the Vedas independently of reason or logical and discursive thought, forms the chief trait of the mysticism of the Vedic type. There is nothing here of feeling or even of intellect, but a blind submission, not to a person but to an impersonal authority which holds within it an unalterable and inscrutable law, the secret of all powers which we may want to wield in our favor.

The next step in the development of this type of mysticism consists in the growth of a school of thought which sought to intellectualise the material sacrifices. It encouraged the belief that it was quite unnecessary actually to perform the sacrifices requiring the expenditure of enormous sums of money for the collection of materials and for labor. The same results might be as well obtained through certain kinds of meditation or reflection. Thus, instead of the actual performance of a horse sacrifice, in which the immolation of a horse is accompanied by other rituals engaging the services of large numbers of men and the expenditure of funds such as kings alone could provide, one might as well think of the dawn as the head of a horse, the sun as its eye, the wind as its life, the heaven as its back, the intervening space as its belly, the sky as its flesh and the stars as its bones.

Such a meditation, or rather concentrated imagining of the universe as a cosmic horse, would, it was maintained, produce all the beneficial results that could be expected from the performance of an actual horse sacrifice. Thus, these attempts to intellectualise sacrifices took the form of replacing by meditation the actual sacrifices, and this substitution was believed to produce results which were equally beneficial. This meditation by substitution gradually took various forms: certain letters of the alphabet had, for example, to be thought of, or meditated upon, as Brahman or some other deity, or as vital functions of the body, or as some personified nature deity. This meditation was supposed to produce beneficial results. It should not be supposed that the sacrificial forms were entirely supplanted by these new forms of substitution-meditations. Rather did they spring up side by side with them. These forms of meditation did not mean prolonged contemplation, or any logical process of thinking, but merely the simple practice of continually thinking of one entity, process, or letter as another entity or process.

Even in modern India there are still many men who believe that the repetition of mystical formulas (apparently meaningless combinations of letters, or the names of some deities) is capable of producing beneficial results. Even the worship of a round or an oval stone as the god Vishnu or Siva, or again the worship of a waterjug or an image as a particular god or goddess, is nothing but a modified form of substitution-meditation, one thing being considered and meditated upon as another. These practices are to be distinguished from the ordinary spells and incantations commonly believed in by uneducated people. These substitution-meditations are often believed to be productive of virtue. They form the normal modes of worship of the ordinary Hindu and have now taken the place of the old sacrifices. Nevertheless the old Vedic sacrifices are also to a certain extent performed on occasions of marriages and other domestic ceremonies, as an indispensable part of those ceremonies which still claim to belong entirely to the Vedic order.

But, refraining from further references to modern India, let us pick up our thread of discussion and note the next stage in the development of the substitution-meditations. Although the latter were in their conception doubtless as mystical and magical as the old sacrifices, they represent an advance. For in them the mystical powers are supposed to reside not in external performances, but in specific forms of meditation or thinking. This represents an approach toward a consciousness of self and toward a recognition of the mystical powers of thought and meditation of a peculiar type. But it was only after an almost endless and fruitless search that the highest idea of self and the highest idea of world mystery and its solution dawned in the minds of the Vedic thinkers. What we find at this stage is merely that the Vedic thinkers had become conscious of the activity of thought and of imagination, and had begun to realise that the activity involved in thinking ought to be considered to be as potent a power as the activity involved in the actual performances of material sacrifices.

Man's inner thought and his performance of sacrificial duties in the world outside are both regarded as capable of producing mysterious changes and transformations in nature which would benefit man. Passages are to be found in the literature where the vital and other inner processes of the self are compared with a sacrifice. The three periods of human life are considered as being the same as the three bruisings of the sacrificial plant soma; and the functions of hungering, eating and begetting are considered to be the same as the different ceremonies of the soma sacrifice. Logical thinking in Vedic times seems to have taken the form of crude generalisation. The fundamental operation of logical thinking is generalisation based on a scrutiny of facts of experience, noting differences and avoiding false identifications. But in the early stages of Vedic thinking, generalisations were very crude and based on insufficient data, slurring points of difference and making bold identifications. Thus from the fact that we perspire through heat, there arose the cosmological belief that out of fire there came water.

From observation of three principal colors, red, white and black (the colors of fire, water and earth) sprang the idea that the universe is made up of the three elements, viz., fire, water and earth. It was thought that wherever there was red, it was due to the existence of fire, wherever there was white it was due to the existence of water, and wherever there was black, it was due to the existence of earth.

By a similar loose process of generalisation the word Brahman came to denote the Vedic verses, truth, sacrifices, and knowledge. Etymologically the word means "The Great." Probably it signified vaguely and obscurely the mysterious power underlying these sacrifices and the substitution-meditations. Both the ideas involved in the conception of Brahman as the highest power and the highest knowledge were derived from the notion of the sacrifices. Thus we read in the celebrated man-hymn of the Rig Veda that the gods offered the supreme man as a sacrifice and that from this great oblation all living creatures, as well as the atmosphere, sky, earth and the four quarters, came into being. Three parts of this supreme man transcend the world while one part of him is the whole world about us; and yet, he is himself both the sacrifice and the object of the sacrifice.

But while I have just emphasised the importance of the mysticism of sacrifice in the development of the mystical conception of Brahman as the supreme being, it would be wrong to hold that the mysticism of the sacrifices is alone responsible for the evolution of the great concept of Brahman. Side by side with the concept found in the Rig Veda of the many gods as personifications of the forces of nature, there was also growing a tendency toward the conception of one supreme being, and this tendency gradually gained in force. Thus, in Rig Veda X. 114.5 we find a verse in which it is said that the deity is one, though he is called by various names. One of the hymns (R. V. X. 129), again, runs as follows:

> "Then there was neither Aught nor Naught, no air nor sky beyond.
> What covered all? Where rested all? In watery gulf profound?
> Nor death was then, nor deathlessness, nor change of night and day.
> That one breathed calmly, self-sustained; naught else beyond it lay.
> Gloom hid in gloom existed first—one sea eluding view.
> The one a void in chaos wrapt, by inward fervor grew.
> Within it first arose desire, the primal germ of mind,
> Which nothing with existence links, as ages searching find.
> The kindling ray that shot across the dark and drear abyss,—
> Was it beneath or high aloft? What bard can answer this?
> There fecundating powers were found and mighty forces strove,
> A self-supporting mass beneath, and energy above.
> Who knows and who ever told, from whence this vast creation rose?
> No gods had then been born. Who then can e'er the truth disclose
> Whence sprang this world, whether framed by hand divine or no,
> Its lord in heaven alone can tell, if he can show."

Again, in the Atharva Veda (X, 7.) we find a hymn dedicated to Skambha where the different parts of this deity are identified not only with the different parts of the material world but also with a number of moral qualities such as faith, austere fervor, truthfulness, etc. All the thirty-three gods of the Vedas are contained within him and bow down to him. He is also called Brahman, "The Great." In the next hymn of the Atharva Veda (X. 8) Brahman is adored and spoken of as presiding over the past and the future, and he is said to be residing within our hearts and to be the self which never decays but is self-existent and self-satisfied. This appears to be very much like the idea of the Upanishads. In the Shatapatha Brahmana, also, we hear of Brahman as having created the gods; and in the Taittiriya Brahmana, Brahman is said to have created the gods and the entire world.

Thus we find that the conception of one great being who created the world and the gods, and who is also the power presiding over our lives and spirits, was gradually dawning in the minds of a few people. And though the sacrificial theory tended to lead away from the ordinary meanings of these Vedic hymns, the development of the sacrificial theory itself also made for the conception of some mysterious force which reconciled the destinies of the world and nature with those of men and their desires. This mysterious power, it was held, is resident not only in things external but also in activities of the inner life; it manifests itself in the power of thought, as is exemplified by the mysterious efficacy of the substitution-meditations. What was the nature of this mysterious power? It is difficult to answer this question. We have seen that its conception varied in significance according to the mode of its development and the sources from which it evolved. But when once the conception was formed, all these constituent notions were mixed together. People regarded Brahman as the highest, but they did not know how Brahman was to be known. Those who started with the sacrificial bias, thought substitution-meditations to be the way to a knowledge of Brahman. And so we find various instructions regarding meditation upon objects, such as the wind, life, fire, etc.,—even upon unmeaning letters.

But parallel with this tendency went another, viz., an intellectual search after Brahman, the highest, which displayed a contempt for sacrifices. We find Brahmins going out of their own sphere to warrior castes and kings for secret instruction about the nature of Brahman. There are narratives in which we find that kings belonging to the warrior caste fill proud Brahmins with a sense of discomfiture by exposing the ignorance of the latter concerning the secret nature of Brahman. Thus Balaki Gargya approached King Ajatashatru with the request to be allowed to explain to him the nature of Brahman. He then tried twelve times in succession to define Brahman as the presiding person in the sun, moon, lightning, ether, wind, fire, water, etc.; and in each case King Ajatashatru refuted him by showing the lower position that such presiding persons occupy in the whole of the universe, whereas

Brahman should be that which is the highest. Again, we find another narrative in which five Brahmins meet and discuss the question, "What is our Atman and what is Brahman?" They proceed to Uddalaka Aruni with the question. When Uddalaka mistrusts his ability to answer the question, all six go to King Ashvapati Kaikeya for instruction. King Ashvapati first asks them what it is that they worship as Atman or Brahman, anticipating their error that they still regard Atman or Brahman as a new kind of external divinity. The six Brahmins explain Atman in succession as the heaven, the sun, the wind, space, water, and the earth, and in so doing assume it to be an objective and an external deity more or less like the old Vedic deities. This shows us a stage of thought in which people somehow understood Brahman to be the highest principle, but yet found it difficult to shake off their old conceptions of external deities or personifications of nature. Again we find Sanatkumara instructing Narada regarding the nature of Brahman. In so doing Sanatkumara starts from "Name," by which he probably understands all conceptual knowledge. With his peculiar logic, which is difficult for us to follow, he observes that speech is greater than name, that mind is greater than speech, that imagination is greater than mind, and so on. Passing in succession through a number of such concepts, from lower to higher, he ultimately stops at that which is absolutely great, the unlimited, beyond which there is nothing and within which is comprehended all that is to be found in the outer and the inner world.

The most important point to be noted in the development of this stage of thought is that worship or prayer is possible only as directed toward a deity conceived with limited powers and as occupying a subordinate position in the universe. But with reference to that which is conceived as the highest truth and the highest power, there is no longer the possibility of external forms of worship. We shall find not only that it is not possible to worship Brahman but that it is not possible to reach Brahman by logical thought or any kind of conceptual apprehension. Thus in a Upanishadic story, referred to by Shankara, we are told of a person who approached a sage Bahva and sought from him instructions regarding the nature of Brahman. Bahva did not speak. He was asked a second time; still he did not speak. Yet again he was asked, but still he did not speak. When the inquirer became annoyed by this, Bahva told him that he was, from the first, by his silence telling him how Brahman was to be described: Brahman is silence and so cannot be represented in speech.

There are, however, unmistakable indications that there were still some who believed that even the highest could be worshipped and adored and that men could still submit themselves to Him as to the highest personal God who comprehends us all and controls us all. But the idea that was gradually gaining ground with some of the most important sages, was that Brahman, as the highest, is no ordinary personal God who can be induced by worship to favor us or who can be approached by the pure intellect or even by feeling. Brahman still retains its mysterious character as the highest power, truth, being and bliss which can neither be worshipped nor known by ordinary means of knowledge. But its nature can be realised, and realised so perfectly that the realisation will be like the bursting of a shell of light, a revelation which will submerge the whole of one's life together with all that it contains.

The Upanishads form the concluding portions of the Vedic literature, both chronologically from the point of view of the development of ideas. They were composed later than the priestly manuals, the Brahmanas, and the manuals of substitution-meditations in the Aranyaka literature, and they form the most authoritative background of all later Hindu philosophical thought. They possess the high authority of the Vedas and are the source of the highest wisdom and truth. The word "Upanishad" has been interpreted etymologically by Shankara to mean "that which destroys all ignorance and leads us to Brahman." It has also been interpreted to mean a secret or mystical doctrine, or a secret instruction, or a secret and confidential sitting. I have elsewhere, in my *History of Indian Philosophy*, shown how all the different systems of orthodox Indian philosophy look to the Upanishads for light and guidance, differently interpreting the Upanishad texts to suit their own specific systems of thought.

Eleven of these, Isha, Kena, Katha, Prashna, Mundaka, Mandukya, Taittiriya, Aitareya, Chandogya, Brihadaranyaka, and Svetashvatara, are probably the oldest. They vary greatly in length: while the Isha Upanishad would occupy but a single printed page, Brihadaranyaka would occupy at least fifty pages. Since the longer ones probably contain compositions of different periods and of different authorship they represent various stages of evolution and exhibit different intentions. Being the concluding portions of the Vedas, they are called the Vedanta. Their interpretations by different later writers gave rise to different systems of Vedanta philosophy. (One of these well-known forms of Vedanta philosophy was made known to the western world for the first time by a gifted Hindu, Svami Vivekananda.) The Upanishads themselves, however, do not seem to have been written in a systematic, well-connected and logical form. They are mystical experiences of the soul gushing forth from within us; they sparkle with the beams of a new light; they quench our thirst, born at their very sight. It was of these that the German philosopher Schopenhauer said: "How does every line display its firm and definite and throughout harmonious meaning. From every sentence deep, original, and sublime thoughts arise and the whole is pervaded by a high and holy and earnest spirit.... In the whole world there is no study, except that of the originals, so beneficial and so elevating as that of the Upanishads. It has been the solace of my life, it will be the solace of my death." Cases are known in which even Christian missionaries, sent out to India to teach church doctrines to clergymen or to preach Christianity among the Indians, became so fascinated by the high and lofty teachings of the Upanishads that they introduced the teaching of the Upanishads in the Church and as a consequence were compelled to resign their posts. To Hindus of all denominations there is nothing higher and holier than the inspired sayings of the Upanishads.

10

THE MYSTICISM OF THE UPANISHADS

Apart from the hymns of the Rig Veda and the Atharva Veda, other hymns might be cited; for instance, the adoration hymn to Hiranyagarbha (R. V. X. 121) who is therein described as the lord of the universe.

"In the beginning rose Hiranyagarbha,
Born as the only lord of all existence.
This earth he settled firm and heaven established:
What god shall we adore with our oblations?
Who gives us breath, who gives us strength, whose bidding
All creatures must obey, the bright gods even;
Whose shade is death, whose shadow life immortal:
What god shall we adore with our oblations?
Who by his might alone became the monarch
Of all that breathes, of all that wakes or slumbers,
Of all, both man and beast, the lord eternal:
What god shall we adore with our oblations?
Whose might and majesty these snowy mountains,
The ocean and the distant stream exhibit;
Whose arms extended are these spreading regions:
What god shall we adore with our oblations?
Who made the heavens bright, the earth enduring,
Who fixed the firmament, the heaven of heavens;
Who measured out the air's extended spaces:
What god shall we adore with our oblations?"

Or one may point to such hymns as the following:

"Who is our father, our creator, maker,

Who every place doth know and every creature,
By whom alone to gods their names were given,
To him all other creatures go to ask him."

But such hymns are not numerous and probably belong to the last epoch of the composition of the Vedic hymns. Most of the Vedic hymns exhibit a conspicuous tendency toward the polytheistic personification of nature. From most of them the monotheistic tendency is well-nigh absent.

So, also, the literature of the sacrificial manuals, the Brahmanas, emphasizes the doctrine of the sacrifice. The adoration hymns of the different gods have lost their independent value and are esteemed only on account of the fact that these verses, sometimes mutilated and torn out of their context, are uttered or chanted in connection with various sacrificial rituals. This literature also contains some passages of a monotheistic or pantheistic character; but the emphasis is almost entirely on the performance of the sacrifices. In the Aranyaka literature, which contains the substitution-meditations, the value and power of thought is realized for the first time. But it is only in the Upanishads that one finds the earliest instances of a sincere and earnest quest after Brahman, the highest and the greatest.

The most important characteristic which distinguishes the science of Brahman from the science of the sacrifices consists in the fact that the former springs entirely from inner, spiritual longings, while the latter is based almost wholly on mundane desires. The science of sacrifice aimed at the acquirement of merit, which could confer all the blessings of life in consequence of due obedience to the Vedic and ritualistic injunctions and prohibitions. The science of Brahman, however, did not seek any ordinary blessings of life. It proceeded from the spiritual needs of our soul which could be satisfied only by attaining the highest aim. All that is mortal, all that is transient and evanescent, all that gives men the ordinary joys of life, such as wealth or fame confer, are but brute pleasures and brute satisfactions, which please only so long as men allow themselves to be swayed by the demands of their senses.

In the hurry and bustle of our modern life, of rapid movements over land, sea and air, in this age of prolific scientific inventions and appliances which add to our material comforts and luxury, in this age of national jealousies and hatreds, which in the name of patriotism and freedom often try to enslave others or monopolize the necessities and luxuries of life for the use of the people of a particular country, it is easy to forget that we have any needs other than the purely material ones. With all the boasted culture of our modern age, with all our advancement of science and progress, do we ever stop to think just what we mean by progress? We have no doubt discovered many new facts of nature, and brought many natural forces under our control. But like vultures soaring high in the air, with greedy eyes fixed on the bones and flesh of the carrion in the field below, are we not, in all our scientific soarings, often turning our greedy eyes to sense gratifications and trying to bind science to the attainment of new comforts and luxuries?

The new comforts and luxuries soon become absolute necessities, and we eagerly press forward to the invention of some other new modes of sense gratification and luxury. Science debased to the end of spreading death and of enslaving humanity, or to the end of procuring newer and newer sensations, a life spent in the whirlpool of fleeting pleasures, varied, subtle, and new, and in the worship of the almighty dollar is what most of us tend to call progress. We live more for the body than for the soul. Our body is our soul; our body is our highest Brahman. The story is told in the Chandogya Upanishads that Virochana and Indra went to Prajapati to receive instructions regarding the nature of the self, or of Brahman the highest. Prajapati gave a course of false instructions, apparently to test the powers of discrimination of his two pupils Virochana and Indra. He asked them to get themselves well-dressed and appear at their best, and then to look into a mirror. When they did so and saw the image of their own bodies in the mirror, Prajapati told them that it was their well-dressed bodies reflected in the mirror that was the true self and the highest Brahman; and they went away satisfied with the answer. Indra, indeed, later returned to Prajapati dissatisfied with the answer; but Virochana (probably an old ancestor of ours) was satisfied with the answer that there is nothing higher than what appears to our senses, our earthly body, and our earthly joys.

But what a different answer do we get from Maitreyi, the wife of Yajnavalkya in the Brihadaranyaka Upanishad II. 4. Yajnavalkya, wishing to become a hermit, explained to his two wives Maitreyi and Katyayani that he wished to divide his wealth between them so that they might live independently while he was away seeking his higher spiritual destiny. But Maitreyi replied: "Well, sir, if you could give me all the wealth of the world, could I become immortal by that?" "No," said Yajnavalkya, "you will only live in pleasure as the rich men do, but I can promise you no hope of immortality through wealth." Maitreyi replied, "Well, sir, what shall I do with that with which I cannot be immortal? Tell me if you know anything by which I may be immortal."

It is this spiritual craving for immortality that distinguishes the mental outlook of the sages of the Upanishads from our own. Yet this desire for immortality is no mere desire for personal survival continuing the enjoyment of pleasures under newer and happier conditions of life, whether in this world or in heaven. This quest for immortality, as it is found in the Upanishads, is in no sense a yearning for personal immortality, the decayless, diseaseless, deathless existence of the individual with his body in full vigor of youth. Neither is it the desire for a bodiless existence of a self fond of sensual joys and sense gratifications and fettered by all the needs and necessities of mundane relations and mundane gratifications. This quest for immortality is identical with the quest of the highest self, the highest truth and reality, the highest Brahman. It is the perception and realization of the inner spring of our life and the inmost spirituality of man as he is within himself, beyond the range of sense and of discursive thought.

If it were a sense-feeling—color, taste, touch, or sound—it might easily be pointed out as this or that sense-datum. It is an ineffable, non-conceptual, inner experience, lying in its own unfathomable depth. When a lump of salt is thrown into the sea, it is entirely dissolved in it; by no means can any part of the lump be recovered in its original form, but every part of the water tastes saline. Similarly, when this stage of supra-consciousness (*prajnana*) is reached, all ordinary experiences are submerged and dissolved in this great, infinite, limitless, homogeneous experience. Like the calm and changeless consciousness of deep, dreamless sleep, is this stage where all duality has vanished: there is no person who knows, nor anything that he is aware of. Ordinary knowledge presupposes a difference between ourselves, our knowledge, and that of which we are aware. When I see a color, there is the "I" which sees, there is the knowledge of the color and also the color itself. When I smell, there is the "I" that smells and the smell; when I think, there is the "I" that thinks and that which is thought; when I speak there is the "I" that speaks and that which is spoken. No one would for a moment think of identifying these. But at this stage of the non-conceptual intuition of the self—an unspeakable, ineffable experience—there is no trace of any duality, and we have one whole of blissful experience wherein is distinguished no one that knows and nothing that he is aware of. All ordinary states of knowledge imply a duality of knower and that which is known; but this is an experience where all duality has vanished.

Nevertheless this experience is not something which is wholly beyond, or wholly out of all relation with, our conscious states of dual experience. For it is the basis, or background, as it were, of all our ordinary knowledge involving the knower and the known. In music, the different notes and tones cannot be grasped separately from and independently of the music itself, and when we are busy in apprehending separately the different notes we miss the music or the harmony which is in itself a whole of experience that cannot be taken in parts, in the multiplicity of the varied notes. So it is with this ineffable experience, which in reality underlies all our ordinary experiences and states of knowledge as the basis or ground of them all; when we are lost in the discursive multiplicity of our ordinary experience, we miss this underlying reality. But when once again we are in touch with it, our so-called personality is as it were dissolved in it, and there ensues that infinitude of blissful experience in which all distinctions are lost. Whatever is dear to me, as e.g., father, mother, wife, money, fame, etc., is so because I love my own self so dearly. It is because I can find the needs of my self best realized through these that I love these. None of these can be ends in themselves; it is only the self that can be an end unto itself, irrespective of any other ulterior end or motive. None of the many-sided interests, desires, and activities of the self represent the self in its entirety or in its essence. It is only this supra-conscious experience, which actually underlies them all, that can be called the real self and that for which everything else exists. Everything else is dear to me because my self is dear to me; but this supra-conscious experience underlies the so-called personality, or self, as its very essence, truth and final reality.

It is indeed difficult for us, with the traditions and associations of our modern world, to believe in the reality of this intuitional experience, unless we attempt to realize it ourselves—unless, by turning our minds entirely away from sense-objects and sense-enjoyments, we deliberately, with faith and firmness, plunge into the depths of this new kind of experience. It cannot be expressed in words or understood by conceptual thought; it reveals itself only to supra-conscious experience. The language of the sages of the Upanishads seems strange to us; but we cannot hope to understand a thing of which we have had no experience. Talk to a child of ten about the romantic raptures of love felt by a pair of lovers, or of the maddening intoxication of sense cravings; what would he understand of it? Talk to a Greenlander about the abominable heat of an African desert; will he be able to imagine it? When an experience is to be realized, the powers of mere logical thinking or of abstraction or of constructive imagination are not sufficient for the purpose. Only another realization of the same experience can testify to its truth.

We are here concerned with an experience which is non-conceptual, intuitive, and ultimate. But, what is more, subtle, fine and formless as it is, it is said to be the source, basis, and ground of everything else. According to a story told in the Chandogya Upanishad VI, when Shvetaketu returned after a stay of twelve years at the house of his preceptor, where he studied all the Vedas, he became arrogant, considered himself to be a wise man, and hardly ever talked with others. His father said to him: "Well, Shvetaketu, what have you learned that you seem to think yourself so wise? Do you know that which when once known everything else becomes known? When you once know what iron is, you know all that can be made out of iron, for these are in essence nothing but iron; we can distinguish the iron vessels from iron only by their specific forms and names. But whatever may be their names and forms, the true essence in them all, whether they be needles, pans or handles, is nothing but iron.

It is only that you find therein so many forms and names. What are these names and forms worth without the essence? It is the essence, the iron, that manifests itself in so many forms and names; when this iron is known, all that is made of iron is also known. It is the ineffable reality, the ultimate being which is the essence of everything else. As rivers which flow into the sea lose all their individuality in it and cannot be distinguished, so all divergent things lose their individuality and distinctness when they are merged in this highest being, the ultimate reality from which they have all sprung forth. Fine and subtle though this experience be, yet it is in reality the entire universe of our knowledge. A small seed of an oak tree when split open reveals nothing that we can call worth noting, yet it is this fine kernel of the seed that holds within it the big oak tree."

The chief features of this Upanishad mysticism are the earnest and sincere quest for this spiritual illumination, the rapturous delight and force that characterize the utterances of the sages when they speak of the realization of this ineffable experience, the ultimate and the absolute truth and reality, and the immortality of all mortal things. Yet this quest is not the quest of the God of the theists. This highest reality is no individual person separate from us, or one whom we try to please, or whose laws and commands we obey, or to whose will we submit with reverence and devotion. It is, rather, a totality of partless, simple and undifferentiated experience which is the root of all our ordinary knowledge and experience and which is at once the ultimate essence of our self and the highest principle of the universe, the Brahman or the Atman. There is, indeed, another current of thought, evident in several passages of different Upanishads, in which Brahman is conceived and described as the theistic God. This will be dealt with separately later on. The special characteristic of the line of thought that has now been described is a belief in a superior principle which enlivens our life, thoughts, actions, desires and feelings, which is the inmost heart of the self of man, the immortal and undying reality unaffected by disease and death, and which is also the ultimate and absolute reality of the universe.

A story is told in the Katha Upanishad according to which King Vajashravasa made a sacrifice involving a gift of all the valuables that he possessed. When everything of the sort had been given away, he made a supplementary gift of his cows which were all old and useless. His son Naciketas, finding that these gifts would be more embarassing than useful to the recipient, disapproved of his father's action. He thought that his father had not finished giving his "all" until he, his son, was also given away. So he asked his father, "To whom are you going to give me?" He was dear to his father; so his father did not like this question and remained silent. But when the question was again and again repeated, the father lost his temper and said, "I give you over to death." Then Naciketas went to the place of Yama, the king of death, where he remained fasting for three days and nights. Yama, willing to appease him, requested him to take any boons that pleased him. Naciketas replied that men do not know what happens to people when they have passed from earthly life, whether they still continue to exist or whether they cease to exist; and he requested Yama to answer this question on which there were so many divergent opinions. Yama in answer said that this was a very difficult question and that even the gods did not know what becomes of man after he passes away from his earthly life; that, therefore, he would rather give Naciketas long life, big estates, gold in abundance, horses, elephants, and whatever else in the way of earthly enjoyment might seem to him desirable. But the philosophical quest was dearer to Naciketas than all the earthly goods that the king of death could bestow upon him. Money, he thought, can not satisfy man; money is of use only so long as a man lives, and he can live only so long as death does not take him away. This quest of the ultimate destiny of man, of his immortal essence, is itself the best and the highest end that our hearts may pursue. So Naciketas preferred to solve this mystery and riddle of life rather than to obtain all the riches of the world and all the comforts that they could purchase.

The king of death appreciated the wisdom of Naciketas' choice. He explained that there are two paths, the path of the good and the path of the pleasant, and that they are different paths, leading to two entirely different goals. The mad hankering after riches can only justify itself by binding us with ties of attachment to sense-pleasures which are short-lived and transitory. It is only the spiritual longing of man after the realization of his highest, inmost, truest, and most immortal essence that is good in itself, though it does not appeal to greedy people who are always hankering after money. Desire for money blinds our eyes, and we fail to see that there is anything higher than the desire for riches, or that there is anything intrinsically superior to our ordinary mundane life of sense-pleasures and sense-enjoyments. The nature of the higher sphere of life and of the higher spiritual experiences cannot be grasped by minds which are always revolving in the whirlpool of mad desires for riches and sense-enjoyments.

As the sage, in his serene enjoyment of spiritual experiences, may well think sense-pleasures dull, insipid, and valueless, so the multitude who live a worldly life of ordinary pleasures and enjoyments, fail to perceive the existence of this superior plane of life and the demands of the spirit for the realization of its immortal essence. They think that nothing exists higher and greater than this mundane life of ordinary logical thought and sense-enjoyments. Most men live on this ordinary level of life; they see, hear, taste, touch and smell. They think and they argue. They have a mind which thinks, feels, and wills, and they have senses which seek their own gratification. They employ the former in the service of the latter and every day discover newer and subtler ways of sense-gratification; they also employ the latter to serve the former by furnishing sense data to guide and check the course of logical thought and the development of science.

The more men, upon comparing opinions, find themselves agreeing that they possess nothing of a more lofty character, the more they cease to believe in the validity and truth of the existence of anything undying in man.

They fail to notice that the life they are living has had the effect of chilling and freezing the clear flowing stream of spiritual experiences and of stifling the spiritual instincts and longings of the soul. Generations of lives spent without once turning the eyes to the spiritual light within have served to build up traditions, beliefs, and tendencies of such an order that faith in the existence of the higher spirituality of man is lost. Discourse about the spirituality of man in its highest sense appears to most men to be no more than a myth of by-gone days or the result of the undue nervous excitation or heated imagination of a religious intoxication. The net result of our modern education, civilization, and culture has been the disappearance of the belief that there is anything higher than the gratification of man's primitive instincts under such checks as society requires, the pursuit of the physical sciences, and the successful employment of the art of reasoning for the satisfaction of all the diverse interests of human beings. So Yama, the king of death, says to Naciketas that the majority of the people do not believe that there is anything higher than the ordinary mundane life, being content with the common concerns and interests of life; that it is only the few who feel this higher call and are happy to respond to it and to pursue a course of life far above the reach of the common man.

But what is this undying spiritual essence, or existence? Cannot our powers of reasoning, as they are employed in philosophical discussion or logical arguments, discover it? If they can, then at its best it can be nothing loftier than thought and can not be considered as the highest principle by which even thought itself and all conscious processes, as well as the functioning of all sense-operations, are enlivened and vitalized. So Yama tells Naciketas that this highest spiritual essence in us cannot be known by discursive reason. Only persons who have realized this truth can point this out to us as an experience which is at once self-illuminating and blissful and which is entirely different from all else that is known to us. Once it is thus exhibited, those who have the highest moral elevation and disinclination to worldly enjoyments can grasp it by an inner intuitive contact with the reality itself (*adhyatmayoga*). This truth is indeed the culmination of all the teaching of the Vedas.

To Naciketas' question as to what becomes of men when they leave this earthly life, Yama's answer is that no one is ever born and no one ever dies. Birth and death pertain only to our physical bodies, but our essence is never born and never dies. The birth and death of the physical body may well be explained by reference to physical causes, and there is not much of a mystery therein. But man cannot be identified with his body, nor can he be identified simply with the life which he has in common with all other animals, and even with plants. Life, in a large measure, seems to be nothing but a harmonious functioning of the inner organs of the body; but no one would say that these movements of the organs can be called "man." There is a superior principle which vitalises and quickens the process of life, enlivens the activity of thought, moves the senses to their normal and regular operations, which is realized, or intuited, as the very essence of our inner illumination, and which is also the highest and ultimate principle underlying all things.

We are here face to face with the real mysticism of the Upanishads. This highest essence of man, the self, the Brahman, is difficult of perception; it is hidden, as in a deep cavern, in that deathless being who exists from the beginning of all time and beyond all time. It is the subtlest, the smallest of the small and yet the greatest of the great. It exists changeless and just the same one when everything else that it has vitalized has ceased to exist. This, our inmost self, cannot be known by much learning or scholarship, nor by sharp intelligence, nor by strong memory. It can only be known, or intuited, by the person to whom it reveals its own nature. In one place we are told that it can be intuited only by an inner, direct, and immediate touch. In another place it is said that it can only be perceived by those who have practised the perceiving of fine truths by a superfine intelligence of the highest order (Katha I. 3.12). The path to this superior intuition is like the edge of a sharp razor, dangerous and difficult. It is beyond all sense-knowledge; and he who intuits this secret truth of the beginningless, endless, unchangeable and eternal overcomes all death. For, once one realizes oneself to be identical with this highest principle, death and the fear of it sink into insignificant, illusory nothingness.

There is, however, another line of thought running through the different Upanishads in which Brahman appears as the supreme Lord from whom everything has proceeded and who is the source of all energy. Thus in the Kena Upanishad we find the query: "By whose will and directed by whom does the mind work, and directed by whom did life first begin? By whose will does the organ of speech work, and led by whom do the eye and the ear perform their respective functions?" Then comes the answer: "It is from Him that the organ of speech, the ear, the eye, the mind and life have all derived their powers; He is the thought of thought, the mind of mind, and the life of life. So neither mind nor eye, neither ear nor speech, can tell us anything about Him, be in form of materialistic pantheism. But this is merely one phase or aspect of the matter. It seems to be contradicted by the idea of Brahman as the creator, ruler, and controller, by whose will everything moves and the order of events is kept in its right place undisturbed. Neither life nor death nor any of the powers of nature can transgress his orders; He is a thundering fear over us all, and yet He is also the bridge by which all the diverse things of the world are connected with one another and with man, their spiritual master. This latter conception, which is present in many passages of the Upanishads, is apparently dualistic and implies a personal God.

The Shvetashvatara Upanishad abounds in passages of an avowedly dualistic character. There it is said that He alone is the Lord of all bipeds and quadrupeds, the protector and master of the universe, and yet is hidden in all beings. The duality between the individual soul and God is also definitely expressed in at least two of the earlier Upanishads, Mundaka 3. 1. 1 and Shvetashvatara 4. 6, where, with reference to Brahman and the individual, it is said that two birds which are alike in nature and friendly to each other reside in the same tree, but that one of them (the individual) eats sweet fruits (i.e. of his own deeds) while the other is happy in itself without eating any fruit whatsoever. In the same Shvetashvatara Upanishad, the sage is described as saying: "I know this great person who resides beyond all darkness (of sin and ignorance), as bright as the sun. He who knows Him escapes death and there is no other way of escape. There is nothing superior to Him, and there is nothing which is greater than Him, and there is nothing smaller than Him. He stands alone by Himself in the Heavens unmoved like a tree, and yet the world is filled by this person." But this also is a passing phase. In a passage immediately preceding that in the Mundaka Upanishad just referred to, it is said that Brahman is right before us in the front; Brahman is behind us in the back; Brahman is on the right and on the left. Again it is said in the Katha Upanishad: "He who perceives diversity in this world suffers the death of all deaths." "He is the controller and the self of all beings; He makes the one form many, being one He satisfies the desires of the many."

The most important emphasis of the Upanishads seems to be on that ineffable experience which lies hidden in the background of all our experiences and at the same time enlivens them all. Yet the experiencer himself is lost, and dissolved as it were, in this superior experience, where there is neither experiencer nor that which is experienced. This experience, or state, cannot be intellectually grasped; it can only be pointed out as different from all that is known, or from all that can be described as "this" or "that". One can only assert that "It is not this," "It is not this." It is like the state of a deep dreamless sleep, like the feeling of intense bliss where neither the knower nor the known can be distinctly felt but where there is only the infinitude of blissful experience.

The various commentators upon the Upanishads belonging to different schools of thought and yet each interested to secure for himself the support of the Upanishads, have been fighting with one another for the last twelve hundred years or more to prove that the Upanishads are exclusively in favor of one party as against the others. Thus some contend that the Upanishads teach that Brahman alone exists and all the rest that appears is false and illusory. Others hold that the Upanishads favor the doctrine of modified duality of man in God and of God in man. Still others maintain that the Upanishads give us exclusively a doctrine of uncompromising duality. And so forth. Passages have often been twisted and perverted, and many new connections and contexts have been introduced or imposed upon the texts, to suit the fancy or the creed of the individual commentator. I think all these interpretations are biassed and one sided, and therefore inexact. The Upanishads reveal to us different phases of thought and experience, not a consistent dogmatic philosophy.

The apparent inconsistency of the different phases of thought is removed if we take a psychological point of view and consider them as different stages of development in the experience of minds seeking to grasp a sublime, ultimate but inexpressible truth. This truth has a logic of its own, different from the logic of discursive thought wherein distinctions are firm and rigid, where concepts are like pieces of brick mortared together by the logical movement of thought. Its logic is that of experience in which the apparently contradictory ideas or thoughts lose their contradictoriness and become parts of one solid whole. The different phases of experience are lived through and enjoyed as inalienable parts of one great experience. When attempts are made to describe any particular phase of this experience it will naturally seem to conflict with the other phases in the eyes of those who have not the capacity of realising the concrete whole experience and who can only look at the phases from an external and a purely intellectual point of view where distinctions cannot be obliterated. When a lover embraces his beloved in his first kiss, he may feel her as the holiest angel, as his own dear life or as the embodiment of all his happiness, as, Shelley says, his "Spouse, Sister Angel, Pilot of the Fate,"

"Of unentangled intermixture, made
By love, of light and motion; one intense
Diffusion, one serene Omnipresence."

But these epithets when applied to a woman can hardly be justified, according to intellectual standards, as properly applied, though the lover may have felt an indescribable sweetness of love in which all these diverse sentiments melted together to form its taste and flavor. The different phases of experience and belief which we find in the Upanishads need not therefore be taken out and pitted against one another. They may all be regarded as stages of experience between which the minds of the sages oscillated in attempting the realisation of a truth which was beyond speech, beyond thought and beyond all sense-perception. It was sometimes felt as the great over-lord, the controller, creator, ordainer, and master of all, sometimes as the blissful spiritual experience, and sometimes as the simple unity in which all duality has vanished.

This truth, person, or absolute—whatever it may be called—was felt as the highest embodiment of moral perfection. It is complete self-illumination, bodiless, faultless, sinless and pure. It is, as it were, covered by a cup of gold in such wise that we, looking at the shiny cup, miss the real treasure that lies concealed beneath. Its illumination reveals itself only when our minds have turned away from all the external lights of the outside world; for where this light is shining, all the other lights of the sun, the moon, and the stars have ceased to give light. The Upanishads tell us again and again that it cannot be perceived by any of our senses and that it cannot be comprehended by reasoning, or by logical and discursive thought, or by discussions, scholarship and much learning, or even by the reading of the scriptures. Only those who have ceased from all sinful actions and have controlled all their sense desires, who are unruffled by passions of all kinds and are at peace with themselves, can have the realization of this great truth by the higher intuitive knowledge (*prajnana,* as distinguished from *jnana,* or cognition).

In Mundaka III. 1, it is said that we can attain this self by truth, control, spiritual fervor and absolute extinction of all sex desires. Only the sages who have purged themselves of all moral defects and faults are capable of perceiving this holy spiritual light within themselves. The Upanishads never tire of repeating that the revelation of this truth is possible only through the most perfect moral purity which results in a natural illumination of intuitive perception when one seeks to attain this partless essence through meditation. Not only can this truth not be perceived by the eye or described in speech; but it cannot even be gained as a boon, or gift, by pleasing the gods or by ascetic practices or by sacrificial performances. It can only be attained by an intuition (*para*) which is superior in kind to the Vedic knowledge of sacrifices, called the lower knowledge (*apara*). By supreme moral elevation and untiring and patient search one can come in touch with Brahman and can enter into Him, but one must abandon all his mundane desires by which he is bound to earthly things. And when through this high moral elevation, control of desires, meditation and the like, one comes face to face with this highest reality, or Brahman, he is lost in it like rivers in the sea; nothing remains of him which he can feel as a separate individual, but he becomes one with Brahman. This is known by the seer through his heart when his senses have ceased to move and when his thought and intellect have come to a dead halt. No one can describe what that existence is; one can only say that it is "being," nothing more. Here all the knots of the heart are untied, all doubts are dispelled, and there is one spiritual light of unity that shines forth in its serene oneness.

11

THE MYSTICISM OF YOGA

The Upanishads regarded the ineffable intuitive experience as absolute and ultimate in nature. The Upanishads, however, indicate no definite method for arriving at the perception of this truth. It is made clear that the pathway consists not in erudition or scholarship, and that it is not traversed by any sharpness of intelligence. The truth is such that it cannot be conceived by the human mind or described by language. One of the fundamental conditions of attaining it is the complete elevation of the moral life, including the absolute control of all passions and desires, the abandonment of worldly ambitions and hopes, and the attainment of an unruffled peace of mind. But the dawning of the supra-consciousness which can reveal this truth does not, even so, depend entirely on our own efforts; there is something like divine mercy that must be awaited.

This self can only be realized by those to whom it reveals itself. The perfecting of our moral life is a prerequisite; but no method deliberately and consciously pursued is sufficient to bring us all the way into the full realization of the highest truth. In at least one or two of the Upanishads indications of a different line of thought and method of realization are to be found. Thus in Katha III, our senses are compared with horses which are always running after their respective sense-objects. He who is not wise but is without control over his own mind cannot control his senses, just as a bad driver cannot control his horses. If anyone wishes to make his way to his highest goal, he should have wisdom for his driver and his mind as the reins of the horses of the senses. In Katha VI, it is said that there is a state in which the five senses, thought, intellect, and mind all cease to operate, and this highest stage of absolute sense-restraint is called "Yoga," or spiritual union.

There are ample literary evidences that from very early times—from at least 700 or 800 B. C.—people were in the habit of concentrating their minds on particular objects and thereby stopping the movement of the mind and the senses and achieving wonderful, miraculous powers. It is difficult to say how the ancient Indians discovered this mode of mental control. But it seems very probable that as at first practised it did not form a part of any metaphysical system of thought but was simply the practice of mental concentration and breath control for the sake of the resulting peace and quietness of mind, as well as of the miraculous powers which could be achieved thereby. The powers of hypnotism, or mesmerism, seem to have been very well known in ancient India and were also included among the powers that could be derived from the yoga practices.

A story is told in the Mahabharata (13.40) that Devasharma, a sage, had a very beautiful wife, named Ruci, whom he carefully guarded from the seductive influences of Indra who desired to possess her. Once he had to go away to perform sacrifices at a distant place, and he left his wife under the protection of his pupil Vipula. The pupil knew that Indra could resort to many clever disguises and that it would be difficult to protect Ruci from him by guarding her by any external means. So he decided to enter into her mind by his powers of yoga and to control her behavior and speech from within. Accordingly, he sat in front of his teacher's wife and remained staring at her eyes, inhibiting all movements of his own body. In this way he entered into her body and remained there awaiting his teacher's return. Nov Indra, thinking that the lady was alone in the house, came there in his fine and radiant form. He saw there the inanimate body of Vipula, the pupil, with its eyes absolutely motionless as if they were painted on canvas. He also saw the lady sitting there in all her resplendent beauty.

On beholding Indra, she wished to rise and greet him; but being controlled from within by her husband's pupil, she could not succeed in doing as she desired. Indra spoke to her in his own charming manner, telling her that he had come there for her and that he was Indra. Perceiving that the lady was showing signs of becoming fascinated, Vipula controlled all her senses and limbs from within in such a way that, though she desired very much by rising from her seat to receive Indra, she could not do so. When Indra found her silent and unresponsive, he again spoke to her and asked her to rise and receive him. Again, though she wanted to welcome him, Vipula controlled her speech so that she told Indra that he had no business to come to her, and she was ashamed that she so spoke against her will. Indra then understood the whole affair and was much afraid. Vipula then returned to his own body and took Indra to task for his misbehavior.

Many other stories, illustrating the various kinds of miraculous powers of yoga, might be repeated. But let us turn to a consideration of the principal use of the yoga practices for the spiritual enlightenment, the ultimate and absolute freedom of man, as described by Patanjali, the great yoga writer of about 150 B. C. Patanjali not only describes the principal yoga practices, but he gives a philosophical basis to the whole system and indicates, for the first time, how yoga may be utilized for the emancipation of man from the bondage of his mind and senses. It was known that the sages of the Upanishads believed in a supra-conscious experience of pure self-illumination as the ultimate principle, superior to and higher than any of our mental states of cognition, willing, or feeling. The nature of this principle is itself extremely mystical; many persons, no doubt, are unable to grasp its character. It has been shown that, even in the days of the Upanishads, it was recognized to be obscure, and that the sages were never tired of saying that it could neither be perceived by the eye nor conceived in thought; but that, nevertheless, the sages believed in its existence as the ultimate being and not as an experience of ecstatic feeling or any other kind of transient psychological state. It was regarded as the real self and the ultimate reality. It is this view of self that is the root, as it were, of Indian mysticism.

If we ask ourselves what we understand by "I", we shall all find that, though it is in the most constant use, it is also the obscurest word in all our dictionaries. About the meaning of the word, in one sense we can never doubt; for there is no person who can ever doubt whether he is himself or another person. But when we try to understand what it definitely and actually means, it appears to be one of the most elusive of words. It certainly cannot designate merely our bodies; nor does it mean any particular idea or feeling of a temporary character. So we have to admit that while we all understand what it means we cannot define it. This is not the place to enter into all the recondite philosophical discussions to which the problem of the nature of the self has given rise. But some attempt must be made to explain what the Indians understood by the immortal and unchangeable self. Some believed this self to be the same in all persons, while others believed it to be many; but the conception of its nature was more or less the same in most of the systems of Indian thought. It was pure, contentless consciousness, altogether different from what we understand by idea, knowledge, or thought. Our thoughts and feelings are changeful; but this mysterious light of pure consciousness was changeless. The ultimate aim of the yoga processes (as of most of the Indian systems of thought) is to dissociate ourselves from our sensations, thoughts, ideas, feelings, etc., to learn that these are extraneous associations, foreign to the nature of self but adhering to it almost so inseparably that the true self cannot be easily discovered as a separate and independent entity.

But with the Indian sages this doctrine of a transcendent self was not merely a matter of speculative philosophy. For philosophy came to them much later than the actual practice of the liberation of this true self from the bondage of the association with all our so-called psychical states, ideas, feelings, emotions, images and concepts. It is very difficult for a Western mind of today to understand, or appreciate, the minds of the Indian seers. They felt a call from within the deep caverns of their selves—a call which must have started from a foretaste of their own true essence—which made all earthly pleasures or hopes of heavenly pleasures absolutely distasteful to them. They could feel satisfied only if they could attain this true freedom, their true self. To appreciate their experience at all one must, in imagination, take a long jump backward of about twenty-five centuries and across the waters of the Atlantic and the Indian oceans, and picture to oneself the valley of the lofty snow-capped peaks of the Himalayas looking high up to the infinite of the heavens and, far beyond, the peaceful groves and cottages where the innocence and forbearance of man had endeared him to trees and beasts alike, where no other sounds disturbed the serene forest-dwellers than the breezy rustling of the lofty Sal trees and the grovy palms.

The necessities of the men who dwelt there were few. They often wore clothes made from birch bark, and ate fruits and vegetables that grew wild in the hermitage and rice which grew without much trouble of cultivation. The cows of the hermitage supplied them with milk and butter. They did not take any animal life for food; the birds ate from their hands, the soft-eyed gazelles roamed about their huts, made of straw or leaves of trees, and the peacocks danced in the shady groves of their forest walks. The clear, transparent waters of the holy river Ganges and other rivers watered their hermitages, and the cool breezes delightfully refreshed their bodies and minds when the wearisome tropical heat had relaxed their nerves and muscles into inaction. These men had no riches, and they did not seek them. Their natural needs were few, and it never occurred to them that these could be augmented or multiplied. They thought, rather, that what needs they had were in themselves too numerous and could be indefinitely curtailed. Even in rather recent times a story is told to the effect that a scholar in Bengal, called Ramnath, was visited by Raja Krishnachandra of Bengal who wanted to bestow riches on him and asked him if he had any wants.

The scholar replied that he had plenty of rice in his house and that he could make his soup out of the sour leaves of the tamarind tree which grew in his yard; the only difficulty that he had was with regard to some intellectual problems which he was still not able to solve. For men who live in a world of sky-scrapers, motor cars and comforts of all sorts, with its varied scientific, political and social ambitions, with its desire for wealth and its highly developed system of trade and commerce, it is inevitably difficult to appreciate, or rightly understand, the minds of those who felt disinclined to all worldly things and were uneasy until they could touch their own inmost self. Theirs, however, was no ordinary pessimism, as is too often supposed by unsympathetic and shallow-minded scholars, who lack the imagination and the will to understand the Indian thought and culture of the past. They felt dissatisfied with the world not because the world had no pleasures or joys to offer, but because their desire for attaining their highest good, their true selves, was so great that it could tolerate no compromise with any other kind of desire. The sole ambition of the yogins, or the seers who practised the yoga discipline, was to become absolutely free from all kinds of bonds and from all kinds of extraneous determination.

The problem of how to become free naturally raised the question as to who is to become free and from what. The logic of the yogins is irresistible. It is the self which has to become free; in fact it is always free. The self is the ultimate principle of pure consciousness, distinct from all mental functions, faculties, powers, or products. By a strange, almost inexplicable, confusion we seem to lose touch with the former so that we consider it as non-existent and characterize the latter with its qualities. It is this confusion which is at the root of all our psychological processes. All mental operations involve this confusion by which they usurp the place of the principle of pure consciousness so that it is only the mind and the mental operations of thought, feeling, willing, which seem to be existing, while the ultimate principle of consciousness is lost sight of.

We call this ultimate principle of consciousness, this true self, "spirit" and designate all our functions of knowing, feeling, and willing collectively as "mind," then we may say that it is only by a strange confusion of mind with spirit that the mind comes to the forefront and by its activities seems to obscure the true light of the spirit. Our senses run after their objects and the mind establishes relations between the sense-data, or sensations, and deals with the concepts formed therefrom as it carries on the processes of logical thought with the aid of memory. The external objects which draw minds to them are not in themselves directly and immediately responsible for obscuring the spirit or in binding it to them. It is, rather, the mind and its activities by which the true nature of the spirit seems to be obscured so that the mind usurps the rightful place of the spirit. What is necessary, therefore, is to control the activities of the mind and to stop all mental processes. If we can in this way kill the mind, all logical thought and all sense processes will be killed with it.

The light of the spirit will then shine alone by itself unshadowed by the darkening influence of thought. The spirit, the ultimate principle of consciousness, and the self are one and the same thing, the three terms expressing the threefold aspect of its nature. But this entity, by whichever name it is called, is to be distinguished from mind, whose activities are thoughts, feelings, etc. We may here employ a simile. We may say that the spirit is like a pure white light covered by the colored dome of the mind. This colored dome hides the pure white light, and, without changing the nature of the white light by its own color, makes the latter appear as colored and wrongfully appears itself to be a source of colored light, though it has no light whatsoever of itself. We fail to recognize the white light within and take it for granted that the colored dome is itself a colored light. The only way to restore the purity of the white light is by smashing the colored dome. Similarly, the only way in which the spirit may be made to realize, in its own non-conceptual way, its own lonely light is by breaking the mind to pieces.

The mind lives by its activities of sensing, perceiving and conceiving. It creates illusions and hallucinations, revives past experiences in memory, and sometimes passes into a state of sleep in which it creates dreams. If the movement of the mind could be entirely stopped, its disintegration would be effected. The process of yoga consists in so controlling the activity of the mind that it ceases to pass through its different states. The cessation of all mental states is yoga. These mental states as they rise and pass away are not altogether lost. They continue in the subconscious mind as impressions which are revived by proper excitations.

As they are thus revived and repeated, and return to the subconscious, the impressions become strengthened, growing more and more powerful and more likely to occur as conscious states. Thus, for example, when we once devote ourselves to making money and to enjoying the comforts it can procure, we become more and more deeply absorbed in earning money and enjoying its comforts. Similarly, the scholar through days and nights of study in his library grows ever more attached to his occupation of study. It is in this way that the tendencies of the mind become strengthened; repeating themselves almost mechanically they keep alive the continual flow of the mind from one state to another. Yoga consists in stopping the conscious and subconscious mental flow entirely and absolutely.

It is easy to see that no one will think of destroying his mind unless his desire for the absolute freedom of the spirit becomes so great that all the activities of the mind, all his sense-enjoyments, all his thoughts and feelings, lose all interest for him and appear to him to be entirely valueless. This disinclination to all worldly things, called *vairagya,* is the first thing which leads the yogin to seek the way of yoga to deliver himself forever from all mundane experiences. The seer is as sensitive as the pupil of the eye. Just as a speck of dust, which passes altogether unnoticed on any other part of the body, causes great pain when it gets into the eye, so the suffering, which is absolutely unnoticed by the ordinary person, is felt keenly by the seer. All ordinary pleasures appear to be distasteful to him. There is nothing in anything worldly that can give him any satisfaction. He is in that mood in which he is dissatisfied with them all and wishes to shun them.

Such a state of mind cannot be produced unless the mind has risen to the highest plane of moral elevation. Unless the mind is made absolutely pure there cannot be any steady disinclination toward worldly things.

A seer must abstain from all injury to living beings. His tenderness should extend not only to all human individuals but to all living beings. He would not willfully take the life of, or injure, any living being. He would not steal the property of any other person. He would be absolutely truthful in thought, word and deed. Veracity consists in the agreement of words and thoughts with facts. But it must always be employed for the good of others and not for their injury. If it proves injurious to living beings, with whatever intention it be uttered it is not truth. Though outwardly such a truthful course may be considered virtuous yet since by his truth he has caused injury to another he has in reality violated the ideal of absolute non-injury. The seer must have a complete control of the sex tendencies. He must not desire anything more than the bare necessities. For the acquisition of things always entails attachment and greed, and injury to others in acquiring and preserving them.

If in performing the great duty of universal non-injury, and in cultivating the other virtues auxiliary to it, a man be troubled by thoughts of sin, he should try to substitute for the sinful ideas those which are contrary to them. Thus, if the old habit of sin tends to drive him along the wrong path, he should, in order to banish it, entertain ideas such as the following: "Being burnt up as I am in the fires of the world, I have taken refuge in the practice of yoga, which gives protection to all. Were I to resume the sins which I have abandoned, I should certainly be behaving like a dog which eats its own vomit—I should be acting as if I were to take up again that which I had once put aside." Thus one should habituate himself to meditation upon the harmful effects of the tendencies which are leading him along the wrong path. The habituation to this contrary tendency consists in continually thinking that these immoral tendencies cause an infinity of pain and error. Pain and error are the unending fruits of these immoral tendencies and in the recognition of this lies the power of righting the trend of our thoughts.

Other moral qualities of a positive character are considered indispensable to a seer toiling on the path of yoga. These are: purity, contentment, indifference to physical difficulties of heat, cold, etc., study and self-surrender to God. Purity here means both physical and mental cleanliness. Contentment means that self-satisfied condition of the mind in which we are at peace with ourselves, having ceased to run after new wants. Indifference to physical difficulties is also a virtue to be acquired by the yogin, who should be able to bear calmly the bodily wants of hunger and thirst, heat and cold. He should also be able to stop his physical movements for a considerable length of time, and be able, as well, to stop his desire to talk with others and to remain absolutely dumb.

On the Upanishadic mysticism, it was shown that when such a high standard of moral elevation is reached and we seek to know the inmost essence of self, the self often reveals its own true nature through a direct intuition which is beyond the grasp of the mind and the senses. The yogins, however, not only emphasized the necessity of the highest moral perfection but they also required a particular course of physical and mental discipline as indispensable to the realization of yoga's high ideal. The yogins emphasized not only the negative aspect of morality, such as abstinence from injury, falsehood and the like, but also such positive moral virtues as purity and contentment.

The four cardinal virtues which a yogin was required to possess were universal friendship (*maitri*), compassion for all who suffer (*karuna*), happiness in the happiness of others (*mudita*), and a sympathetic consideration for the failings of others (*upeksha*). But even these were not deemed sufficient; they were only preliminary acquirements which the yogin must possess before starting with his yoga practices. The acquisition of these moral virtues went, indeed, a long way in restraining the mind from running after sense-objects and from being disturbed by greed, passions and antipathies; for the yogin was self-controlled, contented, pure in mind and body, and peaceable and charitable toward all living beings. But still he must be able to control his bodily movements. He must therefore habituate himself to sitting in one posture for a long time, not only for hours and days but often for months and years together. This implied the attainment of a power to bear calmly hunger and thirst, heat and cold, and all physical hardships.

In order that the movement in the body may be reduced to a minimum, it is necessary to acquire a control over breathing. To practice the science of breath-control, the yogin seats himself firmly, fixes his eyes on an object beyond him, or rather on the tip of his own nose or on the point between his two eye-brows, and slowly inhales a full breath. At first the breath that is taken in is kept perhaps for a minute and then slowly exhaled. The practice is continued for days and months, the period of the retention of the breath taken in being gradually increased. With the growth of breath-control, one may keep his breath suspended, without exhalation or inhalation, for hours, days, months and even years together. With the suspension of the respiratory process the body remains in a state of suspended animation, without any external signs of life. The heart ceases to beat, there is neither taking in of food nor evacuation of any sort, there is no movement of the body.

There is a complete cessation of the respiratory process as, with his mouth shut and his tongue turned backwards behind the tonsils stopping the passage of air firmly like a lid, the yogin sits in his fixed posture in an apparently lifeless condition. Even in modern times there are many well-attested cases of yogis who can remain in this apparently lifeless condition for more than a month. I have myself seen a case where the yogin stayed in this condition for nine days. The case of Saint Haridas is well-known. He remained buried underneath the ground for forty days under strict vigilance of guards. When, after forty days of breathless and foodless condition of suspended animation, he was brought out of the earth, there was apparently no life in him, no movement of breath, no heart-beats. But after his body had been rubbed and much water had been poured on him he again came back to life and began to breathe normally.

Various methods of purifying the body were gradually discovered by which the yogin could so temper the body as to make it immune to diseases. In earlier times, before the elaborate bodily disciplines had been discovered, the yogin prayed to God and depended on His grace for the immunity from disease which was so necessary to the proper performance of his yoga duties. But later on, the yogin tried to be more or less independent of God's grace and discovered a whole system of bodily exercises, breathing exercises, and automatic internal washings by which his body became so tempered that no diseases could easily attack him. These consisted, first, in habituating the body to keeping fixed postures which required various muscular movements.

By this means the yogin could make his body flexible, reduce its unnecessary fat, and attain full control over his voluntary muscles. For these postures required the exercise of all the voluntary muscles. Second, through the breathing exercises which could be performed in different forms and in different degrees of intensity, combined with the different postures, the yogin obtained control over the various involuntary muscles which regulate the operation of the viscera, including the bladder and the excretory organs, the heart, the stomach, etc. Added to these was, third, the thorough washing away of the impurities which, being secreted by some of the internal organs, obstruct their normal activity and lower their power of resistance.

These washings can be easily performed by the control that the yogin acquires over his inner involuntary muscles. Thus, for example, the yogin can take water into the intestines by expelling air from these cavities and thus forcing in water by the downward path from a tub in which he may be sitting at the time. He can expel air from these cavities by means of the control that he has over the muscles of those organs which to a normal person are quite involuntary. Thus, at any time that he likes he can thoroughly wash his stomach, his bladder, urethra, etc. He has thus a thorough access to all the important cavities of the body where impurities may be produced and deposited. In short, by the combined operation of postures, breath-control, breathing exercises, and the voluntary washings of the impurities from all the important cavities of the body, he can so increase his power of physical resistance as to remain practically immune to all diseases.

But these are all merely external preparations to fit the body for the yoga practices. The real yoga practice of the mind can be properly begun only when these preliminaries have been to a large extent acquired so that the chances of external bodily disturbances and internal disturbances due to passions, antipathies, attachments, etc., have been minimized. The yogin begins this superior mental yoga by concentrating at first on any gross physical object. This concentration is not the ordinary concentration of thought as exemplified in any scientific or literary work. For this latter type of concentration consists in the limiting of the mind's activity to matters associated with the object of attention. Thus, if we concentrate on the writing of a poem or the description of scenery, what we do is to restrain the mind from flying off to other objects in which we are not interested at the time and to focus it upon the relations between various associated images and thoughts. The mind is in such cases in a lively state of movement within a limited sphere, always seeking to discover new relations or to intensify the comprehension of relations and facts already known. But yoga concentration aims not to discover any new relations or facts or to intensify any impression; it aims solely to stop the movement of mind and to prevent its natural tendency towards comparison, classification, association, assimilation and the like.

The fixing of the mind on an object is done I with the specific purpose of pinning it to that object and of preventing its transition to any other object. By this process the mind becomes one with the object, and so long as it is pinned to that object its movement is stopped. At the first stage of this union, there is knowledge of the name and the physical form of the object to which the mind has been pinned. But at the next stage nothing is known of the object in its ordinary relations of name and form, but the mind becomes one with the object, steady and absolutely motionless. This state is called a state of *samadhi*, or absorptive concentration. This stage arises when the mind by its steadiness becomes one with its object, divested of all associations of name and concept, so that it is in direct touch with the reality of the thing uncontaminated by associations. In this state, the object does not appear as an object of *my* consciousness but my consciousness, becoming divested of all "I" or "mine," becomes one with the object itself. There is no awareness here that "I know this," but, the mind having become one with the thing, the duality of subject and object disappears, and the result is the transformation of the mind into the object of its concentration.

Our ordinary knowledge of things is full of false and illusory associations which do not communicate to us the real nature of the object; but when such an absorptive union of object and mind takes place, a new kind of intuition is produced, called *prajna*, similar to the Upanishadic intuition, called *prajnana*, and thereby the real nature of the thing is brought home to us. This *prajna* knowledge, which is a new kind of intuition produced by stopping the movement of the mind, is entirely different from the ordinary logical type of cognition of thoughts, images, etc. This intuition is a direct acquaintance, more or less similar to direct perceptual vision but free from the ordinary errors of all sense-perception. Such a steadiness can however be achieved only after continual practice. A yogin must be always watchful, particularly in the first stages, to keep his mind steadily on the object of his concentration. He must have, therefore, an inexhaustible fund of active energy (*virya*).

On the negative side we have, therefore, disinclination to worldly things; on the positive side, firm faith in the efficacy of the yoga process and vigorous energy exercised in steadying the mind in contemplation. Gradually, as the yogin becomes more proficient, he selects subtler and finer objects for his concentration; and at each stage in this refinement, new forms of intuitional prajna, or yoga knowledge, dawn. With' this advancement, the yogin develops many miraculous powers over natural objects and over the minds of men. Truths wholly unknown to others become known to him. Though all these powers confirm his faith in the yoga process, he does not allow himself to be led away by their acquisition, but steadily proceeds toward that ultimate stage in which his mind will be disintegrated and his self will shine forth in its own light and he himself will be absolutely free in bondless, companionless loneliness of self-illumination.

This *prajna,* or yoga intuitional knowledge, may be considered as a new dimension of knowledge wholly different from any other kind of knowledge derived by the movement of the mind. The most fundamental characteristic of yoga mysticism consists, on its negative side, not only in a disbelief in the ability of sense-perception and logical thought to comprehend the ultimate truth about the absolute purity and unattached character of our true self; but also in a disbelief in the possibility of the realisation of this highest truth so long as the mind itself is not destroyed. On its positive side, it implies that intuitional wisdom is able to effect a clear realisation of truth by gradually destroying the so-called intellect. The destruction of mind, of course, also involves the ultimate destruction of this intuition itself. So neither the intuition nor our ordinary logical thought is able to lead us ultimately to self-realisation.

There are thus three stages of knowledge. First, our ordinary sense-knowledge and logical thought which always deal with the world and worldly objects and which appear valueless to us when we are in spiritual exaltation and are anxious to attain the highest truth. Second, the intuitional yoga wisdom, which can only be attained when, as a result of the highest moral elevation and the yoga practices, the mind can be firmly steadied on an object so that it becomes one with that object and all its movements completely cease. This yoga wisdom gives us a direct non-conceptual vision of, or acquaintance with, the ultimate truths concerning all objects on which our minds may be concentrated; and gradually, as the yogin begins to concentrate on subtler and finer objects, such as mind, self, etc., higher and nobler truths concerning these become known to him.

Though we are free to concentrate on any object whatsoever, it is desirable for the quicker attainment of our goal that we should concentrate on God—surrender ourselves to Him. In the most advanced state of this yoga intuition, all the truths regarding the nature of the true self, of the mind and of the material world and its connection with mind, become clear, and as a result of this and also as a result of the gradual weakening of the constitution of the mind, the latter ceases to live and work and is dissociated forever from the spirit or the self. It is then that the spirit shines forth in its own lonely splendor, free from the bondage of the mind which had so long by its activities led it towards false worldly attachments and to a false non-appearance of its own pure nature in all the varied products of ordinary knowledge, feeling and willing which make up our worldly life. The highest and ultimate revelation of truth is therefore not only non-conceptual and non-rational, but also non-intuitional and non-feeling. It is a self-shining which is unique.

12

BUDDHIST MYSTICISM

The process of yoga consists of a threefold course, viz., high moral elevation, physical training of the body for yoga practice, and steady mental concentration associated with the revelation of yoga wisdom, which leads to a knowledge of reality as it is. This system of thought and practice, though not without unique and distinctive features, was largely an adoption from very early times. Thus the heretical school of the Jains, which, like the Buddhistic school, holds to a monastic religion, but which was founded earlier than 500 B.C., the date of the Buddha, also considered yoga as the means of liberation of the soul. For the Jains, the liberated state of the soul is not one of pure, feelingless, non-conceptual, non-intuitional self-illumination, but is a state of supreme happiness in which the liberated self possesses a full perfection of all kinds of knowledge: perceptual, logical, alogical, intuitional and trance cognition. This liberation is attained, they believe, by the performance of yoga.

Yoga with them consists mainly of a high elevation of character and complete cessation from the doing of evil, like the yoga of Patanjali. They lay great emphasis on the principle of non-injury, but they also urge the necessity of the other virtues demanded by the yoga of Patanjali. Here, then, we have a system of thought according to which high moral elevation, by the cessation from all evil-doing and the acquirement of all the positive virtues is supposed to reveal a knowledge of reality as it is, and ultimately to liberate us from the bondage of our deeds and bring us to a state of perfect happiness, perfect knowledge and perfect power. The Jains, like the yogins, also believe that without the control of the mind no one can proceed in the true path. All our acts become controlled when our minds become controlled. It is by attachment and antipathy that man loses his independence. It is thus necessary for the yogin that he should be free from both attachment and antipathy and become independent in the real sense of the term. When a man learns to look upon all beings with an equal eye, he can effect such freedom, in a manner impossible even by the practice of the strictest asceticism through millions of years.

The Buddha himself, as the legendary account of his life tells us, once went out with his friends for a ride on horseback through the fields outside his capital. There he saw that, as the fields were being ploughed by the peasants, many insects were being mutilated and killed with each drive of the plough; and he saw also the sufferings of the poor beasts that were employed in the field. Extremely affected by these sufferings, he dismounted from his horse and sat on the grassy ground to reflect on the ultimate destiny of all beings. He realized that sufferings, diseases, old age and death are evils to which we are all subject. At that moment he saw a monk who said that, being afraid of births and deaths, he had renounced the world for his eternal salvation. The suggestion affected him very deeply. He therefore decided to renounce the world and seek to discover the way to the extinction of all sorrows, sufferings, diseases, old age and death. After testing many ways followed by other people, the Buddha himself adopted the path of yoga for the attainment of the truth that he ultimately discovered. As he sat with fixed determination he was tempted in various ways by Mara, the Buddhist Satan, but all these temptations failed and the Buddha remained firm in his purpose.

In the teachings and instructions found in Pali works ascribed to the Buddha, it is said that we are bound, without and within, by the entanglements of desire and that the only way of loosening these is by the practice of right discipline, concentration and wisdom. Right discipline or sila means the desisting from the commission of all sinful deeds. This is the first prerequisite. Thereby one refrains from all actions prompted by bad desires. Concentration or samadhi is a more advanced effort. By it all the roots of the old vicious tendencies and desires are destroyed, and one is led to the more advanced state of a saint. It leads directly to *prajna* or true wisdom; and by this wisdom one achieves his final emancipation. Here also, as in the yoga of Patanjali, the individual must habituate himself to meditating on the fourfold virtues of universal friendship, universal compassion, happiness in the happiness of all, and indifference to any kind of preferment, whether of himself, his friend, his enemy or a neutral party.

By thus rooting out all misery he will eventually become happy; he will avoid thoughts of death and live cheerfully, and will then pass over to the idea that other beings would also fare similarly. He may in this way habituate himself to thinking that his friends, his enemies and all those with whom he is not connected might all become happy. He may fix himself in this meditation to such an extent that he obliterates all differences between the happiness of himself and that of others. He remembers that if he allows himself to be affected by anger he would weaken the self-restraint which he has been carefully practising. If some one has done a vile action by inflicting an injury, that cannot be a reason why he should himself do the same by being angry with others. If he were finding fault with others for being angry, could he himself indulge in anger? A saint who has thus made his sila or right discipline firm enters into a state of concentration which has four stages of gradual advancement. In the fourth or the last stage both happiness and misery vanish and all the roots of attachment and antipathies are destroyed. With the mastery of this stage of concentration there comes the final state of absolute extinction of the mind and of total cessation of all sorrows and sufferings—Nirvana.

It is easy to see that this system of yoga is very much akin to Patanjali's yoga; and it is not improbable that both Patanjali and Buddha but followed a practice which had been in existence from much earlier times, so that neither of them may be credited with its discovery. But there is one point in which there is at least a good deal of theoretical difference between Buddha's system and that of Patanjali. The ultimate goal of all concentration and its highest perfection with the Buddha is absolute extinction, while with Patanjali it is liberation of the spirit as self-illumination.

It is indeed very difficult to describe satisfactorily the ultimate mystical stage of Buddhistic Nirvana. For in one sense it is absolutely contentless. It is the state of deliverance from all sorrow and from all happiness. Yet, as the ultimate ideal of all our highest strivings and the goal of all our moral perfection and concentration, it was an ideal which was in the highest degree attractive to the Buddhists. Had it been conceived as pure and simple extinction or annihilation, it could not have had the attraction for the Buddhists that it did. In many passages it is actually described as blissful. In other passages it is held to be like the extinction of a flame. Some European scholars have considered the descriptions of Nirvana by the Buddhists to be incoherent or inconsistent.

It is not surprising that European scholars, who are temperamentally often very different from the Buddhists of India, should fall into error in trying to comprehend the mystical state of Nirvana. Whether we read the teachings of the Upanishads or of the yoga of Patanjali, the ultimate state representing the goal of all the spiritual quest and spiritual strivings of the sages is set forth as absolutely contentless and non-conceptual. It is the self no doubt, but this self is entirely different from the self with which we are familiar in all our ordinary worldly concerns. It is the extinction of all our sorrows and pleasures and all our worldly experiences as much as is Nirvana. It is a state of absolute dissolution of all world-process. Though a blissful state, there is no distinction here between the bliss and the enjoyer of the bliss. But still it is just such a non-logical ultimate state that could stimulate the highest strivings of the best men of India. To call it blissful is not to understand bliss in an ordinary way. For this mystical bliss is incomprehensible by the intellect.

Nirvana was conceived as a state similar to that just described. If it was compared to the extinction of a flame, this was quite proper. For is it not a state in which all worldly experiences entirely and absolutely cease to exist? Yet it is blissful in the sense that it can stimulate our spiritual cravings and spiritual strivings to the highest degree. The Hindus thought that at this state there is only the self-luminous self. The Buddhists, however, could not say what exists at this state for they denied the existence of the self. But the teaching of the Hindus is scarcely more comprehensible, except for the fact that at least from the grammatical and literary point of view we have in "the self-luminous self" a positive expression. But this self is as indescribable as is the state of Nirvana, except by the negative method of "not this," "not that." But still this state was rightfully called immortal and blissful because it was looked upon by the Buddhists as the end of all their sufferings, the goal of all their spiritual strivings, and the culmination of spiritual perfection. What is especially emphasized, from the negative point of view, is that it is absolutely non-logical in its nature. It has no describable essence. The mysticism of the Buddhist consists in a belief in this essenceless state of Nirvana 1 as the state of ultimate perfection and ultimate extinction, to be realized by the complete extinction of desires and the supra-intellectual wisdom of the yoga practice.

So, though, for academic and philosophical discussions, the essenceless state of the vacuity of Nirvana is absolutely different from the pure self of yoga liberation, yet from the point of view of mystical experience both are too deep and unfathomable for ordinary comprehension. Both are transcendent, unworldly, and contentless in their nature; and the methods of their realization are also largely similar. In digressing, I shall now turn your attention to other forms of mysticism inviting a belief in non-logical methods of achieving one's highest goal of power, happiness, wisdom or emancipation, and shall speak of Indian asceticism. The Taittiriya Brahmana, which was composed probably as early as 700 B. C. (if not even earlier) speaks of Brahmacharya in the sense of studying the Vedas with due self-control. We find there the story of Bharadvaja who practised Brahmacharya for one whole life which was as long as three lives. Indra approached him and, finding him decayed and old, said, "Bharadvaja, if I were to give you a fourth life, what would you do with it?" He answered, "I would use it in practising Brahmacharya." The word *tapas* etymologically means heat, and in the Atharva Veda (XVII. 1. 24) is actually used in the sense of the heat of the sun. But by an extension of meaning the word was used to denote also the exertion of mental energy for the performance of an action and for the endurance of privations of all kinds, of heat, cold, and the like. It was regarded as a great force which could achieve extraordinary results. Thus it is said in the Taittiriya Upanishad that the Great Being performed *tapas* and having done so created all the world. In Rig Veda (X. 167. 1) Indra is said to have gained Heaven by *tapas*. *Tapas* was thus probably understood from very early times as some kind of austere discipline, the exact nature of which, however, was rather vague, changeable and undefined.

In Ashvaghosha's Buddhacharita, which was written probably during the first century of the Christian era, we find that the Buddha was told by an ascetic in the forest how different ascetics lived like birds, by picking up grains left in the fields; others ate grass like animals; some lived with snakes; some sat still, like ant-hills, with nests of birds in the tangles of their long hair and snakes playing on their bodies; some lived in water, with tortoises eating parts of their bodies, thinking that misery itself is virtue and that the highest happiness in Heaven can be achieved by under-going sufferings of all kinds. Even in recent times Indian ascetics have inflicted on themselves various kinds of self-mortifications for the merits that are supposed to be derived from them. Thus a Brahmin ascetic at Benares is known to have lived for thirty-five years on a flat board studded with iron nails or spikes on which he sits and lies down at full length and which he never leaves night or day. Another common form of self-torture is to raise one or both arms above the head, and to hold them there until they become stiff and atrophied. Some ascetics are known to live with four fires burning very near them on their four sides and with the sun shining over their heads. Others undertake prolonged fastings and take vows of silence for years.

We read in the Puranas that self-mortification by itself was believed to generate a force. By virtue of the force, power or energy of these self-mortifications, an ascetic who performed them could exact from the god he worshipped, any boon that he wanted and the god could not refuse to grant him the boon even though he knew that the effect of granting it would be seriously mischievous. In the Ramayana, the greatest epic of India, the story is told of Ravana, the great demon who carried away Sita, the wife of Rama. Ravana had won the boon from Prajapati that he could not be killed by gods or demons, and it was by virtue of this boon that he could conquer all the gods, though he was ultimately killed by Rama, a man. A story is told of a demon who had a boon from the god Shiva that the person on whose head he would put his hands would he reduced to ashes. When the boon was granted, the demon wanted to test its truth by putting his hands on the head of the god Shiva himself. Shiva was very much afraid and started to fly away with the demon pursuing him in hot haste. But the god Shiva had no power of taking away the favor that he had granted, for it was earned by the force of the *tapas* of the demon. Vishnu, who came to rescue the god Shiva, played a trick upon the demon.

The latter was asked to test the truth of the boon about which he was sceptical on his own head and thus he was reduced to ashes. This *tapas* is often described as a fire. Unless the boon is granted and the ascetic desists from his *tapas*, it is believed that the fire of his *tapas* might even burn the whole world as it were. The force of these stories is that there was a belief that self-mortification is itself a source of great power and that by it one could gain any desire, be it an immortal life in Heaven, the conquest of all the worlds, or any other fanciful desire—even the liberation from all bondage. We thus find that, just as in the Vedic school sacrifice was conceived as a power which could produce any beneficial results that the sacrificer wanted, so in this Puranic school there was the belief that *tapas* as self-mortification could give an individual anything he craved. It was a power by itself. These *tapas* performances were apparently carried out to please certain gods, just as oblations were offered to the Vedic gods in sacrifices; yet the god with reference to whom the *tapas* was performed had no power to refuse the boon. The boons were exacted from the gods by the power of *tapas*, whether or not the gods willed to grant them of their own free volition, just as the effects of sacrifice did not in any way depend on the good will of the gods to whom offerings were made at those sacrifices.

We know that *tapas* as the power of endurance of physical privations and troubles was an indispensable accessory of both the Buddhist yoga and Patanjali's yoga. The gradual abandonment of desires until their ultimate extinction could be effected, was essential both to yoga and to Buddhism. It is true that the Upanishads do not speak of the extinction of desires, but they certainly praise self-control as an indispensable desideratum. There is indeed the law of karma which requires that every person reap the fruits of his actions, whether good or bad, and that if the life of the present birth is not sufficient for the experience of the sufferings or the joys which are put to his account in accordance with the measure of his vice or virtue, he will enjoy or suffer the fruits of his deeds in another birth. So, in an endless chain of births and rebirths, moves on the cyclic destiny of man. All his rebirths are due to the fact that he is filled with desires, and for their fulfillment he performs actions out of attachments, passions, antipathies, etc.

By the law of karma (which acts automatically according to some, and is controlled by the will of God according to others) he enjoys or suffers the fruits of his actions in this or in subsequent births. So if the successive chain of births is to be terminated, the accretion of the fruits of karma must be stopped, and if the accretion of karma is to be stopped, desire must be rooted out. I shall not enter into the subtle question as to whether the place of superior importance belongs to karma or to the extinction of desires in the Hindu, Buddhist and Jaina schemes of life. Whichever of the two may be considered the more important in each particular Hindu or Buddhist system of thought, they are nevertheless indissolubly connected. For out of desires come the actions and their fruits, and out of actions and the enjoyment or suffering of their fruits of pleasures or sorrows come further desires, and so on. However, if one looks at the matter psychologically, the extinction of desires may be considered the more important, since it is for Indian philosophy the indispensable ethical desideratum for all spiritual achievement. If the ultimate freedom of the spirit and the cessation of the cycle of births and rebirths be the ultimate ethical and spiritual goal, this can only be attained by the extinction of desires and the termination of the accretion of the fruits of our deeds.

The development of the ideal of *tapas* is a direct result of this ideal of the extinction of desires. It was probably thought in some circles that control of desires implies on its positive side the idea of self-mortification. Logically it certainly does not. But the mistaken transition is easy. So there grew up a system of practice in which people thought that self-mortifications are of the highest merit and are capable of giving anything that might be desired. Soon degeneration set in. Self-mortifications were probably introduced as supplementary to the control of desires. They then came to be practiced for the indulgence of desires for attaining heaven or superior power, and thus began to perform functions similar to those that were ascribed to sacrifices in Vedic circles.

The Buddha himself, as the legendary account of Ashvaghosha's Buddhacharita relates, directs the same criticisms as the above against the practice of self-mortification. He deplores the fact that, after leaving all worldly comforts, relatives and friends, men should with all these self-mortifications called tapas, desire only the satisfaction of desires. People are afraid of death, but when they seek the satisfaction of desires this leads to births, and thus they again face death of which they are afraid. If self-mortification is by itself productive of virtue, then the enjoyment of pleasures must be vicious. But if it is believed that virtue produces pleasures or happiness, and if pleasures are vices, then virtue produces vice, which is self-contradictory. It is strange, however, that the Buddha himself, when he wanted to attain to the highest wisdom or philosophy, undertook for six years the most rigorous asceticism and with all his limbs emaciated was almost on the point of death. He did not, of course, aim at the fruition of any ordinary desires, but at the discovery of the wisdom by which birth and death and all the sufferings associated with them could be stopped. All the same, he at first followed the custom then prevalent among ascetics and underwent the most austere discipline. But at the end of six years he realized that the performance of asceticism was unnecessary and without value for the attainment of the higher wisdom. He then bethought himself as to how he might regain his former strength and physique.

He thought that by hunger, thirst and fatigue the mind loses its ease, and that if the mind is not at ease one cannot by its use attain the highest wisdom. It is by the due satisfaction of the senses that the mind comes to its ease, and it is the easy, peaceful, and healthy mind in a healthy body that can attain the wisdom of yoga concentration. So the Buddha gave up his old forms of hard ascetic practice and tried to regain his health by proper food, bathing, etc. His associates, however, who probably knew only the old forms of practice, and were therefore shocked over his abandonment of them, left him. It was only after he had thus recovered his health that he could resist all the temptations of Mara, the Buddhistic Satan, and attain by concentration, highest wisdom. The wisdom that the Buddha attained seems to have been more of the nature of logical thought, but the goal that was to be attained by such wisdom was the mystical, inexpressible, essenceless Nirvana; and the direct means by which this could be attained was not logical thought or reasoning or scriptural or other kinds of learning, but the extinction of all desires (*trishna-kshaya*).

The principal virtues of universal friendship, universal compassion, etc., to which reference has already been made, were appreciated early in Buddhism and also in the yoga of Patanjali. But it may well be argued that there was scarcely any place for the active manifestation of universal friendship or universal compassion in a scheme of life which was decidedly individualistic. No one who sought the absolute freedom of his own self, or the extinction of his whole personality like the extinguishing of a flame, and who sought the cessation of his own rebirths and sorrow as the only goal and the only ambition to be realized, could have much scope for any active manifestation of universal friendship. The altruistic ideal can therefore at best be merely a disposition, and can manifest itself merely in a negative way, e.g., in non-injury to any being. But a person who holds such an individualistic notion of salvation cannot, in his scheme of life, have any leisure or opportunity for the doing of active good to others.

In the Hindu Puranas or religio-mythological works, written in poetry, we sometimes come across tales of wonderful self-sacrifice for the good of the gods or even for the good of animals who sought protection. But tales of self-sacrifice from the motive of universal friendship are very rare, and they do not seem to fit in with the Hindu ideal of personal and individual liberation. A story is told that when the gods were in great trouble in their war with Vritra, a demon, they approached the sage Dadhichi. For it was decreed by fate that the demon could be killed with a weapon made of Dadhichi's bones but with nothing else. Dadhichi, in response to the request of the gods, willingly gave up his life, in order that the gods, with a weapon made of his bones, might destroy the demon.

A story is also told of King Shibi, who was tested by the gods Indra and Agni. Agni took the form of a pigeon, and Indra that of a pursuing hawk. The pigeon took shelter with King Shibi. The latter would not give it over to the hawk because the pigeon had taken shelter with him and under these circumstances he would rather give up his own life than allow the pigeon to be killed. At last the hawk said that he would be satisfied if King Shibi would give from his own body flesh of the same weight as that of the pigeon, and the king cut the flesh of his thigh with his own sword. This, however, is a case of the kshatriya's virtue of giving shelter to those who seek it, even at the sacrifice of one's own life. It does not exemplify self-sacrifice for the good of beings in general, out of pure motives of universal friendship. The tale is a Brahmanic adaptation of a Buddhist story called Shibijataka, in which King Shibi is said to have torn out his eyes and made a gift of them out of motives of pure charity alone. In another story in the Mahabharata, Shibi is said to have cut up his own son as food for a Brahmin who desired the son's flesh for dinner; and to please the Brahmin Shibi was prepared to join in eating the dinner consisting of his own son's flesh. The motive here was the supreme duty of pleasing the Brahmins and giving them whatever they wanted.

But though the ideal of universal friendship and compassion does not seem to have been an active creed among the Hindus or among the followers of the Hinayana school of early Buddhism, it assumed a rôle of paramount importance in the Mahayana school of Buddhism. Here universal altruism and universal compassion, and happiness and sorrow in the happiness and sorrow of others, form the dominant principle.

The philosophy of the Mahayana Buddhism was peculiarly idealistic. It taught that matter as such has no existence in any form, and that all things perceived are but creations of the mind, and more like a magic show than reality. Everything, according to it, is essenceless and indescribable, mere phantom creation of the mind. Indeed, mind itself is not ultimately real in any sense, but is as illusory a creation as all other things created by it. It is the realization of this that was called *bodhi* or perfect knowledge. Those who perceive this truth attain perfect knowledge and, like a flame extinguished, reach Nirvana or the final deliverance from all sorrows and rebirths.

There is a lower order of saints called *arhats*, or *pratyekabuddhas*. These *pratyekabuddha* saints are said to be of a lower order because they live alone by themselves like the rhinoceros. By their spiritual endeavors, they obtain a logical understanding of the way in which all worldly things originate and pass away; and by meditation on the essencelessness of all things, they attain perfect knowledge and Nirvana. They are not instructed by any one, nor do they teach others to attain the knowledge that they gain. They are accustomed from the beginning to lead a lonely life like the Hindu yogis, and the instruction of others does not interest them. They are therefore regarded as being only Buddhas or enlightened ones of a lower order. The higher Buddhas are those who aim not only at the vision of truth for destroying their inner notion of self or ego and all desires of existence and non-existence, but also at doing good to all living beings and constantly practicing the great virtues.

Their enlightenment includes not only the possession of the truth indispensable to salvation, but also omniscience, universal knowledge of all details of things, and omnipotence. The perfect Buddha attains these powers not only through his prolonged meditations, by which he gets insight into the principles of all things, but also through his infinite merits of constantly performing the great virtues of charity, patience, etc. The man who aims at the attainment of this superior Buddhahood is called a Bodhisattva (one who is on the way to the attainment of perfect knowledge). His superior aim consists in this that, at the cost of personal sufferings, he wishes the temporal happiness of others. He continually desires for others supreme and temporal happiness, and for himself the Buddhahood as a means of realizing this service to others. Even after the saint attains true enlightenment and knows that there is no essence in anything and that nothing exists, he continues to practice the virtues of charity, morality and patience, and to mature the qualities of his supreme enlightenment.

We sometimes hear very remarkable stories of Buddhist saints, even of actual historical saints, who showed supreme self-control and compassion for others. Thus it is said of Aryadeva, a great Buddhist teacher of the second century, that he once defeated in argument a teacher of non-Buddhistic doctrines. A young disciple of this defeated teacher, greatly enraged over his teacher's defeat, determined to murder Aryadeva and awaited a suitable opportunity. One day Aryadeva was preaching the doctrine of the essencelessness of all things, and was refuting heretical views before his pupils in a solitary forest. After this instruction, while he was taking a walk alone, the enemy stabbed him from ambush, saying, "You conquered my teacher with your knowledge, but I now conquer you with my sword." Aryadeva, holding fast with his hands his stabbed belly, bade the would-be assassin take his three clothes and bowl and escape over the mountains in monk's garb so that others might not capture and punish him. He further told him that he was very sorry for him because of the seeds of sinful deeds that he was sowing. The murderer was deeply moved by the saint's compassion and sympathy, and asked Aryadeva to teach him the doctrine. Even in his wounded condition Aryadeva began to teach him the Buddhist doctrine of the essencelessness of all things. After giving him some instructions Aryadeva fell in a swoon and his assailant escaped. Soon afterwards Aryadeva's pupils came and enquired about the murderer. To them the teacher replied that there was no one who was killed or who killed, no friend and no enemy, no murderer, that everything was a delusion due to ignorance.

He who is kind and good and has a great propensity for doing good to others, and who, though incapable of committing a sinful action for himself, may yet be so moved by love for his fellow beings as to commit a wrong action for them, is fit to take the vow of a Bodhisattva who would spend all his future career for the good of others. His enthusiasm is not for the egoistical calm of the saint who is anxious for his own deliverance; he is moved by the most altruistic of all motives, viz., compassion for all creatures. It is such a person who takes the vow of Bodhisattva or one who aspires to the goal of a future Buddha.

But even then it is one thing to take a vow and another thing to fulfil it. Ordinarily one's unconstrained love is given to himself and it is only by reflection that the Bodhisattva learns to care wholly for the welfare of others. At the lower stages, his nature leaves him at the mercy of his inclination; his knowledge of truth is but slight, and the direct penetrating sight of the yoga meditations is entirely lacking to him. But by a continual repetition of his high aspirations, and by a more and more studious practice of the good works which they involve, he gradually comes to the higher stages of progress. As he enters these, wishing to bear the burden of the sins of all human beings in the hells and elsewhere, he becomes free from all fears of evil reputation, rebirth, death, etc. Becoming more and more perfect, he gradually masters the virtues of faith, compassion, affection for all, disinterestedness, reverence for self and for others. All his actions are for the good of others, and his only thought is that he may be serviceable to all beings.

The person who intends to enter upon the higher career of a Bodhisattva and ultimately to become the perfect Buddha, places himself under the guidance of a religious preceptor, performs the moral or pious works, and undertakes the vow of *bodhi*. He thinks that it is only by a desire to become a perfect Buddha for the salvation of men, and by dedicating himself to the good of all beings, that the sins of his past lives can he wholly removed. He confesses his own guilt and imperfections and deplores them. He wishes to dedicate all the fruits of his virtuous deeds, merit and piety to the good of all creatures and for the attainment of their Bodhi. He wishes to be the bread for those who are hungry, and the drink for those who are thirsty. He devotes himself by his love to all beings; and in his compassion for their sufferings, he gives all that he is, to all creatures.

It is by such determinations that he produces in himself the proper state of mind with which one may start in the high career of a Bodhisattva. He has then to keep a strict vigilance over his thoughts and over the resolutions that he has taken, and keep a continued watchfulness over mind and body. He must also perform the great virtues called *paramitas,* for thinking, though good in itself, is not enough by itself; it must be continually supplemented by the exercise of the great virtues. He should restrain himself from all evil by continued watchfulness over his mind and body, and by self-control attained in this way. But he must also continually perform the great virtues in order to strengthen his life in progressive good.

One of the most important of these virtues is that of giving due scope to compassion (*karuna*). (The aspirant thinks that his neighbour suffers pain as he suffers his.) Why should he be anxious about himself and not about his neighbor? Such a man may even commit a sin if he knows that this will be beneficial to one of his fellow-beings. For the sake of doing good to others he should always be prepared to abandon even his meditations or even his chastity. It is through this universal compassion that he can reconcile all beings to himself—by almsgiving, amiability, obligingness, and sharing the joy and sorrow of others. But he ought also to take care that his tendency to charity do not become so excessive as to stand in the way of his spiritual advancement. For it is only on a high stage of spirituality that he can make himself most genuinely serviceable to others. To give even one's flesh and blood for the good of others is good, but the giving of spiritual food is certainly better. It is not good to sacrifice one's body to satisfy the appetite of a tiger when that body in a sound condition can be utilized for giving spiritual instruction to others.

Careful adherence to morality, consisting of purity of intention, reformation after transgression, and regard for the law of right conduct, is another of the important conditions which a Bodhisattva should strictly meet. Without going into any details, the main principle of morality consists in abstaining from all actions hurtful to others, or the maxim, "Do not do to others what you would not like others to do unto you." But apart from this negative virtue of abstention, he should also acquire the positive virtues of devotion to study, reflection and meditation, reverence to the teacher, nursing the sick, confession of guilt, association with people in their good and useful undertakings and in their difficulties and sicknesses, giving them right teaching, etc.,—in short, doing good to all people in all possible ways.

Another important virtue is patience or control of anger, for anger is the greatest of all sins. He should also practice the virtue of energetically conquering all incapacity of body and mind, all attachment to pleasures and want of firm determination. This he can do by thinking of the evil effects of these traits and by recalling that, unless he can firmly keep himself to the strict path of virtue, he will never be able to cross the ocean of suffering, and that, however low may be his present state, he may by continued exertion raise himself to the highest stage of perfection of the Buddhas. He should also derive additional strength by thinking: first, of his great desire to rid himself and all other beings from all their sins: second, of his great pride over undertaking to bear the burdens of all creatures; third, of his joy in undertaking new tasks as soon as the old ones are finished—his happiness is in action itself, and he seeks in action no other fruit than the pleasure of the action done; fourth, of his self-mastery of attention, and of keeping his mind and body always completely alert. If he for any reason fails once, he must discover the cause and see that he may not fail again.

Two further virtues are contemplation or concentration and the true wisdom which realizes the nothingness of all things. It is surprising how a metaphysics of extreme idealism, of the nothingness and essencelessness of all things, or of nihilism, could set for the achievement of the highest spiritual perfection a program of life and endeavor which is altruistic in the most extreme degree imaginable. What is required is a state of perfection in which the individual esteems the ultimate state of mystical deliverance—Nirvana or extinction—to be of little consequence, and is prepared to undergo all troubles, and refuse to enter Nirvana, unless and until all beings become good and happy and come to the path of deliverance.

Out of the doctrines of self-control and the ideal of the extinction of desires, there has thus come a scheme of life in which desirelessness is attained by magnifying the scope of desires from the individual to the universal, by rejecting personal good for the sake of the good of others. This good is not sought with a view to any selfish aims, for the seer knows that nothing exists and that all forms and names are empty and essenceless. But he takes it upon himself to do this because of his supreme compassion and of his determination to devote himself to the service of his fellow-beings and to bring to them the light of perfection. The milk of human kindness flows through him, and it is this flow of kindness in him which leads him to his highest perfection. With him, as Shantideva (a great authority) says, even contemplation occupies only a lower place. For he attains to his highest only by persisting in the path of compassion.

The two cardinal features of his conduct are a firm conviction of the equality of his self with that of his neighbor and the substitution of his neighbor's self for his self. Each of these features involves a clear insight into the nature of things. If with great strength one can duly exemplify them, he attains all the merits of a Bodhisattva. He understands that our only enemy is our selfish "ego." Thus, he speaks to his own self, "Renounce, O my thought, the foolish hope that I have still a special interest in you. I have given you to my neighbor, thinking nothing of your sufferings. For if I were so foolish as not to give you over to the creatures, there is no doubt that you would deliver me to the demons, the guardians of hell. How often, indeed, have you not handed me over to those wretches, and for what long tortures! I remember your long enmity, and I crush you, O self, the slave of your own interests. If I really love myself, I must not love myself. If I wish to preserve myself, I must not preserve myself."

13

DEVOTIONAL MYSTICISM AND THEIR CLASSICAL FORMS

We have described the ideal of supreme self-control and of the extinction of all desires as an indispensable requirement for the attainment of high perfection. This end is believed to be reached by replacing egoism with unlimited universalism, the individual learning to desire his own good by desiring the good of others. But such an unlimited universalism could hardly be practiced within the limited sphere of the duties and activities of a householder. The ideal yogin who renounced the world and spent a life of supreme self-control and suppression of all desires, and who practiced his yoga courses in which all movements of his body are inhibited, could not live in society and follow the ordinary vocations of life. Cut off from society, he pursued a goal of individualistic perfection.

But the general Hindu system of life was not monistic, individualistic, or separatistic. Hindu society was divided into four castes. We find (1) Brahmins, who followed the scholarly and the priestly line of work, studied the Vedas, gave spiritual instruction and performed the sacrifices; (2) Kshatriyas, the warrior caste who protected the weak from the attacks of the strong, governed kingdoms as kings, and gave to the Brahmins all protection and encouragement in their scholarly and priestly works; (3) Vaishyas, or the trading and pastoral caste, who increased the wealth of the country by trading and farming; and (4) Shudras, or the servant caste, recruited from the non-Aryans who found a home in the Aryan societies and served as menials to the Brahmins, Kshatriyas and Vaishyas.

The Brahmin went to live with his teacher from the age of eight and remained with him until he had completed the study of the Vedas. He then returned from the house of his teacher and was bound according to the injunction of the scriptures to get married, to perform regularly the sacrifices, to be united with his wife and procreate sons, to teach students, and to make gifts or charities to proper persons at auspicious times and at holy places. Upon reaching the age of fifty he had to retire to forest life with his wife, and give himself up to holy thoughts and the leading of a holy life. In the last stage of his life, it was necessary for him to renounce even his forest life of retirement. He had to sever himself from all his attachments, lead the life of a hermit and get his food by begging. Of these four stages of life, called Brahmacharya, Grihastha, Vanaprastha, and Yati, the householder's life was regarded as the best. For this stage (*ashrama*) provided an opportunity for the doing of good to the people of all the other stages of life, by gifts, by the performance of sacrifices, by instruction to teachers, and by the procreation of good sons who might become the future supporters of society. Performance of sacrifices, teaching, and the procreation of sons were regarded as debts with which every Brahmin was born, and no Brahmin had any right to seek the individualistic goal of a hermit's life unless and until he had discharged these duties for the major portion of his life.

Similarly, it was regarded as the duty of a Kshatriya to protect the weak and to fight in a good cause, and of a Vaishya to carry on trading and farming. The performance of the class of duties belonging to each caste at its specific stage of life is the imperative duty (*dharma*); transgression of it was held to be transgression of duty and hence vicious (*adharma*). What was expected of every man was that he follow the specific duties allotted to his caste, satisfy his desires of life, and enjoy the pleasures of life. It was a balance in which equal attention was paid to the performance of the allotted duties and to the satisfaction of personal needs and desires that was regarded as the true ideal of life for all normal persons. Only in exceptional cases did the Hindu scheme of life admit the renouncement of this life (*trivarga*) of threefold duties in a search for the attainment of the goal of liberation (*apavarga*).

The yearning after a higher life was an actual and soul-stirring experience among spiritually-minded persons. They were allowed the privilege of renouncing the life of ordinary pleasures, and of seeking to kill all other desires and to attain true knowledge, by intuition, moral elevation, yoga or even by asceticism. In their case alone, however, was this exception made. But even then the exception was not very readily admitted in orthodox Hindu circles. We remember the great effort that Shankara, the great Vedanta teacher, had to make, especially in his commentary on the Gita, to establish this point. He taught that those who attained higher knowledge (*jnana*) were exempt from the allotted duties of ordinary persons. These duties were obligatory only for those who did not attain the higher knowledge. But Shankara's interpretation of the Gita was objected to by other authorities.

The Gita is a work of great sanctity and popularity among the Hindus. It consists of seven hundred simple verses, of which the first chapter of forty-six verses forms the introduction. It is written in the form of a dialogue between Lord Krishna and Arjuna, the great warrior who, on the battlefield of the terrible Indian civil war described in the classic heroic poem Mahabharata, is appalled at the prospect of the fearful impending destruction and refuses to fight. Lord Krishna tries to persuade him, in the Gita, that as a Kshatriya, (a man of the military caste) it is his duty to fight. To add strength to his persuasion he makes use of many moral and religious arguments. Traditionally this theme forms a part of the fifth canto of the Mahabharata. Though its date is uncertain, it may well be believed to have been written about the. second or the third century B. C. It discards self-mortification and believes in three kinds of *tapas*: first, bodily discipline—respect to gods, Brahmins and the wise, purity, sincerity, chastity and non-injury; second, speech discipline—sweet and truthful speech, and study; and third, mental discipline—contentment, self-control, amiability, purity of mind, and meditation.

But the great solution of the Gita is the compromise its advances between the worldly life of allotted duties and the hermit life of absolute renouncement, and between a life of lawful and proper enjoyment and the absolute extinction of desires. The program that it proposes is, on the one hand, that we purify our minds, purging them of all attachments and passions by dedicating all the fruits of our actions to God; and yet, on the other hand, that we continue to perform all the duties belonging to our particular caste or stage of life. It is not the actions but our own inclinations and passions that really bind us. But if we can augment our faith in and our affection for God to such an extent that in our love for Him we free ourselves from all other attachments while yet we continue to perform the allotted and normal duties, the actions can in no wise bind us to a lower goal. A life dedicated to God, and lived for and in love of Him, is a life which is inevitably ennobled to the highest degree. A seer who has been able to liberate himself from the tendency to self-seeking and from attachment is never over-pleased at any good fortune nor over-sorry at any misfortune. His is a calm and unruffled life. He takes the pleasures and sorrows of life without the least perturbation; he has no fear and no anger; he is firm in himself, unshakeable and unmoved.

Yet he follows the daily routine of social and other duties. The Gita seems to reject the doctrine that the body and mind may be made entirely motionless or inactive. Simple physical conditions could make the body move; and it urges that it is only a false show of morality when the body is controlled and yet one continues to think of doing bad things or to harbor thoughts of attachment. The mysticism of the Gita consists in the belief that the performance of actions without personal attachment or self-seeking motive, and with a dedication of their fruits to God, leads a man to his highest realization or liberation. Knowledge is praised, but only because true knowledge is conducive to the acceptance of such a life of desireless self-surrender to God. A man who has no personal motive in an action really does not perform the action though to all appearances he may seem to be so doing. It is only such a person who my truly be called a yogin. His is a mind that is constantly fixed on God, and he performs all his duties for the sake of duty, out of reverence to the law, and with complete self-surrender to God.

Self-surrender to God, or self-abnegation, however, does not in the Gita involve a personal relationship of communion and love so much as it does the moral qualities of compassion, universal friendship, humility, contentment, want of attachment, self-control and purity. The expectation is emphasized that a person possessed of these moral qualities will be equally unruffled in sorrow and in happiness and that he will be the friend of all. Mind and intellect are to be concentrated on God, and all actions are to be surrendered to Him. This does not necessarily mean a superabundance of love. It may be an offshoot of the old yoga ideal of Patanjali. Here it is enjoined that the mind and intellect be concentrated on God, for, if this is done, God, being satisfied by this attachment, will help the yogin, and by His divine grace the yogin may achieve his goal much more easily than would otherwise be possible.

The idea of the surrender of all actions to God is also to be found in the yoga of Patanjali. Though the writer of the Gita admits breath-control as a discipline, yet his whole emphasis is laid on self-abnegation and self-surrender to God. Breath-control seems to be given only a subordinate value, that of a means of purifying the mind. We have, therefore, in the Gita a new solution of how a man may attain his highest liberation. He may remain a member of society and perform his allotted duties provided he has the right sort of moral elevation, has fixed his mind on God, has dissociated himself from all attachment, and, by self-surrender and self-abnegation, has devoted himself to God. It is faith in the special grace of God to those who have surrendered themselves to Him that forms the essence of the Gita.

Though the idea of love for God does not show itself in any prominent way in early Sanskrit literature, except in the Pancaratra literature, it is very improbable that the idea was not known from very early times. For some of the monotheistic Vedic hymns reveal an intimate personal relation with the deity, implying affection; and in the Buddhist literature we find frequent references to love for the Buddha.

In the Vishnu Purana we are given the story of Prahlada. Because of his devotion to Hari, his father tormented him in various ways and sought to put him to death by throwing him into fire or into the sea, by administering poison, and by various other methods. But he was saved from all these perils by the grace of Hari, and as a true devotee of the great Lord he was not in the least angry with his father. In all the adoration to Hari, whether on the part of Prahlada or as otherwise reported in the Vishnu Purana and in many of the other early Puranas, the great Lord is adored and praised metaphysically or philosophically as the great Being from whom everything has come forth and to whom everything will return, as the great controller of the universe and the great lord who is residing within us and is controlling us, and as the prime mover of the material cosmic world which is only a manifestation of his power.

The subtle and primal cosmic matter is a concrete expression of the energy of the Lord. By His will it is set in active operation and transforms itself into the visible universe. The universe, therefore, though in a sense different from Him, is ultimately sustained and supported by Him; created by Him, it will ultimately return to Him. Many are the hymns in the Puranas which praise God in this philosophical manner and extol His great powers. There are also numberless instances in which God is said to be pleased by philosophic meditation, and in consequence appears to the devotee, to speak with him, and to grant him the boon he seeks.

The earlier literature does not always emphasize the feeling element in devotion. In the Vishnu Purana, however, we find that when God came face to face with Prahlada and asked him if he had a boon to crave, he besought the same attachment for the Lord that ordinary people have for sense enjoyments. The devotion that Prahlada had previously shown was a concentration on God and a serene contemplation in which he became one, as it were, with the Lord. Ramanuja, the great Vedanta commentator of the 11th century, also defines devotion (bhakti) as a contemplation of God unbroken as the smooth and ceaseless flow of oil. But that such a contemplation necessarily implies love of God as its inner motive cannot be denied, and Ramanuja also describes this ceaseless contemplation as having its main source in love for God, who was so dear to the devotee. But all that I wish to point out in this connection is that, in this aspect of devotion, contemplation and communion are more prominent than any exuberance of feeling. Prahlada was attached to God by his love of Him; God was the dearest of all dear things to him. It was this inmost and most deep-seated love for God that stirred him to withdraw his mind from all other things and to enter into such a contemplation of God that he became absorbed in Him, his whole personality lost in an ecstatic trance unity with God. But this did not satisfy Prahlada. He desired such a devotion to God that the very thought of Him would bring the same sort of satisfaction that persons ordinarily have in thinking of sense-objects. He desired not only contemplative union but longed also to taste God's love as one tastes the pleasures of the senses.

It is the contemplative union with God that we find in the Gita, and the transition to it from the state of yoga concentration is not difficult to understand. Self-surrender to God, the higher moral elevation, and concentration on God are all present in Patanjali's yoga. But here the objective was the destruction of the mind through psychical exercises accompanied by the complete inhibition of bodily and mental activity. Later the devotee seeks to attain liberation through the special grace of the Lord, which he can hope to acquire by such contemplative union.

In later Indian thought the method of yoga on the one hand receded in favor of that of bhakti or devotion; on the other hand, its pure form became greatly complicated by the development of many mysterious doctrines and rites which became associated with it, sought its support, and claimed to be forms of it. But my time is limited and I cannot enter into these latter forms of mysticism. Nor can I describe those mystical religious movements which, arising as a reaction against the dominant religious ideal of extreme sense-control and the practice of desirelessness, tried to formulate certain principles and methods by which one could attain his highest goal not by sense-control but by sense-enjoyments. In these schemes, sense-indulgence under certain specified conditions was considered not only harmless but an indispensable desideratum.

They probably started among some of the Buddhist schools and they soon became very common among certain sects of the Hindus. I shall, therefore, leave them and pass directly to the development of the mysticism of love to God, as it is presented in the Bhagavata Purana and other relevant later literature.

It is in the Bhagavata Purana, whose date is probably the eleventh century A. D., that we first meet with the idea of devotion as the supreme source of a bliss or spiritual enjoyment that is itself the highest goal and so completely usurps the place of wisdom or philosophical knowledge. Even in the Gita true wisdom was regarded as a fire which reduces to ashes, as it were, all the past deeds whose fruits were not yet on the point of being enjoyed. But in the Bhagavata we read (11.14) that it is bhakti which destroys all the past sins. The old principle of self-surrender to God and a life spent in God-intoxication is the happiest of all lives. A man of such self-surrender has nothing else but God as his possession: he is supremely self-controlled, and the enjoyment that he has from his constant association with God keeps him absolutely happy and content with all things. Such a man does not aspire to any heavenly happiness or even to liberation. Devotion is regarded as having also a protective virtue.

Even an ordinary devotee who is often led away by his sense attachments is so purified by this devotion that he is no longer overcome by external attachments or passions. The Lord can be realized by bhakti and by nothing else. Neither the performance of the allotted duties nor knowledge combined with the austere discipline of tapas can purify a man who is devoid of all bhakti. This bhakti, however, is no longer the old contemplative meditation of God, stirred by a deep-seated love. It is the ebullition of feelings and emotions of attachment to God. It manifests itself in the soft melting of the heart and expresses itself in tears, inarticulate utterances of speech, laughter, songs and dances, such as can only be possible through a mad intoxication of love. This kind of bhakti is entirely different from the calm contemplative life of complete self-abnegation and self-surrender to God and a mind wholly immersed in God and the thought of God.

The Bhagavata Purana is aware of the three methods of approach by knowledge, work and devotion, and also of the approach through yoga. Moreover, while emphasizing the superiority of devotion, it does not deny the efficacy of the other methods of approach. The latter are also described in the Gita; indeed, the Gita also emphasizes the bhakti method. Both the Gita and Bhagavata criticize the older course of the Vedic sacrifices, but neither of them has the boldness to pass an unconditional condemnation. The Gita says that one should perform these sacrifices, which are obligatory, with a pure and desireless mind. The fault of those who devote themselves to sacrifices is that they are filled with ordinary desires for pleasures and are not acquainted with any higher goal of life. To one who is infused with the higher ideal of life and can emancipate himself from desires by self-surrender to God, the performance of sacrifices, as of any other kinds of action, can do no harm. Indeed, it is good that under these circumstances one should not forsake his allotted duties.

The Bhagavata holds that the only efficacy of the Vedic restrictions and prohibitions is to be found in the fact that they offer a check on the natural inclinations of man and ultimately help him to desist from sense-activities and sense-propensities. The promise of heavenly rewards as the result of the performance of sacrifices is only a trick to incline people to accommodate themselves to modes of life offering only a restricted scope of sense-gratification. Its appeal is therefore only to those of the lowest plane. Those who are of the next higher order and have been able to accommodate themselves to a life of desirelessness would perform the obligatory duties without in the least looking forward to their fruits. In the next higher stage, a man may follow the path of yoga, or the path of wisdom respecting the supreme unity of Brahman, or any other line of devotion.

The path of devotion, however, is most fitted for those who are neither too much attached to sense-desires nor too much detached from them. Such men may adopt the line of bhakti and thereby purify their minds and, by self-surrender to God and the taste of supreme human happiness in their love, become averse to all other desires and enjoyments. Thus they learn to live a life of supreme devotion. They come to experience such intense happiness that all their limbs and senses become saturated therewith and their minds swim, as it were, in a lake of such supreme bliss that even the bliss of ultimate liberation loses its charm. Such an individual desires to live on, enjoying the love of God with heart, soul and body. When he acquires such a bhakti, it purifies his mind from all passions and impurities, and destroys all the bonds of his deeds and their fruits. For such a person is so attached to God that there is nothing else for which he cares; without any effort on his part, other attachments and inclinations lose their hold over him. So great is his passion for God that it consumes all his earthly passions. It is so great that it is its own satisfaction; it seeks nothing beyond itself. It stands by itself. As a great spring of happiness, it is ultimate and self-complete.

The bhakta who is filled with such a passion does not experience it merely as an undercurrent of joy which waters the depths of his heart in his own privacy, but as a torrent that overflows the caverns of his heart into all his senses. Through all his senses he realizes it as if it were a sensuous delight; with his heart and soul he feels it as a spiritual intoxication of joy. Such a person is beside himself with this love of God. He sings, laughs, dances and weeps. He is no longer a person of this world. The germ of this love is already found in the Vishnu Purana, where Prahlada seeks as a boon that bhakti which is an attachment for God no less strong than the attraction to sense-objects felt by ordinary sensual persons.

Vallabha, a later writer, defines bhakti as a great, firm feeling of love, associated with a sense of God's superiority and greatness. It places the bhakta or the devotee in a subordinate position. The latter is described as approaching God as one approaches his master, desiring mercy and protection and soliciting His special grace. But this idea of seeking protection and special grace, with a sense of God's supreme superiority, and finding oneself happy in thinking of the greatness of the superior Being, is by no means restricted to Hindu circles. There are numerous evidences of Buddhists praising the Buddha and seeking his protection, and finding great joy in extolling his great qualities and powers. Bhaktishataka of Ramachandra Bharati of the 13th century may be referred to as a typical instance.

This kind of bhakti is also associated with the doctrine of prapatti, or taking refuge in God, and is to be found among many classes of Vaishnavas, including the followers of Ramanuja. Prapatti consists in taking refuge in God with great faith and with the strong conviction that it is God and God alone who can help one to attain one's end. Like the fabled bird Chataka that would rather die of thirst than drink any water other than that falling from the clouds, the devotee looks to God for succor, and would seek no other help. Believing that God alone is the saviour, the devotee depends entirely on Him, and refuses to take any other course than that of remaining in entire dependence upon Him. God, for him, is the great master of whom he is the humble servant; God is the controller alike of his mind and his body.

This is only a detailed method of the self-surrender already referred to in the Gita. Naturally the latter also is based on a belief in the great mercy of God, who is sure to free the devotee who with complete reliance has taken refuge in Him as his master and Lord. But in this case the prapatti or taking refuge in God is always with a purpose. It is for the realization of an end that the devotee relies on the mercy, goodness or grace of God. He believes that he can by this means alone attain what he wants. But the bhakti praised in the Bhagavata is of a sort superior to this. It is a devotion without motive of any kind.

It is the love of God proceeding directly from the heart and not prompted by any reason. The true bhakta does not love God because he seeks something from Him, but

he loves Him freely and spontaneously. He sacrifices everything for this love. It is his only passion in life and he is filled with God. God is attracted by such love and always abides with such a bhakta and encourages his great love for him. All distinctions of caste, creed or social status vanish for those who are filled with this true and sincere devotion to God. It is a great leveller. To the eye of a true bhakta all beings are but manifestations of God's power, and they are all equal. Impelled by this idea of universal equality and by the idea of God being in all things and all things in God, he is filled with such a sweetness of temper that howsoever he may be tyrannized over by any one he cannot think of inflicting any injury in return. Nor can he remain unaffected when he sees the sufferings of his fellow-beings, however lowly or depraved they may be.

The question is sometimes asked whether such devotional systems of mysticism are pantheistic. To this no satisfactory reply can be given without a proper definition of pantheism. Without entering into any discussion regarding the meaning of this term or the distinctive metaphysical features of the different systems of Vaishnavism, I can here say only that all these systems in a manner agree as to the duality of God and man. They consider man as a manifestation of the power of God. Though ultimately sustained and always controlled by God, man is for all empirical purposes different from Him. This psychological, logical and ontological difference between God and man is the basis of devotion and worship. In the development of devotion there may, however, come a stage in the mind of the devotee when he becomes one with the Lord in the exuberance of his feelings. But at the next instant the experience may again be differentiated into a feeling of duality and of distinction between him and God.

The devotee may then come to regard himself as a servant of God or His son, or friend, or spouse. It cannot be said, in this inner dialectic of feeling, which of the phases is the truer and has a greater claim to our acceptance. For we have here an alternation of feeling which sometimes expresses itself as an experience of communion or contemplative unity with God and then by its own inner movement passes for its own realization into the various other modes of relationships through which ordinary human love expresses itself. It is a circular movement. At one stage within it, man becomes God, but, at the other, God slowly becomes man and participates with him in diverse human relationships of love and its joys.

Love of God is not a thing which we produce in ourselves by excessive brooding or by self-hypnotism or by any other method. It is a permanent flame, slowly burning in the caverns of all our hearts. Only, however, when it gains strength through study, and through association with other devotees at an opportune moment, do we come to know of it. The basis of all religions is this love of God. For if this love of God were not vital to us, all that the great prophets have been trying to preach would have been unreal and futile. If it were not a real experience which in some sense is shared by us all, an experience which ennobles us and raises us far above the selfish pettinesses of life, no prophet and no religious deed would be able to appeal to our higher natures and establish the claims of religion. Religion is by nature an other-worldly attitude of life—one which we have along with our worldly attitude. "Man does not live by bread alone," is a very elastic proposition. If we by nature wanted only that which satisfies our appetites, there would have been no art, no philosophy, and no religion. Our being is such that side by side with the tendencies that take us to the satisfaction of our appetites or to sense-gratifications, there are others which in an unaccountable manner lift us higher. The senses when properly exercised give us sense pleasures; the mind, through its activities of logical thinking, affords the corresponding joys and the satisfaction of truth-seeking; and the spirit longs to associate itself with some higher ideal, with a greater and superior being, or with a transcendent unspeakable something of which it has at first only an indistinct vision.

Reason moves within a circle and cannot get beyond it. When the ultimate reason of reasoning is to be sought, we have to rest in a tendency, temperament or feeling. Ask a philosopher why he engages in philosophical speculation. He may say that he seeks to know the truth of some particular or some universal problem. But ask him again why he so seeks and he will probably say that he does it because he finds therein a special satisfaction. The satisfaction, though not measureable in physical terms, is yet enough for him. He possesses intellectual curiosity and it must be gratified. Ask a scientist and you will probably receive the same answer. One can never explain our endeavors in any of the higher planes of life, philosophy, art or religion, by reference to any of the ordinary needs and objects of life. These higher activities are apparently without any reason, but still they justify themselves and they are our very existence. That bread alone should not satisfy man is part of his very nature and there is no getting away therefrom.

It is an absolute fact with man. The case of religion is very similar. There is a spiritual longing in the heart of man, indistinct and undefined, but steady like a flame tapering upwards to some divine goal. The mystics of the Bhagavata Purana of whom I am now speaking called it the love of God. They felt that there is nothing higher than the culture of this love. The seed of it they regarded as latent within the individual. Hearing and singing the praises of God stimulates its growth—sprinkles it with water, as it were—until it ascends higher and higher and eventually reaches God. Like an expert gardener the individual has always to see that no beast of a sin, tramples this tender creeper, and that no offshoots, no branches of worldly desires, obstruct its upward growth. Whenever he is tempted by worldly desires or to pray to God for worldly good, he is allowing offshoots to grow on the body of the tender creeper of God's love and to interfere with its upward growth. He must cut them off and make the creeper of love grow freely in one direction, until it connects him with God and he thus comes to enjoy its sweet fruits.

The type of bhakti which is preached in the Bhagavata Purana is well illustrated in the life of Chaitanya, who was born in Navadvip, in Bengal, in 1486 and died in 1534. In his life we find an exemplification of how love of God may be cultivated for its own sake, without any kind of ulterior motive whether of liberation or of happiness. In the accounts which his biographers have given of his mysticism, a distinction is drawn between the experience of God's love as self-surrender to Him, or taking refuge in Him through attachment to Him, and a driving passion of love for God, i.e., between what they call *rati* and *preman*. A distinction is also drawn between a course of attachment and love of God adopted out of a sense of duty or of reverence for the scriptures and a passion of love which springs spontaneously and overflows unrestrainedly.

A distinction is further made between love of God with an overwhelming sense of His greatness and superiority, awe and reverence, and love of God as an easy flow of affection to one who is nearest and dearest to us. Real intimacy with God is only possible in the case of the latter alternative, when a free flow of passionate love springing spontaneously from within associates us with God as the most intimate friend and beloved without whom we cannot live. Chaitanya acknowledges, of course, the peaceful calm and tender love for God called *shanta,* and the submission of the heart to God in obligation and service to Him, called the service attitude, *dasya;* but to look upon God as one's own most intimate friend, *sakhya,* is regarded by him as higher than either of the first two attitudes. To look upon God as one's dearest beloved or lover, or to love Him with a feminine love as that with which a woman loves her beloved, he considers the deepest, sweetest and most perfect love, *madhura*.

According to the legend, Lord Krishna was born of Devaki and Vasudeva in a prison-house where the King Kansa, who was afraid of the birth of the infant who was foretold to be his future destroyer, had confined his mother Devaki. Later Krishna was carried to the house of a cowherd chief, Nanda. There he grew up, having as his associates cowherd boys with whom he was very friendly. He came to be regarded as God incarnate, as the result of a number of miracles which he performed. The wives of most of the cowherd people, who were, in reality but the female incarnations of God's energy, became attached to him and loved him dearly. They were sorely pained over the separation when he later on left for Mathura, a city at some distance from Brindaban, the scene of his early activities. Krishna's early life illustrates the love for him of his fostermother Yashoda, wife of the cowherd chief Nanda, the love for him of his cowherd friends, and the love of the cowherd girls for him as their lover. Inasmuch as Krishna was considered to be God, these three kinds of love for Krishna as described in the tenth chapter of the Bhagavata Purana, together with the other two time-honored modes of loving God, viz., the peaceful quiet love of God and the love of God as God's servant, came to be considered as the five fundamental modes of loving God. The attention of the later Vaishnavas was so much drawn to the excellence of the three kinds of love described in the Bhagavata, and particularly of the love of God as one's lover, that no less than fourteen commentaries have been published dealing with this portion of the Bhagavata Purana. Love of Krishna was the most absorbing passion of Chaitanya's life and, though he came to taste all the different ways of loving God, it was the sweet love of Krishna as the lover, husband and Lord that was the most important feature of his life.

Chaitanya's elder brother had turned a recluse. So his mother Sachi Devi would not at first send Chaitanya to school, since she believed that it is through knowledge that one learns the transitoriness of all things, and she thought it better that her son should grow untutored than that he become learned and renounce the world. So Chaitanya, or Nimai as he was called in his early life, grew wild. But he gradually grew so wild that he could no longer be tolerated, and so he was sent to school. He mastered Sanskrit grammar and logic very thoroughly and at twenty started a school himself. Numerous anecdotes are told by his biographers of his great scholarship and of occasions when he defeated reputed scholars in open debates. At this period he scoffed at all religions and was considered by many to be absolutely godless. In the meanwhile he had settled down in life. His first wife having died, he married again. But at this time Chaitanya's deeper nature began to reveal itself and he wanted to visit the temple of the God Krishna at Gaya, several hundred miles distant from his village. On his way thither he met a great Vaishnava saint and at his sight his higher spiritual life was stirred into life. When he reached the temple of Gaya he experienced a rapturous fervor of love for Krishna, and he became an entirely different man. "Where is my God Krishna," became his chief cry.

In thinking of Krishna, in seeking Him, in relating his vision of Him, he would be so overpowered as often to become unconscious. It was in this condition that he was brought home from Gaya by his friends. He spent his days and nights in reciting and singing the name of God. He, his intimate friend Nityananda, and his other friends used thus to sing the name of God and to dance about with a particular type of music produced by special musical instruments. This music touched the inner, spiritual chords of life and brought on a great religious intoxication in all the hearers, and particularly in Chaitanya and his followers. Chaitanya lived continually in this state of religious intoxication. He had no respect for caste or creeds but was a friend of all. He could not continue this sort of life midst the worldly conditions of his native village. Hence he renounced the world to preach the love of God all over India. In this work he spent the rest of his years, going about from place to place, thousands of miles, on foot. The vision of God was always before him in the form of Lord Krishna. His whole life was a passionate flow of love for this deity, and this emotion was generally so intense that as he sang and danced like a mad man he often became unconscious. He had so thoroughly identified himself as a partner in the episodes of the life of Krishna as described in the Bhagavata that the slightest incidents deriving either from personal conversations and relations or from the scenes of nature sufficed to suggest to him similar adventures or events in the life of Krishna.

Chaitanya described God's love in its most exalted form as being like the love of a woman in deep attachment to a man, where the attachment is so deep that all sex considerations have ceased a love so intense that only an insatiable desire of union in love remains and all the earthly relations of man and woman have ceased. God, he taught, is himself a great controller of us all, and in His eternal love is always attracting us, drawing us up toward greater and greater perfection. Love is His very nature. So it is only through a passionate love of Him that we can enjoy His deep love for us. The older ideals of liberation, of heavenly happiness, of the destruction of the mind and the like were considered by Chaitanya to be absolutely insignificant for a person whose mind has been fired by a great passion that flows in torrents to God, the great ocean of love, who washes away all his sins and defects. In the end, Chaitanya, in an outbreak of divine passion which he was unable to restrain, jumped into the deep blue ocean on the South and was lost forever to human eyes. So passed away one drop of God's love in human shape into that eternal and limitless Ocean of divine love from which it had descended upon the earth.

POPULAR DEVOTIONAL MYSTICISM

The chief features of the passionate devotion for God are its spontaneity and its transference of human relations and emotions to God through the medium of the Krishna legend described in the Bhagavata Purana. It presupposes the theory of the incarnation of God as man, which makes it possible to think of God in human relations and in human ways. The idea of God as father is indeed as old as the Vedas. It is expressed also in several passages of the Gita (9.17, 11.43, 11.44, 14.4) and in the Puranas, in the Nyaya-bhashya of Vatsyayana, as well as elsewhere. Nevertheless it did not, during this period, seem to gain much strength in the way of fostering an intimate relation with God or of affecting worship.

Wherever it appears it seems to be but one of the many passing phases in which God's relation to man is viewed when God is praised and extolled in His greatness as Lord and Master. But in the new school of bhakti the conception of God as creator, supporter, father, lord and master, or as the ultimate philosophical principle, is subordinated to the conception of God as the nearest and dearest. The most important feature is His nearness to and His intimacy with us—not His great powers, which create a distance between Him and us. That He is the greatest of the great and the Highest of the high, that there is nothing greater and higher than Him is admitted by all. His greatness, however, does not reveal the secret of why He should be so dear to us. He may be the greatest, highest, loftiest and the most transcendent, but yet He has made His home in our hearts and has come down to our level to give us His affection and love. Indeed He is conceived as so near to us that we can look upon Him and love Him with the love of a very dear friend, or with the devotion and the intensity of love of a spouse. Love is a great leveller; the best way of realizing God is by making Him an equal partner in life by the force of intense love.

The legend of Krishna supplies a human touch to God's dealings with men. With the help of this legend the bhaktas of the new school, by a peculiar mystical turn of mind, could conceive of God as at once a great being with transcendent powers and also as an intimate friend or a dear lover maintaining human relations with his bhaktas. The episodes of Krishna's life in Brindaban are spiritualized. They are often conceived to happen on a non-physical plane where both Krishna and his partners are thought to play their parts of love and friendship in non-physical bodies. Thus they are not regarded as particular events that took place at specific points of time in the life of a particular man, Krishna. They are interpreted as the eternal, timeless and spaceless play of God with His own associates and His energies, with whom He eternally realizes Himself in love and friendship.

The part that his bhaktas had to play was to identify themselves, by a great stretch of sympathy, as partners in or spectators of God's love-play, and find their fullest satisfaction in the satisfaction of God. For a true bhakta, it is not necessary, therefore, that his sense-inclinations should be destroyed. What is necessary is merely that these should be turned towards God and not towards himself, i.e., that he uses his senses not for his own worldly satisfaction but to find enjoyment and satisfaction in the great love-drama of God by identifying himself with one of the spiritual partners of God in his love-play. Hence it is not essential that all desires and sense-functions, as the Gita says, be destroyed, or that the individual behave as if he had desires while yet being absolutely desireless. It was required that the bhakta have the fullest satisfaction of his sense and inclinations by participating in the joys of Krishna in his divine love-play. For such participation and vicarious enjoyment was regarded as true love (*preman*), while the satisfaction of one's own senses or of one's own worldly purposes was viewed as a vicious passion. Thus here we have a new scheme of life. The ideal of desirelessness and absolute self-control is replaced by that of participation in a drama of divine joy, and the desires are given full play in the direction of God. Desires are not to be distinguished; only their directions are to be changed.

Though this form of bhakti has in various circles at times been debased and encroached upon by diverse kinds of eroticism or erotic mysticism, it cannot be denied that many of the immediate and later followers of Chaitanya achieved great spiritual success in this form of bhakti-worship. In the Narayaniya chapter of the fifth canto of the Mahabharata God is spoken of as a father, mother and teacher; and in the Yoga Sutra of Patanjali and elsewhere the idea is often expressed that God originally taught the Vedas to the sages and that He is therefore the original teacher. In all these writings, however, the love of God supercedes deep reverence. The true bhakta looked upon God as the divine dispenser; he considered all that he had—kingdoms, riches, wife and all that he could call his own—to be God's. Love of God as the mother of the world plays an important part in the religious attitude of many bhakti worshippers. This is particularly true in the case of Ramprasad and others, notably the sage Ramakrishna of recent times. And in this attribution of motherliness to God both Ramprasad and Ramakrishna view Him as a tender mother who is always helping her child, condoning his sins and transgressions, partial to his weaknesses and concerned to better him. Nevertheless He cannot be attained by mere formal worship but only through a whole-hearted worship, with a proper control of the sense-inclinations.

The theory of bhakti seems to have its original source in the Pancaratra school of Vaishnavism. However, the doctrine of supreme self-surrender to Narayana, Hari or Krishna as the one and only God in disregard of all other mythical gods, represents a teaching of the Gita, the chief work of the Ekanti school of Vaishnavas; and this doctrine forms the universal basis of all kinds of bhakti worship, though among the Shaktas or Shaivas the supreme deity went by the name of Shakti or Shiva. The Gita plainly teaches, that there is no other God but Narayana or Krishna, that He alone is great and that we should lay aside all other modes of religious worship and take refuge in Him.

In Chaitanya this devotion to God developed into a life-absorbing passion; yet in all advanced forms of bhakti the chief emphasis is on supreme attachment to God. The sort of bhakti which Prahlada asked as a boon from Hari was such an attachment for Him as worldly persons have for the objects of their senses. Such a bhakti, as described in the Bhagavata or the Shandilya sutra, is not worship out of a sense of duty or mere meditation on God or mere singing of His name, but it is deep affection (*anurakti*). It is therefore neither knowledge nor any kind of activity, but is a feeling. And the taking of refuge (*prapatti*) in God is also not motivated by knowledge but by a deep affection which impels the individual to take his first and last stay in Him. But though a feeling, this bhakti does not bind anyone to the world. For the world is but a manifestation of God's maya, and God so arranges for those who love Him that His maya cannot bind His bhakta to the world.

But how is such a bhakti possible? For this also we have ultimately to depend on God. There is a passage in the Upanishads (Katha II. 23) which states that He can be attained by him whom He (God) chooses. This text has often been cited to indicate that it is only the chosen man of God who has the privilege of possessing a special affection for God. Vallabha declares this special favor (*pushti*) of God indispensable for the rise of such an affection for God. He further holds that according to the different degrees of the favor of God one may have different degrees of affection for Him, though by avoiding the commission of sinful actions, by cleansing the mind of the impurities of worldly passions, and by inclining the mind towards God, one may go a great way in deserving His special favor. It is only by the highest special favor of God that one's affection or attachment for Him can become an all-consuming and all-engulfing passion. True devotion to God, affection or love for Him, must always be an end in itself and never a means to any other end, not even salvation or liberation, so much praised in the classical systems of philosophy. This all-absorbing passion for God is the bhakta's eternal stay in God, and dearer to him than liberation or any other goal of religious realization.

It is not out of place here to mention that among various Hindu sects it was held that an engrossing passion of any kind may so possess the whole mind that all other mental functions may temporarily be suspended, and that gradually, through the repeated occurrence of such a passion, the other mental functions may be altogether annihilated. Thus, absorption in a single supreme passion may make the mind so one-pointed that all other attachments are transcended and the individual attains Brahmahood. In the Upanishads (Brihadaranyaka IV. 3.21) we find that the bliss of Brahman is compared with the loving embrace of a beloved woman. To love one's husband and to serve him as a god was regarded from very early times as the only spiritualizing duty for a woman. Hence the idea that ordinary man-and-woman love may be so perfected as to become a spiritual force easily won acceptance in certain circles.

This man-and-woman love developed an absorbing and dominant passion, completely independent and unaided by other considerations of marital and parental duties. In its non-marital forms, it was considered to be capable of becoming so deep as to become by itself a spiritualizing force. Moreover, it was thought that the transition from human love to divine love was so easy that a man who had specialized in the experience of deep man-and-woman love of a non-marital type could easily change the direction of his love from woman to God, and thus indulge in a passionate love for God. The story is told that in his early career the saint Bilvamangala became so deeply attached to a courtesan named Cintamani that one night he swam across a river supported by a floating corpse, then scaled a high wall by holding on to the tail of a serpent, and finally well-nigh broke his limbs in jumping down from the wall into the yard of Cintamani. The woman, however, rebuked him, saying that if he entertained toward

God a little of the love that he had for her he would be a saint. This produced such a wonderful change in Bilvamangala that he forthwith became a God-intoxicated man. Later, in his saintly life, when he once again felt attracted by a woman, he plucked out his eyes so that external forms and colors might not further tempt him. This blind saint became one of the best-reputed among all the saints, devoting his life to the love of God.

Thus there grew up a school of mystics, including the great poet Candidas and others, who devoted themselves to the cultivation of the spirituality of love and the deification of human love, and who thought that more could be learned through such efforts than through any other mode of worship. "There is no god or goddess in Heaven who can teach spiritual truths more than the person whom one loves with the whole heart." The goddess Basuli whom Candidas worshipped is said to have admonished him to adhere to his love for the washerwoman Rami, saying that Rami would be able to teach him truths that no one else could, and to lead him to such bliss as not even the creator himself might do. A somewhat similar idea of the purificatory power of intense human love is found in the Vishnupurana. In describing the illicit love of a cowherd-girl for Krishna, the Vishnupurana says that at her separation from him she underwent so much suffering that all her sins were expiated, and that in thinking of him in her separation from him she had so much delight as would be equal to the collective culmination of all the happiness that she could enjoy as a reward of her virtuous actions.

By the combination of the suffering and the bliss, she exhausted all the fruits of her bad and good deeds, and thus by her thoughts of Krishna she attained her liberation. Somewhat allied with the idea of human worship, though not of the man-and-women type just mentioned, is a certain attitude sometimes adopted toward man as a religious teacher. The latter was considered in many circles as the representative of God on earth, and self-surrender, love and devotion to him was considered to lead one to God. This sort of worship was prevalent among the Hindus and the Buddhists from pretty early times. One fact should be noted. It was associated with reverence and a sense of the religious teacher's superiority, whereas the other type of worship (through romantic love) raised the man and woman by their constancy and sufferings for each other and the happiness that each enjoys in the company and thought of the other.

In this latter case, love is religion, and all pain endured for the beloved, joy. With the exception of the phase of love-mysticism just mentioned, I have thus far confined myself to a description of different forms of mysticism as portrayed in Sanskrit writings. I shall now turn to the mysticism of divine love that found expression in the vernaculars of North India and of the South. But this is a vast subject and I can say only a few words. Let me advert first to the Alvar saints of the South, the earliest of whom belonged to the second and the latest to the tenth century, A. D. They all wrote psalms or songs in Tamil, a Dravidian tongue of South India. They were inspired by the teachings of Vaishnavism when it travelled from the North to the South.

Their doctrines were more or less similar to those in connection with the bhakti mysticism of the Bhagavata Purana and the Gita. They are embodied in psalms and not in any connected philosophical treatise. Describing his insatiable love of God, Nam Alvar says:

"As I dote on the Lord of Katkarai (God)
Whose streets with scarlet lily are perfumed
My heart for his wonderful graces melts
How then can I, my restless love suppress?"

With reference to Nam Alvar, Govindacarya has said: "Briefly, Saint Nam Alvar declares that when one is overcome by bhakti exaltation, trembling in every cell of his being, he must freely and passively allow this influence to penetrate his being, and carry him beyond all known states of consciousness; never from fear or shame that bystanders may take him for a madman, ought the exhibition of this bhakti-rapture that deluges his being, to be suppressed. The very madness is the means of distinguishing him from the ordinary mortals to whom such beatific vision is necessarily denied. The very madness is the bhakta's pride. In that very madness, the saint exhorts, "run, jump, cry, laugh and sing, and let every man witness it." Let us now pass on to other saints of the South, Namdev and Tukaram. The bhakti school and most of the other branches of this school, developed under purely Brahminic traditions and in the shadow of Brahminic scriptures, the Puranas and the like. And though in the Bhagavata we find that even the foreign and aboriginal races of the Kiratas, Hunas, Andhras, Pulindas, Pukkasas, Abhiras, Suhmas, Yavanas, Khasas, etc., become pure if they are attached to God, yet the Brahminic civilization had such a hold over the country that the cult of bhakti grew up around the traditional cult of Rama, or Krishna, Shiva or Shakti. Representation of God in images and their worship by the bhaktas, faith in the legends of Krishna and other inferior deities as told in the Puranas, preferential treatment of the Brahmin caste, respect to the Vedas, etc., became very intimately associated with the doctrine of bhakti preached in the Puranas and other Sanskrit scriptures. We know, of course, that the bhakti cult spread also among foreigners. Thus, in the second century B. C., the Greek king Heliodorus, son of Dios, dedicated to Vasudeva a flagstaff bearing an image of the bird Garuda, on which the God Vasudeva or Krishna was said to ride. Now, though the sons of some demons are also known to have been great bhaktas, as described in the Puranas, yet the latter all accepted the traditional God Vasudeva and they regarded the legends associated with Krishna or Vasudeva as real episodes of his life. In the thirteenth century A.D., we find that Visoba Khecar, the teacher of the bhakta Namdev, denounced the worship of images as a substitute for the God Krishna or for any other god. He is said to have instructed Namdev to abandon image-worship, saying: "A stone god never speaks". What possibility then of his removing the disease of mundane existence?

A stone image is regarded as God, but the true God is wholly different. If a stone god fulfills desires, how is it he breaks when struck? Those who adore a god made of stone, lose everything through their folly. Those who say and hear that a god of stone speaks to his devotees are both of them fools. Whether a holy place is small or large there is no god but stone or water. There is no place which is devoid of God. That God has shown Nama in his heart and thus Khecar conferred a blessing on him." Namdev was a tailor by caste and he worshipped the idol at Pandharpur in the Maratha country in South India. However, he had a full knowledge of the true nature of God, as had other bhaktas of Sanskritic traditions. Thus he says: "The Veda has to speak by Thy might and the Sun has to move round; such is the might of Thee, the Lord of the Universe. Knowing this essential truth I have surrendered myself to Thee.

By Thy might it is that the clouds have to pour down rain, mountains to rest firm and the wind to blow." Again: "Vows, fasts and austerities are not at all necessary; nor is it necessary for you to go on a pilgrimage. Be you watchful in your hearts and always sing the name of Hari. It is not necessary to give up eating food or drinking water; fix your mind on the foot of Hari. Neither is it necessary for you to contemplate the one without attributes. Hold fast to the love of the name of Hari." "Recognize him alone to be a righteous man, who sees Vasudeva in all objects, eradicating all pride or egoism. The rest are entangled in the shackles of delusion. To him all wealth is like earth, and the nine gems are mere stones. The two, desire and anger, he has thrown out, and he cherishes in his heart quietude and forgiveness." Again he says: "Firmly grasp the truth which is Narayana. Purity of conduct should not be abandoned; one should not be afraid of the censure of people and thus accomplish one's own purpose. Surrender yourself to your loving friend (God) giving up all ostentation and pride. The censure of people should be regarded as praise and their praise not heeded. One should entertain no longing for being respected and honored, but should nourish in oneself a liking for devotion. This should be rendered firm in the mind and the name of God should not be neglected even for a moment."

The essence of the teachings of Namdev, as of almost all the other bhaktas of whom I shall now be speaking, is purity of mind, speech, and deed, utter disregard of castes, creeds and other social distinctions, a tendency to leave all for God, and in love and joy to live in God always, utterly ignoring all social, communal and religious prejudices, narrowness, dogmas and bigotry. It is held that God is omnipotent and omnipresent and that He cannot be identified with any particular deity or his character properly narrated by any particular legendary or mythical ways of thinking. At the same time it is contended that we may call him by any name we like, for He is always the same in all.

Another great Maratha saint was Tukaram of the seventeenth century. Tukaram was a low class Hindu. His father was a petty trader. When his father, in his old age, wanted to give over his business to his eldest son Savji, the latter refused the task since he did not wish a worldly life. So the business was entrusted to Tukaram when he was at the age of thirteen. Four years later his father died. Then Tukaram was imposed upon by crafty persons and his business was wrecked. His wife, however, procured a loan; the business was restored and then he began to prosper. Once, however, while he was returning home, Tukaram met a man who was on the point of being dragged to prison for his debts. Tukaram at once gave all that he had to this debtor in order to achieve his release. From that time on Tukaram renounced all worldly vocations and devoted his life to singing the glories of God and the dearness of our relations to Him. He employed a particular kind of verse which he often composed extempore and in which he frequently spoke.

Thus Tukaram says: "God is ours, certainly ours, and is the soul of all souls. God is near to us, certainly near, outside and inside. God is benignant, certainly benignant, and fulfills every longing even of a longing nature." Again he says: "This thy nature is beyond the grasp of the mind or of words, and therefore I have made devoted love a measure. I measure the endless by the measure of love. He is not to be truly measured by any other means. Thou art not to be found by processes of concentration, sacrificial rites, practice of austerities, or any bodily exertions, or by knowledge. Oh Kesava, accept the service which we render to thee in the simplicity of our hearts." Still again: "The Endless is beyond, and between him and me there are lofty mountains of desire and anger. I am not able to ascend them, nor do I find any pass. Insurmountable is the ascent of my enemies. What possibility is there of my attaining my friend Narayana (God)?" He expresses his heart full of longing for God in the following words:

"As on the bank the poor fish lies
And gasps and writhes in pain,
Or, as a man with anxious eyes
Seeks hidden gold in vain,—
So is my heart distressed and cries
To come to thee again.
Thou knowest, Lord, the agony
Of the lost infant's wail
Yearning his mother's face to see.
(How oft I tell this tale.)

O, at thy feet the mystery
Of the dark world unveil.
The fire of this harassing thought
Upon my bosom prays.
Why is it I am thus forgot?
(O, who can know thy ways?)
Nay, Lord, thou seest my hapless lot;
Have mercy, Tuka says."

Desolate and disconsolate for the love of God he prays at His door:

"A beggar at thy door,
Pleading I stand;
Give me an alms, O God,
Love from thy loving hand.
Spare me the barren task,
To come, and to come for nought.
A gift poor Tuka craves,
Unmerited, unbought."

Again:

"O save me, save me, Mightiest,
Save me and set me free.
O let the love that fills my breast
Cling to thee lovingly.
Grant me to taste how sweet thou art;
Grant me but this, I pray,
And never shall my love depart
Or turn from thee away.
Then I thy name shall magnify
And tell thy praise abroad,
For very love and gladness I
Shall dance before my God.
Grant to me, Vitthal, that I rest
Thy blessed feet beside;
Ah, give me this, the dearest, best,
And I am satisfied."

Leaving this bhakti movement of the South, which dates from the thirteenth to the seventeenth century, from Jnanesvar and Namdev to Tukaram, we pass to the bhakti movement of North India, represented by Kabir, Nanak and others. It followed the line traced by the Gita and the Bhagavata. Having been developed in the vernacular, however, it appealed directly to the masses. It largely dissociated itself from the complex entanglements of Hindu mythology which had enmeshed the devotional creed of spiritual loyalty to God in the legend of Krishna and his associates.

Kabir (1440-1518) was an abandoned child, probably because of the illegitimacy of his birth. He was brought up by a weaver, Niru, and his wife, Nina. Throughout his life he lived in Benares, probably himself following the profession of a weaver. He is said to have been a disciple of Ramananda, a disciple of Ramanuja, the great Vaishnava teacher of the South. But he likewise came into touch with some Mohammedan Pirs and was also probably acquainted with certain forms of Sufism. His was a religion which derived its life from what was best among both the Hindus and the Mohammedans. However, he disliked the bigotry and superstitions of all formal religions and was consequently persecuted by both the Hindus and the Mohammedans. With him and his followers, such as Ruidas and Dadu, we find a religion which shook off all the traditional limitations of formal religions, with their belief in revealed books and their acceptance of mythological stories, and of dogmas and creeds that often obscure the purity of the religious light and contact with God. Kabir considered the practice of yoga, alms, and fasting, and the feeding of Brahmins, not only useless but improper without the repetition of God's name and love for Him. He discarded the Hindu ideas regarding purity, external ablutions and contact with so-called impure things with as much force as he rejected the Mohammedan belief in circumcision or the requirement that a Brahmin should wear a holy thread, or any other marks of caste. When Kabir's parents found that they could not subdue his Hindu tendencies they wanted to circumcise him, and at this he said:

> "Whence have come the Hindus and Mussulmans? Who hath put them in their different ways,
> Having thought and reflected in thy heart, answer this—who shall obtain Heaven and who Hell."

Now we know that the doctrine of bhakti had a great levelling influence. Even according to the Gita and the Bhagavata Purana, bhakti removed all inequalities of caste and social status. We know that Haridas (his Mohammedan name is not known) was converted from Mohammedanism to Vaishnavism by Chaitanya and Nityananda. In lauding him Chaitanya once said: "Your holy thoughts are as the streams of the Ganges in which your soul bathes every hour. Your pious acts earn for you that virtue which the people seek in sacrificial rites prescribed in the scriptures. You are constantly in touch with the loftiest of ideals which give you the same merit as the study of the Vedas. What sadhu or Brahmin is there who is good and great as you are?" In the Brihat Naradiya Purana we find that even a candala (the lowest caste among the Hindus) becomes the greatest of all Brahmins if he loves God. So the new religious ideal of bhakti, in all its enthusiastic circles, dispensed with the considerations of caste, creed, and social status.

There was, therefore, nothing particularly novel in Kabir's insistence that the time-honored distinctions of caste, creed and social status are absolutely valueless or in his emphasis upon the need of bhakti for all, as that which alone exalts a man. But in Kabir we find a reformatory zeal. He never tires of reiterating the worthlessness of all these superstitions of caste, creed, social status, external purity and impurity, penances, asceticism, and all sorts of formalities which passed by the name of religion though in fact having nothing to do with it. Thus Kabir says:

"If union with God be obtained by going about naked,
All the deer of the forest shall be saved.
What mattereth it whether man goeth naked or weareth a deerskin,
If he recognize not God in his heart?
If perfection be obtained by shaving the head,
Why should not sheep obtain salvation?
If, O brethren, the continent man is saved,
Why should not a eunuch obtain the supreme reward?
Saith Kabir, hear, O my brethren,
Who hath obtained salvation without God's name?"

Again he says:

"They who battle in the evening and the morning
Are like frogs in the water.
When men have no love for God's name,
They shall all go to the god of death.
They who love their persons and deck themselves out in various guises,
Feel not mercy even in their dreams.
Many leading religious men call them quadrupeds,
And say that only holy men shall obtain happiness in this ocean of trouble.
Saith Kabir, why perform so many ceremonies?
Forsaking all other essences quaff the great essence of God's name."

These allusions to bathing and other activities refer to religious practices followed by many Hindus but vigorously denounced by Kabir.

To a Yogin who said to Kabir that one could not attain deliverance without chastening his heart by the performance of yoga Kabir said:

"Without devotion the qualities of the heart cling to the heart,
Who secured perfection by merely chastening his heart?
What holy man has succeeded in chastening his heart?
Say who bath saved any one by merely chastening his heart.
Every one thinketh in his heart that he is going to chasten it,

But the heart is not chastened without devotion.
Saith Kabir, let him who knoweth this secret
Worship in his heart God, the lord of the three worlds."

Kabir in speaking of the search after God says:

"When I turned my thoughts toward God, I restrained my mind
and my senses, and my attention became lovingly fixed on Him.
O Bairagi, search for Him who neither cometh nor goeth, who neither dieth nor is.
My soul turning away from sin, is absorbed in the universal soul."

Describing the view that God is not confined to any mosque, church or temple, Kabir says:

"If God dwell only in the mosque, to whom belongeth the rest of the country?
They who are called Hindus say that God dwelleth in an idol:
I see not the truth in either sect.
O God, whether Allah or Ram, I live by Thy name,
O Lord, show kindness unto me.
Hari dwelleth in the south, Allah hath his place in the west.
Search in thy heart, search in thy heart of hearts; there is his place and abode.
The Brahmins yearly perform twenty-four fastings... the Mussulmans fast in the month of Ramzan.
... Kabir is a child of Ram and Allah and accepteth all gurus and Pirs."

Describing his great love and intoxication for God, Kabir says:

"I am not skilled in book knowledge, nor do I understand controversy:
I have grown mad reciting and hearing God's praises.
O father, I am mad; the whole world is sane; I am mad;
I am ruined; let not others be ruined likewise;
I have not grown mad out of my own will; God hath made me mad—
The true guru hath dispelled my doubts—
I am ruined, and have lost my intellect;
Let nobody be led astray in doubts like mine.
He who knoweth not himself is mad;
When one knoweth himself he knoweth the one God.
He who is not intoxicated with divine love in this human birth shall never be so.
Saith Kabir, I am dyed with the dye of God."

Thus, on the one hand, Kabir waged war against the prevailing superstitions, rituals and litanies of all religions and religious sects; and, on the other hand, he dived deep in the depth of God's love and he beheld nothing but God on all sides, becoming as it were one with Him in spiritual union. Thus, he says:

"With both mine eyes I look,
But I behold nothing save God;
Mine eyes gaze affectionately on Him."

The motto of his life was, as he often said, "Remember God, Remember God, Remember God, my brethren;" and in his own life he felt that he was absorbed in the Infinite.

Rui Das (also called Ravi Das), a shoe-maker by caste, was another great disciple of Ramananda. His songs and hymns are full of humility and devotion. However, he evidences none of the reformatory zeal that animated Kabir. I shall quote the translation of only one hymn which seems to me typical of Rui Das's attitude of love towards God. He says:

"There is none so poor as I, none so compassionate as Thou;
For this what further test is now necessary?
May my heart obey thy words, fill thy servant therewith.
I am a sacrifice to thee, O God;
Why art thou silent?
For many births have I been separated from Thee, O God;
This birth is on thine own account.
Saith Rui Das, putting my hopes in Thee, I live; it is long since I have seen thee."

Still another great saint of love was Mira Bai, a princess of Rajputana, who from her childhood (born about 1504 A. D.) was devoted to an image of Lord Krishna called Girdharlal. Her marriage proved unhappy. At the time of going to her husband's place she became very disconsolate. She wept until she became unconscious at the idea of leaving the image of Girdharlal behind. So her parents gave her the image as a part of her marriage dowry. It proved that Mira could not get on well with the family of her father-in-law, for she was always given to the adoration and worship of her little image, representing to her Lord Krishna, and it was this image that she considered as her husband. Her father-in-law made attempts to kill her, but she was miraculously saved. Ultimately she left his abode and went to Brindaban, the place of Lord Krishna's activities, to have her passion for Krishna realized. Here again, in the case of this princess saint who left her all for Krishna, we find the potency of the Krishna legend.

I shall quote here the translation of one of Mira Bai's hymns which show her great attachment for Krishna, in an image of whom, at Dvaraka, she was, as the tradition says, ultimately lost. Her soul was so full of deep longing for Lord Krishna, or Girdhar as she called him, that she proclaims:

"I have the god Girdhar and no other;
He is my spouse on whose head is a crown of peacock feathers,

Who carrieth a shell, discus, mace and lotus, and who weareth a necklace;
I have forfeited the respect of the world by ever sitting near holy men.
The matter is now public; everybody knoweth it.
Having felt supreme devotion I die as I behold the world.
I have no father, son, or relation with me.
I laugh when I behold my beloved; people think I weep.
I have planted the vine of love and irrigated it again
and again with the water of tears,
I have cast away my fear of the world, what can anyone do to me
Mira's love for her god is fixed, come what may."

India is a land of saints. There are hundreds of them of whom one could say much. But my time is limited and I have well-nigh exhausted your patience. Yet I cannot conclude without referring briefly to Tulsidas, the greatest Hindu poet of India and a great saint.

Tulsidas lived in the seventeenth century. He did not inaugurate any new faith, but accepted the Hindu mythology and the theory of the incarnation of God, the appearance of the attributeless God as a God of infinite attributes. In his view Rama was the incarnation of God, the savior and father of mankind. An all-surrendering devotion to him, he believed, is our only duty and the sole legitimate passion of life. God is great not only in His greatness, but also in his mercy. He knows the sins and the frailties of men, and is always prepared to help them repel their temptations. To run counter to the will of God is sin, and it is only by acknowledging our sins and taking an all-surrendering refuge in Him, in love and faith, that we can be saved. Connected herewith was the doctrine of the brotherhood of man and of our duty toward our neighbors. Tulsidas is said to have been very much attached to his wife in his early life. On one occasion he followed her to her father's place, much to her annoyance, and she said that if he had as much love for God Rama as he had for her he would be saved. This struck Tulsidas to the heart and he renounced the world. By his great strength of character, his remarkable poetic gifts which he applied to religious subjects, and by his strong faith, Tulsidas soon endeared himself to his countrymen. No one has exercised a greater influence than he over the Hindi-speaking people of North India.

I have now described, though but briefly, some of the main types of Indian mysticism in their mutual relations; others could not be so much as touched upon owing to the limitations of time. I am fully alive to the imperfections of my treatment. Great as they are, they must have appeared to you even greater on account of the difficulty that you must have experienced in placing yourselves on the mental plane of these mystics. The subtle metaphysical and philosophical background of these different types of mysticism I have here been compelled to disregard. But I have elsewhere undertaken an historical survey of all the different systems of Indian Philosophy. Through oral instruction, tradition, and the example of great men who renounced the world in pursuance of the high ideals of philosophy, the essence of these different systems, with their spiritual longings and their yearnings after salvation and the cessation of rebirth, have gradually been filtering down into the minds of the masses of the population. The tiller of the soil and the grocer in the shop may be uneducated and often wholly illiterate, but even they, while tilling the ground, driving a bullock cart or resting after the work of the day, will be singing songs full of mystical meaning, and for the moment transporting themselves to regions beyond the touch of material gains and comforts:

"The sky and the earth are born of mine own eyes.
The hardness and softness, the cold and the heat are the products of my own body;
The sweet smell and the bad are of my own nose."

Or,

"Nobody can tell whence the bird unknown
Comes into the cage and goes out.
I would feign put round its feet the fetter of my mind
Could I but capture it."

A traveller in the village of Bengal or on board the steamers plying the rivers of the interior of rural Bengal, may often hear a middle-aged or old Mohammedan or a Hindu singing mystical, philosophical or mythical songs of the love of Krishna and Radha, or of the renouncement of the world by Chaitanya, while a large crowd of men is assembled around the singer listening to him with great reverence and feeling. The singer is probably describing the world as a mirage or a mere phantom show of *maya,* or is expressing the futility of his worldly life on account of his having lost his friendship with his own self.

"My hope of the world is all false,
What shall be my fate, O kind, good lord?
I am not in love with him (self) with whom
I have come to live in this house (body)
O kind, good lord."

So the sublime teachings of philosophy and the other-worldly aspirations of mysticism, with their soothing, plaintive and meditative tendencies, have watered the hearts of Bengal right into the thatched cottages of this land. Wealth and comfort they all appreciate as do people everywhere, but they all know that money is not everything, and that peace of mind and the ultimate good of man cannot be secured through it or any other worldly thing. They are immersed in the world; but still the wisdom of the ages and the teachings of the saints have not been in vain, and at times they are drawn away from the world—their souls unknowingly long for deliverance and find a mystic delight in it. It is only the educated or Anglicized Hindu who, dazzled by the gay colors of the West, sometimes turns a deaf ear to the old tune of his country—the flute of Krishna calling from afar through the rustling leaves of bamboos and the cocoanut groves of the village homes—and, in the name of patriotism and progress, installs a foreign god of money and luxury in the ancestral throne of the god of the Indian heart—the god of deliverance.

The thoughts and aspirations of the ages, our myths, our religions, our philosophies, our songs and poetry, have all interpenetrated and formed a whole which cannot be expressed through a portrayal of its elements. They represent a unique experience which I feel with my countrymen, but which is incommunicable to any one who is unable imaginatively to bring himself into tune with that spirit. The British in India have understood as much of the country as is necessary for policing it, but no foreigner has ever adequately understood our land. Those of you who see India through newspapers and the strange tales and stories of tourists who "do" India in a month, can hardly hope to go right to the place where the heart of India lies.

But, you may perhaps ask, what may I gain by knowing India as it really is at its heart? Well, that is a different matter. Perhaps you may derive gain, perhaps not. You may further ask what is it that one gains through such spiritual longing, realization, or mystical rapture. And I shall frankly confess that one certainly gains nothing that will show itself in one's bank account. But with all my appreciation and admiration of the great achievements of the West in science, politics and wealth, the Upanishad spirit in me may whisper from within: What have you gained if you have not gained yourself, the immortal, the infinite? What have you gained if you have never tasted in your life the deep longing for deliverance and supreme emancipation? And the spirit of the saints of ages whispers in my ears: What have you gained if you have not tasted the joys of self-surrender, if your heart has not longed to make of you a flute in the hands of Krishna, that master musician of the universe, and if you have not been able to sweeten all your miseries with a touch of God?

14

MYSTICISM IN SUFISM

Sufism, is the mystical dimension of Islam. A practitioner of this tradition is generally known as a Sûfî, though some adherents of the tradition reserve this term only for those practitioners who have attained the goals of the Sufi tradition. Another name sometimes used for the Sufi seeker is dervish.

Classical Sufi scholars have defined Sufism as:

"a science whose objective is the reparation of the heart and turning it away from all else but God."

Or, in the words of the renowned Darqawi Sufi teacher Ahmad ibn Ajiba:

"a science through which one can know how to travel into the presence of the Divine, purify one's inner self from filth, and beautify it with a variety of praiseworthy traits."

The Sufi movement has spanned several continents over a millennium, at first expressed through Arabic, then through Persian, Turkish, and a dozen other languages. Sufi orders, most of which are Sunni in doctrine, trace their origins from the Prophet of Islam, Muhammad, through his cousin Ali or his father-in-law Abu Bakr.

According to some modern proponents, Sufi philosophy is rooted prior to the modern day religions and is universal in nature. However, mainstream Sufis vehemently reject the notion of Sufism without Islam.

ETYMOLOGY

The lexical root of Sufi is variously traced to the Arabic word for wool, referring either to the simple cloaks the early Muslim ascetics wore, or possibly to the Arabic word *safâ*, meaning purity. The two were combined by al-Rudhabari who said, "The Sufi is the one who wears wool on top of purity."

Others suggest the origin of of the word *Sufi* is from *Ashab as-Suffa* (*"Companions of the Porch"*), who were a group of impoverished Muslims during the time of the Prophet Mohammad who spent much of their time on the veranda of the Prophet's mosque, devoted to prayer and eager to memorize each new increment of the Qur'ân as it was revealed. Yet another etymology, advanced by the 10th century Persian historian Biruni is that the word is linked with the word sophia.

BASIC VIEWS

While all Muslims believe that they are on the pathway to God and will become close to God in Paradise—after death and after the "Final Judgment"—Sufis also believe that it is possible to draw closer to God and to more fully embrace the Divine Presence in this life. The chief aim of all Sufis is to seek the pleasure of God by working to restore within themselves the primordial state of *fitra*, described in the Qur'an and similar to the concept of Buddha nature. In this state nothing one does defies God, and all is undertaken by the single motivation of love of God. A secondary consequence of this is that the seeker may be led to abandon all notions of dualism or multiplicity, including a conception of an individual self, and to realize the Divine Unity.

Thus Sufism has been characterized as the science of the states of the lower self (the ego), and the way of purifying this lower self of its reprehensible traits, while adorning it instead with what is praiseworthy, *whether or not* this process of of cleansing and purifying the heart is in time rewarded by esoteric knowledge of God. This can be conceived in terms of two basic types of law (*fiqh*), an outer law concerned with actions, and an inner law concerned with the human heart. The outer law consists of rules pertaining to worship, transactions, marriage, judicial rulings, and criminal law — what is often referred to, a bit too broadly, as *shariah*. The inner law of Sufism consists of rules about repentance from sin, the purging of contemptible qualities and evil traits of character, and adornment with virtues and good character.

To enter the way of Sufism, the seeker begins by finding a teacher, as the connection to the teacher is considered necessary for the growth of the pupil. The teacher, to be genuine, must have received the authorization to teach (*ijazah*) of another Master of the Way, in an unbroken succession (*silsilah*) leading back to Sufism's origin with the Prophet Muhammad. It is the transmission of the divine light from the teacher's heart to the heart of the student, rather than of worldly knowledge transmitted from mouth to ear, that allows the adept to progress. In addition, the genuine teacher will be utterly strict in his adherence to the Divine Law.

Scholars and adherents of Sufism are unanimous in agreeing that Sufism cannot be learned through books. To reach the highest levels of success in Sufism typically requires that the disciple live with and serve the teacher for many, many years. For instance, Baha-ud-Din Naqshband Bukhari, considered founder of the Naqshbandi Order, served his first teacher, Sayyid Muhammad Baba As-Samasi, for 20 years, until as-Samasi died. He subsequently served several other teachers for lengthy periods of time. The extreme arduousness of his spiritual preparation is illustrated by his service, as directed by his teacher, to the weak and needy members of his community in a state of complete humility and tolerance for many years. When he believed this mission to be concluded, his teacher next directed him to take care for animals, curing their sicknesses, cleaning their wounds, and assisting them in finding provision. After many years of this he was next instructed to spend many years in the care of dogs in a state of humility, and to ask them for support.

As a further example, the prospective adherent of the Mevlevi Order would have been ordered to serve in the kitchens of a hospice for the poor for 1,001 days prior to being accepted for spiritual instruction, and a further 1,001 days in solitary retreat as a precondition of completing that instruction.

Some teachers, especially when addressing more general audiences, or mixed groups of Muslims and non-Muslims, make extensive use of parable, allegory, and metaphor. Although approaches to teaching vary among different Sufi orders, Sufism as a whole is primarily concerned with direct personal experience, and as such has sometimes been compared to other, non-Islamic forms of mysticism (e.g., as in the books of Seyyed Hossein Nasr).

HISTORY OF SUFISM

Origins

In its early stages of development Sufism effectively referred to nothing more than the interiorization of Islam. According to one perspective, it is directly from the Qur'an, constantly recited, meditated, and experienced, that Sufism proceeded, in its origin and its development. Others have held that Sufism is the strict emulation of the way of Muhammad, through which the heart's connection to the Divine is strengthened.

From the traditional Sufi point of view, the esoteric teachings of Sufism were transmitted from the Prophet Muhammad to those who had the capacity to acquire the direct experiential gnosis of God, which was passed on from teacher to student through the centuries. Some of this transmission is summarized in texts, but most is not. Important contributions in writing are attributed to Uwais al-Qarni, Harrm bin Hian, Hasan Basri and Sayid ibn al-Mussib are regarded as the first Sufis in the earliest generations of Islam. Harith al-Muhasibi was the first one to write about moral psychology. Rabia Basri was a female Sufi and known for her love and passion for God, expressed through her poetry. Bayazid Bastami was among the first theorists of Sufism; he concerned himself with *fanâ* and *baqâ,* the state of annihilating the self in the presence of the divine, accompanied by clarity concerning worldly phenomena derived from that perspective.

Sufism had a long history already before the subsequent institutionalization of Sufi teachings into devotional orders (*tarîqât*) in the early Middle Ages. Almost all extant Sufi orders trace their chains of transmission (*silsila*) back to Prophet Muhammad via his cousin and son-in-law Ali. The Naqshbandi order is a notable exception to this rule, as it traces the origin of its teachings from the Prophet Muhammad to the first Islamic Caliph Abu Bakr.

Different devotional styles and traditions developed over time, reflecting the perspectives of different masters and the accumulated cultural wisdom of the orders. Typically all of these concerned themselves with the understanding of subtle knowledge (gnosis), education of the heart to purify it of baser instincts, the love of God, and approaching God through a well-described hierarchy of enduring spiritual stations (*maqâmât*) and more transient spiritual states (*ahwâl*).

Formalization of Doctrine

Towards the end of the first millennium CE, a number of manuals began to be written summarizing the doctrines of Sufism and describing some typical Sufi practices. Two of the most famous of these are now available in English translation: the *Kashf al-Mahjûb* of Hujwiri, and the *Risâla* of Qushayri.

Two of Imam Al Ghazali's greatest treatises, the "Revival of Religious Sciences" and the "Alchemy of Happiness," argued that Sufism originated from the Qur'an and was thus compatible with mainstream Islamic thought, and did not in any way contradict Islamic Law — being instead necessary to its complete fulfillment. This became the mainstream position among Islamic scholars for centuries, challenged only recently on the basis of selective use of a limited body of texts. Ongoing efforts by both traditionally-trained Muslim scholars and Western academics are making Imam Al-Ghazali's works available in English translation for the first time, allowing readers to judge for themselves the compatibility between Islamic Law and Sufi doctrine.

These remarks concern written sources. It is to be remembered that Sufism is transmitted from the heart of the teacher to the heart of the student, not through texts; and also, that texts may not convey everything, or may be read by different seekers on different levels. Therefore the notion of a "formalization of doctrine" in Sufism is not strictly correct.

Growth of Sufi Influence in Islamic Cultures

The spread of Sufism has been considered a definitive factor in the spread of Islam, and in the creation of integrally Islamic cultures, especially in Africa and Asia. Recent academic work on these topics has focused on the role of Sufism in creating and propagating the culture of the Ottoman world, and in resisting European imperialism in Africa and South Asia.

Between the 13th and 16th centuries CE, Sufism produced a flourishing intellectual culture throughout the Islamic world, a sort of "Golden Age" whose physical artifacts are still present. In many places, a lodge (known variously as a *zaouia*, *khanqah*, or *tekke*) would be endowed through a pious foundation in perpetuity (*waqf*) to provide a gathering place for Sufi adepts, as well as lodging for itinerant seekers of knowledge. The same system of endowments could also be used to pay for a complex of buildings, such as that surrounding the Süleymaniye Mosque in Istanbul, including a lodge for Sufi seekers, a hospice with kitchens where these seekers could serve the poor and/or complete a period of initiation, a library, and other structures. No important domain in the civilization of Islam remained unaffected by Sufism in this period.

Contemporary Sufism

Sufism suffered many setbacks in the modern era, particularly (though not exclusively) at the hands of European imperialists in the colonized nations of Asia and Africa. The life of the Algerian Sufi master Emir Abd al-Qadir is instructive in this regard. Notable as well are the lives of Amadou Bamba and Hajj Umar Tall in sub-Saharan Africa, and Sheikh Mansur Ushurma and Imam Shamil in the Caucasus region.

Sufism being the central organizing principle of many traditional Islam cultures, It is not surprising that colonial powers attacked Sufi masters as one means of undermining the forces of indigenous self-determination.

In some countries today, the institutional expression of Sufism is simply illegal. Most famous as an example is the case of Turkey, where in 1925 Mustafa Kemal Atatürk imposed a law outlawing and disbanding the Sufi orders. This law remains in effect, and the famous "whirling dervishes" are tolerated only as a form of folk entertainment, a politically acceptable remnant of the once-prominent Mevlevi Order.

In spite of this recent history of official repression, there remain many places in the world with vital Sufi traditions. Sufism is popular in such African countries as Senegal, where it is seen as a mystical expression of Islam in Senegal. Mbacke suggests that one reason Sufism has taken hold in Senegal is because it can accommodate local beliefs and customs, which tend toward the mystical.

In South Asia, four major Sufi orders persist, namely the Chishti Order, the Qadiriyyah, the Naqshbandiyya, and the Suhrawardiyya. The Deobandis (i.e., adherents of the Darul Uloom Deoband) and Barelwi are two significant Islamic movements in this region whose followers often belong to one of these orders.

For a more complete summary of currently active groups and teachers, readers are referred to links in the site of Dr. Alan Godlas of the University of Georgia.

A number of Westerners have embarked with varying degrees of success on the path of Sufism. One of the first to return to Europe as an official representative of a Sufi path, and with the specific purpose to spread Sufism in Western Europe, was the Swedish-born wandering Sufi Abd al-Hadi Aqhili. The ideas propagated by such spiritualists may or may not conform to the tenets of Sufism as understood by orthodox Muslims, as for instance with G. I. Gurdjieff. On the other hand, American—and British-born teachers such as Nuh Ha Mim Keller, Hamza Yusuf, and Abdal Hakim Murad have been instrumental in spreading messages that conform fully with the normative tenets of Islam.

Other noteworthy Sufi teachers who have been active in the West in recent years include Riaz Ahmed Gohar Shahi, Muhammad Emin Er, Nazim al-Qubrusi, Javad Nurbakhsh, and Muzaffer Ozak.

THEORETICAL PERSPECTIVES IN SUFISM

Traditional Islamic scholars have recognized two major branches within the practice of Sufism, and use this as one key to differentiating among the approaches of different masters and devotional lineages.

On the one hand there is the path from the signs to the Signifier (or from the arts to the Artisan). In this branch, the seeker begins by purifying the lower self of every corrupting influence that stands in the way of recognizing all of creation as the work of God, as God's active Self-disclosure or theophany. This is the way of Imam Al-Ghazali and of the majority of the Sufi orders.

On the other hand there is the path from the Signifier to His signs, from the Artisan to His works. In this branch, the seeker experiences divine attraction (*jadhba*), and is able to enter the path with a glimpse of its endpoint, of direct apprehension of the Divine Presence towards which all spiritual striving is directed. This does not replace the striving to purify the heart, as in the other branch; it simply stems from a different point of entry into the path. This is the way primarily of the masters of the Naqshbandi and Shadhili orders.

Contemporary scholars may also recognize a third branch, attributed to the late Ottoman scholar Said Nursi and explicated in his vast Qur'ân commentary called the

Risale-i Nur. This approach entails strict adherence to the way of the Prophet Muhammad, in the understanding that this wont, or *sunnah,* proposes a complete devotional spirituality adequate to those without access to a master of the Sufi way.

Contributions to other Domains of Scholarship

Sufism has contributed significantly to the elaboration of theoretical perspectives in many domains of intellectual endeavor. For instance, the doctrine of "subtle centers" or centers of subtle cognition (known as *Lataif-e-sitta*) addresses the matter of the awakening of spiritual intuition in ways that some consider similar to certain models of *chakra* in Hinduism. In general, these subtle centers or *latâ'if* are thought of as faculties that are to be purified sequentially in order to bring the seeker's wayfaring to completion. A concise and useful summary of this system from a living exponent of this tradition has been published by Muhammad Emin Er. Sufi psychology has influenced many areas of thinking both within and outside of Islam, drawing primarily upon three concepts. Ja'far al-Sadiq (both an imam in the Shia tradition and a respected scholar and link in chains of Sufi transmission in all Islamic sects) held that human beings are dominated by a lower self called the *nafs*, a faculty of spiritual intuition called the *qalb* or spiritual heart, and a spirit or soul called *ruh*. These interact in various ways, producing the spiritual types of the tyrant (dominated by *nafs*), the person of faith and moderation (dominated by the spiritual heart), and the person lost in love for God (dominated by the *ruh*).

Of note with regard to the spread of Sufi psychology in the West is Robert Frager, a Sufi teacher authorized in the Halveti Jerrahi order. Frager was a trained psychologist, born in the United States, who converted to Islam in the course of his practice of Sufism and wrote extensively on Sufism and psychology. Sufi cosmology and Sufi metaphysics are also noteworthy areas of intellectual accomplishment.

SUFI PRACTICES

The devotional practices of Sufis vary widely. This is because an acknowledged and authorized master of the Sufi path is in effect a physician of the heart, able to diagnose the seeker's impediments to knowledge and pure intention in serving God, and to prescribe to the seeker a course of treatment appropriate to his or her maladies. The consensus among Sufi scholars is that the seeker cannot self-diagnose, and that it can be extremely harmful to undertake any of these practices alone and without formal authorization.

Prerequisites to practice include rigorous adherence to Islamic norms (ritual prayer in its five prescribed times each day, the fast of Ramadan, and so forth). Additionally, the seeker ought to be firmly grounded in supererogatory practices known from the life of the Prophet Muhammad (such as the so-called "sunna prayers"). This is in accordance with the words, attributed to God, of the following, a famous Hadith Qudsi:

My servant draws near to Me through nothing I love more than that which I have made obligatory for him. My servant never ceases drawing near to Me through supererogatory works until I love him. Then, when I love him, I am his hearing through which he hears, his sight through which he sees, his hand through which he grasps, and his foot through which he walks.

It is also necessary for the seeker to have a correct creed (*Aqidah*), and to embrace with certainty its tenets. The seeker must also, of necessity, turn away from sins, love of this world, the love of company and renown, obedience to satanic impulse, and the promptings of the lower self. (The way in which this purification of the heart is achieved is outlined in certain books, but must be prescribed in detail by a Sufi master.) The seeker must also be trained to prevent the corruption of those good deeds which have accrued to his or her credit by overcoming the traps of ostentation, pride, arrogance, envy, and long hopes (meaning the hope for a long life allowing us to mend our ways later, rather than immediately, here and now).

Sufi practices, while attractive to some, are not a *means* for gaining knowledge. The traditional scholars of Sufism hold it as absolutely axiomatic that knowledge of God is not a psychological state generated through breath control. Thus, practice of "techniques" is not the cause, but instead the *occasion* for such knowledge to be obtained (if at all), given proper prerequisites and proper guidance by a master of the way. Furthermore, the emphasis on practices may obscure a far more important fact: The seeker is, in a sense, to become a broken person, stripped of all habits through the practice of (in the words of Imam Al-Ghazali words) solitude, silence, sleeplessness, and hunger.

Dhikr

Dhikr is the remembrance of God commanded in the Qur'an for all Muslims. To engage in dhikr is to practice consciousness of the Divine Presence (some would say "to seek a state of godwariness") according to a variety of means. Some types of dhikr are prescribed for all Muslims, and do not require Sufi initiation or the prescription of a Sufi master because they are deemed to be good for every seeker under every circumstance. Other types of dhikr require specific instruction and permission.

Dhikr as a devotional act includes the repetition of divine names, supplications and aphorisms from hadith literature, and sections of the Qur'an. More generally, any activity in which the Muslim maintains awareness of God is considered dhikr.

Some Sufi orders stress and extensive reliance upon Dhikr and termed it the source to attain Divine Love likewise in Qadri Al-Muntahi Sufi tariqa, which was originated by Riaz Ahmed Gohar Shahi. This practice of Dhikr called Dhikr-e-Qulb(remembrance of Allah by Heartbeats). The basic idea of this practice is to visualize the Arabic name of God, Allah as having been written on the disciple's heart.

Some Sufi orders engage in ritualized dhikr ceremonies, the liturgy of which may include recitation, singing, instrumental music, dance, costumes, incense, meditation, ecstasy, and trance.

Muraqaba

The practice of *muraqaba* can be likened to the practices of meditation attested in many faith communities. The word *muraqaba* is derived from the same root (*r-q-b*) occurring as one of the 99 Names of God in the Qur'an, al-Raqîb, meaning "the Vigilant" and attested in verse 4: 1 of the Qur'an. Through *muraqaba,* a person watches over or takes care of the spiritual heart, acquires knowledge about it, and becomes attuned to the Divine Presence, which is ever vigilant.

While variation exists, one description of the practice within a Naqshbandi lineage reads as follows:

He is to collect all of his bodily senses in concentration, and to cut himself off from all preoccupation and notions that inflict themselves upon the heart. And thus he is to turn his full consciousness towards God Most High while saying three times: "*Ilahî anta maqsûdî wa-ridâka matlûbî* — my God, you are my Goal and Your good pleasure is what I seek." Then he brings to his heart the Name of the Essence — Allâh — and as it courses through his heart he remains attentive to its meaning, which is "Essence without likeness." The seeker remains aware that He is Present, Watchful, Encompassing of all, thereby exemplifying the meaning of his saying (may God bless him and grant him peace): "Worship God as though you see Him, for if you do not see Him, He sees you." And likewise the prophetic tradition: "The most favored level of faith is to know that God is witness over you, wherever you may be."

Sufi Pilgrimages

In popular Sufism (i.e., devotional practices that have achieved currency in world cultures through Sufi influence), one common practice is to visit the tombs of saints, great scholars, and righteous people. This is a particularly common practice in South Asia, where famous tombs include those of Khoja Afâq, near Kashgar, in China; Sachal Sarmast, in Sindh, Pakistan; and the Darbar-e-Gohar Shahi in Kotri Sharif. Likewise, in Fez, Morocco, a popular destination for such pious visitation is the Zaouia Moulay Idriss II.

Visitors may invoke blessings upon those interred, and seek divine favor and proximity. This practice is said to conform to the advice of some of the masters of the Sufi path: "Be with God in your heart, and if you are not able to do that, then be in your heart with the one who is with God."

ISLAM AND SUFISM

Many Sufi masters in the past as well as the present day have also been acknowledged masters of Islamic Law. The claim that Sufism is a heretical innovation within Islam has always been a fringe position, gaining traction mainly among partisans of Islamic Modernism who have not had access to rigorous training in the traditional sources of Islamic learning. Even today, most Islamic madrassa continue teaching from books authored by renowned Sufis.

Sufism and Islamic Law

Scholars and adherents of Sufism sometimes describe Sufism in terms of a threefold approach to God as explained by a tradition (*hadîth*) attributed to the Prophet Muhammad,*"The Shariah is my words, the tariqa is my actions, and the haqiqa is my interior states". Shariah, tariqa* and *haqiqa* are mutually interdependent. The *tariqa,* the 'path' on which the mystics walk, has been defined as 'the path which comes out of the *Shariah,* for the main road is called *shar,* the path, *tariq.*' No mystical experience can be realized if the binding injunctions of the Shariah are not followed faithfully first. The path, *tariqa,* however, is narrower and more difficult to walk. It leads the adept, called *sâlik* (wayfarer), in his *sulûk* (wayfaring), through different stations (*maqâmât*) until he reaches his goal, the perfect *tawhîd,* the existential confession that God is One. This perspective is also emphasized by Imam Malik, founder of the Maliki School in Islamic Law, who stated that the one who attempts to practice Sufism without learning Sacred Law corrupts his faith, while he who learns Sacred Law without practicing Sufism corrupts himself.

While virtually all classical Islamic scholars agreed with the understanding of Imam Al-Ghazali that the practice of Sufism is personally obligatory for Muslims as a way to purify the intention (*niyya*) behind one's actions, a growing number of Muslims in the present day reject this view. A concise summary of both sides of this recent controversy is available on line.

Traditional Islamic thought and Sufism

The literature of Sufism emphasizes highly subjective matters that resist outside observation, such as the subtle states of the heart. Often these resist direct reference or description, with the consequence that the authors of various Sufi treatises took recourse to allegorical language. For instance, much Sufi poetry refers to intoxication, which Islam expressly forbids. This usage of indirect language and the existence of interpretations by people who had no training in Islam or Sufism led to doubts being cast over the validity of Sufism as a part of Islam. Also, some groups emerged that considered themselves above the Sharia and discussed Sufism as a method of bypassing the rules of Islam in order to attain salvation directly. This was disapproved of by traditional scholars.

For these and other reasons, the relationship between traditional Islamic scholars and Sufism is complex and a range of scholarly opinion on Sufism in Islam has been the norm. Some scholars, such as Al-Ghazali, helped its propagation while other scholars, such as Ibn Taymiyyah, opposed it. W. Chittick explains the position of Sufism and Sufis this way:

> In short, Muslim scholars who focused their energies on understanding the normative guidelines for the body came to be known as jurists, and those who held that the most important task was to train the mind in achieving correct understanding came to be divided into three main schools of thought: theology, philosophy, and Sufism. This leaves us with the third domain of human existence, the spirit. Most Muslims who devoted their major efforts to developing the spiritual dimensions of the human person came to be known as Sufis.

Traditional and Non-traditional Sufi Groups

The traditional Sufi orders, which are in majority, emphasize the role of Sufism as a spiritual discipline within Islam. Therefore, the Sharia (traditional Islamic law) and the Sunnah (customs of the Prophet) are seen as crucial for any Sufi aspirant. One proof traditional orders assert is that almost all the famous Sufi masters of the past Caliphates were experts in Sharia and were renowned as people with great Iman (faith) and excellent practice. Many were also Qadis (Sharia law judges) in courts. They held that Sufism was never distinct from Islam and to fully comprehend and practice Sufism one must be an observant Muslim.

In recent decades there has been a growth of non-traditional Sufi movements in the West. Examples include the Universal Sufism movement, the Golden Sufi Center, the Sufi Foundation of America, the neo-sufism of Idries Shah, and Sufism Reoriented. Rumi has become one of the most widely read poets in the United States, thanks largely to the translations published by Coleman Barks.

Islamic Positions on Non-Islamic Sufi Groups

The use of the title *Sufi* by non-traditional groups to refer to themselves, and their appropriation of traditional Sufi masters (most notably Jalaluddin Rumi) as sources of authority or inspiration, is not accepted by Muslims who are Sufi adherents.

Some traditional Sufis also object to interpretations of classical Sufis texts by writers who have no grounding in the traditional Islamic sciences and therefore no prerequisites for understanding such texts. These are considered by certain conventional Islamic scholars as beyond the pale of the religion. This being said, there are Islamic Sufi groups that are open to non-Muslim participation, and even membership.

Criticism within Islam

Critics of Sufism from within Islam tend to be adherents of Islamic Modernism, above all those committed to Salafism or Wahhabism. Traditional Sunni Muslims may also condemn certain Sufi practices, though never condemning Sufism as a whole.

The Modernist criticisms of Sufism emphasize the claim that Sufi masters have introduced special prayers and devotional acts into their schools that are not part of early Islam, or even that Sufi Muslims have contrived entirely new beliefs. Such criticisms may also be accompanied by the unsubstantiated claim that Sufism has never played a part in normative Islam.

The allegorical and often abstruse language used by Sufis in their texts, when interpreted by persons without proper qualification and guidance, may at times create potential for misunderstanding of the orthodoxy of traditional Sufism. For instance, some critics consider the concept of "unity of being" (Wahdat-ul-wujood) to be a form of pantheism and therefore incompatible with Islam. Sufi masters in many of their introductory texts caution aspirants from reading and interpreting texts by themselves, and explicitly correct mistaken impressions of pantheistic tendency. They hold that the subject can only be taught by a master to a student under strict guidance and supervision owing to its delicate nature. This discussion only scratches the surface of a delicate and subtle issue that remains a matter of contention among Muslim polemicists.

Riaz Ahmed Gohar Shahi was heavily criticized by orthodox theological scholars in Pakistan and abroad. Shahi's books were banned by the Government of Pakistan, public meetings are not allowed to his followers and no press coverage is allowed to either Gohar Shahi or to his followers due to charges of blasphemy law violations. Many attempts were made on Shahi's life including a petrol bomb attack, thrown into his Manchester residence, and an attack with a hand grenade during the discourse at his home in Kotri, Pakistan. Gohar Shahi was booked in 1997 on alleged charges of murdering a woman who had come to him for spiritual treatment. Gohar Shahi, and many of his followers, were later convicted under Islamic blasphemy laws by an antiterrorist court in Sindh. Gohar Shahi was convicted in absentia—as then he was in England—resulting in sentences that totaled approximately 59 years. Gohar Shahi died abroad, prior to any decision on appeals filed with the High Court of Sindh.

Perception Outside Islam

Sufi mysticism has long exercised a fascination upon the Western world, and especially its orientalist scholars. Figures like Rumi have become household words in the United States, where sufism is perceived as quietist and non-political.

The Islamic Institute in Mannheim, Germany, which works towards the integration of European muslims, sees sufism as particularly suited for interreligious dialogue and intercultural haromonisation in democratic and pluralist societies; it has described sufism as a symbol of tolerance and humanism in Islam – undogmatic, flexible and non-violent. The Indian government has likewise praised sufism as the tolerant form of Islam, in contrast to its more militant manifestations.

MAN IS A MIRROR WHICH, WHEN POLISHED, REFLECTS GOD

The God that the Sufis discover is a God of love and the way to him is through Love: " whoever knows God, loves him; whoever knows the world turns away from him. " "If you wish to be free, become a prisoner of Love."

This is not unfamiliar music to the ears of the Christian mystics. In this respect, it is curious to note the similarities between Sufism and other philosophic or religious trends. Originally, Sufism was influenced by Pythagorean thought and by the Zoroastrian religion of Persia. The Sufi initiation rite, which opens up the possibility of a spiritual rebirth, is not entirely unlike Christian baptism and one could even identify some Buddhist echos in the Sufic formula "man is non-existent before God".

There is the same diversity and the same imagination in the spiritual techniques of Sufism. The search for God through symbolism, in the case of some Sufis, passes through music or dance which, they believe, transcends thought. This was practised by Djalal ed din Roumi, according to Mevlana, the founder of the whirling dervishes. In the case of other Sufis, symbolism is an intellectual exercise in which one meditates on the numerical value of letters as the Cabbalistic Jews do. Sometimes also, it is through an endless repetition of the invocation of the names of God that the Sufi seeks union with Him.

And so Sufism brings to Islam a poetic and mystical dimension that one could never find in the exegetes' pernickety analysis of the texts of the Koran. For this reason the latter, irritated by this over-zealous fervour, seek to marginalise Sufism. This is also why the Sufis set such store by their practices and trace them back to the prophet himself. They hold that Mohammed received, at the same time as the Koran, esoteric revelations which he revealed only to some of his companions. In this way, the Sufi masters all link their teaching to a long line of predecessors who give them authenticity.

However, this legitimacy through reference to the prophet does not give rise to uniformity in the Sufi movement. There are many different schools and each one has its own style and practices. In French, these schools are generally designated under the name of confraternities. Before going on to study some of these schools, it is necessary first to keep in mind that the confraternities have become, not an institution, but at least one way of living Islam in a manner so widely accepted that all kinds of movements, mystical or not, assume the title of confraternity in order to practise their activities. One should not therefore be surprised at times to come across rather unmystical confraternities with a rudimentary spirituality that is far removed from the elevated speculations that have made Sufism one of the major components of universal spirituality.

SUFISM, MYSTICISM AND ESOTERISM

Sufism covers a multitude of very different realities in Islam. We would like to highlight just a few distinctions between " the mystical " and " the esoterical". "Mysticism" in the literal sense means living as closely united to God as possible. An example of this can be found in Mary of the Incarnation, a French religious in the 17th century who had been married, had children and was widowed. She had managed a transport business before entering the Ursuline convent. She was then sent to Canada where she built a school for French and Indian girls. She was constantly in union with God, whether at the attorney's office to sign deeds or with the builders to oversee the construction. Even when, one Winter the building caught fire and it was not possible to extinguish the fire because of the temperature of 20° below freezing which meant the water was frozen, Mary of the Incarnation fell to her knees in the snow and praised God. This is what the mystical life means; living in constant union with God in the events of daily life, whether one is a religious or a lay person. In a sense, one is already living hidden with God, one has already entered into the endless mystery of eternal life, life with God. King Baudoin of Belgium tried to live his public and private life in this way without giving any sign of failing in the duties of his public responsibilities nor in his conjugal love as a husband.

Understood in this way, mystical life is open to all, it is a matter of letting God, in love, live in us. As St. Paul says, it is no longer I but Christ who lives in me. The mystic is not someone whose very person disappears. He or she retains the same character, history, even the same brilliance, and everything that makes the person unique and loveable.

Do all religions have a mystical dimension? Evidence shows that it is only those who have encountered God as a person and giver of life. In this sense, it is not impossible for Muslims to live a mystical life, whether Sufic or not. Sufism certainly emphasises this union with God. But is this always so in conditions worthy of God and of man? It is here that the necessity arises of seeing the radical difference between "mysticism" and "esoterism". For Esoterism effectually turns its back on Mysticism. While mysticism is an opening up to God, to his revelation and his love, esoterism claims to provide the power to acquire God, indeed to become God through one's own efforts by reaching degrees of "knowledge" reserved for the "initiated" who keep these powers to themselves.

It is surely not difficult to understand that if God really exists He is more "person" than Mankind. He therefore also has a certain freedom. And if He is free to give himself, how could one grasp him through "knowledge "and" inititiation rites ". God can only be reached if it is he who takes the initiative and gives himself and if he is then well received.

Esoterism is a willed spiritual power achieved through "secrets" or techniques. Far from liberating man, these secrets and techniques create an artificial spiritualism within which the "man with knowledge" locks himself up. The illusion of " knowing " prevents one from hearing God who reveals himself by speaking to those who are sufficiently humble to want to know him as he himself tells us he is. And so some people enclose themselves in a theory of numerology, others in the various boxes of determinist characterology; yet others in horoscope columns, others in meditation techniques.

The true God makes man free and he offers his friendship to all, not only to a few initiates. "Since he clings to me, I rescue him, I raise him high since he acknowledges my name." He calls to me and I answer him: "This God entered into human history by the door of humble folk, by becoming a little child, in Bethlehem two thousand years ago."

15

MYSTICISM IN CHRISTIANITY

Christianity is reverent and alive if one listens to the call from inside. The dull habit of preaching, giving sermons, patronizing, condemning or judging others as insufficient is the ego talking about Christ, not the religion of Christ. Descriptions about Jesus are not the spiritual ideas Jesus described. The experience of joy and the supernatural enlightenment of Christ is not about sins, hell or Satan, but the glorious energy of the soul. A healer doesn't rifle through the lives of others, but brings one from the outer personality to the inner-self arousing one from immaturity and prejudice to wholeness.

This solo mystical journey evolves from location to position, from view to vision onward towards total understanding. It is passed from mind to mind, a flame passed from candle to candle. There is nothing to buy, join or donate. A Christian vision beyond personality opens the eye to a new awareness, cultivating good qualities, internal clarity and introspection. It encourages one to believe the truth that is experienced and not necessarily to join. When one is tired of reading the menu, it is time for the inner spiritual meal to be experienced, a deeper reality beyond the normal worldly existence of guilt, pain and pleasure. Looking from the inside out the veil of ideological and religious conflict is parted giving clues to unity and wholeness.

Christian mysticism looks at the world from a different angle giving meaning to life, not rejecting anything or waving a fist with scorn and resentment. One does not have to point a finger when the experience is direct because the power of Christ consciousness is accessible to provide the means to love in every form, enjoying, not judging what is encountered. These deeper understandings value love and see more to the physical world than what is in it. These windows look out on the path we are traveling to our destination, a spiritual experience that sooths the personality.

A consciousness focused on the core and not the superficial facade or surface personality aligns the personality with the soul. Watching the mind's intentions for what they are helps one to recognize a cold heart beneath polished and pleasing words and good intentions behind an unwise approach. Consciousness has the ability to seize the whole and not error in efforts to witness and read human nature so it refuses to go along with any cruelty. The surface of a thing is not the whole of it so Christian mysticism is the discovery that there are depths beyond depths of truth.

To many modern Christians, words like "meditation," "mystic," and "mysticism" bring to mind Eastern religions, not Christianity. Certainly Eastern religions are known for their mysticism, however, mysticism is not only a vital part of the Christian heritage as well, but it is actually the *core* of Christian spirituality. Mysticism simply means the spirituality of the direct experience of God. It is the adventure of "the wild things of God."

The direct experience of God is a kind of knowing, which goes beyond intellectual understanding. It is not a matter of "belief." It is marked by love and joy, but it is not "emotional experience." In many ways, it is better described by what it is not. To describe what it is, we must use metaphors—the marriage of the soul to Christ, the death of the "old man" and birth of the "new man," being the "body of Christ."

Jesus proclaimed "I and the Father are one," (Jn. 10.30) showing the world what the union of God and man can be. Christian mysticism is about nothing else but this transforming union.

Christ is the sole end of Christian mysticism. Whereas all Christians have Christ, call on Christ, and can (or should) know Christ, the goal for the Christian mystic is to become Christ—to become as fully permeated with God as Christ is, thus becoming like him, fully human, and by the grace of God, also fully divine. In Christian teaching this doctrine is known by various names—theosis, divinization, deification, and transforming union.

A common misconception about mysticism is that it's about "mystical experiences," and there are many volumes on such experiences in religious literature. But true mysticism is not focussed on "experiences" (which come and go) but with the lasting experience of God, leading to the transformation of the believer into union with God.

To know God directly shows that mysticism is different from any passive or legalistic kind of Christianity. It means:

- That while we honor the Scriptures, we want to know God directly, not just through Scripture.
- While we respect our heritage of teachings about God, we want to know God directly, not through doctrines and teachings.

- While we gather in communal worship, we want to know God directly, not just through the Church.

Some readers may find this unsettling. Maybe you believe it doesn't apply to you, because you "know" that your church is purer and more correct than others. Even if that were true, is it a substitute for knowing God directly? Or, you might also feel that trusting the Bible alone gives you knowledge of God directly from the Source. But it was written by mystics, listening to God speaking his Word in their hearts. Is it possible for you to read it directly, without the conceptions of your language, time, culture, and personal history? Are you sure you wouldn't understand it very differently if you were reading it, say, in third-century Damascus?

The religion we call "Christianity" changes, but God is eternal. Mystical faith wants to know this unchanging God to whom Christianity leads us, the One behind the beliefs and the words, the One whom beliefs and words cannot describe. We want to follow Jesus' example more closely, and go beyond the religion about Jesus, and take the religion of Jesus: the knowledge of the Father and unconditional love he had, and urged us to have.

Christian mysticism is traditionally practised through the disciplines of:

- prayer (including oratio, meditation and contemplation);
- self-denial, including fasting, broadly called asceticism; and
- service to others, broadly called almsgiving.

In the tradition of Mystical Theology, Biblical texts are typically interpreted metaphorically, for example in Jesus' "Sermon on the Mount" (Matthew 5–7) the text, in its totality, is held to contain the way for direct union with God. Also, in the contemplative and eremitic tradition of the Carmelite "Book of the First Monks", 1 Kgs. 17:3-4 is the central Biblical text around which the work is written.

Whereas Christian doctrine generally maintains that God dwells in all Christians and that they can experience God directly through belief in Jesus, Christian mysticism aspires to apprehend spiritual truths inaccessible through intellectual means, typically by emulation of Christ. William Inge divides this *scala perfectionist* into three stages: the "purgative" or ascetic stage, the "illuminative" or contemplative stage, and the "unitive" stage, in which God may be beheld "face to face."

BIBLICAL FOUNDATIONS

The tradition of Christian Mysticism is as old as Christianity itself. At least three texts from the New Testament set up themes that recur throughout the recorded thought of the Christian mystics. The first, Galatians 2:20, says that:

I am crucified with Christ: nevertheless I live, yet not I, but Christ liveth in me, and the life which I now live in the flesh I live by the faith of the Son of God, who loved me, and gave himself for me. (KJV)

The second important scriptural text for Christian mysticism is 1 John 3:2:

Beloved, now we are the sons of God, and it doth not yet appear what we shall be: but we know that, when he shall appear, we shall be like him; for we shall see him as he is.

The third such text, especially important for Eastern Christian mysticism, is found in II Peter 1:4:

...[E]xceedingly great and precious promises [are given unto us]; that by these ye might be *partakers of the divine nature,* having escaped the corruption that is in the world through lust.

Two major themes of Christian mysticism are (1) a complete identification with, or *imitation of Christ,* to achieve a unity of the human spirit with the spirit of God; and (2) the perfect vision of God, in which the mystic seeks to experience God "as he is," and no more "through a glass, darkly." (1 Corinthians 13:12)

Other mystical experiences are described in other passages. In 2 Corinthians 12:2–4, Paul sets forth an example of a possible out-of-body experience by someone who was taken up to the "third heaven", and taught unutterable mysteries:

I knew a man in Christ above fourteen years ago, (whether in the body, I cannot tell or whether out of the body, I cannot tell: God knoweth) such a one caught up to the third heaven. And I knew such a man, (whether in the body, or out of the body, I cannot tell: God knoweth;) how that he was caught up into paradise, and heard unspeakable words, which it is not lawful for a man to utter.

Perhaps a similar experience occurred at the Transfiguration of Jesus, an incident confirmed in each of the Synoptic Gospels. Here Jesus led three of his apostles, Peter, John, and James, to pray at the top of a mountain, where he became transfigured. Jesus's face shone like the sun, and he was clad in brilliant white clothes. Elijah and Moses appeared with Jesus, and talked with him, and then a bright cloud appeared overhead, and a voice from the cloud proclaimed, "This is my beloved Son: hear him."

PRACTICE

While such phenomena are associated with mysticism in general, including the Christian variety, for Christians the major emphasis concerns a spiritual transformation of the egoic self, the following of a path designed to produce more fully realized human persons, "created in the Image and Likeness of God" and as such, living in harmonious communion with God, the Church, the rest of humanity, and all creation, including oneself. For Christians, this human potential is realized most perfectly in Jesus and is manifested in others through their association with Him, whether conscious, as in the case of Christian mystics, or unconscious, with regard to persons who follow other traditions, such as Gandhi. The Eastern Christian tradition speaks of this transformation in terms of theosis or divinization, perhaps best summed up by an ancient aphorism usually attributed to Athanasius of Alexandria: "God became human so that man might become God."

Going back at least to Evagrius Ponticus and Pseudo-Dionysius, Christian mystics have pursued a threefold path in their pursuit of holiness. While the three aspects have different names in the different Christian traditions, they can be characterized as *purgative, illuminative, and unitive,* corresponding to body, soul (or mind), and spirit. The first, the way of purification, is where aspiring Christian mystics start. This aspect focuses on discipline, particularly in terms of the human body; thus, it emphasizes prayer at certain times, either alone or with others, and in certain postures, often standing or kneeling. It also emphasizes the other disciplines of fasting and alms-giving, the latter including those activities called "the works of mercy," both spiritual and corporal, such as feeding the hungry and sheltering the homeless.

Purification, which grounds Christian spirituality in general, is primarily focused on efforts to, in the words of St. Paul, "put to death the deeds of the flesh by the Holy Spirit" (Romans 8:13). The "deeds of the flesh" here include not only external behavior, but also those habits, attitudes, compulsions, addictions, etc. (sometimes called *egoic passions*) which oppose themselves to true being and living as a Christian not only exteriorly, but interiorly as well. Evelyn Underhill describes purification as an awareness of one's own imperfections and finiteness, followed by self-discipline and mortification. Because of its physical, disciplinary aspect, this phase, as well as the entire Christian spiritual path, is often referred to as "ascetic," a term which is derived from a Greek word which connotes athletic training. Because of this, in ancient Christian literature, prominent mystics are often called "spiritual athletes," an image which is also used several times in the New Testament to describe the Christian life. What is sought here is salvation in the original sense of the word, referring not only to one's eternal fate, but also to healing in all areas of life, including the restoration of spiritual, psychological, and physical health.

It remains a paradox of the mystics that the passivity at which they appear to aim is really a state of the most intense activity: more, that where it is wholly absent no great creative action can take place. In it, the superficial self compels itself to be still, in order that it may liberate another more deep-seated power which is, in the ecstasy of the contemplative genius, raised to the highest pitch of efficiency. *Mysticism: A Study in Nature and Development of Spiritual Consciousness* by Evelyn Underhill (Public Domain)

The second phase, the path of illumination, has to do with the activity of the Holy Spirit enlightening the mind, giving insights into truths not only explicit in scripture and the rest of the Christian tradition, but also those implicit in nature, not in the scientific sense, but rather in terms of an illumination of the "depth" aspects of reality and natural happenings, such that the working of God is perceived in all that one experiences. Underhill describes it as marked by a consciousness of a transcendent order and a vision of a new heaven and a new earth.

The third phase, usually called contemplation in the Western tradition, refers to the experience of oneself as in some way united with God. The experience of union varies, but it is first and foremost always associated with a reuniting with Divine *love*, the underlying theme being that God, the perfect goodness, is known or experienced at least as much by the heart as by the intellect since, in the words 1 John 4:16: "God is love, and he who abides in love abides in God and God in him." Some approaches to classical mysticism would consider the first two phases as preparatory to the third, explicitly mystical experience, but others state that these three phases overlap and intertwine.

Author and mystic Evelyn Underhill recognizes two additional phases to the mystical path. First comes the awakening, the stage in which one begins to have some consciousness of absolute or divine reality. Purgation and illumination are followed by a fourth stage which Underhill, borrowing the language of St. John of the Cross, calls the dark night of the soul. This stage, experienced by the few, is one of final and complete purification and is marked by confusion, helplessness, stagnation of the will, and a sense of the withdrawal of God's presence. It is the period of final "unselfing" and the surrender to the hidden purposes of the divine will. Her fifth and final stage is union with the object of love, the one Reality, God. Here the self has been permanently established on a transcendental level and liberated for a new purpose.

Another aspect of traditional Christian spirituality, or mysticism, has to do with its communal basis. Even for hermits, the Christian life is always lived in communion with the Church, the community of believers. Thus, participation in corporate worship, especially the Eucharist, is an essential part of Christian mysticism. Connected with this is the practice of having a spiritual director, confessor, or "soul friend" with which to discuss one's spiritual progress. This person, who may be clerical or lay, acts as a spiritual mentor.

What is a Mystic?

I believe that everyone who wants to love *unconditionally* is a mystic. All children are born mystics, and if you were once a child, you were once a mystic. Christian mysticism is following the example of Christ as he followed the Father. And mysticism is not by any means restricted to Christianity: the Bible says, "everyone who loves is begotten of God, and knows God." (*1 Jn.* 4.7) God speaks in various ways, in every time and every place to "whosoever will." Other pages on this site treat non-Christian mysticism.

Mystics range the gamut of walks of life, from intellectual priests such as Frs. Pierre Teilhard de Chardin and Matthew Fox, to laywomen like Bernadette Roberts and Katherine Nelson. The mystic way is old, but timeless—it is alive, and ever-new for each one who chooses it. It may be inviting you to begin this adventure of divine transformation and discovery.

The term mysticism derives from *The Mystical Theology*, a tiny treatise written by the greatest Christian writer of the sixth century, Dionysius the Areopagite, a.k.a. Pseudo-Dionysius or St. Denys [the Areopagite]. But Dionysius is in no way the "founder" of Christian mysticism. That honor belongs to none but Jesus the Christ himself. But there was mysticism long before Jesus was born. God "strolled in the Garden" with man (Heb. *'adam*). Jacob saw heaven opened. God spoke to Joseph through dreams. Moses communed with God on Sinai. David lost himself in dancing for the Lord.

But when Jesus declared "I and the Father are one," (*Jn.* 10.30) he proclaimed in himself the union of God and humankind, and he offers it to all who follow him (he gave the power to become sons of God to all who believe. (*Jn.* 1.12).

From there, the mystic heart is seen in the letters of the apostles: Paul reached the divinized state of losing his "self": *I no longer live, but Christ lives in me!* (*Gal.* 2.20) James wrote that every good and perfect gift comes from the Father of Lights, in whom there is no variation nor shadow of turning. (*Jas.* 1.17) Peter proclaimed that Christ even descended to hell to liberate imprisoned souls, (*1 Pet.* 3.19) and John understood the most sublime truth of God's essence: God is Love! (*1 Jn.* 4.8,16). This is only the beginning. Every century has been influenced by Christian mystics—from apostles and martyrs, Church Fathers and Desert Mothers, to monks and nuns of religious orders, to the lay mystics—men and women and boys and girls in every century, in every denomination, in every walk of life.

A Christian Mystic is on a spiritual journey towards unity and a new way of living. This is a compassionate path that recognizes and respects our diversity and interconnectedness. A consciousness of unity gives a new concept of life which helps form a new humanity on the individual and community level for Christians and non-Christians. Unity transcends biological evolution and starts spiritual evolution. Spiritual evolution is not evolution with biological genes, but with ideas because they can transform fear to joy and frustration to fullfillment.

Unity is love so emphasis on religious differences, race or intolerance rather than the unity of God is a strange god indeed and can be a challenge for us to overcome so we need to invoke the unity of God in all things. This unity is an innocence that sees a fresh world in a new way giving life, awareness, and ideas that love so kindness can replace judgement.

Without a doubt the mind of God is everywhere in pure consciousness and in the individual consciousness of all living things. The spirit of God is the principal partner in the human compound of body, mind and spirit, but it is usually ignored because it does not come across as the voice of authority especially to those who like things cut and dried. Organized religion is the voice of authority and it can meddle, tinker and mean well, but to break up old patterns of thought and behavior, we need to open ourselves to new possibilities. With the highest exercise of our intellect we know the purpose of our existence and can proceed to live intelligently according to it, if we direct our physical and mental activities to the pure consciousness of God. We know we are on the right path because God's pure consciousness makes cheerful every action and person contacted. Once we are in touch with the spirit within we can offer more to others, religion or the church.

CHRISTIAN MYSTICS

Some examples of Christian mystics:

- St. Paul
- St. John the Baptist
- St. John the Apostle
- St. Peter
- Valentinus (c.100–c.153)
- St. Clement of Alexandria
- St. Athanasius (c293–373)
- Evagrius Ponticus (345–399)
- St. Augustine of Hippo (354–430)
- Pseudo-Dionysius the Areopagite (5th century)
- St. John Climacus (525–606)
- St. Gregory I (590–604)
- St. Isaac the Syrian (c.700)
- St. Anastasius Sinaita
- St. Symeon the New Theologian (949–1022)
- Saint Anselm (1033–1109)
- Hugh of Saint Victor (1096–1141)

- Richard of St. Victor
- Hildegard of Bingen (1098–1179)
- St. Francis of Assisi (1181–1226)
- St. Clare of Assisi (1194–1253)
- St. Anthony of Padua (1195–1231)
- Beatrice of Nazareth (1200-1268)
- Mechthild of Magdeburg (1210–1279)
- St. Bonaventure of Bagnoregio (1221–1274)
- Angela of Foligno (1248–1309)
- Gertrude the Great (1256–1301)
- Marguerlte Porete
- Meister Eckhart (c. 1260–1327/8)
- John of Ruysbroeck (1293–1381)
- St. Gregory Palamas (1296–1359)
- Johannes Tauler (1300–1361)
- Henry Suso (1300–1366)
- St. Bridget of Sweden (1302–1373)
- St. Julian of Norwich (1342–c.1416)
- St. Catherine of Sienna (1347–1380)
- William Langland
- Margery Kempe (c.1373–1438)
- Thomas à Kempis (1380–1471)
- St. Ignatius of Loyola (1491–1556)
- St. Teresa of Avila (1515–1582)
- St. John of the Cross (1542–1591)
- St. Francis de Sales (1567–1622)
- Jakob Böhme (1575–1624)
- Maria de Agreda (1602–1665)
- Sir Thomas Browne (1605–1682)
- Brother Lawrence (1614–1691)
- Angelus Silesius (1624–1677)
- George Fox (1624–1691)

- Jane Leade (1624–1704)
- Miguel de Molinos (c. 1628–1697)
- Sarah Wight
- Madame Guyon (1648–1717)
- Johannes Kelpius (1667–1708)
- Emanuel Swedenborg (1688–1772)
- John Woolman (1720–1772)
- William Blake (1757–1827)
- George Rapp (1757-1847)
- St. Seraphim of Sarov (1759–1833)
- Anna Catherine Emmerich (1774–1824)
- Jakob Lorber (1800–1864)
- Phineas Parkhurst Quimby (1802-1866)
- St. John of Kronstadt (1829–1908)
- St. Bernadette Soubirous (1844–1879)
- Max Heindel (1865–1919)
- Sergei Bulgakov (1871–1944)
- St. Therese of Lisieux (1873–1897)
- Evelyn Underhill (1875–1941)
- Pope Pius XII (1876–1958)
- Antonin Gadal (1877–1962)
- Pierre Teilhard de Chardin (1881–1955)
- St. Pio of Pietrelcina (1887–1968)
- T. S. Eliot (1888–1965)
- Sadhu Sundar Singh (1889–1929)
- St. Theresa-Benedicta of the Cross (Edith Stein) (1891–1942)
- St. John Maximovitch (1896–1966)
- Jan van Rijckenborgh (1896–1968)
- Maria Valtorta (1897–1961)
- Aiden Wilson Tozer (1897–1963)
- Adrienne von Speyr (1902–1967)
- Catharose de Petri (1902–1990)

- St. Faustina Kowalska (1905–1938)
- Dag Hammarskjöld (1905–1961)
- Eugenia Ravasio (1907-1990)
- Simone Weil (1909–1943)
- Thomas Merton (1915–1968)
- Vernon Howard (1918–1992)
- Thomas Keating (1923)
- Henri Nouwen (1932-1996)
- Vassula Ryden (1942)
- Guy Finley (1949)
- Erwin McManus (1958)
- Richard Foster

16

JAIN MYSTICISM

Jain philosophy deals extensively with the problems of metaphysics, reality, cosmology, ontology, epistemology and divinity. Jainism is essentially a transtheistic religion of ancient India. It is a continuation of the ancient Shramana tradition which co-existed with the Vedic tradition since ancient times. The distinguishing features of Jain philosophy are its belief on independent existence of soul and matter, denial of creative and omnipotent God, potency of karma, eternal and uncreated universe, a strong emphasis on non-violence, accent on relativity and multiple facets of truth, and morality and ethics based on liberation of soul. Jain philosophy attempts to explain the rationale of being and existence, the nature of the Universe and its constituents, the nature of bondage and the means to achieve liberation. It has often been described as an ascetic movement for its strong emphasis on self-control, austerities and renunciation. It has also been called a model of philosophical liberalism for its insistence that truth is relative and multifaceted and for its willingness to accommodate all possible view-points of the rival philosophies. In this regard it is also compared to Western concepts of subjectivism and moral relativism. Jainism strongly upholds the individualistic nature of soul and personal responsibility for one's decisions; and that self-reliance and individual efforts alone are responsible for one's liberation. In this matter, it is similar to individualism and objectivism.

Throughout its history, the Jain philosophy remained unified and single, although as a religion, Jainism was divided into various sects and traditions. The contribution of Jain philosophy in developing the Indian philosophy has been significant. Jain philosophical concepts like Ahimsa, Karma, Moksa, Samsara and like have been assimilated into the philosophies of other Indian religions like Hinduism and Buddhism in various forms. While Jainism traces its philosophy from teachings of Mahavira and other Tirthankaras, various Jain philosophers from Kundakunda and Umasvati in ancient times to Yasovijaya in recent times have contributed greatly in developing and refining the Jain and Indian philosophical concepts.

JAIN COSMOLOGY

Jain cosmology denies the existence of a supreme being responsible for creation and operation of universe. According to Jainism, the universe and its constituents are eternal and uncreated.

Jain Conception of the Universe

According to Jainism, this *loka* or Universe is an uncreated entity, existing since infinity, immutable in nature, beginningless and endless. Jain texts describe the shape of the Universe as similar to a man standing with legs apart and arm resting on his waist. The Universe according to Jainism is narrow at top and broad at middle and once again becomes broad at the bottom. Mahâpurâna of Âcârya Jinasena is famous for this quote:

> "Some foolish men declare that the creator made the world. The doctrine that the world was created is ill advised and should be rejected.
> If god created the world, where was he before the creation? If you say he was transcendent then and needed no support, where is he now?
> How could god have made this world without any raw material? If you say that he made this first, and then the world, you are faced with an endless regression."

The Constituents of Reality

This Universe is made up of what Jains call the six *dravyas* or substances which are the basic constituents of reality and are classified as follows:

- ***Jîva—The Living Substances***

Jains believe that souls (*Jîva*) exist as a reality, having a separate existence from the body that houses it. *Jîva* is characterised by *cetana* (consciousness) and *upayoga* (knowledge and perception). Though the soul experiences both birth and death, it is neither really destroyed nor created. Decay and origin refer respectively to the disappearing of one state of soul and appearance of another state, these being merely the modes of the soul.

- ***Ajîva—Non-Living Substances***

  o ***Pudgala*-Matter**—Matter is classified as solid, liquid, gaseous, energy, fine Karmic materials and extra-fine matter or ultimate particles. Paramânu or ultimate particles are considered the basic building block of all matter. One of the qualities of the *Paramânu* and *Pudgala* is that of permanence and indestructibility. It combines and changes its modes but its basic qualities remain the same. According to Jainism, it cannot be created nor destroyed.

- **Dharma-tattva-Medium of Motion and Adharma-tattva–Medium of Rest**— Also known as *Dharmâstikâya* and *Adharmâstikâya,* they are unique to Jain thought depicting the principles of motion and rest. They are said to pervade the entire universe. *Dharma-tattva* and *Adharma-tattva* are by themselves not motion or rest but mediate motion and rest in other bodies. Without *dharmâstikâya* motion is not possible and without *adharmâstikâya* rest is not possible in the universe.
- ***Âkâsa*** **- Space**—Space is a substance that accommodates souls, matter, the principle of motion, the principle of rest, and time. It is all-pervading, infinite and made of infinite space-points.
- ***Kâla*** **- Time**—Time is a real entity according to Jainism and all activities, changes or modifications can be achieved only through time. In Jainism, the time is likened to a wheel with twelve spokes divided into descending and ascending halves with six stages, each of immense duration estimated at billions of sagaropama or ocean years. According to Jains, sorrow increases at each progressive descending stage and happiness and bliss increase in each progressive ascending stage.

These are the uncreated existing constituents of the Universe which impart the necessary dynamics to the Universe by interacting with each other. These constituents behave according to the natural laws and their nature without interference from external entities. *Dharma* or true religion according to Jainism is *vatthu sahâvo dhammo* translated as "the intrinsic nature of a substance is its true religion."

Ontology and Metaphysics

Jain ontology postulates existence of principle of sentient or consciousness called as *Jiva* or soul characterized by knowledge and perception. There are infinite independent souls categorized into: liberated and non-liberated. Infinite knowledge, perception and bliss are the intrinsic qualities of a soul. These qualities are fully enjoyed unhindered by liberated souls, but obscured by karmas in the case of non-liberated souls resulting in karmic bondage. This bondage further results in a continuous co-habitation of the soul with the body. Thus, an embodied non-liberated soul is found in four realms of existence—heavens, hells, humans and animal world – in a never-ending cycle of births and deaths also known as *samsâra.* The soul is in bondage since beginningless time; however, it is possible to achieve liberation through rational perception, rational knowledge and rational conduct.

According to Jainism, the soul is the master of its own destiny. One of the qualities of the soul is complete lordship of its own destiny. The soul alone chooses its actions and soul alone reaps its consequences. No god, prophet or angel can interfere in the actions or the destiny of the soul. Furthermore, it is the soul alone who makes the necessary efforts to achieve liberation without any divine grace. Amongst the twelve contemplations *(anupreksâs)* of Jains, one of them is the loneliness of one's soul and nature of the Universe and transmigration. Hence only by cleansing our soul by our own actions can we help ourselves.

Jain metaphysics is based on seven (sometimes nine, with subcategories) truths or fundamental principles also known as *tattva,* which are an attempt to explain the nature and solution to the human predicament. The first two are the two ontological categories of the soul and the non-soul, namely the axiom that they exist. The third truth is that through the interaction, called *yoga,* between the two substances, soul and non-soul, karmic matter flows into the soul *âsrava,* clings to it, becomes converted into karma and the fourth truth acts as a factor of bondage *bandha,* restricting the manifestation of the consciousness intrinsic to it. The fifth truth states that a stoppage (*samvara*) of new karma is possible through asceticism through practice of right conduct, faith and knowledge. An intensification of asceticism burns up the existing karma – this sixth truth is expressed by the word nirjarâ. The final truth is that when the soul is freed from the influence of karma, it reaches the goal of Jaina teaching, which is liberation or *mokca.* Some authors add two additional categories: the meritorious and demeritorious acts related to karma *(punya and pâpa).* These nine categories of cardinal truth, called *navatattva,* form the basis of entire Jain metaphysics.

Epistemology and Logic

Jainism made its own unique contribution to this mainstream development of philosophy by occupying itself with the basic epistemological issues, namely, with those concerning the nature of knowledge, how knowledge is derived, and in what way knowledge can be said to be reliable. Knowledge for the Jains takes place in the soul, which, without the limiting factor of karma, is omniscient. Humans have partial knowledge – the object of knowledge is known partially and the means of knowledge do not operate to their full capacity. According to *Tattvârthasûtra,* the knowledge of the basic Jaina truths can be obtained through :

- **Pramana** means or instruments of knowledge which can yield a comprehensive knowledge of an object, and
- **Naya** particular standpoints, yielding partial knowledge.

Pramana are of five kinds:

- *mati* or "sensory knowledge",
- *Sruta* or "scriptural knowledge",
- *avadhi* or "clairvoyance",

- *manahparyaya* or "telepathy", and
- *kevala" or "omniscience"*

The first two are described as being indirect means of knowledge *(paroksa)*, with the others furnishing direct knowledge *(pratyakca)*, by which it is meant that the object is known directly by the soul.

As per Jainism, the truth or the reality is perceived differently from different points of view, and that no single point of view is the complete truth. Jain doctrine states that, an object has infinite modes of existence and qualities and, as such, they cannot be completely perceived in all its aspects and manifestations, due to inherent limitations of the humans. Only the *Kevalins*—the omniscient beings—can comprehend the object in all its aspects and manifestations, and that all others are capable of knowing only a part of it. Consequently, no one view can claim to represent the absolute truth. In the process, the Jains came out with there doctrines of relativity used for logic and reasoning:

- ***Anekântavâda***—the theory of relative pluralism or manifoldness;
- ***Syâdvâda***—the theory of conditioned predication and;
- ***Nayavâda***—The theory of partial standpoints.

These philosophical concepts have made most important contributions to the ancient Indian philosophy, especially in the areas of skepticism and relativity.

Morality and Ethics

The Jain morality and ethics are rooted in its metaphysics and its utility towards the soteriological objective of liberation. Jaina ethics evolved out of the rules for the ascetics which are encapsulated in the *mahavratas* or the five great vows :

- ***Ahimsa***, non-violence
- ***Aparigrah***, non-possession
- ***Asteya***, non-stealing
- ***Satya***, truth
- ***Brahmacarya***, celibacy

The ethics are governed not only through the instrumentality of physical actions, but also through verbal action and thoughts. Thus, ahimsa has to be observed through mind, speech and body. The other rules of the ascetics and laity are derived from these five major vows. Jainism does not invoke the fear of God as a reason for moral behavior. The observance of the moral code is not necessary simply because it is a commandment of a God or any other supreme being. Neither, is its observance necessary simply because it is conducive to general welfare of the state or the community. While it is true that in Jainism, the moral and religious injunctions were laid down as law by *Arhats* who have achieved perfection through their supreme moral efforts, their adherence is just not to please a God, but because the life of the Arhats has demonstrated that such commandments were conductive to *Arhat's* own welfare, helping him to reach spiritual victory. Just as *Arhats* achieved *mokca* or liberation by observing the moral code, so can anyone, who follows this path.

Karma: Law of Causation

Karma in Jainism conveys a totally different meaning as commonly understood in the Hindu philosophy and western civilization. It is not the so called inaccessible mystic force that controls the fate of living beings in some inexplicable way. It does not mean "deed", "work", nor invisible, mystical force (adrsta), but a complexes of very fine matter, imperceptible to the senses, which interacts with the soul and causes great changes in it. The karma, then, is something material (*karmapaudgalam*), which produces in the soul certain conditions, even as a medical pill which, when introduced into the body, produces therein manifold effects. According to Robert Zydendos, karma in Jainism can be considered a kind of system of laws, but natural rather than moral laws. In Jainism, actions that carry moral significance are considered to cause certain consequences in just the same way as, for instance, physical actions that do not carry any special moral significance. When one holds an apple in one's hand and then let go of the apple, the apple will fall: this is only natural. There is no judge, and no moral judgment involved, since this is a mechanical consequence of the physical action.

Hence in accordance with the natural karmic laws, consequences occur when one utters a lie, steals something, commits acts of senseless violence or leads the life of a debauchee. Rather than assume that moral rewards and retribution are the work of a divine judge, the Jains believe that there is an innate moral order to the cosmos, self-regulating through the workings of karma. Morality and ethics are important not because of the personal whim of a fictional god, but because a life that is led in agreement with moral and ethical principles is beneficial: it leads to a decrease and finally to the total loss of karma, which means: to ever increasing happiness.

The karmas can be said to represent a sum total of all unfulfilled desires of a soul. They enable the soul to experience the various themes of the lives that it desires to experience. They ultimately mature when the necessary supportive conditions required for maturity are fulfilled. Hence a soul may transmigrate from one life form to another for countless of years, taking with it the karmas that it has earned, until it finds conditions that bring about the fruits. Hence whatever suffering or pleasure that a soul may be experiencing now is on account of choices that it has made in past.

The following quote in *Bhagavatî Ârâdhanâ* (1616) sums up the predominance of karmas in Jain doctrine:

"There is nothing mightier in the world than karma;
karma tramples down all powers, as an elephant a clump of lotuses."

The Nature of Divinity and God

The undercurrent of non-creationism and absence of omnipotent God and divine grace runs strongly in all the philosophical dimensions of Jainism, including its cosmology, karma, moksa and its moral code of conduct. Jainism shows how a religious and virtuous life is possible without the idea of a creator god to whom one can turn to. Models for ethical life in Jainism are provided by the biographies of the twenty-four Jinas, the conquerors of the passions, of whom Mahâvîra was the last. They are worshipped as divine beings, as their lives serve as a guiding principle and an emulation of their virtues can lead one to the same goal of liberation that they achieved. According to Jainism, gods, that are worthy of worship and emulation, can be categorized into :

- ***Tîrthankara***, the ford makers
- ***Arhats*** or ordinary Kevalin, and
- ***Siddha***, the liberated beings

Jainism considers, demi-gods and goddesses who dwell in heavens owing to meritorious deeds in their past lives, as unliberated beings who are subject to further re-incarnations. Worship of such gods is considered as *mithyâtva* or wrong belief leading to bondage of karmas. However, many Jains are known to worship such gods for material gains.

Soteriolog : The Path to Moksha

Jainism is essentially a soteriological path where all the practices and beliefs are geared towards attainment of the ultimate objective—liberation of the soul. Jainism is also known as mokcamârga – the path to liberation. Mokca is a blissful state of existence of a soul, completely free from the karmic bondage, free from samsara, the cycle of birth and death. A liberated soul is said to have attained its true and pristine nature of infinite bliss, infinite knowledge and infinite perception. Such a soul is called siddha or paramatman and considered as supreme soul or God. In Jainism, it is the highest and the noblest objective that a soul should strive to achieve. In fact, it is the only objective that a person should have, other objectives are contrary to the true nature of soul. With right faith, knowledge and efforts all souls can attain this state.

Contributions to Indian Philosophy

Jainism had a major influence in developing a system of philosophy and ethics that had a major impact on all aspects of Indian culture in all ages : from Upanishads to Mahatma Gandhi. The scholarly research and evidences have shown that philosophical concepts that are considered typically Indian – Karma, Ahimsa, Moksa, reincarnation and like—either have their origins in the sramana school of thought or were propagated and developed by the Jaina teachers. These concepts were later assimilated in Hinduism and other religions, often in a different form and sometimes having a different meaning. The sramanic ideal of mendicancy and renunciation, that the worldly life was full of suffering and that emancipation required giving up of desires and withdrawal into a lonely and contemplative life, was in stark contrast with the brahmanical ideal of an active and ritually punctuated life based on sacrifices, household duties and chants to deities. Sramanas developed and laid emphasis on ahimsa, karma, moksa and renunciation. Early Upanishad thinkers like Yajnavalkya were acquainted with the sramanic thinking and tried to incorporate these ideals into the vedic thought implying a disparagement of the vedic ritualism and recognising the mendicancy as an ideal.

Schools and Traditions

Jain philosophy arose from the Sramana philosophy. In its 2,500 years post-Mahavira history, Jain philosophy remained, more or less, fundamentally the same as preached by Mahavira, who preached essentially the same religion as the previous Tirthankaras. However, he modified the four vows of Parsva by adding a fifth vow of celibacy. Jain texts like Uttaradhyana Sutra speak of parallel existence the order of Parsva which was ultimately merged into Mahaviras order. For a few centuries after Mahavira, the Jain religion remained united. The schisms into Svetâmbara and Digambara traditions arose mainly on account of differences in question of practice of nudity amongst monks and liberation of women. Apart from these minor differences in practices, there are no major philosophical differences between the different sects of Jainism. Tattvârthasûtra which encapsulates the major philosophical doctrine of Jainism is accepted by all traditions of Jainism. This coherence in philosophical doctrine and consistency across different schools has led many scholars like Jaini to remark that in the course of history of Jainism no heretical movements like Mahayana, tantric or bhakti movement developed outside mainstream Jainism. Thus, we have many traditions within the Jainism, but basically the same philosophy that is at the core of all the sects and sub-sects.

Earlier Traditions

As per the tradition, Jain Sangh was divided into two major sects, a few centuries after the nirvana of Mahavira :

- **Svetâmbara**—Svetambaras believe that women can attain liberation and that nudity is optional. Úvetâmbara scriptures support both *acelakatva,* nudity in monks and *sacelakatva,* the wearing of white clothes by ascetics. They also hold that Jain canon were not lost.

- **Digambara**—Digambaras hold that nudity is necessary for liberation and only men can attain the final stage of non-attachment to the body by remaining nude. They also hold that the canonical literature was eventually lost.

The now defunct, Yapaniya sect followed Digambara nudity and eating from the hands while standing up; along with several svetâmbara beliefs and texts. They are now believed to have been absorbed in the Digambara community during the medieval period.

Medieval Traditions

The period of 16th to 18th century was a period of reforms in Jainism. The later schools arose against certain practices and belief that were perceived as corrupting and not sanctioned by scriptures. The following schools arose during this period :

- **Sthanakvasi** – Sthanakvasi arising from Svetambara tradition rejected idol worship as not sanctioned by scriptures.
- **Terapanthi (Digambara)** – Digambara Terapantha movement arose in protest against the institution of Bhattarakas (Jain priestly class), usage of flowers and offerings in Jain temples, and worship of minor gods.
- **Terapanthi (Svetâmbara)** – Terapanthi, also a non-iconic sect, arose from Sthanakvasi on account of differences in religious practices and beliefs.

Recent Developments

Dissatisfaction with the monkhood and its related emphasis on austerities saw rising of two new sects within Jainism in 20th Century. These were essentially led by laity rather than ascetics and soon became a major force to be reckoned with. The non-sectarian cult of Srimad Rajcandra, who was one of the major influences on Mahatma Gandhi is now one of the most popular cults amongst the Jains. Another cult founded by Kanjisvami laying stress on determinism and "knowledge of self" has gained a large following among Jains.

Jain Philosophers

Jains hold the Jain doctrine to be eternal and based on universal principles. In the current time cycle, they trace the origins of its philosophy to Rsabha, the first Tîrthankara. However, the tradition holds that the ancient Jain texts and Purvas which documented the Jain doctrine were lost and hence, historically, the Jain philosophy can be traced from Mahâvîras teachings. Post Mahâvîra many intellectual giants amongst the Jain ascetics contributed and gave a concrete form to the Jain philosophy within the paramaters set by Mahavira. Following is the partial list of Jain philosophers and their contributions:

- **Kundakunda** (1st Century CE)—exponent of Jain mysticism and Jain nayas dealing with the nature of the soul and its contamination by matter, author of *Pañcâstikâyasâra* (Essence of the Five Existents), the *Pravacanasâra* (Essence of the Scripture), the *Samayasâra* (Essence of the Doctrine), *Niyamasâra* (Essence of Discipline), *Atthapâhuda* (Eight Gifts), *Dasabhatti* (Ten Worships) and *Bârasa Anuvekkhâ* (Twelve Contemplations).
- **Samantabhadra** (2nd Century CE)—first Jain writer to write on *nyâya*, (Apta-Mimâmsâ), which has had the largest number of commentaries written on it by later Jain logicians. He also composed the *Ratnakaranda Srâvakâcâra* and the *Svayambhu Stotra*.
- **Umâsvâti** or **Umasvami** (2nd Century CE)—author of first Jain work in Sanskrit, Tattvârthasûtra, expounding the Jain philosophy in a most systematized form acceptable to all sects of Jainism.
- **Siddhasena Divâkara** (3rd Century CE)—Jain logician and author of important works in Sanskrit and Prakrit, such as, *Nyâyâvatâra* (on Logic) and *Sanmatisûtra* (dealing with the seven Jaina standpoints, knowledge and the objects of knowledge).
- **Akalanka** (4th-5th Century CE)—key Jain logician, whose works such as *Laghiyastraya, Pramânasangraha, Nyâyaviniscaya-vivarana, Siddhiviniscaya-vivarana, Astasati, Tattvârtharâjavârtika,* et al are seen as landmarks in Indian logic. The impact of Akalanka may be surmised by the fact that Jain *Nyâya* is also known as *Akalanka Nyâya*.
- **Pujyapada** (6th Century CE)—Jain philosopher, grammarian, Sanskritist. Composed *Samadhitantra, Ishtopadesha* and the *Sarvarthasiddhi*, a definitive commentary on the *Tattvârthasûtra* and *Jainendra Vyakarana*, the first work on Sanskrit grammar by a Jain monk.
- **Manikyanandi** (6th Century CE)—Jain logician, composed the *Parikshamaukham*, a masterpiece in the *karika* style of the Classical Nyaya school.
- **Jinabhadra** (6-7th Century) - author of *Avasyaksutra* (Jain tenets) *Visesanavati* and *Visesavasyakabhasya* (Commentary on Jain essentials) He is said to have followed Siddhasena and compiled discussion and refutation on various views on Jaina doctrine.
- **Mallavadin** (8th Century) - author of *Dvadasaranayacakra* (Encyclopedia of Philosophy) which discusses all the school of Indian Philosophy. Mallavadin was known as a *vadin* i.e. a logician and he is said to have defeated many Buddhist monks on the issues of philosophy.

- **Haribhadra** (8th Century CE)—Jain thinker, author, philosopher, satirist and great proponent of anekântavâda and classical yoga, as a soteriological system of meditation in the Jain context. His works include *ba darœanasamuccaya, Yogabindu* and *Dhurtakhyana.* he pioneered the *Dvatrimshatika* genre of writing in Jainism, where various religious subjects were covered in 32 succinct Sanskrit verses.
- **Prabhacandra** (8th-9th Century CE)—Jain philosopher, composed a 106-Sutra Tattvarthasutra and exhaustive commentaries on two key works on Jain Nyaya, *Prameyakamalamartanda,* based on Manikyanandi's *Parikshamukham* and *Nyayakumudacandra* on Akalanka's *Laghiyastraya.*
- **Abhayadeva** (1057 CE to 1135 CE)—author of *Vadamahrnava* (Ocean of Discussions) which is a commentary of *Sanmartika* and considered a great treatise on logic.
- **Hemacandra** (1089–1172 CE)—Jain thinker, author, historian, grammarian and logician. His works include *Yogaúâstra* and *Trishashthishalakapurushacaritra* and the *Siddhahemavyakarana.* He also authored an incomplete work on Jain Nyâya, titled *Pramâna-Mimâmsâ.*
- **Vadideva** (11th Century) – He was a senior contemporary of Hemacandra and is said to have authored *Paramananayatattavalokalankara* and its voluminous commentary *syadvadaratnakara* that establishes the supremacy of doctrine of syadvada.
- **Vidyanandi** (11th Century CE)—Jain philosopher, composed the brilliant commentary on Acarya Umasvami's Tattvarthasutra, known as *Tattvartha-shlokavartika.*
- **Yaœovijaya** (1624–88 CE)—Jain logician and considered one of the last intellectual giant to contribute to Jain philosophy. He specialised in *Navya-Nyâya* and wrote Vrttis (commentaries) on most of the earlier *Jain Nyâya* works by Samantabhadra, Akalanka, Manikyanandi, Vidyânandi, Prabhâcandra and others in the then-prevalent *Navya-Nyâya* style. Yaœovijaya has to his credit a prolific literary output—more than 100 books in Sanskrit, Prakrit, Gujarati and Rajashtani. He is also famous for *Jnanasara* (essence of knowledge) and *Adhayatmasara* (essence of spirituality).

BIBLIOGRAPHY

Alston, W.P. (1991) *Perceiving God: The Epistemology of Religious Experience*, Ithaca, NY: Cornell University Press.

Amore, Roy C. and Larry D. Shinn (1981) *Lustful Maidens and Ascetic Kings: Buddhist and Hindu Stories of Life*. New York: Oxford University Press.

Buitenen, J.A.B. van. *Tales of Ancient India (1959)* Chicago: University of Chicago Press.

Burghart, Richard and Audrey Cantlie (eds.) (1985) *Indian Religion*, London: Curzon; New York: St. Martin.

Certeau, M. de (1992) *The Mystic Fable, Vol. 1: The Sixteenth and Seventeenth Centuries*, Chicago, IL: University of Chicago Press.

Chattopadhyaya, D. (1964) *Indian Philosophy: A Popular Introduction*, Delhi: People's Publishing House; reprint. 1972.

Coomaraswamy, Ananda K. and Sister Nivedita (1967) Myths *of the Hindus & Buddhists*, New York: Dover.

Davis, C.F. (1989) *The Evidential Force of Religious Experience*, Oxford: Clarendon.

De Bary, and William T. (ed.) (1988) *Sources of Indian Tradition*, New York: Columbia University Press.

Embree, Ainslie T. (1990) *Utopias in Conflict: Religion and Nationalism in Modern India*, Berkeley, CA: University of California Press.

Flew, A. (1966) God and Philosophy, New York: Delta Books.

Forman, R.A.C. (1990) *The Problem of Pure Consciousness: Mysticism and Philosophy*, New York: Oxford University Press.

Gale, R.M. (1991) *On the Nature and Existence of God*, New York: Cambridge University Press.

Halbfass, W. (1991) *Tradition and Reflection: Explorations in Indian Thought*, New York: State University of New York Press.

Hepburn, R.W. (1976) 'Mysticism, Nature and Assessment' in P. Edwards (ed.) *Encyclopedia of Philosophy*, New York: Macmillan.

Inge, W.R. (1899) *Christian Mysticism*, London: Methuen.

James, W. (1902) *The Varieties of Religious Experience: A Study in Human Nature*, New York: Modern Library.

Katz, S.T. (ed.) (1978) *Mysticism and Philosophical Analysis*, New York: Oxford University Press.

——————— (ed.) (1983) *Mysticism and Religious Traditions*, New York: Oxford University Press.

Lopez, Donald S., Jr., (ed.) (1995) *Religions of India in Practice.* Princeton, NJ: Princeton University Press.

Madan, T. N. (ed.) (1992) *Religion in India,* New Delhi: Oxford University Press.

Marechal, J. (1926, 1937) *Studies in the Psychology of Mystics,* trans. A. Thorld, Albany, NY: Magi Books, 1964.

Maritain, J. (1944) 'The Natural Mystical Experience and the Void', in *Redeeming the Time,* London: Geoffrey Bles Centenary Press.

Martin, C.B. (1959) *Religious Belief,* Ithaca, NY: Cornell University Press.

McGinn, B. (1991) *The Presence of God, A History of Western Christian Mysticism, vol. 1*: New York: Crossroad.

Mohanty, J. (1992) *Reason and Tradition in Indian Thought: An Essay on the Nature of Indian Philosophical Thinking,* Oxford: Clarendon Press.

Otto, R. (1958) The *Idea of the Holy,* New York: Oxford University Press.

Philips, S.H. (1995) *Classical Indian Metaphysics: Refutations of Realism and the Emergence of New Logic,* La Salle, IL: Open Court.

Pike, N. (1992) *Mystic Union: An Essay in the Phenomenology of Mysticism,* Ithaca, NY: Cornell University Press.

Potter, K.H. (1963) *Presupposition of Indian Philosophies,* Englewood Cliffs, NJ: Prentice-Hall.

Proudfoot, W. (1985) *Religious Experience,* Berkley, CA: University of California Press.

Ranher, K. (1983) *The Practice of Faith: A Handbook of Contemporary Spirituality,* New York: Crossroad.

Smart, N. (1965) 'Interpretation and Mystical Experience', *Religious Studies* 1: 75-87.

Stace, W.T. (1960a) *Mysticism and Philosophy,* London: Macmillan.

————————(1960b) *The Teachings of Mystics,* New York: New American Library.

Swineburn, R. (1979) *The Existence of God,* Oxford: Clarendon Press.

Underhill, E. (1965) *Mysticism: A Study in the Nature and Development of Man's Spiritual Consciousness,* Cleveland: OH, and New York.

Wainewright, W.J. (1981) *Mysticism: A Study of its Nature, Cognitive Value and Moral Implications,* Madison, WI: University of Wisconsin Press.

Woods, R. (ed.) (1980) *Understanding Mysticism,* Garden City, NY: Doubleday.

Yandell, K.E. (1993) *The Epistemology of Religious Experience,* New York: Cambridge University Press.

Zaehner, R.C. (1961) *Mysticism: Sacred and Profane: An Inquiry into Some Varieties of Preternatural Experience,* New York: Oxford University Press.

INDEX

P

Q

R

S